£5
c

YORKSHIRE'S
22
CHAMPIONSHIPS

YORKSHIRE'S 22 CHAMPIONSHIPS

1893–1946

by

E. L. ROBERTS

Including

YORKSHIRE PROFILES

by J. M. KILBURN

LONDON

EDWARD ARNOLD & CO.

" Yorkshire cricket is a thing of which not only every Yorkshireman but every Englishman must be proud."

LORD HAWKE

PRINTED IN GREAT BRITAIN BY HUGH PATON AND SONS LTD., EDINBURGH

CONTENTS

	Page
Introduction	9

PART I

Beginnings and Foundations (1833–1872)	11
Chronology	14

PART II

First Championship, 1893	18
Interregnum—1894, 1895	23
Second Championship, 1896	25
Interregnum—1897	34
Third Championship, 1898	35
Interregnum—1899	43
Fourth Championship, 1900	44
Fifth Championship, 1901	53
Sixth Championship, 1902	63
Interregnum—1903, 1904	73
Seventh Championship, 1905	75
Interregnum—1906, 1907	85
Eighth Championship, 1908	87
Interregnum—1909, 1910, 1911	95
Ninth Championship, 1912	99
Interregnum—1913, 1914	106

World War I, 1914–1918

Tenth Championship, 1919	109
Interregnum—1920, 1921	115
Eleventh Championship, 1922	118
Twelfth Championship, 1923	128
Thirteenth Championship, 1924	136
Fourteenth Championship, 1925	144
Interregnum—1926, 1927, 1928, 1929, 1930	152
Fifteenth Championship, 1931	156
Sixteenth Championship, 1932	165
Seventeenth Championship, 1933	176
Interregnum—1934	183
Eighteenth Championship, 1935	185
Interregnum—1936	192
Nineteenth Championship, 1937	194
Twentieth Championship, 1938	202
Twenty-first Championship, 1939	210

World War II, 1939·1945

Twenty-second Championship, 1946	221
Summary	229
The Best Side	229
Making a Yorkshire Cricketer	231

Contents

PART III

Yorkshire Profiles, by J. M. Kilburn

	Page
Lord Hawke (1881–1911)	233
R. Peel (1882–1897)	234
D. Hunter (1888–1909)	234
E. Wainwright (1888–1902)	235
J. T. Brown (1889–1904)	236
E. Smith (1889–1907)	236
G. H. Hirst (1889–1921)	237
Sir F. S. Jackson (1890–1907)	238
J. Tunnicliffe (1891–1907)	238
D. Denton (1894–1920)	239
F. Mitchell (1894–1904)	240
S. Haigh (1895–1913)	240
W. Rhodes (1898–1930)	241
T. L. Taylor (1899–1906)	242
E. R. Wilson (1899–1923)	242
A. Dolphin (1905–1927)	243
R. Kilner (1911–1927)	243
P. Holmes (1913–1933)	244
H. Sutcliffe (1919–1939)	245
E. Robinson (1919–1931)	245
M. Leyland (1920–1946)	246
G. G. Macaulay (1920–1935)	247
A. Mitchell (1922–1939)	247
A. Wood (1927–1947)	248
W. E. Bowes (1929–1947)	249
H. Verity (1930–1939)	249
A. B. Sellers (1932–)	250
T. F. Smailes (1932–)	251
L. Hutton (1934–)	252
N. W. D. Yardley (1936–)	252

PART IV

The County Cricket Championship, 1893–1946 . . .	254
Yorkshire v. The Counties	255
Yorkshire v. " The Big Five "	256
Ten Batsmen	256
Ten Bowlers	256
Ten Fielders	257
Three Wicketkeepers	257
Fifty Runs in Each Innings	257
Five Wickets in Each Innings	258
Averages	260
100 Yorkshire Records	266
Index	273

ILLUSTRATIONS

	FACING PAGE
LORD HAWKE	32
F. S. JACKSON	33
YORKSHIRE COUNTY CRICKETERS at one of Lord Hawke's parties at Wighill Park	48
THE YORKSHIRE TEAM OF 1901	49
J. T. BROWN	96
J. TUNNICLIFFE	96
G. H. HIRST	97
W. RHODES	97
GEORGE MACAULAY, ARTHUR DOLPHIN and MAURICE LEYLAND	112
THE YORKSHIRE TEAM OF 1922	113
HEADINGLEY CRICKET AND FOOTBALL GROUND, LEEDS, from the air	160
ROY KILNER	161
SCHOFIELD HAIGH	161
HOLMES and SUTCLIFFE, at Leyton in 1932, after their record first wicket partnership	176
THE YORKSHIRE TEAM OF 1933	177
LEN HUTTON	208
DAVID DENTON	208
GEORGE HIRST demonstrating bowling to young cricketers	209
HEDLEY VERITY	224
W. E. BOWES	224
A. B. SELLERS	225
N. W. D. YARDLEY	225

INTRODUCTION

CRICKET historians of the future may not unreasonably agree to call the period from 1893 to 1946—both years inclusive—the Golden Age of Yorkshire cricket. Justification for such a distinction is ample and obvious. In the forty-four seasons included in the period (ten seasons were stolen from cricket by war) Yorkshire won the County Cricket Championship twenty-two times, a record no other county has approached and one which appears unapproachable in anything but the very distant future. In the pages that follow, the progress of the Yorkshiremen in building up this outstanding achievement is examined a little more closely than has hitherto been done. Much has been written about Yorkshire cricket and cricketers, but the spotlight has not previously been directed at Yorkshire's 22 Championships.

In 1873 the County Cricket Championship was inaugurated with nine contestants—Derbyshire (whose place was later taken by Somerset), Gloucestershire, Kent, Lancashire, Middlesex, Nottinghamshire, Surrey, Sussex and Yorkshire—but for the first twenty years of the competition Yorkshire never succeeded in finishing at the top of the table. On occasion only the vagaries of the methods of reckoning points defeated the Yorkshiremen, but the fact remains that it was not until 1893 that the first of Yorkshire's Championships was won. Then, having tasted blood and liked it, Yorkshire cricketers proceeded to make a practice of periodically finishing at the top of the Championship table. In 1896 and 1898 the success of 1893 was repeated, and after the lapse of a season three consecutive Championships were won—in 1900, 1901 and 1902. And so cricket's greatest success story continued until in 1946, for the twenty-second time, Yorkshire were Champions in the first post-war season.

At the moment of writing (May 1948) only a super-optimist would anticipate the imminent winning of the twenty-third Championship. In every county's history there comes a time when team-building has to be given priority. The stars who carry a side to success drop out, and their successors have to be found, tested, groomed and welded into a *team*. Championships are seldom won while this process of development is in progress, so Yorkshire may have to wait for their next success until the " new boys " have found their feet. But in the meantime the potential stars of to-day and to-morrow can study the glorious tradition built up by Yorkshire cricketers during the last fifty years.

9

Such periods of almost uninterrupted success never fail to produce great personalities. In Yorkshire's case the first in chronological order was Lord Hawke, founder of the Yorkshire tradition and good friend of professional cricketers. For fifty-five years as Captain and President of the County Club (Captain from 1883 to 1910 and President from 1898 until his death in 1938) he was the chief architect and builder of that imposing edifice—Yorkshire County Cricket. Though never a great cricketer in the sense that A. C. MacLaren was great, Lord Hawke's value to Yorkshire as a leader, reformer and administrator was incalculable. It may be noted here that in the last eighty-six years the County Club has had only five Presidents, and three of them (Mr M. J. Ellison, Lord Hawke and Sir F. S. Jackson) held office in all but two of those years.

Yorkshire has always had great cricketers in the side—especially opening batsmen, left-hand slow bowlers or all-rounders ; and in their best seasons the XI.'s had all three. Sir F. S. Jackson (better known to Yorkshire crowds as " Jacker "), George Hirst, Wilfred Rhodes, John Tunnicliffe, Herbert Sutcliffe, Hedley Verity and " Bill " Bowes were something more than Yorkshire cricketers—they were household words wherever cricket was played or talked. Four of them were cartooned by " Spy " in *Vanity Fair*, and E. C. Bentley, the ingenious inventor of " Clerihews," composed the following tribute to the prowess of George Hirst :

> " When I faced the bowling of Hirst
> I ejaculated : ' Do your worst ! '
> He said : ' Right you are, Sid ! '
> And he did."

Yes, they and their fellows were great cricketers, and great men ; and the standards of play and conduct they set up on and off the field will remain an inspiration for their successors.

In common with most authors of books about cricket, the Compiler is indebted to the various issues of *Wisden's Cricketers' Almanac*, and also to the admirable series of Yorkshire Year-books issued to the members of the County Club. He is grateful to the Yorkshire Secretary, Mr J. H. Nash, for information and help with illustrations, and especially for providing in his busiest month notes on Yorkshire's method of discovering the raw material which, after treatment, becomes Yorkshire cricketers. Help in the matter of illustrations given by Mr C. R. Yeomans (*Yorkshire Evening Post*) and Mr R. A. Sparling (*Sheffield Telegraph*) must also be acknowledged.

Special thanks are due to Mr J. M. Kilburn for his series of " Yorkshire Profiles." As Cricket Correspondent of the *Yorkshire Post* he has come into personal contact with most of the subjects of the " Profiles," which are so full of insight and understanding.

E. L. R.

PART I

BEGINNINGS AND FOUNDATIONS

THE beginnings of Yorkshire cricket, like most cricket, stretch back in a mist of rumour and conjecture for two hundred years or more, but it is much later that real facts begin to emerge.

In 1825 an All-England XI. played 22 of the Rest of Yorkshire on the Darnall ground, Sheffield. The title of this match rather suggests that no Sheffield players were included in the Rest team, but whatever its composition and in spite of its numerical advantage, the Yorkshiremen ost by 28 notches. Even in those days it was difficult to prevent the inhabitants of the county from watching cricket, for it is recorded that over 14,000 spectators were present on the second day of the match.

Sheffield was the great cricket centre of Yorkshire in early times, and the series of matches between Sheffield and Nottingham, beginning in 1771 and ending in 1860, was the forerunner of the county matches of a later period.

The star of these matches in the eighteen-twenties was Tom Marsden, perhaps the first of Yorkshire's famous collection of left-handed cricketers. Marsden was an all-rounder who bowled a very insidious lob, and he came into prominence in 1826 when he scored 227 out of 379 in 8 hours for Sheffield and Leicester v. Nottingham. Marsden was 21 at the time and was appearing in his first match against Nottingham. Moreover, the only other double hundred recorded at that time was William Ward's famous 278 at Lord's in 1820. Marsden's achievement evidently impressed the authorities, for he played in the Gentlemen–Players match in the following season. Unfortunately, he did not retain his form very long, and rarely produced a big innings away from Yorkshire. It was not long before he was overshadowed by men like Sam Dearman and Harry Sampson, each of whom beat him in single-wicket matches.

A milestone was reached in 1833 when Yorkshire's first *county* match was played on the Hyde Park ground at Sheffield, Norfolk providing the opposition and Yorkshire winning by 120 runs. The reason that Norfolk was chosen for this innovation was probably the fact that Fuller Pilch, who was a member of the East Anglian side, had played much of his early cricket with the Sheffield Wednesday club. He never played in the Sheffield–Nottingham matches owing to lack of birth qualification, but his inclusion in the Norfolk XI. was clearly an attraction from a gate point of view. Five matches were played by the two counties, and in spite of getting " spectacles " in one of them, Fuller Pilch scored 385 runs in his eight innings.

Between 1833 and 1855 Yorkshire met Lancashire, Sussex, Kent and Surrey, in addition to Norfolk, and also played a number of matches against the All-England XI. and the United All-England XI. Nearly all the games played in Yorkshire took place in Sheffield on the Darnall ground (opened in 1821), the Hyde Park ground (1826) or Bramall Lane, where county matches are still played. It may be noted here that Bramall Lane is the only Football League ground on which county cricket is played.

In 1861 a step forward in the direction of the formation of a County Club was taken. At a meeting held in Sheffield a Public Match Fund Committee was formed, Mr M. J. Ellison being elected President and Treasurer, but this idea hung fire. Apart from three Sheffield clubs, Scarborough was the only other Yorkshire club that rallied to the call, and as a result shortage of funds severely limited the Committee's activities.

In January 1863 the final step was taken—it was decided to form a County Club " to consist of an unlimited number of members, the lowest subscription being 10s. 6d." ; its object being " to provide funds for playing first-class matches either in Sheffield or in other towns of the County." Mr T. R. Barker was the first President, Mr M. J. Ellison being Treasurer, and at last the good ship " Yorkshire County " was launched, and, weathering the perils of local rivalries and rifts between committee and players, was, by 1866, setting a straight course for success.

Administrative troubles had not interrupted the important business of team-building. In 1865 George Freeman came on the scene, and in the following year another great Yorkshire bowler, Tom Emmett, made his début against Nottinghamshire. The difference made to the Yorkshire side by the inclusion of these two cricketers was soon felt ; in 1867 Freeman took fifty-one wickets for 7 runs each in seven matches, and Emmett thirty wickets at a cost of 5 runs each.

In 1868 another valuable recruit joined the ranks. Included almost at the last moment in the Yorkshire side at the Oval, Ephraim Lockwood opened the innings with his uncle, John Thewlis, and the two Lascelles Hall cricketers scored 175 runs before they were parted. Lockwood was Yorkshire's greatest batsman for many years, scoring his highest innings, 208 against Kent, in 1883. With Lockwood to score the runs, and Freeman, Emmett and, later, Alan Hill to take the wickets, Yorkshire enjoyed a number of successful seasons.

W. G. Grace and Gloucestershire made their first appearance in county matches against Yorkshire at Sheffield in 1872. This was not W. G.'s first visit to the county ; in 1869 he had scored 122 for South v. North at Sheffield. On the second occasion he opened the Gloucestershire innings with T. G. Matthews, and scored 150 of the 238 runs made during the partnership.

In 1873 the County Championship was instituted, and as the various counties concerned agreed on rules governing qualifications cricket really began to get organised. The methods adopted for deciding the Championship read strangely to the modern accustomed to percentages, averages and other fearsome mathematical combinations, but they possessed at least the virtue of simplicity. From 1873 to 1886 the county with fewest defeats was the Champion county; from 1887 to 1889 one point was given for a win and half a point for a draw; from 1890 to 1894, when the number of first-class counties was increased, losses were deducted from wins, drawn matches being ignored.

These simple systems were easily understood by the cricket public, but on occasion the equity of the results they produced was not always apparent; and in spite of having the best professional batsman in England (Lockwood), a wicketkeeper like Pinder, fine bowlers like Emmett and Hill, and promising colts like George Ulyett and Louis Hall, Yorkshire failed to come up to expectations. The team developed a habit of starting the season badly and finishing it like champions— a method which rarely wins championships. The cricketers were there, and on many occasions they played magnificent cricket, but leadership was lacking, and this fault was not rectified until Lord Hawke, then the Hon. M. B. Hawke, became captain in 1883.

But in spite of disappointments Yorkshire was still producing fine cricketers. In 1875 T. Armitage, a sound batsman and tricky lob bowler, appeared in the side. W. Bates, a greater all-rounder, followed in 1877. Then in quick succession came Joseph Hunter (1878), E. Peate (1879), R. Peel (1882), David Hunter (1883), and others less well known. There was no shortage of cricketers.

One point about Yorkshire cricket in the 'eighties may be noted with surprise in view of more recent cricket history: the fielding was, on the whole, poor. Indeed, it was not until Lord Hawke took over the captaincy, and discipline began to be tightened up, that this vital part of any cricket team's equipment showed improvement.

In 1891 Yorkshire were last but one in the Championship and pessimism in the county was deep and dark. As a result of much agitation the Sheffield monopoly was broken, and the County Committee selected on a broader basis. Sheffield had done much for Yorkshire cricket, but the time had come when it was necessary to face the fact that Yorkshire was greater than any one part of Yorkshire. And the proof of the pudding was in the eating: two years after Yorkshiremen had been in the doldrums of failure they rose to the zenith of success by winning the County Championship in 1893. Such a change was ample justification for the agitation that put the County Club on its present democratic basis.

CHRONOLOGY

1893. FIRST CHAMPIONSHIP. Captain, Lord Hawke. At the end of the season G. Ulyett retired after playing for Yorkshire since 1873.

1894. Peel's Benefit at Bradford (Yorkshire v. Lancashire) produced £2,000. D. Denton made his first appearance for the county.

1895. C. L. Townsend, 18 years of age, took 15 wickets for 184 runs for Gloucestershire at Cheltenham. S. Haigh made his first appearance.

1896. SECOND CHAMPIONSHIP. At Birmingham, Yorkshire scored 887 v. Warwickshire, then the highest total on record, and still the highest in a county match.

1897. In Derbyshire's first innings at Bradford Haigh took 5 wickets, including a hat-trick, in 10 balls for no runs. Peel's last season in the Yorkshire side.

1898. THIRD CHAMPIONSHIP. Lord Hawke elected President of the County Club. First appearance of Wilfred Rhodes. At Chesterfield J. T. Brown and J. Tunnicliffe shared a record first wicket partnership—554—v. Derbyshire.

1899. At the Oval, Surrey (551 for seven wickets) and Yorkshire (704) scored 1,255 runs for 17 wickets, each wicket taken costing 73·82. E. R. Wilson made his first appearance.

1900. FOURTH CHAMPIONSHIP. Rhodes took 206 wickets in Championship matches, Tunnicliffe made 46 catches, and Yorkshire won without losing a match.

1901. FIFTH CHAMPIONSHIP. Yorkshire won 20 county matches and lost 1—against Somerset, who scored 630 in their second innings at Leeds. Tunnicliffe made 62 catches in 27 matches. Nottinghamshire dismissed for 13 at Nottingham.

1902. SIXTH CHAMPIONSHIP. Haigh took 123 wickets for 11·99 runs each, 91 being bowled and 10 lbw.

1903. F. C. Toone was appointed Secretary. G. H. Hirst headed the batting and bowling averages, obtaining a " double " in Championship matches. In all matches during the season Rhodes completed the first of his 16 " doubles."

1904. Hirst's Benefit at Leeds, Yorkshire v. Lancashire, realised £3,703. J. T. Brown dropped out of the side after appearing in one match, and died later in the year.

1905. SEVENTH CHAMPIONSHIP. E. Smith scored the finest 0 in cricket history v. Essex at Leyton. Rhodes had a great season : 2 hundreds and 9 other innings over 50, 10 wickets in a match 3 times, 5 wickets in an innings 10 times, 50 runs and 5 wickets in a match 4 times, and 35 catches.

1906. Gloucestershire won at Bristol by one run. Against Somerset at Bath, Hirst scored a hundred in each Yorkshire innings, and took 5 or more wickets in each Somerset innings—the all-rounder's perfect " double." In all Yorkshire matches he scored 2,164 runs and took 201 wickets.

1907. Hon. F. S. Jackson and J. Tunnicliffe made their last appearances in Yorkshire cricket.

1908. EIGHTH CHAMPIONSHIP. Another Championship won without losing a match. Northamptonshire were dismissed for 27 and 15 at Northampton. Hirst scored 50 runs and took 5 wickets in the same match 9 times.

1909. At the Oval, Yorkshire were all out for 26 runs in their second innings—their lowest total.

1910. Lord Hawke, after 28 years as captain, resigned. Hirst headed the batting and bowling averages.

1911. Captain, E. J. Radcliffe. C. J. B. Wood carried his bat through each Leicestershire innings *v*. Yorkshire at Bradford for 107 and 117. R. Kilner made his first appearance in the side.

1912. NINTH CHAMPIONSHIP. Captain, Sir A. W. White. In a wet season Denton scored 1,831 runs (average 53·85), including 6 hundreds, in Championship matches.

1913. Gloucestershire beat Yorkshire by 2 runs at Sheffield. Batting No. 9, E. R. Wilson scored 104 not out *v*. Essex at Bradford. Haigh retired. P. Holmes made his first appearance.

1914. In consecutive matches *v*. Gloucestershire and Somerset, M. W. Booth and A. Drake bowled unchanged in each innings. In Somerset's second innings Drake took all 10 wickets for 35 runs, and earlier in the season had taken 4 Derbyshire wickets in 4 balls at Chesterfield.

1915-1918. FIRST WORLD WAR.

1919. TENTH CHAMPIONSHIP. Captain, D. C. F. Burton. Holmes and Sutcliffe opened the Yorkshire innings for the first time against Kent at Leeds on June 30. A. Waddington took 100 wickets in his first season.

1920. G. G. Macaulay made his first appearance in the Yorkshire eleven. Holmes scored 126 and 111 *v*. Lancashire at Manchester, and later 302 not out *v*. Hampshire at Portsmouth. Denton retired.

1921. At the end of the season Hirst retired after scoring over 32,000 runs and taking more than 2,500 wickets in Yorkshire matches. He made his first appearance for the county in 1889.

1922. ELEVENTH CHAMPIONSHIP. Captain, G. Wilson. Sussex were dismissed for 20 runs at Hull, Waddington taking 7 wickets for 6 runs.

1923. TWELFTH CHAMPIONSHIP. Yorkshire won 25 of their 32 Championship matches. Six batsmen each scored 1,000 runs, and the first four bowlers took 503 wickets for 12·46 runs each.

1924. THIRTEENTH CHAMPIONSHIP. Yorkshire were all out for 33 in the second innings *v.* Lancashire at Leeds, and lost by 24 runs. P. Holmes scored 315 not out *v.* Middlesex at Lord's.

1925. FOURTEENTH CHAMPIONSHIP. Captain, A. W. Lupton. Yorkshire won 21 of the 32 county matches, and were unbeaten.

1926. Holmes and Sutcliffe scored 105 and 265 (unfinished) for Yorkshire's first wicket *v.* Surrey at the Oval. For the sixteenth and last time Rhodes scored 1,000 runs and took 100 wickets in a season, in his forty-ninth year.

1927. Macaulay and Robinson bowled unchanged in each Worcestershire innings at Leeds, Waddington scoring 114 in the Yorkshire innings. R. Kilner died before the season started.

1928. Captain, W. A. Worsley. Against Nottinghamshire at Nottingham, Holmes and Sutcliffe scored over 100 for the first wicket in each innings.

1929. In his fifty-second year, Rhodes took 12 Essex wickets for 80 runs at Leyton in the first county match of the season. W. E. Bowes made his first appearance in the team.

1930. Captain, A. T. Barber. After a career extending over 29 seasons, Rhodes retired at the end of the summer. Verity made his first appearance in the Yorkshire side in 1930, and finished top of the County and England bowling averages. Sutcliffe headed the England batting averages. J. H. Nash was appointed Secretary.

1931. FIFTEENTH CHAMPIONSHIP. Captain, F. E. Greenwood. At the end of the season, Emmott Robinson retired. In a wet season, Sutcliffe scored 3,006 runs and averaged 96·96 in first-class cricket.

1932. SIXTEENTH CHAMPIONSHIP. H. Sutcliffe scored his hundredth 100 in first-class cricket—132 *v.* Gloucestershire at Bradford. Verity took 10 wickets for 10 runs in the second innings *v.* Nottinghamshire. H. Fisher did the hat-trick *v.* Somerset, all three batsmen being lbw.

1933. SEVENTEENTH CHAMPIONSHIP. Captain, A. B. Sellers. Leyland scored 210 not out and took 5 wickets for 84 runs *v.* Kent at Dover. Northamptonshire were all out for 27 at Kettering. Holmes retired at the end of the season after scoring 26,216 runs (average 41·94). Verity took 17 wickets in a day at Leyton.

1934. L. Hutton scored his maiden hundred—196 *v.* Worcestershire at Worcester. Warwickshire won by one wicket at Scarborough after being all out for 45 in their first innings.

1935. EIGHTEENTH CHAMPIONSHIP. Yorkshire were all out before lunch on two consecutive days *v.* Essex at Huddersfield, scoring 31 and 99. M. S. Nichols scored 146 and took 11 wickets for 54 runs for Essex. At the Oval, Wood kept wicket in his 222nd consecutive Championship match. Macaulay retired at the end of the season.

1936. Verity took 15 wickets for 38 runs *v.* Kent at Sheffield—6 for 26 and 9 for 12. Worcestershire won by 11 runs at Stourbridge. In all first-class cricket, Verity scored 855 runs, took 216 wickets and made 21 catches.

1937. NINETEENTH CHAMPIONSHIP. For the third time in consecutive seasons, Verity took 200 wickets—202 wickets (average 15·68).

1938. TWENTIETH CHAMPIONSHIP. E. P. Robinson made 6 catches in an innings *v.* Leicestershire at Bradford. Yorkshire beat Glamorgan by 12 runs at Hull.

1939. TWENTY-FIRST CHAMPIONSHIP. Rt. Hon. Sir F. S. Jackson was elected President. In 21 inter-war seasons Sutcliffe completed 50,000 runs. During the season he carried his bat through the innings for the first hundred of the season and scored 4 hundreds in consecutive innings. In the last innings of the last first-class match played " between the wars," Yorkshire dismissed Sussex for 33 at Hove, Verity taking 7 wickets for 9 runs.

1940-1945. SECOND WORLD WAR.
In the summer of 1943 Hedley Verity died of wounds in a prisoner-of-war camp in Italy. In 1945 Yorkshire and Lancashire played a Verity Memorial match at Bradford in aid of the Verity Memorial Fund, which realised £8,233.

1946. TWENTY-SECOND CHAMPIONSHIP. In his first full season, A. Booth (43 years of age) headed the English bowling averages with 111 wickets for 11·61 runs each. Yorkshire beat Worcestershire by one wicket at Leeds.

PART II

FIRST CHAMPIONSHIP

1 8 9 3

Captains : Lord Hawke and G. Ulyett

After twenty years Yorkshire won their first County Cricket Championship with considerable ease, the runners-up being Yorkshiremen's Enemy No. 1—Lancashire. Nine counties competed, and the only blot on Yorkshire's record was the fact that Lancashire beat them twice.

THE FIRST SIX

	Played	Won	Lost	Drawn	Points
Yorkshire	16	12	3	1	9
Lancashire	16	9	5	2	4
Middlesex	16	9	6	1	3
Kent	16	6	4	6	2
Surrey	16	7	8	1	− 1
Nottinghamshire	16	5	7	4	− 2

METHOD OF SCORING : Losses deducted from wins.

MATCH SCORES AND RESULTS

Yorkshire *v.*	Ground	Yorkshire		Opponents		Result
		1st Inns.	2nd Inns.	1st Inns.	2nd Inns.	
Gloucestershire	Gloucester	385	3 (1)	235	152	Y. won by 9 wickets.
Sussex	Leeds	111	76 (6)	125	61	Y. won by 4 wickets.
Middlesex	Lord's	304	145 (7)	169	279	Y. won by 3 wickets.
Surrey	Sheffield	98	91	72	59	Y. won by 58 runs.
Somerset	Taunton	469	—	227	191	Y. won by inns. and 51 runs.
Lancashire	Leeds	107	53	169	—	L. won by inns. and 9 runs.
Surrey	Oval	125	238	356	10 (0)	S. won by 10 wickets.
Nottinghamshire	Bradford	220	120 (3)	*321 (8)	—	Draw.
Somerset	Sheffield	300	—	161	126	Y. won by inns. and 13 runs.
Nottinghamshire	Nottingham	182	—	124	38	Y. won by inns. and 20 runs.
Gloucestershire	Huddersfield	162	4 (0)	74	91	Y. won by 10 wickets.
Kent	Blackheath	220	—	77	132	Y. won by inns. and 11 runs.
Lancashire	Manchester	58	51	64	50	L. won by 5 runs.
Middlesex	Bradford	234	184	191	82	Y. won by 145 runs.
Kent	Sheffield	211	80 (2)	161	127	Y. won by 8 wickets.
Sussex	Brighton	203	185 (2)	192	194	Y. won by 8 wickets.

* Innings declared closed.

Yorkshire beat Gloucestershire, Kent, Middlesex, Somerset, Sussex twice ; and Nottinghamshire, Surrey once.

Yorkshire were beaten by Lancashire twice ; Surrey once.

Yorkshire drew with Nottinghamshire once.

18

SUMMARY

	Yorkshire	Opponents
Runs scored	4619	4310
Average per wicket	19·99	15·01
Hundreds	3	2
Other innings over 50	24	16
Ten wickets in match	3	5
Five wickets in innings	16	16
Highest total	469 v. Somerset	356 (Surrey)
Lowest total	51 v. Lancashire	38 (Nottinghamshire)
Totals over 400	1	—
Totals under 100	5	10

PRINCIPAL AVERAGES

	Inns.	Not Out	Runs	Highest Inns.	100's	50's	Aver.
J. T. Brown	26	1	712	84	—	6	28·48
J. Tunnicliffe	26	3	653	77	—	3	28·39
A. Sellers	25	—	678	105	2	3	27·12
G. H. Hirst	23	9	287	43	—	—	20·50

	Balls	Balls per Wkt.	Runs	Wkts.	5 Wkts. in Inns.	Aver.
E. Wainwright	3000	33·33	1130	90	6	12·55
R. Peel	3137	48·26	922	65	6	14·18
G. H. Hirst	2837	48·08	963	59	2	16·32

NOTES

For Yorkshire v. Surrey at Sheffield, T. Wardall took nine wickets for 19 runs (four for 6 and five for 13) ; and in the two Surrey innings Tunnicliffe made 6 catches.

J. Briggs took eight wickets for 19 runs in Yorkshire's second innings against Lancashire at Leeds.

At the Oval, W. H. Lockwood scored 61 not out and took eleven wickets for 120 runs.

When Lancashire won by 5 runs at Manchester, the match was played on a bowler's wicket, 223 runs being scored for the loss of forty wickets. Peel and Briggs had field-days, the former taking ten for 39 and the Lancastrian eleven for 60.

George Ulyett, after playing for the county for twenty years, made his last appearance in the side in 1893.

Yorkshire dismissed Notts for 38, Lancashire for 50 and 64, Surrey for 59 and 72, Sussex for 61, Gloucestershire for 74 and Kent for 77.

HOW IT WAS DONE

	100's	50's	10 Wkts. in Match	5 Wkts. in Inns.	50 Runs & 5 Wkts. in Match
J. T. Brown	–	6	–	–	–
G. H. Hirst	–	–	–	2	–
F. S. Jackson	–	1	–	1	1
R. Peel	–	1	2	6	–
A. Sellers	2	3	–	–	–
J. Tunnicliffe	–	5	–	–	–
G. Ulyett	–	3	–	–	–
E. Wainwright	–	4	1	6	2
T. Wardall	1	–	–	1	–
Total	3	23	3	16	3

FIELDING (125 Catches)

No. of Catches		No. of Catches	
31	J. Tunnicliffe	5	R. Moorhouse
19	E. Wainwright	5	E. Smith
12	G. Ulyett	4	F. S. Jackson
11	G. H. Hirst	3	J. Mounsey
11	A. Sellers	1	Lord Hawke
9	J. T. Brown		
6	R. Peel	1	" Sub "
6	T. Wardall		

WICKETKEEPING

	Stumped	Caught	Total
D. Hunter	9	29	38
H. Hayley	–	1	1
Total	9	30	39

TOTALS

400 Runs and Over

Yorkshire (1)

469 *v.* Somerset at Taunton

Opponents (0)
None.

Under 100 Runs

Yorkshire (5)

98 and 91 *v.* Surrey at Sheffield   58 and 51 *v.* Lancashire at Manchester
53 *v.* Lancashire at Leeds

Opponents (10)

61, Sussex, Leeds   77, Kent, Blackheath
72 and 59, Surrey, Sheffield   64 and 50, Lancashire, Manchester
38, Notts, Nottingham   82, Middlesex, Bradford
74 and 91, Gloucestershire, Huddersfield

FIRST WICKET PARTNERSHIPS

None.

50 RUNS AND 5 WICKETS

Scores	Analyses	Player	Against	Ground
51	5-32, 4-58	E. Wainwright	Kent	Blackheath
59	5-42	F. S. Jackson	Nottinghamshire	Nottingham
78	4-49, 4-39	E. Wainwright	Somerset	Taunton

MATCH OF THE SEASON

Yorkshire v. Lancashire

Manchester, August 7, 8

Lancashire won by 5 runs

When Yorkshire and Lancashire met at Old Trafford on August 7 they were first and second respectively in the County Championship table. On the first day a record crowd of 25,000 watched some sensational cricket.

Winning the toss, Lancashire took first innings but were immediately in difficulties with fine Yorkshire bowling and fielding, four wickets falling for 22 runs before rain stopped play. On the resumption another wicket fell without addition to the total, and in spite of a stand by Ward and Baker only 64 runs were on the board when the last wicket fell. Peel (four for 15) and E. Smith (three for 10) were mainly responsible for this modest total.

Yorkshire found run-getting just as difficult, only Brown, Tunnicliffe and Peel reaching double figures. Briggs (six for 35) and Mold four for 20) bowled unchanged, and when the last Yorkshireman was out Lancashire had a lead of 6 runs.

During the day 129 runs were scored for the loss of twenty wickets in 260 minutes, Lancashire leading by 13 runs when stumps were drawn.

The second day produced even more thrills and sensations than the first. Rain during the night followed by a hot sun made the pitch tricky, and when the last Lancastrian was out only 50 runs had been scored. Peel, who made his match analysis ten wickets for 39 runs, and Wainwright, four for 8 in 35 balls, were the destructive agents, only MacLaren and Ward scoring more than 10 runs.

Needing only 57 to win Yorkshire began well, Sellers and Jackson scoring 24 in sixteen minutes before the latter was run out. Smith knocked up 12 runs quickly, but at lunch six wickets were down and 15 runs were still required. After lunch the last four Yorkshire wickets fell for 9 runs in twenty-five minutes, the most sensational battle of " the Wars of the Roses " ending when Ward caught a potential six by Ulyett on the boundary, which a shorter man might have been unable to reach.

Lancashire

A. C. MacLaren c Hirst b Peel	1	c Hunter b Peel	16
A. Ward c Ulyett b Smith	19	c Hunter b Peel	12
F. H. Sugg c Tunnicliffe b Hirst	3	c Tunnicliffe b Peel	0
J. Briggs lbw, b Hirst	0	c Tunnicliffe b Peel	9
S. M. Crosfield run out	10	c Hunter b Wainwright	6
A. Tinsley c Tunnicliffe b Peel	0	c Tunnicliffe b Peel	3
G. R. Baker b Peel	21	st. Hunter b Wainwright	0
G. Yates c Hunter b Smith	2	b Wainwright	0
A. T. Kemble b Smith	4	b Wainwright	0
W. Oakley not out	0	not out	3
A. Mold b Peel	1	c Tunnicliffe b Peel	1
Extras	3		
	64		50

Yorkshire

A. Sellers b Briggs	0	b Oakley	13
F. S. Jackson c and b Briggs	1	run out	12
E. Smith c Ward b Briggs	4	c Crosfield b Briggs	12
J. T. Brown b Briggs	17	b Oakley	0
J. Tunnicliffe c Ward b Briggs	11	c Oakley b Mold	2
E. Wainwright b Mold	4	lbw, b Briggs	3
R. Peel b Mold	12	lbw, b Mold	1
R. Moorhouse c Tinsley b Mold	4	st. Kemble b Briggs	0
G. Ulyett c Baker b Briggs	0	c Ward b Briggs	7
G. H. Hirst b Mold	1	c Baker b Briggs	0
D. Hunter not out	1	not out	1
Extras	3		
	58		51

Yorkshire Bowling

	Overs	Mdns.	Runs	Wkts.		Overs	Mdns.	Runs	Wkts.
Hirst	24	11	36	2	...	4	2	4	0
Peel	29.3	20	15	4	...	19.3	9	24	6
Smith	6	2	10	3	...	8	4	14	0
Wainwright						7	2	8	4

Lancashire Bowling

	Overs	Mdns.	Runs	Wkts.		Overs	Mdns.	Runs	Wkts.
Briggs	22	8	35	6	...	14.2	3	25	5
Mold	21.3	10	20	4	...	9	5	13	2
Oakley						5	1	13	2

APPEARANCES

The following 18 cricketers appeared for Yorkshire in Championship matches, the number of appearances being in parentheses :

J. T. Brown (16)
R. W. Frank (1)
R. Hayley (1)
Lord Hawke (6)
G. H. Hirst (16)
D. Hunter (16)
F. S. Jackson (6)
R. Moorhouse (15)
J. Mounsey (6)

R. Peel (15)
A. Sellers (15)
E. Smith (6)
J. Tunnicliffe (16)
G. Ulyett (15)
E. Wainwright (16)
G. Waller (1)
T. Wardall (8)
Lees Whitehead (1)

POST MORTEM

Without showing the overwhelming superiority of some subsequent seasons—1900 for example—Yorkshire were undoubtedly entitled to first place. Their all-round strength was greater and more consistent than that of any other county. Brown, Tunnicliffe, Sellers, Wainwright and Jackson could generally be relied on to make sufficient runs, and the bowling was very strong with Peel, Wainwright and Hirst as the spearhead. Usually going in No. 9, G. Ulyett produced several useful innings in his last season as a Yorkshire cricketer.

INTERREGNUM

1894, 1895

1894

But for bad weather luck Yorkshire might have shared the Championship with Surrey, being only one point behind with one match—*v.* Kent at Bradford—abandoned without a ball being bowled. However, as Surrey beat the Yorkshiremen, both at the Oval and Bramall Lane, they clearly had better claims to the Championship.

Some great performances were recorded for Yorkshire during the season :

> *v. Sussex at Dewsbury* : Wainwright took thirteen wickets for 38 runs (six for 18 and seven for 20), nine being clean bowled.

> *v. Notts at Leeds* : F. S. Jackson scored 43 and 145, and in the second innings of Notts took five wickets for 37 runs.

> *v. Somerset at Huddersfield* : Hirst took five wickets for 9 runs in Somerset's first innings and ten for 49 in the match.

> *v. Lancashire at Bradford* : Peel's Benefit produced record receipts —£2,000.

> *v. Middlesex at Sheffield* : In the second innings of Middlesex, Wainwright took nine wickets for 66 runs.

> *v. Middlesex at Lord's* : Middlesex scored 92 and 63.

> *v. Lancashire at Manchester* : Briggs's Benefit—Lancashire scored 50 and 98, Peel and Hirst bowling unchanged in the first innings.

In a wet season the highest batting average was F. S. Jackson's 28·15, but the bowling figures were impressive : E. Wainwright, 97 wickets (average 10·17 ; R. Peel, 79 (11·14) ; G. H. Hirst, 56 (13·05) ; F. S. Jackson 25 (13·44).

1895

Yorkshire were third in the Championship, Surrey finishing first and Lancashire second. Fourteen counties competed, the new comers being Derbyshire, Warwickshire, Essex, Hampshire and Leicestershire.

Eight Yorkshiremen averaged 20 runs an innings, but the bowling was not, perhaps, quite as consistently destructive as in 1894. But it was as least as good as any other county's attack, Peel, Jackson, Hirst and Wainwright all taking fifty or more wickets for fewer than 20 runs each.

The following were some of the highlights of the season :

v. Surrey at the Oval : Yorkshire won by an innings and 30 runs, Surrey being dismissed for 136 and 78, Hirst taking four wickets for 7 runs in the second innings.

v. Somerset at Leeds : Peel took fifteen wickets for 50 runs, Yorkshire winning by 103 runs.

v. Gloucestershire at Cheltenham : Gloucestershire won by seven wickets, C. L. Townsend scoring 42 and taking fifteen wickets for 184 runs. Townsend was 18 years of age at the time.

v. Surrey at Bradford : Splendid fast bowling by Richardson—thirteen wickets for 134 runs—and a hundred by Hayward were mainly responsible for a Surrey win by eight wickets.

v. Middlesex at Leeds : A very strong Middlesex eleven was beaten by 205 runs, fine bowling by Hirst (twelve wickets for 89 runs) and Peel (four for 12 in the second innings) keeping the Middlesex totals to 103 and 57.

v. Somerset at Taunton : In a match in which 1,049 were scored Somerset gained a narrow win by 29 runs, thanks to L. C. H. Palairet's 165 out of 253, in their second innings, and the persistent bowling of Tyler, who took fourteen wickets (seven in each innings) for 247 runs in 87·4 overs.

v. Kent at Canterbury : Yorkshire won by seven wickets, F. S. Jackson scoring 35 and 18, and taking twelve wickets for 91 runs. When Yorkshire went in to score 50 runs, W. Wright took three wickets for 3 runs in 4 overs (3 maidens).

SECOND CHAMPIONSHIP

1896

Captain : Lord Hawke

In the first half of the season Yorkshire and Surrey were well ahead in the Championship race, but Surrey cracked and finished fourth below Yorkshire, Lancashire and Middlesex. On all kinds of wickets and in varying conditions, Yorkshire were more consistent than any other county.

THE FIRST SIX

	Played	Won	Lost	Drawn	Points	Percent.
Yorkshire	26	16	3	7	13	68·42
Lancashire	22	11	4	7	7	46·66
Middlesex	16	8	3	5	5	45·45
Surrey	26	17	7	2	10	38·46
Essex	12	5	4	3	1	11·11
Nottinghamshire	16	5	5	6	0	00·00

METHOD OF SCORING : 1 point for a win; 1 point deducted for each loss. Championship decided by the greatest proportionate number of points in finished matches.

MATCH SCORES AND RESULTS

Yorkshire v.	Ground	Yorkshire		Opponents		Result
		1st Inns.	2nd Inns.	1st Inns.	2nd Inns.	
Lancashire	Manchester	123	168 (8)	150	139	Y, 2 wickets
Warwickshire	Birmingham	887	—	203	48 (1)	Draw
Somerset	Taunton	400	132 (5)	323	208	Y, 5 wickets
Gloucestershire	Bristol	234	57 (1)	131	158	Y, 9 wickets
Sussex	Bradford	543	22 (0)	265	296	Y, 10 wickets
Middlesex	Lord's	381	147 (0)	384	142	Y, 10 wickets
Kent	Leeds	459	23 (1)	205	275	Y, 9 wickets
Nottinghamshire	Nottingham	450	—	279	328	Draw
Surrey	Bradford	135	*134 (7)	147	75 (6)	Draw
Essex	Bradford	80	85 (3)	109	55	Y, 7 wickets
Leicestershire	Leicester	660	—	165	193	Y, inns. and 302 runs
Derbyshire	Derby	416	43 (1)	281	*450 (8)	Draw
Derbyshire	Sheffield	298	86 (1)	109	55	Y, 9 wickets
Warwickshire	Leeds	329	—	167	148	Y, inns. and 14 runs
Nottinghamshire	Huddersfield	90	193	226	58 (6)	N, 4 wickets
Essex	Leyton	203	133	205	134 (6)	E, 4 wickets
Hampshire	Southampton	307	235 (8)	515	—	Draw
Lancashire	Leeds	190	209	169	107	Y, 123 runs
Somerset	Dewsbury	251	—	78	167	Y, inns. and 6 runs
Gloucestershire	Sheffield	141	296	79	92	Y, 266 runs
Surrey	Oval	172	206	439	—	S, inns. and 61 runs
Hampshire	Harrogate	266	32 (0)	176	121	Y, 10 wickets
Leicestershire	Scarborough	184	*130 (8)	93	59	Y, 162 runs
Middlesex	Bradford	363	143 (1)	332	—	Draw
Sussex	Brighton	407	—	191	260 (2)	Draw
Kent	Tonbridge	184	*124 (7)	98	103	Y, 107 runs

* Innings declared closed.

25

Yorkshire beat Gloucestershire, Kent, Lancashire, Leicestershire, Somerset twice ; and Derbyshire, Essex, Hampshire, Middlesex, Sussex, Warwickshire once.

Yorkshire were beaten by Essex, Nottinghamshire, Surrey once.

Yorkshire drew with Derbyshire, Hampshire, Middlesex, Nottinghamshire, Surrey, Sussex, Warwickshire once.

SUMMARY

	Yorkshire	Opponents
Runs scored	10751	9672
Average per wicket	31·90	20·75
Hundreds	18	13
Other innings over 50	47	33
Ten wickets in match	7	5
Five wickets in innings	24	18
Highest total	887 v. Warwickshire	515 (Hampshire)
Lowest total	80 v. Essex	55 (Essex)
Totals over 400	8	3
Totals under 100	2	7

PRINCIPAL AVERAGES

	Inns.	Not Out	Runs	Highest Inns.	100's	50's	Aver.
J. T. Brown	41	7	1556	203	4	7	45·76
F. S. Jackson	25	1	1030	117	3	5	42·91
R. Peel	35	3	1135	210*	3	3	35·46
G. H. Hirst	34	3	1018	107	1	10	32·83
J. Tunnicliffe	45	4	1223	99	—	9	29·82

	Balls	Balls per Wkt.	Runs	Wkts.	5 Wkts. in Inns.	Aver.
S. Haigh	2428	34·19	1085	71	7	15·28
E. Wainwright	3847	42·74	1685	90	6	18·72
R. Peel	5404	55·71	1850	97	6	19·07
G. H. Hirst	4304	53·80	1913	80	3	23·91

* Not out.

NOTES

During the season 9 Yorkshiremen scored over 500 runs in county matches, 12 averaged over 20 runs an innings, 7 took over 20 wickets and averaged less than 20 runs per wicket.

In the second match of the season (May 7, 8, 9) Yorkshire scored the record total in county cricket—887 v. Warwickshire at Birmingham.

R. Peel completed a " double " in all Yorkshire matches in 1896, scoring 1,193 runs and taking 108 wickets. He missed a " double " in county matches by three wickets.

Tunnicliffe made 52 catches in Championship games.

When Yorkshire scored 660 v. Leicestershire at Leicester every contributor, including " extras," reached double figures, and the runs were scored in 480 minutes.

For Kent at Leeds, F. Marchant scored 128 and 88 out of totals of 205 and 275.

F. S. Jackson scored 115 and 83 *v.* Middlesex at Bradford, and with ✓ Tunnicliffe made 127 for the first wicket in the second innings.

Against Middlesex at Lord's, J. T. Brown scored 203 and 81 in an unfinished second innings opening partnership with Tunnicliffe (63 not out) of 147.

In Lohmann's Benefit match at the Oval, which Surrey won by an innings and 61 runs, Peel scored 74 and 18, and took five wickets for 94 runs in 252 balls.

For Derbyshire at Derby, W. Storer scored 100 and 100 not out. In their second innings the Derbyshire batsmen collared the Yorkshire bowling, scoring 450 for eight wickets before declaring.

Against Hampshire at Southampton, Milligan, Mounsey and Hirst scored 58, 55, 55 in the first innings and 52, 64, 68 in the second, these being Yorkshire's only innings over 50. The three players were Nos. 6, 7 and 8 in the batting order. For Hampshire, who registered the biggest total of the season (515) against Yorkshire, E. G. Wynyard scored 268.

For the first time in a first-class match four individual hundreds were scored in an innings when Yorkshire made their record score against Warwickshire at Birmingham : Peel, 210 not out ; Lord Hawke, 166 ; E. Wainwright, 126 ; and F. S. Jackson, 117.

At Brighton, K. S. Ranjitsinhji scored 100 and 125 not out in one day. He went in on the second day of the match but had not scored when rain stopped play, and scored his first run on the third day.

HOW IT WAS DONE

	100's	50's	10 Wkts. in Match	5 Wkts. in Inns.	50 Runs & 5 Wkts. in Match
J. T. Brown	4	7	–	–	–
D. Denton	1	3	–	–	–
S. Haigh	–	–	2	7	–
Lord Hawke	2	–	–	–	–
G. H. Hirst	1	10	–	3	4
F. S. Jackson	3	5	–	–	2
F. W. Milligan	–	2	–	–	–
R. Moorhouse	1	3	–	–	–
J. Mounsey	–	2	–	–	–
R. Peel	3	3	3	6	1
E. Smith	1	1	–	2	–
J. Tunnicliffe	–	9	–	–	–
E. Wainwright	2	2	2	6	1
Total	18	47	7	24	8

FIELDING (168 Catches)

No. of Catches		No. of Catches	
46	J. Tunnicliffe	7	S. Haigh
22	E. Wainwright	7	F. W. Milligan
16	J. T. Brown	6	Lord Hawke
16	G. H. Hirst	6	R. Moorhouse
12	F. S. Jackson	5	J. Mounsey
11	D. Denton	4	E. Smith
9	R. Peel	1	J. Shaw

WICKETKEEPING

	Stumped	Caught	Total
D. Hunter	13	48	61
A. L. Bairstow	1	6	7
W. Earnshaw	1	1	2
Total	15	55	70

TOTALS

400 Runs and Over

Yorkshire (8)

887 *v*. Warwickshire, Birmingham
660 *v*. Leicestershire, Leicester
543 *v*. Sussex, Bradford
459 *v*. Kent, Leeds

450 *v*. Nottinghamshire, Nottingham
416 *v*. Derbyshire, Derby
407 *v*. Sussex, Brighton
400 *v*. Somerset, Taunton

Opponents (3)

515, Hampshire, Southampton
450 (8),* Derbyshire, Derby

439, Surrey, Oval

* Innings declared closed.

Under 100 Runs

Yorkshire (2)

80 *v*. Essex, Bradford

90 *v*. Nottinghamshire, Huddersfield

Opponents (7)

55, Essex, Bradford
93 and 59, Leicestershire, Scarborough
78, Somerset, Dewsbury

79 and 92, Gloucestershire, Sheffield
98, Kent, Tonbridge

FIRST WICKET PARTNERSHIPS

Scores	Partners	Against	Ground
139, 147*	J. T. Brown, J. Tunnicliffe	Middlesex	Lord's
143	F. S. Jackson, J. Tunnicliffe	Sussex	Brighton
139	J. T. Brown, J. Tunnicliffe	Leicestershire	Leicester
127	F. S. Jackson, J. Tunnicliffe	Middlesex	Bradford

* Unfinished.

50 RUNS AND 5 WICKETS

Scores	Analyses	Player	Against	Ground
90	3-51, 3-67	G. H. Hirst	Sussex	Bradford
21, 41	2-21, 4-30	F. S. Jackson	Lancashire	Manchester
74, 18	5-94	R. Peel	Surrey	Oval
68	2-47, 4-43	G. H. Hirst	Derbyshire	Derby
62, 25	2-66, 6-49	E. Wainwright	Somerset	Taunton
85	8-59	G. H. Hirst	Warwickshire	Birmingham
77	3-27, 3-49	F. S. Jackson	Leicestershire	Leicester
107	5-67, 1-46	G. H. Hirst	Leicestershire	Leicester

MATCHES OF THE SEASON

Yorkshire v. *Lancashire*

Manchester, May 4, 5, 6

Yorkshire won by two wickets

One of the most exciting matches of 1896 was played in the first week of the season, when Yorkshire beat Lancashire by two wickets.

On the first day each side completed an innings, Lancashire having lead of 27 runs. F. H. Sugg's 74 was the only batting highlight. Peel, Hirst, Wainwright and Jackson all took wickets cheaply for Yorkshire, Briggs and Hallam being the most successful Lancastrians.

When play ended on the second day Yorkshire, with Mounsey and Hirst not out and only Hunter to follow, still needed 18 runs. But on the following morning the runs were obtained without difficulty, and the Yorkshiremen had defeated the ancient enemy.

In Lancashire's second innings Paul scored 52 in three hours.

Lancashire

A. N. Hornby c Hunter b Peel	1	c Hunter b Jackson	5
A. Ward c Hunter b Peel	13	c Hirst b Milligan	14
A. Paul st. Hunter b Wainwright	16	c Wainwright b Milligan	52
F. H. Sugg c Denton b Hirst	74	c Tunnicliffe b Milligan	16
G. R. Baker c Tunnicliffe b Hirst	1	b Jackson	4
C. H. Benton b Jackson	1	c Tunnicliffe b Milligan	0
J. Briggs c Milligan b Jackson	8	c Wainwright b Jackson	4
C. Smith not out	12	st. Hunter b Jackson	17
W. R. Cuttell lbw, b Peel	2	not out	8
A. W. Hallam b Hirst	0	b Peel	0
A. Mold b Peel	11	b Peel	4
Extras	11	Extras	15
	150		139

Yorkshire

F. S. Jackson c Sugg b Briggs	21	b Briggs	41
J. Tunnicliffe b Briggs	0	c Smith b Mold	6
J. T. Brown b Briggs	4	b Briggs	10
D. Denton b Briggs	18	b Mold	25
R. Moorhouse c Hornby b Hallam	43	lbw, b Briggs	1
E. Wainwright b Briggs	11	b Mold	47
R. Peel c Paul b Hallam	12	c and b Mold	0
F. W. Milligan b Mold	4	b Baker	8
J. Mounsey not out	1	not out	15
G. H. Hirst b Hallam	5	not out	11
D. Hunter c and b Mold	0		
Extras	4	Extras	4
	123		168

Yorkshire Bowling

	Overs	Mdns.	Runs	Wkts.		Overs	Mdns.	Runs	Wkts.
Peel	29.4	12	54	4	...	21	8	21	2
Hirst	25	13	47	3	...	18	7	29	0
Wainwright	9	5	17	1	...	15	8	16	0
Jackson	5	2	21	2	...	25	15	30	4
Milligan						18	6	28	4

Lancashire Bowling

	Overs	Mdns.	Runs	Wkts.		Overs	Mdns.	Runs	Wkts.
Mold	12	3	32	2	...	22	6	49	4
Briggs	23	8	44	5	...	35.3	16	55	3
Hallam	12	4	22	3	...	11	1	30	0
Cuttell	9	2	21	0	...	5	0	12	0
Baker						9	2	18	1

Yorkshire v. *Warwickshire*

Birmingham, May 7, 8, 9

Draw

Yorkshire travelled from Manchester to a perfect wicket at Birmingham and proceeded to compile the highest total ever recorded in a county match, and only beaten in England by England's 903 *v.* Australia in 1938. Few other cricket records have remained unbroken for fifty-two years.

Only rarely have Yorkshire allowed themselves to forget their main objective—winning the match—in order to set up a record, but on this occasion the partnerships of Wainwright and Peel, followed by one of 240 between Peel and Lord Hawke, probably induced the Yorkshire captain to bat for two days.

All the Yorkshiremen, except Denton and Hunter, scored runs, and for the first time in first-class cricket four individual hundreds were scored in an innings. Peel's 210 not out was the highest innings of his career.

When Warwickshire went in, Hirst took eight wickets for 59 runs, but there was, of course, not sufficient time to get Warwickshire out twice on a good wicket.

Yorkshire

F. S. Jackson c Law b Ward	117
J. Tunnicliffe c Pallett b Glover	28
J. T. Brown c Hill b Pallett	23
D. Denton c W. G. Quaife b Santall	6
R. Moorhouse b Ward	72
E. Wainwright run out	126
R. Peel not out	210
F. W. Milligan b Pallett	34
Lord Hawke b Pallett	166
G. H. Hirst c Glover b Santall	85
D. Hunter b Pallett	5
Extras	15
	887

Warwickshire

H. W. Bainbridge c Hunter b Hirst	5	b Wainwright	29
W. Quaife b Hirst	0	not out	18
W. G. Quaife not out	92		
A. Law c Jackson b Hirst	7		
A. A. Lilley b Hirst	0		
J. E. Hill b Hirst	4		
E. J. Diver b Peel	27		
H. J. Pallett c Wainwright b Jackson	25		
S. J. Santall b Hirst	29		
A. C. S. Glover b Hirst	1		
W. Ward b Hirst	3		
Extras	10	Extras	1
	203		48

Warwickshire Bowling

	Overs	Mdns.	Runs	Wkts.
Santall	65	9	223	2
Ward	62	11	175	2
Glover	30	1	154	1
Pallett	75.3	14	184	4
W. G. Quaife	8	1	33	0
Bainbridge	6	1	17	0
Hill	3	0	14	0
Lilley	6	1	13	0
W. Quaife	9	1	18	0
Diver	10	1	41	0

Yorkshire Bowling

	Overs	Mdns.	Runs	Wkts.		Overs	Mdns.	Runs	Wkts.
Hirst	40.1	16	59	8					
Peel	31	21	27	1	...	3	2	4	0
Jackson	18	9	23	1					
Wainwright	16	7	35	0	...	2.1	1	4	1
Milligan	13	5	14	0	...	5	1	15	0
Brown	4	0	24	0					
Moorhouse	4	1	11	0	...	4	0	24	0

Yorkshire v. *Leicestershire*

Leicester, June 18, 19, 20

Yorkshire won by an innings and 302 runs

Yorkshire's match against Leicestershire at Leicester has two interesting features : every member of the side, including " extras," scored double figures, the individual scores ranging from 131 to 19 ; and the runs were scored in 480 minutes—a rate of 82 runs per hour.

When Leicester batted, Hirst took five wickets and Tunnicliffe made four catches in the slips in the first innings.

Yorkshire

J. T. Brown c Tomlin b Pougher	131
J. Tunnicliffe c Holland b Geeson	79
F. G. Jackson c Tomlin b Geeson	77
D. Denton b Coe	73
R. Moorhouse c de Trafford b Woodcock	19
E. Wainwright b Woodcock	23
G. H. Hirst c Coe b de Trafford	107
F. W. Milligan c Pougher b de Trafford	48
J. Mounsey c Whiteside b Pougher	21
S. Haigh not out	32
D. Hunter c sub. b Pougher	31
Extras	19
	660

Leicestershire

C. E. de Trafford b Haigh	24	b Jackson	18
J. Holland c Denton b Hirst	9	c Hunter b Jackson	10
A. E. Knight c Tunnicliffe b Hirst	16	not out	45
A. D. Pougher c Wainwright b Hirst	4	b Moorhouse	39
C. J. B. Wood c Hunter b Hirst	2	lbw, b. Brown	10
S. Coe b Jackson	16	c Haigh b Jackson	13
W. Tomlin b Milligan	62	c Milligan b Hirst	37
L. Brown c Tunnicliffe b Hirst	0	st. Hunter b Brown	8
F. Geeson c Tunnicliffe b Jackson	13	run out	4
A. Woodcock c Tunnicliffe b Jackson	2	st. Hunter b Brown	1
J. P. Whiteside not out	10	run out	0
Extras	7	Extras	8
	165		193

Leicestershire Bowling

	Overs	Mdns.	Runs	Wkts.
Pougher	63.2	22	135	3
Woodcock	51	4	147	2
Geeson	46	12	160	2
Coe	22	3	114	1
Tomlin	2	0	5	0
Wood	2	0	19	0
de Trafford	7	0	47	2
Holland	2	0	14	0

Yorkshire Bowling

	Overs	Mdns.	Runs	Wkts.		Overs	Mdns.	Runs	Wkts.
Hirst	23	10	67	5	...	19	5	46	1
Haigh	17	4	40	1	...	10	4	17	0
Jackson	14	2	27	3	...	19	2	49	3
Wainwright	5	0	23	0					
Milligan	2.4	1	1	1	...	10	2	37	0
Moorhouse						4	2	9	1
Brown						7.4	0	20	3
Mounsey						4	2	7	0

LORD HAWKE

From a cartoon by 'Spy'

F. S. JACKSON

(The Rt. Hon. Sir Stanley Jackson)

From a cartoon by 'Spy'

APPEARANCES

The following 19 cricketers appeared for Yorkshire in Championship matches, the number of appearances being in parentheses :

A. L. Bairstow (2)
J. T. Brown (24)
D. Denton (23)
W. Earnshaw (1)
S. Haigh (13)
Lord Hawke (20)
G. H. Hirst (25)
D. Hunter (23)
F. S. Jackson (16)
S. Kilburn (1)

F. W. Milligan (16)
R. Moorhouse (20)
J. Mounsey (16)
R. Peel (24)
J. Shaw (1)
E. Smith (9)
J. Tunnicliffe (26)
E. Wainwright (25)
C. E. M. Wilson (1)

POST MORTEM

Without showing any overwhelming superiority, Yorkshire were without question the best all-round county side in England. Five of their batsmen scored 1,000 runs in county matches and seven bowlers took twenty or more wickets. In Jackson, Peel, Wainwright, Hirst, Milligan and E. Smith, Yorkshire had a solid foundation of all-rounders unequalled by any other county, and in Tunnicliffe they had the finest slip fielder in the country. The bowling was not, perhaps, quite as devastating as in 1893—Derbyshire and Hampshire showed that it could be hit—but it had variety and there was plenty of it, and 1896 was a season in which the weather and wickets favoured batsmen. Lord Hawke captained the side in twenty of the Championship matches with his customary skill and sagacity.

C

INTERREGNUM

1897

Lancashire won the County Championship in 1897, Surrey being second, Essex third and Yorkshire fourth. Yorkshire scored the highest total—681 for five wickets—against Sussex at Sheffield, but lost 5 matches—to Essex twice, Gloucestershire, Sussex and Lancashire. On July 17 Yorkshire was well in the running, having won 9 matches and lost 1 out of 13 matches, but of the remaining 13 games 4 were lost.

The batting was as good as in 1896, six batsmen scoring 1,000 runs and ten averaging 20 or more per innings ; but the bowling was less effective. Peel, Haigh, Jackson, Hirst and Wainwright all took over fifty wickets, but none of them took wickets for less than 20 runs each.

Here are some of the most outstanding performances of the season :

v. Surrey at Sheffield : Yorkshire won by 100 runs, Haigh taking seven wickets for 17 runs in Surrey's first innings. In the match, Richardson took fifteen wickets for 154 runs, ten being clean bowled.

v. Sussex at Sheffield : Brown (311) and Tunnicliffe (147) set up a new first wicket record by scoring 378 before they were parted.

v. Lancashire at Bradford : Hunter's Benefit realised £1,950.

v. Essex at Huddersfield : The most sensational match of the season, Essex winning by one run. Scores—Essex, 139 and 294 ; Yorkshire, 135 and 297.

v. Derbyshire at Bradford : In Derbyshire's first innings 120 runs had been scored for four wickets. Haigh then took five wickets in 10 balls without a run being scored off him, the last three wickets being taken with consecutive balls.

J. T. Brown headed the batting averages with 1,431 runs (average 43·36), the most successful bowler being Peel, with fifty-six wickets for 20·01 runs each. This was Peel's sixteenth, and last, season with Yorkshire.

THIRD CHAMPIONSHIP

1898

Captain : Lord Hawke

Yorkshire, in spite of being beaten by Surrey and Middlesex in August, always seemed to have a little in hand. Actually, they won the Championship rather more easily than is suggested by the difference between the first two percentages.

THE FIRST SIX

	Played	Won	Lost	Drawn	Points	Percent.
Yorkshire	26	16	3	7	13	68·42
Middlesex	18	10	3	5	7	53·84
Gloucestershire	20	9.	3	8	6	50·00
Surrey	24	11	4	9	7	46·66
Essex	20	10	6	4	4	25·00
Lancashire	26	9	6	11	3	20·00

METHOD OF SCORING : As in 1896.

MATCH SCORES AND RESULTS

Yorkshire v.	Ground	Yorkshire 1st Inns.	Yorkshire 2nd Inns.	Opponents 1st Inns.	Opponents 2nd Inns.	Result
Somerset	Bath	163	*174 (7)	104	35	Y, 198 runs
Gloucestershire	Bristol	263 (3)	—	—	—	Draw
Hampshire	Southampton	157	—	42	36	Y, inns. and 79 runs
Warwickshire	Leeds	112	85 (0)	218	*50 (5)	Draw
Essex	Leyton	118	129 (7)	78	168	Y, 3 wickets
Surrey	Bradford	*297 (9)	—	139	37	Y, inns. and 121 runs
Hampshire	Huddersfield	226	—	45	83	Y, inns. and 98 runs
Kent	Sheffield	289	*229 (3)	218	171	Y, 129 runs
Middlesex	Lord's	445	—	118	318	Y, inns. and 9 runs
Nottinghamshire	Leeds	143	56 (6)	215	*105 (4)	) Draw
Leicestershire	Leicester	449	—	57	126	Y, inns. and 226 runs
Essex	Bradford	278	—	64	176	Y, inns. and 38 runs
Leicestershire	Dewsbury	178	—	56	98	Y, inns. and 24 runs
Sussex	Bradford	282	126 (3)	189	218	Y, 7 wickets
Lancashire	Sheffield	316	*253 (2)	288	140 (5)	Draw
Kent	Maidstone	199	124	199	127 (4)	K, 6 wickets
Somerset	Scarborough	397	54 (4)	208	242	Y, 6 wickets
Gloucestershire	Sheffield	331	—	192	127	Y, inns. and 12 runs
Derbyshire	Harrogate	252	*321 (9)	238	219 (3)	Draw
Warwickshire	Birmingham	448	—	406	102 (4)	Draw
Surrey	Oval	78	186	536	—	S, inns. and 272 runs
Nottinghamshire	Nottingham	277	—	90	90 (1)	Draw
Lancashire	Manchester	114	63 (0)	112	64	Y, 10 wickets
Middlesex	Leeds	142	45	128	62 (2)	M, 8 wickets
Derbyshire	Chesterfield	662	—	118	157	Y, inns. and 387 runs
Sussex	Brighton	428	*166 (7)	311	91	Y, 192 runs

* Innings declared closed.

35

Yorkshire beat Essex, Hampshire, Leicestershire, Somerset, Sussex twice; and Derbyshire, Gloucestershire, Kent, Lancashire, Middlesex, Surrey once.

Yorkshire were beaten by Kent, Middlesex, Surrey.

Yorkshire drew with Nottinghamshire, Warwickshire twice; and Derbyshire, Gloucestershire, Lancashire once.

SUMMARY

	Yorkshire	Opponents
Runs scored	9035	7411
Average per wicket	28·23	16·95
Hundreds	15	5
Other innings over 50	32	22
Ten wickets in match	5	2
Five wickets in innings	24	15
Highest total	662 v. Derbyshire	536 (Surrey)
Lowest total	45 v. Middlesex	35 (Somerset)
Totals under 400	5	2
Totals under 100	2	14

PRINCIPAL AVERAGES

	Inns.	Not Out	Runs	Highest Inns.	100's	50's	Aver.
J. Tunnicliffe	38	5	1538	243	4	8	46·60
F. S. Jackson	32	3	1326	160	5	2	45·72
J. T. Brown	40	2	1389	300	3	2	36·55
Lord Hawke	30	6	797	134	2	4	33·20

	Balls	Balls per Wkt.	Runs	Wkts.	5 Wkts. in Inns.	Aver.
W. Rhodes	5000	39·68	1745	126	11	13·84
E. Wainwright	2161	38·58	802	56	4	14·32
F. S. Jackson	3488	43·60	1217	80	4	15·21
S. Haigh	3735	42·44	1618	88	4	18·38

NOTES

In his first county match—v. Somerset at Bath—Rhodes took thirteen wickets for 45 runs (seven for 24 and six for 21).

At Bradford, Surrey were all out for 37 in the second innings, Rhodes (seven for 24) and Wainwright (three for 10) bowling unchanged. Rhodes and Hunter (st. 3, ct. 2) disposed of the last five Surrey batsmen.

In their second innings v. Middlesex at Leeds, Yorkshire scored only 45 runs, A. E. Trott taking seven wickets for 13 runs.

In their two matches against Yorkshire, Hampshire scored 36, 42, 45 and 83—206 runs for the loss of forty wickets. (Average 5·12.)

At Chesterfield on August 18, 19, 20, J. T. Brown (300) and J. Tunnicliffe (243) set up a new world record for the first and any wicket in first-class cricket (554).

C. B. Fry carried his bat through the Sussex innings (311) for 179 at Brighton.

The Hampshire-Yorkshire match at Southampton in 1898 was H. Baldwin's Benefit, but unfortunately for the beneficiary it was rained off on the first day and begun and finished on the second. Yorkshire scored 157, and then dismissed Hampshire for 42 and 36, Haigh taking fourteen wickets for 43 runs.

Against Leicestershire at Leicester, F. S. Jackson scored 147 and took five wickets for 20 and three for 34.

HOW IT WAS DONE

	100's	50's	10 Wkts. in Match	5 Wkts. in Inns.	50 Runs & 5 Wkts. in Match
J. T. Brown sen.	3	2	–	1	–
D. Denton	–	4	–	–	–
S. Haigh	–	2	1	4	–
Lord Hawke	2	4	–	–	–
G. H. Hirst	1	–	–	–	–
F. S. Jackson	5	2	–	4	3
F. W. Milligan	–	5	–	–	–
W. Rhodes	–	3	3	11	1
J. Tunnicliffe	4	8	–	–	–
E. Wainwright	–	2	1	4	1
Total	15	32	5	24	4

FIELDING (153 Catches)

No. of Catches		No. of Catches	
28	J. Tunnicliffe	12	E. Wainwright
20	F. S. Jackson	9	F. W. Milligan
19	G. H. Hirst	6	R. Moorhouse
15	J. T. Brown sen.	4	Lord Hawke
13	S. Haigh	1	E. Smith
13	W. Rhodes	1	C. E. M. Wilson
12	D. Denton		

WICKETKEEPING

	Stumped	Caught	Total
D. Hunter	17	29	46
A. L. Bairstow	5	7	12
J. Binns	3	–	3
Total	25	36	61

TOTALS

400 Runs and Over

Yorkshire (5)

662 *v.* Derbyshire, Chesterfield   445 *v.* Middlesex, Lord's
448 *v.* Leicestershire, Leicester   428 *v.* Sussex, Brighton
448 *v.* Warwickshire, Birmingham

Opponents (2)

536, Surrey, Oval   406, Warwickshire, Birmingham

Under 100 Runs

Yorkshire (2)

45 *v.* Middlesex, Leeds   78 *v.* Surrey, Oval

Opponents (13)

35, Somerset, Bath   64, Essex, Bradford
42 and 36, Hampshire, Southampton   64, Lancashire, Bradford
45 and 83, Hampshire, Huddersfield   78, Essex, Leyton
56 and 98, Leicestershire, Dewsbury   90, Nottinghamshire, Nottingham
57, Leicestershire, Leicester

FIRST WICKET PARTNERSHIPS

Score	Partners	Against	Ground
554	J. T. Brown sen., J. Tunnicliffe	Derbyshire	Chesterfield
133	J. T. Brown sen., J. Tunnicliffe	Sussex	Brighton
100	J. T. Brown sen., J. Tunnicliffe	Essex	Bradford

50 RUNS AND 5 WICKETS

Scores	Analyses	Player	Against	Ground
38, 13	5-46, 0-33	F. S. Jackson	Essex	Leyton
46, 31	2-28, 3-42	F. S. Jackson	Kent	Sheffield
147	5-20, 3-34	F. S. Jackson	Leicestershire	Leicester
50*	6-32, 1-26	W. Rhodes	Nottinghamshire	Nottingham

* Not out.

MATCHES OF THE SEASON

Yorkshire v. *Hampshire*
Southampton, May 26, 27

Yorkshire won by an innings and 79 runs

After the first day had been lost owing to rain, the match between Yorkshire and Hampshire was begun and finished in six hours.

Going in first, Hampshire collapsed and were all out for 42, D. A. Steele (10) being the only Hampshire batsman to reach double figures in the match. Haigh and Rhodes bowled unchanged, the former taking eight wickets for 21 runs. Five Hampshire men failed to score.

In view of the conditions, Yorkshire's 157 was a very good performance, Tunnicliffe, who was in throughout the innings, scoring a fine 58, and Rhodes, Hirst and Haigh giving useful assistance.

Hampshire's second innings was even more disastrous than their first, the whole side being out for 36, including four more " ducks."

In the match, Haigh took fourteen wickets for 43 runs, ten of his wickets being clean bowled.

Hampshire

C. G. Ward c Denton b Haigh	6	b Haigh	5
V. A. Barton b Haigh	7	c Brown b Haigh	3
A. J. L. Hill c Jackson b Rhodes	0	b Haigh	7
W. Andrews b Haigh	0	b Haigh	0
A. Webb c Jackson b Haigh	0	b Jackson	7
B. Lamb b Haigh	0	b Jackson	3
C. Heseltine b Haigh	6	not out	5
D. A. Steele c Jackson b Haigh	10	run out	0
C. Robson not out	6	b Haigh	0
H. Baldwin b Haigh	6	b Haigh	0
E. Light b Haigh	0	st. Hunter b Haigh	4
Extras	1	Extras	2
	42		**36**

Yorkshire

J. T. Brown b Baldwin	4
J. Tunnicliffe b Baldwin	58
F. S. Jackson b Andrews	9
D. Denton c Barton b Baldwin	3
E. Wainwright st. Robson b Light	8
G. H. Hirst st. Robson b Light	18
F. W. Milligan c Barton b Hill	2
W. Rhodes c Andrew b Hill	28
Lord Hawke c Ward b Hill	0
S. Haigh c Lamb b Baldwin	17
D. Hunter not out	4
Extras	6
	157

Yorkshire Bowling

	Overs	Mdns.	Runs	Wkts.		Overs	Mdns.	Runs	Wkts.
Haigh	15.4	10	21	8	...	13.2	7	22	6
Rhodes	15	8	20	2	...	7	3	10	1
Jackson						6	4	2	2

Hampshire Bowling

	Overs	Mdns.	Runs	Wkts.
Andrew	15	4	30	1
Baldwin	12.1	1	37	4
Light	11	0	44	2
Hill	18	6	34	3
Heseltine	2	0	6	0

Yorkshire v. *Surrey*

Bradford, June 6, 7, 8

Yorkshire won by an innings and 21 runs

Yorkshire's match with Surrey at Bradford was, perhaps, the most remarkable of the season. After a blank first day Surrey scored 139 and

Yorkshire 142 for eight wickets, Hirst and Haigh being not out at close of play.

On the third day the two not outs added 155 runs before Abel caught Haigh with his score at 85. The innings was then declared closed, Hirst being 130 not out. The two Yorkshire bowlers had added 192 runs, and Surrey needed 158 to save the innings defeat.

They scored 37, Richardson (9) being the top scorer. With batsmen like Abel, Hayward, Brockwell, Baldwin, Jephson and Key in the side such a collapse was astonishing, and can only be attributed to extraordinarily fine bowling by Rhodes and Wainwright, who bowled unchanged.

In Surrey's second innings, Rhodes and Hunter (st. 3, c 2) dismissed the last five batsmen.

Surrey

R. Abel st. Hunter b Wainwright	51	c Jackson b Rhodes	6
W. Brockwell b Wainwright	19	lbw, b Wainwright	5
T. Hayward st. Hunter b Rhodes	1	b Wainwright	2
C. Baldwin c and b Wainwright	3	b Wainwright	0
D. L. A. Jephson c and b Wainwright	4	c Brown b Rhodes	0
K. J. Key c Jackson b Rhodes	32	not out	8
A. E. Street c Tunnicliffe b Rhodes	0	st. Hunter b Rhodes	4
W. H. Lockwood st. Hunter b Rhodes	2	c Hunter b Rhodes	0
W. Lees b Wainwright	18	st. Hunter b Rhodes	0
H. Wood not out	8	st. Hunter b Rhodes	0
T. Richardson c Denton b Rhodes	0	c Hunter b Rhodes	9
Extras	1	Extras	3
	139		37

Yorkshire

J. T. Brown b Lockwood	0
J. Tunnicliffe run out	21
F. S. Jackson c and b Lockwood	3
D. Denton b Lockwood	11
E. Wainwright lbw, b Richardson	5
G. H. Hirst not out	130
R. Moorhouse c Hayward b Lockwood	12
Lord Hawke b Lees	5
W. Rhodes c Jephson b Richardson	13
S. Haigh c Abel b Brockwell	85
D. Hunter did not bat.	
Extras	12
	297*

* Innings declared closed.

Yorkshire Bowling

	Overs	Mdns.	Runs	Wkts.		Overs	Mdns.	Runs	Wkts.
Haigh	13	3	28	0					
Jackson	16	6	21	0					
Rhodes	30.3	12	46	5	...	19.1	9	24	7
Wainwright	27	11	43	5	...	20	14	10	3

Surrey Bowling

	Overs	Mdns.	Runs	Wkts.
Lockwood	41	18	74	4
Hayward	13	3	36	0
Richardson	29	7	64	2
Lees	18	8	41	1
Jephson	8	0	30	0
Brockwell	6.2	1	18	1
Abel	4	1	8	0
Street	5	0	14	0

Yorkshire v. *Derbyshire*

Chesterfield, August 18, 19, 20

Yorkshire won by an innings and 387 runs

The match at Chesterfield provided Brown and Tunnicliffe with an opportunity to produce their *magnum opus*—a first wicket stand of 554 runs.

This great partnership put several new records into *Wisden*: (1) It was the highest partnership for the first or any wicket in first-class cricket ; (2) it was the first stand exceeding 500 runs in a first-class match ; (3) it was scored in 305 minutes—a rate of scoring of 105 runs per hour. When Brown completed his 300 he hit his wicket, and Yorkshire proceeded to the serious business of winning the match.

Each of the partners scored 48 fours.

Yorkshire

J. T. Brown hit wkt b Storer	300
J. Tunnicliffe c F. Davidson b Storer	243
Lord Hawke c Walker b Storer	14
D. Denton b F. Davidson	45
G. H. Hirst c G. Davidson b Walker	0
F. S. Jackson c Storer b Walker	14
W. Rhodes c Storer b Walker	6
F. W. Milligan c Chatterton b F. Davidson	4
E. Smith c Storer b Walker	4
S. Haigh c Ashcroft b F. Davidson	13
D. Hunter not out	0
Extras	19
	662

Derbyshire

S. H. Evershed c Hunter b Jackson	18	b Smith	12
L. G. Wright c Hawke b Hirst	0	st. Hunter b Rhodes	5
H. Bagshaw c Haigh b Jackson	20	b Jackson	2
W. Storer c Denton b Milligan	13	c Rhodes b Jackson	25
W. Chatterton b Milligan	6	c and b Rhodes	54
G. Davidson b Jackson	36	lbw, b Jackson	2
E. M. Ashcroft c Hunter b Jackson	1	not out	21
W. Sugg c Brown b Smith	8	b Rhodes	3
F. Davidson c Haigh b Smith	3	retired hurt	5
A. Charlesworth c Haigh b Rhodes	7	absent hurt	0
G. G. Walker not out	0	b Haigh	7
Extras	6	Extras	21
	118		157

Derbyshire Bowling

	Overs	Mdns.	Runs	Wkts.
Davidson (G.)	1	0	3	0
Walker	55	11	199	4
Davidson (F.)	39.3	9	133	3
Sugg	5	0	27	0
Bagshaw	11	1	50	0
Storer	26	1	142	3
Ashcroft	6	1	21	0
Evershed	3	0	13	0
Wright	3	0	24	0
Charlesworth	7	0	31	0

Yorkshire Bowling

	Overs	Mdns.	Runs	Wkts.		Overs	Mdns.	Runs	Wkts.
Hirst	10	3	19	1					
Jackson	28	12	52	4	...	37	22	26	3
Milligan	12	3	36	2	...	4	2	6	0
Smith	7.1	6	5	2	...	21	10	35	1
Rhodes	1	1	0	1	...	29	13	47	3
Brown						4	1	9	0
Haigh						7.1	4	13	1

APPEARANCES

The following 19 cricketers appeared for Yorkshire in Championship matches, the number of appearances being in parentheses :

J. T. Brown sen. (26)
J. T. Brown jun. (1)
A. L. Bairstow (3)
J. Binns (1)
D. Denton (26)
S. Haigh (26)
Lord Hawke (25)
H. Hayley (1)
G. H. Hirst (23)
D. Hunter (22)
F. S. Jackson (23)
F. W. Milligan (23)
R. Moorhouse (9)
W. Rhodes (26)
E. Smith (4)
T. Tait (1)
J. Tunnicliffe (24)
E. Wainwright (21)
C. E. M. Wilson (1)

POST MORTEM

One of the secrets of Yorkshire's success in 1898 was the fact that practically the same side appeared in every match—and every one of these eleven " regulars " averaged over 14 runs an innings. Another deciding factor was the discovery of a new slow left-hand bowler to take the place of Peel. Few, if any, young cricketers have enjoyed more successful first seasons than Rhodes in 1898. He scored 472 runs with an average of 21·45 and took 126 wickets in county matches at a cost of 13·84 runs each. In the English averages only J. T. Hearne was above Yorkshire's new star. Of the other bowlers, Hirst had a poor season, but Wainwright, Jackson and Haigh were able and willing assistants in the task of getting the other side out cheaply. Lord Hawke supervised this operation with his usual skill.

INTERREGNÙM

1899

Yorkshire finished third in the Championship with a percentage of 55·55 to Surrey's 66·66, Middlesex with 57·14 just beating the Yorkshiremen for second place. Right up to the last week of the summer Yorkshire seemed certain to win.

The season's play produced some remarkable performances:

v. Worcestershire at Worcester : The first match of the season resulted in a narrow Yorkshire win by 11 runs, Wainwright being top scorer in each innings (35, 86) and J. T. Brown jun., taking six Worcester wickets for 19 runs in the second innings. In the match, G. A. Wilson took ten Yorkshire wickets for 139 runs.

v. Somerset (Bath), Gloucestershire (Bristol), Essex (Leyton) : In consecutive innings, Rhodes took twenty-nine wickets for 3·37 runs each—five for 11 *v.* Somerset, six for 16 and three for 15 *v.* Gloucestershire, nine for 28 and six for 28 *v.* Essex.

v. Middlesex at Lord's : Middlesex won by an innings and 2 runs, P. F. Warner scoring 150, and A. E. Trott, in addition to an innings of 164, taking nine wickets for 228 runs in 81 overs.

v. Surrey at the Oval : Every wicket obtained by the perspiring bowlers in this match cost 73·82 runs. Yorkshire scored 704 and Surrey 551 for seven wickets, the highlights being partnerships of 340 by Wainwright (228) and Hirst (186) for Yorkshire ; and 448 by Hayward (273) and Abel (193) for Surrey.

v. Sussex at Harrogate : Rhodes scored 81 not out in Yorkshire's second innings and took five wickets for 57 runs in the first innings of Sussex. C. B. Fry scored 162 not out in the second innings.

v. Somerset at Hull : E. R. Wilson made his first appearance for the county, scoring 55 and 0 and taking three wickets for 50 runs.

v. Leicestershire at Leicester : E. Wainwright scored 153 and took six wickets for 44 runs in Leicestershire's second innings.

The batting was stronger than ever, seven batsmen scoring 1,000 runs and twelve averaging over 20, of whom eight averaged 31 or more. In his second season Rhodes headed the bowlers with 129 wickets for 15·66 runs each, but the remainder of the bowling was scarcely on the same high level.

FOURTH CHAMPIONSHIP

1 9 0 0

Captain : Lord Hawke

The County Championship of 1900 soon developed into a new "War of the Roses," both Yorkshire and Lancashire being unbeaten after three months' play. The unexpected defeat of Lancashire by Gloucestershire in the last week of July was the turning point. Lancashire did not crack, but they lost a second match, whereas Yorkshire sailed past the winning post with an unbeaten record.

THE FIRST SIX

	Played	Won	Lost	Drawn	Points	Percent.
Yorkshire	28	16	0	12	16	100·00
Lancashire	28	15	2	11	13	76·47
Kent	22	8	4	10	4	33·33
Sussex	24	4	2	18	2	33·33
Nottinghamshire	18	7	4	7	3	27·27
Warwickshire	18	3	2	13	1	20·00

METHOD OF SCORING : As in 1896.

MATCH SCORES AND RESULTS

Yorkshire v.	Ground	Yorkshire 1st Inns.	Yorkshire 2nd Inns.	Opponents 1st Inns.	Opponents 2nd Inns.	Result
Worcestershire	Bradford	99	—	43	51	Y, inns. and 5 runs
Kent	Catford	163	260	112	180	Y, 131 runs
Derbyshire	Sheffield	259 (8)	—	175	9 (1)	Draw
Leicestershire	Huddersfield	302	61 (0)	262	100	Y, 10 wickets
Warwickshire	Leeds	359	86 (3)	228	294	Draw
Middlesex	Lord's	307	98 (4)	202	202	Y, 6 wickets
Leicestershire	Leicester	241	15 (0)	162	93	Y, 10 wickets
Lancashire	Bradford	230	64 (6)	96	—	Draw
Essex	Leyton	152	102(4)	132	120	Y, 6 wickets
Surrey	Sheffield	195	31 (1)	242	146	Draw
Hampshire	Hull	460	—	128	61	Y, inns. and 271 runs
Derbyshire	Derby	195	—	69	102	Y, inns. and 24 runs
Somerset	Dewsbury	137	191	140	48	Y, 140 runs
Kent	Leeds	132	51 (3)	230	42 (2)	Draw
Nottinghamshire	Scarborough	311	—	279	72 (6)	Draw
Sussex	Sheffield	*489 (9)	—	232	164	Y, inns. and 93 runs
Hampshire	Portsmouth	372	133 (4)	202	299	Y, 6 wickets
Worcestershire	Worcester	189	349 (8)	237	143 (5)	Draw
Lancashire	Manchester	235	146	228	20 (1)	Draw
Gloucestershire	Bradford	409	187	269	287	Y, 40 runs
Surrey	Oval	380	—	360	52	Draw
Nottinghamshire	Nottingham	270	197 (3)	335	—	Draw
Essex	Harrogate	171	42 (1)	65	52	Y, 96 runs
Warwickshire	Birmingham	158 (2)	—	84	43 (7)	Draw
Middlesex	Leeds	235	96	192	76	Y, 63 runs
Gloucestershire	Cheltenham	305	—	101	160	Y, inns. and 44 runs
Somerset	Taunton	*518 (8)	—	250	148	Y, inns. and 120 runs
Sussex	Brighton	214	199 (8)	268	—	Draw

* Innings declared closed.

Yorkshire beat Essex, Gloucestershire, Hampshire, Leicestershire, Middlesex, Somerset twice; and Derbyshire, Kent, Sussex, Worcestershire once.

Yorkshire drew with Lancashire, Nottinghamshire, Surrey, Warwickshire twice; and Derbyshire, Kent, Sussex, Worcestershire once.

SUMMARY

	Yorkshire	Opponents
Runs scored	9795	8287
Average per wicket	27·28	16·84
Hundreds	13	6
Other innings over 50	49	28
Ten wickets in match	7	3
Five wickets in innings	36	24
Highest total	518 (8) v. Somerset	360 (Surrey)
Lowest total	96 v. Middlesex	43 (Worcester)
Totals over 400	4	—
Totals under 100	2	9

PRINCIPAL AVERAGES

	Inns.	Not Out	Runs	Highest Inns.	100's	50's	Aver.
T. L. Taylor	18	3	740	147	1	6	49·33
G. H. Hirst	42	6	1573	155	4	11	43·69
J. Tunnicliffe	43	4	1428	158	4	6	36·61
E. Smith	25	6	553	116*	1	2	29·10
D. Denton	44	4	1111	96	–	8	27·77
J. T. Brown sen.	37	3	812	128	1	3	23·88

* Not out.

	Balls	Balls per Wkt.	Runs	Wkts.	5 Wkts. in Inns.	Aver.
W. Rhodes *	6991	33·93	2532	206	21	12·29
S. Haigh	4954	34·16	2054	145	10	14·16
J. T. Brown jun.	1225	53·26	529	23	2	23·00
G. H. Hirst	2702	55·14	1227	49	1	25·04
E. Smith	1561	53·82	751	29	2	25·89

* Rhodes was the first Yorkshire bowler to take 200 wickets in county matches in a season.

NOTES

The first county match of the season, v. Worcestershire at Bradford, was begun and finished in one day, Yorkshire winning by an innings and 5 runs, neither side scoring 100, and the match aggregate being 193. Ten batsmen failed to score, Wainwright's 34 being the biggest innings. Rhodes and Haigh bowled unchanged throughout the match.

Against Leicestershire at Leicester, Tunnicliffe made seven catches, five in the first innings.

J. Tunnicliffe captained an all-professional Yorkshire XI. against Hampshire at Hull.

At the Oval, Haigh took six wickets (all bowled) for 21 runs in Surrey's first innings (52).

G. L. Jessop scored 104 and 139 (88 minutes) for Gloucestershire at Bradford.

On three occasions Rhodes took fourteen wickets in a match—fourteen for 66 v. Hampshire at Hull, fourteen for 192 v. Gloucestershire at Bradford, and fourteen for 68 v. Essex at Harrogate.

In each Yorkshire–Surrey match, D. L. A. Jephson scored a hundred.

For Middlesex at Leeds, C. M. Wells took thirteen wickets for 68 runs, Haigh taking thirteen for 94. In the second innings of Middlesex, Haigh bowled six of the last seven batsmen and got the other lbw.

For Somerset at Dewsbury, Cranfield took thirteen wickets for 159 runs.

HOW IT WAS DONE

	100's	50's	10 Wkts. in Match	5 Wkts. in Inns.	50 Runs & 5 Wkts. in Match
J. T. Brown sen.	1	3	–	–	–
J. T. Brown jun.	–	–	–	2	–
D. Denton	–	8	–	–	–
S. Haigh	–	3	1	10	1
Lord Hawke	–	1	–	–	–
G. H. Hirst	4	11	–	1	1
D. Hunter	–	1	–	–	–
W. Rhodes	–	2	6	21	1
E. Smith	1	2	–	2	–
T. L. Taylor	1	6	–	–	–
J. Tunnicliffe	4	6	–	–	–
E. Wainwright	2	2	–	–	–
I. Washington	–	1	–	–	–
Lees Whitehead	–	3	–	–	–
Total	13	49	7	36	3

FIELDING (203 Catches)

No. of Catches		No. of Catches	
46	J. Tunnicliffe	7	I. Washington
33	E. Wainwright	6	J. T. Brown jun.
20	G. H. Hirst	6	W. Rhodes
18	S. Haigh	6	T. L. Taylor
14	E. Smith	5	" Sub."
12	D. Denton	4	Lees Whitehead
12	Lord Hawke	2	C. Oyston
11	J. T. Brown sen.	1	W. Riley

WICKETKEEPING

	Stumped	Caught	Total
D. Hunter	25	35	60
A. L. Bairstow	6	5	11
Total	31	40	71

TOTALS

400 Runs and Over

Yorkshire (4)

518 (8)* *v.* Somerset, Taunton   460 *v.* Hampshire, Hull
489 (9)* *v.* Sussex, Sheffield   409 *v.* Gloucestershire, Bradford

* Innings declared closed.

Opponents (0)
None.

Under 100 Runs

Yorkshire (2)

96 *v.* Middlesex, Leeds   99 *v* Worcestershire, Bradford

Opponents (11)

43 and 51, Worcestershire, Bradford   69, Derbyshire, Derby
48, Somerset, Dewsbury   76, Middlesex, Leeds
52, Surrey, Oval   84, Warwickshire, Birmingham
65 and 52, Essex, Harrogate   96, Lancashire, Bradford
61, Hampshire, Hull

FIRST WICKET PARTNERSHIPS

Score	Partners	Against	Ground
148	J. T. Brown sen., J. Tunnicliffe	Hampshire	Hull
132	J. T. Brown sen., J. Tunnicliffe	Middlesex	Lord's

50 RUNS AND 5 WICKETS

Scores	Analyses	Player	Against	Ground
53	7-32, 4-45	W. Rhodes	Derbyshire	Derby
55	2-30, 5-57	S. Haigh	Hampshire	Portsmouth
71	6-49, 1-36	G. H. Hirst	Sussex	Sheffield.

MATCHES OF THE SEASON

Yorkshire v. *Worcestershire*
Bradford, May 7

Yorkshire won by an innings and 5 runs

This match, the first of the season, was a cricket *rara avis* for two reasons : first, it was begun and finished in one afternoon ; second, although the losers lost by an innings, the winners scored less than 100 runs.

After Worcestershire had been skittled out for 43, of which E. G. Arnold scored 20, Yorkshire made an equally bad start, losing Tunnicliffe, Brown sen., Denton and Washington for 11 runs. Wainwright (34),

Hirst (24) and Haigh (15) brightened the outlook, and when the innings ended Yorkshire led by 56 runs.

Worcestershire's second innings lasted only an hour, Rhodes (seven for 20) being practically unplayable.

Rhodes and Haigh bowled unchanged in each innings, taking eleven wickets for 36 runs and seven for 49 respectively.

Worcestershire

H. K. Foster b Rhodes	6	b Haigh	6
J. Howard b Haigh	0	c Tunnicliffe b Rhodes	1
E. G. Arnold c Hunter b Rhodes	20	b Rhodes	13
F. L. Bowley b Haigh	5	st. Hunter b Rhodes	12
J. Fereday run out	0	c Hawke b Haigh	0
A. W. Izaac st. Hunter b Rhodes	2	c Haigh b Rhodes	12
A. Bird b Haigh	2	st. Hunter b Rhodes	0
A. F. Bannister b Rhodes	0	not out	4
G. A. Wilson c Washington b Haigh	1	c Denton b Rhodes	0
T. Straw not out	0	lbw, b Rhodes	0
S. Gethin absent	0	b Haigh	1
Extras	7	Extras	2
	43		51

Yorkshire

J. Tunnicliffe b Wilson	5
J. T. Brown c Bowley b Wilson	2
D. Denton b Wilson	0
I. Washington c sub. b Wilson	0
E. Wainwright c Straw b Bannister	34
G. H. Hirst c Bird b Bannister	24
S. Haigh b Bird	15
W. Rhodes c and b Bannister	0
Lord Hawke c Foster b Bannister	0
J. T. Brown jun. c Bird b Bannister	9
D. Hunter not out	6
Extras	4
	99

Yorkshire Bowling

	Overs	Mdns.	Runs	Wkts.		Overs	Mdns.	Runs	Wkts.
Rhodes	13	6	16	4	...	11.1	4	20	7
Haigh	12.3	5	20	4	...	11	0	29	3

Worcestershire Bowling

	Overs	Mdns.	Runs	Wkts.
Arnold	10	4	21	0
Wilson	15	7	25	4
Bannister	13.5	5	30	5
Bird	8	2	19	1

YORKSHIRE COUNTY CRICKETERS AT ONE OF LORD HAWKE'S PARTIES AT WIGHILL PARK

[*Photo : Yorkshire Evening Post*]

Back row : J. T. Brown, W. Rhodes, R. Moorhouse, J. B. Wostinholm, (county sec.), Rev. E. J. Carter, Turner, (scorer), Schofield Haigh;
Middle row : George Hirst, John Tunnicliffe, Ted Wainwright; *Front row* : F. Milligan, David Hunter, Lord Hawke, David Denton

THE YORKSHIRE TEAM OF 1901

Back row: E. Wainwright, L. Whitehead, W. Rhodes, D. Hunter; *Middle row*: G. Hirst, E. Smith, Lord Hawke, F. Mitchell, I. Tunnicliffe.

Yorkshire v. *Gloucestershire*
Bradford, July 23, 24, 25

Yorkshire won by 40 runs

One of the most remarkable matches of the season ended in a narrow win for Yorkshire after fine batting by Hirst, two displays of hard hitting by Jessop, and match-winning bowling by Rhodes in spite of Jessop's attentions.

On the first innings Yorkshire gained a lead of 140 runs, thanks mainly to Hirst.   But although the latter scored 92 in the second innings, Gloucestershire required only 327 to win when they went in for the second time.

The earlier Gloucestershire batsmen did little, but on the arrival of Jessop the balloon went up.   He reached his hundred without offering a chance, and when caught by Tunnicliffe off Rhodes had scored 139 in 88 minutes and had hit Rhodes out of the ground for 6 seven times. Although he received heavy Jessopian punishment in each innings, Rhodes took fourteen wickets for 192 runs.

A feature of the game was the fine fielding of Gloucestershire.

Yorkshire

Lord Hawke c Board b Roberts	32	c Roberts b Paish	6
J. Tunnicliffe b Townsend	25	b Roberts	0
D. Denton c Townsend b Roberts	85	c Wrathall b Roberts	19
T. L. Taylor lbw, b Townsend	64	c Townsend b Fargus	35
G. H. Hirst c Jessop b Paish	111	c Townsend b Fargus	92
E. Wainwright c Champain b Fargus	19	run out	4
I. Washington b Paish	16	c Jessop b Townsend	8
J. Haigh c Paish b Fargus	2	c Paish b Townsend	8
W. Rhodes not out	23	not out	11
D. Hunter c and b Paish	11	c Paish b Townsend	0
C. Oyston c Jessop b Paish	0	c Jessop b Townsend	2
Extras	21	Extras	2
	409		**187**

Gloucestershire

G. O. H Sewell c Hawke b Rhodes	4	lbw, b Rhodes	10
W. S. A. Brown c Hunter b Rhodes	0	c Tunnicliffe b Rhodes	3
N. O. Taggart c Hunter b Oyston	25	c Hunter b Haigh	4
J. H. Board c Oyston b Rhodes	4	b Haigh	10
C. L. Townsend b Haigh	42	b Haigh	22
H. Wrathall c Wrainwright b Rhodes	42	c Haigh b Rhodes	31
G. L. Jessop c Hawke b Rhodes	104	c Tunnicliffe b Rhodes	139
F. H. B. Champain c Hunter b Rhodes	22	c Taylor b Rhodes	53
A. H. C. Fargus st. Hunter b Rhodes	8	c Wainwright b Haigh	5
A. Paish c Denton b Rhodes	8	b Rhodes	2
F. G. Roberts not out	0	not out	2
Extras	10	Extras	6
	269		**287**

Yorkshire Bowling

	Overs	Mdns.	Runs	Wkts.		Overs	Mdns.	Runs	Wkts.
Hirst	17	1	80	0	...	9	1	44	0
Rhodes	20.5	6	72	8	...	24.4	5	120	6
Oyston	10	0	45	1	...	2	0	3	0
Haigh	18	3	62	1	...	27	4	114	4

Gloucestershire Bowling

	Overs	Mdns.	Runs	Wkts.		Overs	Mdns.	Runs	Wkts.
Jessop	13	5	29	0	...	7	2	20	0
Paish	37.3	4	154	4	...	11	4	27	1
Roberts	20	5	55	2	...	13	3	44	4
Townsend	10	0	39	2	...	11	0	58	4
Brown	11	4	30	0	...	5	0	20	0
Fargus	19	4	81	2	...	10	5	16	2

Yorkshire v. *Essex*

Harrogate, August 2, 3, 4

Yorkshire won by 96 runs

A very fine example of Yorkshire's knack of winning a match most counties would regard as a predestined draw.

On the first day there was play for only 2½ hours, rain made the second day a blank. When play started on Saturday, Yorkshire had scored 159 for nine wickets, and a definite result seemed out of the question barring a miracle.

As has so often happened in Yorkshire's matches, the miracle materialised. Yorkshire's unfinished innings ended when the total reached 171. Then the Yorkshire machine got busy. Essex were bowled, caught, stumped and run out at top speed—total 65, and Yorkshire had to bat again.

Lord Hawke sent in Ernest Smith, Denton and Hirst, and when 42 runs had been scored quickly declared—and in 65 minutes Essex were in and out for a second time for 52. Yorkshire had won by clever captaincy and fine bowling, Rhodes having taken fourteen wickets for 68 runs.

Yorkshire

E. Smith b Mead	26	b Mead	22
J. Tunnicliffe b Mead	21		
D. Denton b Reeves	18	not out	7
T. L. Taylor b Mead	3		
G. H. Hirst b Reeves	14	not out	13
E. R. Wilson b Mead	0		
E. Wainwright lbw, b Reeves	50		
S. Haigh c Buckenham b Young	16		
Lord Hawke b Mead	7		
W. Rhodes c and b Mead	9		
A. L. Bairstow not out	3		
Extras	4	Extras	0
	171		*42

* Innings declared closed.

Essex

H. G. Owen b Haigh	3	st. Bairstow b Rhodes	0
H. Carpenter c Haigh b Rhodes	4	st. Bairstow b Rhodes	0
P. A. Perrin run out	7	c Hirst b Rhodes	10
C. McGahey c Bairstow b Rhodes	19	c Bairstow b Haigh	12
C. P. Buckenham b Haigh	6	b Rhodes	0
W. Reeves st. Bairstow b Rhodes	4	st. Bairstow b Rhodes	0
J. H. Inns b Rhodes	0	c Hirst b Rhodes	0
T. M. Russell c Wainwright b Rhodes	0	b Rhodes	8
F. G. Bell c Smith b Rhodes	8	b Rhodes	8
W. Mead b Smith	10	b Haigh	10
Young not out	0	not out	3
Extras	4	Extras	1
	65		52

Essex Bowling

	Overs	Mdns.	Runs	Wkts.		Overs	Mdns.	Runs	Wkts.
Mead	32	6	65	6	...	4	0	15	1
Bull	11	1	29	0					
Reeves	15	1	54	3	...	2	0	15	0
Young	6	1	19	1	...	2	0	12	0

Yorkshire Bowling

	Overs	Mdns.	Runs	Wkts.		Overs	Mdns.	Runs	Wkts.
Rhodes	16.2	5	40	6	...	12.5	4	28	8
Haigh	13	6	20	2	...	12	4	23	2
Wainwright	1	1	0	0					
Smith	2	1	1	1					

APPEARANCES

The following 19 players appeared for Yorkshire in Championship matches, the number of appearances being in parentheses :

A. L. Bairstow (3)
J. T. Brown sen. (23)
J. T. Brown jun. (9)
D. Denton (28)
F. W. Elam (1)
S. Haigh (28)
Lord Hawke (25)
G. H. Hirst (28)
D. Hunter (25)
C. Oyston (3)

W. Rhodes (26)
W. Riley (3)
E. Smith (17)
T. L. Taylor (12)
J. Tunnicliffe (27)
E. Wainwright (27)
I. Washington (13)
Lees Whitehead (6)
E. R. Wilson (4)

POST MORTEM

In winning their fourth Championship, Yorkshire produced all-round cricket of a very high standard—solid batting down to No. 11, splendid bowling which was never collared, good offensive fielding and wicket-keeping, all co-ordinated by the experienced and astute captaincy of Lord Hawke.

Of the 19 cricketers who appeared in county matches, 12 had batting averages ranging from 49·33 to 15·68 for 12 or more innings, and with

Rhodes and Haigh in devastating form right through the season, no liberties could be taken with the bowling. Only Surrey at the Oval and Notts at Trent Bridge succeeded in reaching the third hundred in an innings. And it must be noted that this success was achieved without the assistance of F. S. Jackson, who had headed the batting averages in 1899.

The secret of Yorkshire's success was the bowling of Rhodes and Haigh, backed up by sound batting, good fielding and clever leadership.

FIFTH CHAMPIONSHIP

1901

Captain : Lord Hawke

The County Championship of 1901 was a case of "Eclipse first and the rest nowhere." Yorkshire won 20 of their 28 matches (one abandoned) and no other county won more than 11. By the time Somerset brought off their sensational win at Leeds in July, Yorkshire had piled up such a big lead that the unexpected defeat had no effect on the Championship Table.

THE FIRST SIX

	Played	Won	Lost	Drawn	Points	Percent.
Yorkshire	27	20	1	6	19	90·47
Middlesex	18	6	2	10	4	50·00
Lancashire	28	11	5	12	6	37·50
Sussex	24	8	4	12	4	33·33
Warwickshire	16	7	4	5	3	27·27
Surrey	27	7	6	14	1	7·69

METHOD OF SCORING : As in 1896.

MATCH SCORES AND RESULTS

Yorkshire v.	Ground	Yorkshire 1st Inns.	Yorkshire 2nd Inns.	Opponents 1st Inns.	Opponents 2nd Inns.	Result
Gloucestershire	Bristol	224	16 (0)	150	89	Y, 10 wickets
Somerset	Taunton	391	241 (9)	349	281	Y, 1 wicket
Worcestershire	Dewsbury	205	245	218	142	Y, 90 runs
Derbyshire	Huddersfield	*481 (8)	—	106	93	Y, inns. and 282 runs
Lancashire	Manchester	134	44 (1)	133	44	Y, 9 wickets
Leicestershire	Leicester	348	—	84	136	Y, inns. and 128 runs
Hampshire	Bournemouth	365	—	75	208	Y, inns. and 82 runs
Middlesex	Lord's	398	54 (3)	168	282	Y, 7 wickets
Surrey	Bradford	290	157 (7)	172	431	Draw
Warwickshire	Birmingham	*401 (5)	—	320	—	Draw
Essex	Leeds	252	—	97	95	Y, inns. and 60 runs
Nottinghamshire	Nottingham	204	—	13	173	Y, inns. and 18 runs
Kent	Sheffield	201	309	218	80	Y, 80 runs
Derbyshire	Glossop	213	*359 (5)	141	186	Y, 245 runs
Sussex	Bradford	158	50 (0)	52	155	Y, 10 wickets
Leicestershire	Scarborough	562	—	103	212	Y, inns. and 247 runs
Worcestershire	Worcester	530	—	156	162	Y, inns. and 212 runs
Somerset	Leeds	325	113	87	630	S, 279 runs
Warwickshire	Bradford	237	281 (2)	401	—	Draw
Nottinghamshire	Sheffield	528	—	151	151	Y, inns. and 226 runs
Surrey	Oval	186	Abandoned		184	Y, 55 runs
Gloucestershire	Hull	186	123	70	184	Y, 55 runs
Lancashire	Leeds	319	175 (5)	413	—	Draw
Hampshire	Harrogate	439	—	204	154	Y, inns. and 81 runs
Middlesex	Sheffield	363	—	62 (3)	—	Draw
Essex	Leyton	104	—	30	41	Y, inns. and 33 runs
Sussex	Brighton	92	107 (0)	*560 (5)	—	Draw
Kent	Canterbury	251	265	206	63	Y, 247 runs

* Innings declared closed.

53

Yorkshire beat Derbyshire, Essex, Gloucestershire, Hampshire, Kent, Leicestershire, Nottinghamshire, Worcestershire twice; and Lancashire, Middlesex, Somerset, Sussex once.

Yorkshire were beaten by Somerset.

Yorkshire drew with Warwickshire twice; and Lancashire, Middlesex, Surrey, Sussex once.

SUMMARY

	Yorkshire	Opponents
Runs scored	10740	8731
Average per wicket	31·22	18·34
Hundreds	17	13
Other innings over 50	45	25
Ten wickets in a match	12	2
Five wickets in an innings	38	15
Highest total	562 *v.* Leicestershire	630 (Somerset)
Lowest total	92 *v.* Sussex	13 (Nottinghamshire)
Totals over 400	6	4
Totals under 100	1	15

PRINCIPAL AVERAGES

	Inns.	Not Out	Runs	Highest Inns.	100's	50's	Aver.
F. Mitchell	38	4	1674	162*	7	6	49·23
G. H. Hirst	36	1	1174	214	2	6	33·54
J. T. Brown sen.	42	4	1263	134*	3	5	33·23
T. L. Taylor	27	1	783	156	2	3	30·11
J. Tunnicliffe	42	4	1075	145	1	6	28·28
D. Denton	36	1	967	86	—	6	27·62
S. Haigh	26	4	606	159	1	2	27·54
Lord Hawke	30	3	691	89	—	6	25·59

* Not out.

	Balls	Balls per Wkt.	Runs	Wkts.	5 Wkts. in Inns.	Aver.
W. Rhodes	6923	35·37	2664	196	20	13·59
G. H. Hirst	5093	37·72	2262	135	12	16·75
S. Haigh	2169	44·26	1082	49	3	22·08
J. T. Brown sen.	1835	42·67	1074	43	1	24·97
E. Wainwright	1456	60·66	633	24	1	26·37

NOTES

After a great struggle, Yorkshire beat Somerset by one wicket at Taunton. Rhodes took twelve wickets for 182 runs for Yorkshire and Braund ten for 288 in 79.3 overs for Somerset. L. C. H. Palairet (103) and S. M. J. Woods (60, 90) were the batting successes for Somerset.

Hirst took twelve wickets for 77 runs against Lancashire at Manchester, and was top scorer for Yorkshire (40).

In successive matches, F. Mitchell scored 100 *v.* Hampshire, 100 *v.* Middlesex, 106 *v.* Surrey and 162 not out *v.* Warwickshire—484 runs (average 121·00).

When Notts were put out for 13 at Nottingham the individual innings were : 0, 1, 2, 4, 1, 2, 0, 0, 0, 2, 1 (no extras). Rhodes took six wickets for 4 runs in 47 balls, and Haigh four for 8.

In Leicestershire's second innings at Scarborough, Tunnicliffe made 5 slip catches. In three other innings he made 4, and against Hampshire at Harrogate made 3 catches in each innings.

L. C. H. Palairet and Braund opened the innings for Somerset at Leeds. Each failed to score in the first innings and made a hundred in the second.

Rhodes took seven wickets for 20 runs in 20.2 overs in Gloucestershire's first innings at Hull.

The Yorkshire–Essex match at Leyton produced only 175 runs, Yorkshire winning by an innings and 33 runs.

Sussex was the only county, other than Somerset, that really collared the Yorkshire bowling in 1901. At Brighton, C. B. Fry scored 209, Killick 200 and K. S. Ranjitsinhji 86 not out, the innings being declared with the score 560 for five wickets.

Hirst took seven wickets for 24 runs in Kent's second innings at Canterbury.

In Championship matches in 1901, G. H. Hirst completed a " double " —1,174 runs (average 33·54) and 135 wickets (average 16·75).

HOW IT WAS DONE

	100's	50's	10 Wkts. in Match	5 Wkts. in Inns.	50 Runs & 5 Wkts. in Match
J. T. Brown sen.	3	5	–	1	1
J. T. Brown jun.	–	–	–	1	–
D. Denton	–	6	–	–	–
S. Haigh	1	2	–	3	–
Lord Hawke	–	6	–	–	–
G. H. Hirst	2	6	4	12	4
F. Mitchell	7	6	–	–	–
W. Rhodes	–	1	8	20	3
E. Smith	–	1	–	–	–
T. L. Taylor	2	3	–	–	–
J. Tunnicliffe	1	6	–	–	–
E. Wainwright	1	2	–	1	–
Lees Whitehead	–	1	–	–	–
	17	45	12	38	8

FIELDING (197 Catches)

No. of Catches		No. of Catches	
62	J. Tunnicliffe	12	F. Mitchell
21	E. Wainwright	9	T. L. Taylor
20	W. Rhodes	8	Lord Hawke
16	G. H. Hirst	6	Lees Whitehead
13	S. Haigh	3	E. Smith
12	J. T. Brown sen.	2	J. T. Brown jun.
12	D. Denton	1	H. Myers

WICKETKEEPING

	Stumped	Caught	Total
D. Hunter	27	34	61
T. L. Taylor	2	4	6
J. Higgins	1	—	1
Total	30	38	68

TOTALS

400 Runs and Over

Yorkshire (6)

562 v. Leicestershire, Scarborough   481 (8)* v. Derbyshire, Huddersfield
530 v. Worcestershire, Worcester   439 v. Hampshire, Harrogate
528 v. Nottinghamshire, Sheffield   401 (5)* v. Warwickshire, Birmingham

Opponents (4)

650 (5),* Sussex Brighton   413, Lancashire, Leeds
630 Somerset, Leeds   401, Warwickshire, Bradford
* Innings declared closed.

Under 100 Runs

Yorkshire (1)

92 v. Sussex, Brighton

Opponents (15)

13, Nottinghamshire, Nottingham   80, Kent, Sheffield
30 and 40, Essex, Leyton   84, Leicestershire, Leicester
44, Lancashire, Manchester   87, Somerset, Leeds
52, Sussex, Bradford   89, Gloucestershire, Bristol
63, Kent, Canterbury   93, Derbyshire, Huddersfield
70, Gloucestershire, Hull   97 and 95, Essex, Leeds
75, Hampshire, Bournemouth

FIRST WICKET PARTNERSHIPS

Score	Partners	Against	Ground
121	J. T. Brown, J. Tunnicliffe	Derbyshire	Glossop
113	J. T. Brown, J. Tunnicliffe	Derbyshire	Huddersfield
107*	J. T. Brown, J. Tunnicliffe	Sussex	Brighton

* Unfinished.

50 RUNS AND 5 WICKETS

Scores	Analyses	Player	Against	Ground
64	2-38, 3-18	G. H. Hirst	Gloucestershire	Bristol
11, 40	4-77, 2-61	G. H. Hirst	Worcestershire	Dewsbury
81	6-42, 0-39	G. H. Hirst	Hampshire	Bournemouth
61	7-21, 3-93	G. H. Hirst	Leicestershire	Scarborough
61	5-33, 3-36	J. T. Brown sen.	Derbyshire	Huddersfield
17, 35*	3-60, 5-34	W. Rhodes	Kent	Sheffield
40, 36	3-74, 6-54	W. Rhodes	Worcestershire	Dewsbury
53	4-45, 2-35	W. Rhodes	Worcestershire	Worcester

* Not out.

MATCHES OF THE SEASON

Yorkshire v. *Somerset*
Taunton, May 13, 14, 15

Yorkshire won by one wicket

Yorkshire's match against Somerset at Taunton produced one of the most exciting finishes of the season. On the last afternoon, when Yorkshire's ninth wicket fell, 2 runs were still required, and were obtained three minutes before time.

When each side had completed an innings, Yorkshire had a lead of 42 runs, L. C. H. Palairet having scored a fine hundred for Somerset. In their second innings the home county's earlier batsmen failed, but good batting by S. M. J. Woods (90), Robson (58) and Gill (40) pulled the game round, and when the innings ended Yorkshire had to get 240 runs to win.

With six Yorkshire wickets down for 119 the odds were on Somerset, but a stand of 93 by Wainwright and Lord Hawke retrieved the situation.

In the match, Rhodes took twelve wickets for 182 runs and Braund ten for 268, S. M. J. Woods (60 and 90) for Somerset, and T. L. Taylor, Wainwright and Lord Hawke providing the batting highlights.

Somerset

L. C. H. Palairet b Hirst	103	c and b Rhodes	38
A. E. Lewis lbw, b Rhodes	39	lbw, b Hirst	13
L. C. Braund c Hunter b Brown	23	lbw, b Rhodes	10
F. A. Phillips c Hawke b Rhodes	37	b Hirst	13
S. M. J. Woods st. Hunter b Rhodes	60	c Tunnicliffe b Rhodes	90
E. Robson c Denton b Rhodes	37	c Wainwright b Rhodes	58
G. Gill b Rhodes	4	run out	40
G. Fowler b Hirst	8	b Wainwright	0
B. Cranfield st. Hunter b Brown	2	not out	5
E. Grant not out	13	c Mitchell b Rhodes	3
W. L. Price c and b Rhodes	10	c Haigh b Rhodes	0
Extras	13	Extras	11
	349		**281**

Yorkshire

J. T. Brown b Cranfield	0	b Braund	27
J. Tunnicliffe b Braund	80	c Grant b Braund	12
D. Denton b Braund	30	b Braund	11
T. L. Taylor c Palairet b Braund	97	lbw, b Braund	8
F. Mitchell b Gill	1	b Braund	24
G. H. Hirst c Wood b Cranfield	16	lbw, b Braund	17
E. Wainwright c and b Braund	41	c Woods b Cranfield	70
Lord Hawke b Gill	25	b Cranfield	52
S. Haigh b Cranfield	21	b Cranfield	6
W. Rhodes b Cranfield	38	not out	11
D. Hunter not out	7	not out	2
Extras	35	Extras	1
	391		**241**

Yorkshire Bowling

	Overs	Mdns.	Runs	Wkts.		Overs	Mdns.	Runs	Wkts.
Hirst	33	9	98	2	...	21	6	67	2
Rhodes	38.2	10	115	6	...	28	7	67	6
Haigh	17	1	83	0	...	7	2	15	0
Brown	16	2	40	2	...	15	1	99	0
Wainwright						7	1	22	1

Somerset Bowling

	Overs	Mdns.	Runs	Wkts.		Overs	Mdns.	Runs	Wkts
Cranfield	35.2	8	94	4	...	26	4	79	3
Braund	49	11	155	4	...	30.3	2	113	6
Grant	2	0	10	0					
Gill	23	4	64	2	...	6	1	20	0
Robson	7	0	33	0	...	9	2	28	0

Yorkshire v. *Nottinghamshire*

Nottingham, June 20, 21

Yorkshire won by an innings and 18 runs

This match produced the sensation of the season, Notts being all out for 13 in their first innings—a low level for county cricket until Gloucestershire dismissed Northamptonshire for 12 in 1907.

Winning the toss, Yorkshire were all out late on the first day for the moderate total of 204. One Notts wicket fell for a single before close of play, and next day when play started, after a delay of an hour, the batsmen were helpless against Rhodes and Haigh, the innings lasting 55 minutes, during which one 4, a 2 and seven singles were scored.

When Notts followed on Hirst came into the picture with six wickets for 26 runs, and Notts were all out for 178. During their two innings only A. O. Jones, J. Gunn and Iremonger reached double figures.

One unusual incident may be noted. An hour after the start of the match Shrewsbury split his hand in fielding a ball, and Lord Hawke allowed Harrison to take his place in the Notts side.

Yorkshire

J. T. Brown c Anthony b Wass	6
J. Tunnicliffe b Dixon	31
D. Denton c W. Gunn b J. Gunn	73
F. Mitchell c and b J. Gunn	22
E. Wainwright b J. Gunn	20
G. H. Hirst c Harrison b J. Gunn	2
L. Whitehead c W. Gunn b Hallam	27
Lord Hawke c and b Wass	1
S. Haigh c Carlin b J. Gunn	5
W. Rhodes c Wass b Hallam	11
D. Hunter not out	3
Extras	3
	204

Nottinghamshire

C. E. Dench c Wainwright b Rhodes	0	c Hunter b Hirst	0
A. W. Hallam c Tunnicliffe b Rhodes	1	b Hirst	0
W. Gunn c Hunter b Rhodes	2	c and b Haigh	2
A. O. Jones b Haigh	4	c Mitchell b Wainwright	47
J. A. Dixon c Tunnicliffe b Rhodes	1	b Rhodes	8
J. Carlin c Tunnicliffe b Rhodes	2	b Wainwright	8
J. Gunn c Hawke b Haigh	0	c Hunter b Hirst	35
J. Iremonger not out	0	not out	55
I. Harrison c Haigh b Rhodes	0	b Hirst	
G. Anthony b Haigh	2	b Hirst	5
T. Wass st. Hunter b Rhodes	1	b Hirst	0
Extras	0	Extras	17
	13		173

Nottinghamshire Bowling

	Overs	Mdns.	Runs	Wkts.
Wass	26	3	84	2
Hallam	16.5	6	34	2
J. Gunn	33	15	49	5
Dixon	9	2	23	1
Jones	3	1	11	0

Yorkshire Bowling

	Overs	Mdns.	Runs	Wkts.		Overs	Mdns.	Runs	Wkts.
Hirst	1	0	1	0	...	12.1	2	26	6
Rhodes	7.5	4	4	6	...	22	4	53	1
Haigh	7	2	8	4	...	16	3	53	1
Wainwright						13	6	28	2

Yorkshire v. *Somerset*
Leeds, July 15, 16, 17

Somerset won by 279 runs

There are few better examples of the ups and downs of cricket than Yorkshire's return match with Somerset at Leeds. When each side had completed an innings heavy odds would have been laid on a Yorkshire win, but a wonderful second innings by Somerset and an unexpected collapse by Yorkshire gave the western county an almost miraculous victory.

Hirst, Rhodes and Haigh got rid of Somerset cheaply for 87, and the same three cricketers were mainly responsible for Yorkshire's total of 325, scoring 201 of the 307 runs made by the bat.

Then came the beginning of the transformation scene. Palairet and Braund scored 222 runs in 140 minutes for Somerset's first wicket. F. A. Phillips, S. M. J. Woods, V. T. Hill and Robson continued the good work with considerable gusto. The Yorkshire bowling was collared, and when the last Somerset wicket fell the total was 630, and Yorkshire were 392 behind. Then came their collapse, and Somerset had won one of the most amazing victories in cricket history.

Somerset

L. C. H. Palairet b Hirst	0	c and b Brown	173
L. C. Braund b Rhodes	0	b Haigh	107
A. E. Lewis c Tunnicliffe b Rhodes	10	b Rhodes	12
F. A. Phillips b Hirst	12	b Wainwright	122
S. M. J. Woods c Hunter b Haigh	46	c Tunnicliffe b Hirst	66
V. T. Hill run out	0	c Hirst b Rhodes	53
E. Robson c Hunter b Rhodes	0	c Tunnicliffe b Rhodes	40
G. Gill c Hunter b Rhodes	4	st. Hunter b Rhodes	14
A. E. Newton b Haigh	0	c Taylor b Rhodes	4
G. Burrington c Brown b Rhodes	11	st. Hunter b Rhodes	15
B. Cranfield not out	1	not out	5
Extras	3	Extras	19
	87		630

Yorkshire

J. T. Brown c Braund b Cranfield	24	c sub. b Gill	5
J. Tunnicliffe c Newton b Gill	9	c Palairet b Braund	44
D. Denton c Woods b Gill	12	b Braund	16
T. L. Taylor b Cranfield	1	absent hurt	0
F. Mitchell b Gill	4	b Braund	21
G. H. Hirst c Robson b Cranfield	61	lbw, b Braund	6
E. Wainwright b Gill	9	c Lewis b Cranfield	1
Lord Hawke b Robson	37	c Burrington b Cranfield	4
S. Haigh c Robson b Cranfield	96	not out	2
W. Rhodes c Lewis b Robson	44	st. Newton b Cranfield	0
D. Hunter not out	10	c Woods b Cranfield	0
Extras	18	Extras	14
	325		113

Yorkshire Bowling

	Overs	Mdns.	Runs	Wkts.		Overs	Mdns.	Runs	Wkts.
Hirst	12	5	36	2	...	37	1	189	1
Rhodes	16	8	39	5	...	46.5	12	145	6
Haigh	4	0	9	2	...	20	4	78	1
Wainwright						34	3	107	1
Brown						18	1	92	1

Somerset Bowling

	Overs	Mdns.	Runs	Wkts.		Overs	Mdns.	Runs	Wkts.
Cranfield	27	5	113	4	...	18	5	34	4
Gill	23	2	105	4	...	4	1	23	1
Braund	5	0	33	2	...	15	3	41	4
Robson	10	1	35	0					
Woods	5	1	21	0					
Palairet	1	1	0	0					

Yorkshire v. *Essex*

Leyton, August 15, 16

Yorkshire won by an innings and 33 runs

On a bowler's wicket twenty-seven wickets fell on the first day, the whole match being finished by noon on the second morning.

Essex won the toss, and in an hour were all back in the pavilion, the total being 30. Hirst and Rhodes had bowled unchanged and the former swerved so surprisingly as to be practically unplayable. An analysis of seven wickets (six bowled) for 12 runs tells its own story.

The Yorkshiremen found Mead (six for 40) almost equally difficult, only Tunnicliffe, Mitchell and Taylor, who scored a fine 44, being able to make much headway. Still, 104 was a vast improvement on 30.

When Essex went in again they found Hirst as puzzling as ever, and when play ended for the day the Yorkshire all-rounder had five of the seven wickets that had fallen. Next morning Rhodes quickly took the three outstanding wickets, Essex being all out for 41.

Hirst (twelve wickets for 29 runs) and Rhodes (six for 37) bowled unchanged in both innings, and, apart from Taylor's 44, no batsman scored more than 12.

Essex

F. L. Fane b Hirst	1	b Hirst	3
H. Carpenter b Hirst	0	b Hirst	0
P. A. Perrin c Hunter b Hirst	0	c Hawke b Hirst	9
C. McGahey b Hirst	11	lbw, b Rhodes	1
J. H. Douglas b Hirst	0	b Hirst	0
A. P. Lucas run out	3	c and b Hirst	0
G. Tossetti b Hirst	3	c and b Rhodes	9
W. Reeves c Denton b Rhodes	10	st. Hunter b Rhodes	12
T. M. Russell c Taylor b Rhodes	0	retired hurt	1
H. Young not out	1	not out	0
W. Mead b Hirst	0	st. Hunter b Rhodes	2
Extras	1	Extras	4
	30		41

Yorkshire

J. T. Brown lbw, b Mead	3
J. Tunnicliffe b Mead	10
D. Denton c Mead b Young	5
T. L. Taylor b Reeves	44
F. Mitchell b Mead	10
G. H. Hirst c Reeves b Mead	0
E. Wainwright c Young b Reeves	4
E. Smith c Fane b Reeves	8
Lord Hawke b Mead	7
W. Rhodes not out	9
D. Hunter lbw, b Mead	4
	104

Yorkshire Bowling

	Overs	Mdns.	Runs	Wkts.		Overs	Mdns.	Runs	Wkts.
Hirst	8.1	3	12	7	...	10	6	17	5
Rhodes	8	0	17	2	...	10	2	20	4

Essex Bowling

	Overs	Mdns.	Runs	Wkts.
Young	12	3	28	1
Mead	22	8	40	6
Reeves	10	3	36	3

The following 16 cricketers appeared for Yorkshire in Championship matches, the number of appearances being in parentheses :

J. T. Brown sen. (27)	F. Mitchell (27)
J. T. Brown jun. (1)	H. Myers (1)
D. Denton (25)	W. Rhodes (27)
S. Haigh (21)	E. Smith (6)
Lord Hawke (24)	T. L. Taylor (20)
J. Higgins (2)	J. Tunnicliffe (27)
G. H. Hirst (27)	E. Wainwright (26)
D. Hunter (24)	Lees Whitehead (13)

POST MORTEM

Yorkshire had a runaway victory in the Championship of 1901, winning 20 out of 27 matches played, and losing only 1—the extraordinary match against Somerset at Leeds. Yorkshire's success becomes even more commendable when it is remembered that F. S. Jackson, the leading batsman in 1900, was unable to give any assistance in 1901.

The long series of wins in 1901 was brought about by a number of factors :

1. Team-work—11 of the 16 players who appeared in county matches averaged 24 matches each.

2. Of the 13 principal players, 12 averaged over 20 runs an innings, and the 14th, Hunter, averaged 14.

3. F. Mitchell's consistent batting, Rhodes's magnificent bowling and the all-round figures of Hirst were largely responsible for laying the foundations of success.

4. In the 27 Championship matches, Hirst and Rhodes bowled 2,004.2 of the 3,126.3 overs delivered, and took 331 out of 468 wickets taken.

5. The captaincy of Lord Hawke, who played in 24 of the 27 matches, was a vital factor.

The 11 players who did the bulk of the work made up a team that compares favourably with any side in the history of Yorkshire cricket : J. T. Brown, J. Tunnicliffe, F. Mitchell, D. Denton, G. H. Hirst, T. L. Taylor, E. Wainwright (or E. Smith), Lord Hawke, W. Rhodes, S. Haigh, D. Hunter.

Seven of the above made one or more hundreds during the season, all except Hunter averaged over 20 and ten scored over 500 runs. And the deciding factor was the bowling of Rhodes and Hirst—331 wickets for 14·88 runs each.

SIXTH CHAMPIONSHIP

1902

Captain : Lord Hawke

In spite of the first three matches being drawn owing to bad weather and an early beating from Somerset, there was never much doubt about the destination of the Championship in 1902, and at the end of the season Yorkshire had won their third consecutive Championship almost as comfortably as in 1901, but with 13 wins and 11 draws instead of 20 wins and 6 draws in the previous season. Actually, the result was just as creditable, as Test match calls on Yorkshire were heavy, F. S. Jackson and Rhodes playing in five Tests, Hirst in four, while T. L. Taylor and Haigh were both included in " twelves " from which Test elevens were chosen. With such a demand for their stars, it is surprising that Yorkshire should have gone through their county programme with only one defeat.

THE FIRST SIX

	Played	Won	Lost	Drawn	Points	Percent.
Yorkshire	25	13	1	11	12	85·71
Sussex	24	7	3	14	4	40·00
Nottinghamshire	20	6	3	11	3	33·33
Surrey	28	8	5	15	3	23·07
Lancashire	23	7	5	11	2	16·16
Warwickshire	18	6	5	7	1	9·09

METHOD OF SCORING : As in 1896.

MATCH SCORES AND RESULTS

Yorkshire v.	Ground	Yorkshire 1st Inns.	Yorkshire 2nd Inns.	Opponents 1st Inns.	Opponents 2nd Inns.	Result
Essex	Leyton	171 (3)	—	89	—	Draw
Sussex	Leeds	302	*182 (5)	232	126 (3)	Draw
Leicestershire	Huddersfield	*323 (6)	—	228	10 (1)	Draw
Lancashire	Sheffield	148	—	72	54	Y, inns. and 22 runs
Kent	Bradford	337	—	100	129	Y, inns. and 108 runs
Derbyshire	Dewsbury	393	—	23 (2)	—	Draw
Derbyshire	Chesterfield	150	309	64	24 (3)	Draw
Middlesex	Bradford	175	—	73	80	Y, inns. and 22 runs
Somerset	Sheffield	74	84	86	106	S, 34 runs
Warwickshire	Birmingham	208	—	100	45	Y, inns. and 63 runs
Nottinghamshire	Hull	184	346	155	148	Y, 228 runs
Surrey	Leeds	*362 (8)	—	188	72	Y, inns. and 102 runs
Sussex	Brighton	372	84 (6)	455	—	Draw
Essex	Bradford	504	—	281	193	Y, inns. and 30 runs
Nottinghamshire	Nottingham	497	—	328	255 (2)	Draw
Gloucestershire	Leeds	253	—	46	166	Y, inns. and 91 runs
Worcestershire	Worcester	257	248 (8)	230	—	Draw
Warwickshire	Sheffield	135	270	207	98	Y, 100 runs
Surrey	Oval	470	363 (3)	359	—	Draw
Lancashire	Manchester	499 (5)	—	243	—	Draw
Leicestershire	Leicester	Abandoned				
Worcestershire	Harrogate	79	134 (4)	82	130	Y, 6 wickets
Gloucestershire	Cheltenham	261	—	104	55	Y, inns. and 102 runs
Somerset	Taunton	129	63 (1)	104	—	Draw
Middlesex	Lord's	125	68 (6)	99	93	Y, 4 wickets
Kent	Catford	97	78 (1)	71	100	Y, 9 wickets

* Innings declared closed.

Yorkshire beat Gloucestershire, Kent, Middlesex, Warwickshire twice; and Essex, Lancashire, Nottinghamshire, Surrey, Worcestershire once.

Yorkshire were beaten by Somerset.

Yorkshire drew with Derbyshire, Sussex twice; and Essex, Lancashire, Leicestershire, Nottinghamshire, Somerset, Surrey, Worcestershire once.

SUMMARY

	Yorkshire		Opponents	
Runs scored	8734		5903	
Average per wicket	28·54		15·09	
Hundreds	14		5	
Other runs over 50	46		20	
Ten wickets in match	9		2	
Five wickets in innings	29		14	
Highest total	504	v Essex	455	(Sussex)
Lowest total	74	v. Somerset	45	(Warwickshire)
Totals over 400	4		1	
Totals under 100	3		15	

PRINCIPAL AVERAGES

	Inns.	Not Out	Runs	Highest Inns.	100's	50's	Aver.
T. L. Taylor	31	3	1276	142*	4	8	45·57
G. H. Hirst	28	3	1025	134	2	6	41·00
Hon. F. S. Jackson	19	2	544	101*	1	4	32·00
D. Denton	34	4	934	127	2	3	31·13
I. Washington	35	5	906	100*	1	5	30·20
J. Tunnicliffe	37	—	1079	127	3	5	29·16
J. T. Brown sen.	36	2	868	91	—	6	25·52

* Not out.

	Balls	Balls per Wkt.	Runs	Wkts.	5 Wkts. in Inns.	Aver.
S. Haigh	3652	29·69	1475	123	12	11·99
W. Rhodes	5260	37·57	1748	140	12	12·48
Hon. F. S. Jackson	1466	40·72	525	36	3	14·58
G. H. Hirst	2850	53·77	1089	53	3	20·54

NOTES

After three draws owing to rain Yorkshire beat Lancashire by an innings and 22 runs in the Whitsuntide match at Sheffield. Only two Lancashire batsmen reached double figures, and in their second innings S. F. Barnes was top scorer with 9 not out. In the match, F. S. Jackson scored 33 and took eight wickets for 13 runs (three for 5 and five for 8).

In consecutive completed innings Yorkshire dismissed Lancashire for 72 and 54, Kent for 100 and 129, Derbyshire for 64, Middlesex for 73 and 80, Somerset for 86, and Warwickshire for 100 and 45—an average total of 80.

Against Derbyshire at Chesterfield, Hirst (5) and Haigh (2) clean-bowled the first seven batsmen.

In the second innings of Middlesex at Bradford, Haigh bowled six of the first seven batsmen, who between them scored 17 runs.

When Somerset beat Yorkshire at Sheffield, L. C. Braund scored 31 and 34 in totals of 86 and 106, and took fifteen wickets for 71 runs (six for 30 and nine for 41). In 1901 and 1902 Somerset beat Yorkshire twice, lost a match by one wicket and drew the fourth match. In these four matches Braund scored 248 runs (average 35·42) and took thirty-four wickets for 13·44 runs each.

In Shrewsbury's last season he scored 66 and 52 not out against Yorkshire at Nottingham.

Yorkshire's amateurs provided the side's batting highlights in Hayward's Benefit at the Oval; T. L. Taylor scored 64 and 88 not out, Hon. F. S. Jackson 77 and 81 not out, and Lord Hawke (batting No. 9) 126 in the first innings.

In Gloucestershire's second innings at Cheltenham, Haigh took four wickets for 10 runs in 69 balls.

In the second innings of the two matches against Middlesex, Haigh and Rhodes had the following curiously similar figures :

	Haigh	Rhodes
Bradford	7 bowled	2 caught, 1 hit wkt
	(seven for 47)	(three for 32)
Lord's	6 bowled, 1 lbw	3 caught
	(seven for 40)	(three for 34)

Haigh's bowling figures in 1902 have seldom, if ever, been equalled. He took 123 wickets for 11·99 runs each in county matches, and 101 (82 per cent.) were taken without help from the field—91 bowled, 10 lbw. In three consecutive matches v. Middlesex, Somerset and Warwickshire, he took 26 wickets, 1 being lbw and 20 bowled.

It may be noted that at Lord's in 1902 Yorkshire dismissed M.C.C. for 27 (ten of the batsmen scored 13 between them), and at Leeds dismissed the Australians for 23 (Hirst five for 9 and Jackson five for 12).

HOW IT WAS DONE

	100's	50's	10 Wkts. in Match	5 Wkts. in Inns.	50 Runs & 5 Wkts. in Match
J. T. Brown sen.	–	6	–	–	–
D. Denton	2	3	–	–	–
S. Haigh	–	4	3	12	–
Lord Hawke	1	–	–	–	–
G. H. Hirst	2	6	1	2	1
Hon. F. S. Jackson	1	4	–	3	–
W. Rhodes	–	1	5	12	–
E. Smith	–	1	–	–	–
T. L. Taylor	4	8	–	–	–
J. Tunnicliffe	3	5	–	–	–
I. Washington	1	5	–	–	–
Lees Whitehead	–	2	–	–	–
E. R. Wilson	–	1	–	–	–
Total	14	46	9	29	1

E

FIELDING (117 Catches)

No. of Catches		No. of Catches	
32	J. Tunnicliffe	8	Hon. F. S. Jackson
10	J. T. Brown sen.	7	Lord Hawke
10	D. Denton	7	G. H. Hirst
9	S. Haigh	7	I. Washington
9	T. L. Taylor	6	W. Rhodes
9	Lees Whitehead	3	E. Smith

WICKETKEEPING

	Stumped	Caught	Total
D. Hunter	16	29	45
J. Higgins	1	2	3
Total	17	31	48

TOTALS

400 Runs and Over

Yorkshire (4)

504* v. Essex, Bradford   497 v. Nottinghamshire, Nottingham
499 (5)* v. Lancashire, Manchester   470 v. Surrey, Oval

Opponents (1)

455, Sussex, Brighton

* Innings declared closed.

Under 100 Runs

Yorkshire (3)

74 and 84 v. Somerset, Sheffield   97 v. Kent, Catford

Opponents (15)

45, Warwickshire, Birmingham
46, Gloucestershire, Leeds
72 and 54, Lancashire, Sheffield
55, Gloucestershire, Cheltenham
64, Derbyshire, Chesterfield
71, Kent, Catford

72, Surrey, Leeds
73 and 80, Middlesex, Bradford
82, Worcestershire, Harrogate
86, Somerset, Sheffield
89, Essex, Leyton
99 and 93, Middlesex, Lord's

FIRST WICKET PARTNERSHIPS

Score	Partners	Against	Ground
115	J. T. Brown, J. Tunnicliffe	Nottinghamshire	Hull

50 RUNS AND 5 WICKETS

Scores	Analyses	Player	Against	Ground
19, 52	7-68, 3-60	G. H. Hirst	Nottinghamshire	Hull

MATCHES OF THE SEASON

Yorkshire v. *Lancashire*
Sheffield, May 19, 20

Yorkshire won by an innings and 22 runs

Owing to rain only 60 minutes' play was possible on the first day, but the Yorkshiremen were in such fine form that the match ended before close of play on the second day.

Taking first innings, Lancashire had scored 52 before their third wicket fell, but then Rhodes, Haigh and Jackson skittled out the next seven Lancastrians for the addition of 20 runs, Jackson taking three wickets for 5 runs in 20 balls.

When Yorkshire batted, nobody but F. S. Jackson reached 20, but seven of the side contributed additions ranging from 17 to 11. As a result, Lancashire went in again 76 runs behind.

This second innings was disastrous, no batsman reaching double figures and the bowlers being on top from start to finish. Jackson again had an extraordinary analysis—five wickets for 8 runs in 42 balls. In the match he made the top score (33) and took eight wickets for 13 runs.

Lancashire

A. C. MacLaren lbw, b Rhodes	7	st. Hunter b Rhodes	1
A. Ward c Washington b Haigh	22	b Haigh	3
J. T. Tyldesley b Hirst	9	c Brown sen. b Rhodes	3
J. Hallows b Rhodes	14	c Tunnicliffe b Jackson	7
A. Eccles b Haigh	0	b Rhodes	8
C. R. Hartley b Haigh	2	b Jackson	1
W. R. Cuttell c Hawke b Rhodes	8	b Jackson	6
E. E. Steel b Jackson	2	st. Hunter b Rhodes	0
S. F. Barnes b Jackson	3	not out	9
S. Webb not out	4	c and b Jackson	3
R. Thomas b Jackson	0	b Jackson	0
Extras	1	Extras	13
	72		54

Yorkshire

J. T. Brown sen. c and b Steel	15
J. Tunnicliffe c Steel b Barnes	13
Hon. F. S. Jackson c Thomas b Barnes	33
T. L. Taylor st. Thomas b Barnes	16
D. Denton run out	11
G. H. Hirst c Ward b Barnes	6
I. Washington b Barnes	0
S. Haigh b Barnes	1
Lord Hawke b Cuttell	11
W. Rhodes not out	17
D. Hunter c MacLaren b Steel	13
Extras	12
	148

Yorkshire Bowling

	Overs	Mdns.	Runs	Wkts.		Overs	Mdns.	Runs	Wkts.
Hirst	12	4	17	1					
Rhodes	26	14	29	3	...	13	4	25	4
Haigh	11	3	20	3	...	7	2	8	1
Jackson	3.3	2	5	3	...	7	2	8	5

Lancashire Bowling

	Overs	Mdns.	Runs	Wkts.
Barnes	20	4	39	6
Webb	9	2	27	0
Cuttell	28	10	43	1
Steel	9.2	1	27	2

Yorkshire v. *Middlesex*

Bradford, June 9, 10

Yorkshire won by an innings and 22 runs

On a difficult wicket at Bradford, Middlesex were beaten by the same margin as Lancashire at Sheffield at Whitsuntide.

MacGregor sent his hitters in first but the policy paid poor dividends, seven wickets being down with only 34 runs on the board. Littlejohn stayed in for an hour, but the last wicket fell at 73, Rhodes having taken seven wickets for 24 runs.

Yorkshire also went in for hitting but with better results. Brown and Tunnicliffe scored 56 in 50 minutes before Brown was out for 17. Tunnicliffe continued to bat well and found a useful partner in Hirst, who was 46 not out when the innings closed for 175 on the second morning.

Haigh was the destructive agent when Middlesex started their second innings. The first six batsmen scored 17 runs and Haigh clean-bowled five of them. In the innings he took seven wickets, all bowled, and Middlesex were all out for 80.

Middlesex

B. J. T. Bosanquet c Hunter b Rhodes	5	b Haigh	7
G. W. Beldam c Tunnicliffe b Rhodes	11	c Tunnicliffe b Rhodes	0
A. E. Trott c Hirst b Rhodes	0	b Haigh	2
W. P. Robertson c and b Jackson	9	b Haigh	2
C. P. Foley c Hawke b Rhodes	4	b Haigh	6
G. S. F. Griffin c Denton b Rhodes	0	b Haigh	0
G. MacGregor b Rhodes	2	not out	14
E. S. Littlejohn lbw, b Haigh	14	b Haigh	0
J. T. Rawlin b Rhodes	7	b Haigh	21
R. O. Schwarz b Haigh	6	hit wkt, b Rhodes	27
J. T. Hearne not out	6	c Taylor b Rhodes	0
Extras	9	Extras	1
	73		80

Yorkshire

J. T. Brown b Trott	17
J. Tunnicliffe b Bosanquet	64
Hon. F. S. Jackson b Trott	1
T. L. Taylor lbw, b Trott	4
D. Denton c Bosanquet b Trott	13
G. H. Hirst not out	46
I. Washington b Hearne	9
S. Haigh c and b Hearne	12
Lord Hawke lbw, b Hearne	0
W. Rhodes c Griffin b Trott	3
D. Hunter lbw, b Trott	0
Extras	6
	175

Yorkshire Bowling

	Overs	Mdns.	Runs	Wkts.		Overs	Mdns.	Runs	Wkts.
Hirst	5	1	9	0					
Rhodes	22	11	24	7	...	16	3	32	3
Jackson	15	7	25	1					
Haigh	4	2	6	2	...	15.5	6	47	7

Middlesex Bowling

	Overs	Mdns.	Runs	Wkts.
Hearne	22	11	40	3
Trott	18.5	1	69	6
Rawlin	12	2	36	0
Bosanquet	7	1	24	1

Yorkshire v. *Somerset*

Sheffield, August 16, 17, 18

Somerset won by 34 runs

For the second time in two successive seasons Somerset beat Yorkshire on their own ground. In 1901 the defeat of the Champions was due to heavy run-getting in the giant-killers' second innings, but in 1902 a low-scoring match was a triumph for Somerset's all-rounder, L. C. Braund, who scored 31 and 34 and took fifteen wickets for 71 runs—an obvious match-winning performance.

Somerset went in first, but after Palairet and Braund had scored 44 for the first wicket, the rest of the side could only add another 42 runs, the last wicket falling at 86.

Yorkshire's initial effort was even more meagre. Denton hit up 20 and Brown 13, but no one else could get beyond 8, and when the innings closed Somerset led by 12 runs.

After another good opening partnership by Palairet and Braund, only a fine bout of hitting by Gill (41) saved a sensational Somerset collapse, the other eight batsmen scoring only 7 runs. For this debacle

Haigh was mainly responsible, clean-bowling the last five batsmen and taking six wickets for 19 runs in 43 balls.

Requiring 119 runs to win, Yorkshire never looked like doing anything but lose. Cranfield took Brown's wicket, but Braund bowled his leg-breaks so well that he took the other nine wickets, and Yorkshire were all out for 84.

Somerset

L. C. H. Palairet b Jackson	25	c and b Jackson	24
L. C. Braund c and b Rhodes	31	c Jackson b Haigh	34
E. Robson b Jackson	0	b Jackson	0
P. R. Johnson b Jackson	0	run out	3
S. M. J. Woods lbw, b Rhodes	14	c Hirst b Rhodes	0
A. E. Lewis c Haigh b Rhodes	1	b Haigh	4
G. Gill lbw, b Jackson	1	b Haigh	41
F. M. Lee c Denton b Rhodes	1	b Haigh	0
A. E. Newton b Jackson	0	b Haigh	0
B. Cranfield b Jackson	5	not out	0
D. L. Evans not out	6	b Haigh	0
Extras	2	Extras	0
	86		106

Yorkshire

J. T. Brown b Cranfield	13	c Johnson b Cranfield	8
J. Tunnicliffe b Braund	4	c Robson b Braund	11
D. Denton b Robson	20	b Braund	6
T. L. Taylor c Newton b Braund	8	st. Newton b Braund	18
Hon. F. S. Jackson b Braund	5	b Braund	6
G. H. Hirst c Evans b Braund	0	c Palairet b Braund	9
I. Washington b Robson	0	b Braund	3
S. Haigh b Braund	9	b Braund	6
W. Rhodes b Braund	5	c and b Braund	5
Lord Hawke lbw, b Robson	1	b Braund	6
D. Hunter not out	1	not out	0
Extras	8	Extras	6
	74		84

Yorkshire Bowling

	Overs	Mdns.	Runs	Wkts.		Overs	Mdns.	Runs	Wkts.
Hirst	7	3	8	0	...	2	0	5	0
Rhodes	26	10	39	4	...	12	0	44	1
Jackson	24.2	12	29	6	...	21	7	38	2
Haigh	4	2	8	0	...	7.1	1	19	6

Somerset Bowling

	Overs	Mdns.	Runs	Wkts.		Overs	Mdns.	Runs	Wkts.
Cranfield	7	0	34	1	...	9	0	22	1
Braund	13	2	30	6	...	17.3	5	41	9
Robson	6	5	2	3	...	9	3	15	0

Yorkshire v. Middlesex

Lord's, August 21, 22

Yorkshire won by four wickets

For the second time in the season, Middlesex were dismissed by Yorkshire for less than 100 runs in each innings, and once again Rhodes and Haigh were responsible for the result.

In the two matches Rhodes and Haigh took 38 of the forty Middlesex wickets, Rhodes having seventeen for 8·05 runs each and Haigh twenty-one for 6·28.

The critical period arrived at the start of the second innings of Middlesex, when Haigh clean-bowled the first five batsmen and got a sixth lbw. Wells and Foley tried to retrieve the situation, but when the last wicket fell Yorkshire only required 68 runs. When the fourth went down with 24 on the board Middlesex seemed to have a chance, but a little judicious pulling by Hirst and a back-to-the-wall partnership by Smith and Haigh brought the ship safely to port.

Middlesex

P. F. Warner b Haigh	16	b Haigh		18
J. Douglas c Smith b Haigh	3	b Haigh		13
G. W. Beldam lbw, b Haigh	1	b Haigh		3
R. N. Douglas c Hirst b Rhodes	5	b Haigh		0
B. J. T. Bosanquet c Tunnicliffe b Rhodes	3	b Haigh		1
C. M. Wells c Brown b Rhodes	7	not out		28
A. E. Trott b Haigh	11	lbw, b Haigh		0
G. MacGregor c Tunnicliffe b Rhodes	27	c Hunter b Rhodes		3
C. P. Foley b Haigh	16	b Haigh		13
R. O. Schwarz run out	1	c Tunnicliffe b Rhodes		3
J. T. Hearne not out	2	c Hunter b Rhodes		0
Extras	7	Extras		11
	99			**93**

Yorkshire

J. Tunnicliffe c Schwarz b Wells	13	b Trott		10
J. T. Brown b Trott	13	c Bosanquet b Beldam		5
I. Washington b Beldam	39	st. MacGregor b Beldam		3
D. Denton c Schwarz b Hearne	39	c J. Douglas b Beldam		2
Hon. F. S. Jackson c and b Bosanquet	0	b Hearne		8
G. H. Hirst c MacGregor b Bosanquet	4	c Wells b Trott		17
E. Smith b Bosanquet	5	not out		12
S. Haigh b Bosanquet	0	not out		10
W. Rhodes b Bosanquet	0			
L. Whitehead c Hearne b Bosanquet	8			
D. Hunter not out	0			
Extras	4	Extras		1
	125			**68**

Yorkshire Bowling

	Overs	Mdns.	Runs	Wkts.		Overs	Mdns.	Runs	Wkts.
Rhodes	26.5	10	47	4	...	25.2	10	34	3
Haigh	23	9	39	5	...	26	12	40	7
Hirst	1	1	0	0	...	6	3	8	0
Jackson	3	1	6	0					

Middlesex Bowling

	Overs	Mdns.	Runs	Wkts.		Overs	Mdns.	Runs	Wkts.
Hearne	12	2	25	1	...	14.2	8	19	1
Trott	12	3	30	1	...	7	0	18	2
Wells	9	1	25	1					
Bosanquet	13.1	3	28	6	...	3	2	5	0
Beldam	10	5	13	1	...	10	3	25	3

APPEARANCES

The following 20 cricketers appeared for Yorkshire in Championship matches, the number of appearances being in parentheses :

J. T. Brown sen. (24)
J. T. Brown jun. (1)
W. Brown (1)
D. Denton (25)
F. W. Elam (1)
S. Haigh (23)
Lord Hawke (16)
J. Higgins (2)
G. H. Hirst (21)
D. Hunter (20)
Hon. F. S. Jackson (15)
C. Oyston (3)
W. Rhodes (20)
W. Ringrose (2)
E. Smith (5)
T. L. Taylor (22)
J. Tunnicliffe (25)
I. Washington (23)
Lees Whitehead (11)
E. R. Wilson (1)

POST MORTEM

In spite of the loss of F. Mitchell—their best batsman in 1901—who had gone to South Africa, Yorkshire put as strong a side as ever into the field, the return of F. S. Jackson adding to the all-round strength of the team.

Although 1902 was wetter than 1901, Yorkshire had eight regular members of the XI. with averages ranging from 45·57 to 22·92, and all the " regulars " had double-figure averages.

Rhodes was as consistently efficient as ever in taking wickets, but Haigh took up the role of chief assistant which had been filled by Hirst in the previous season. In fact, Haigh was probably the most dangerous bowler in England during the season, an extraordinary number of his victims (82 per cent.) being bowled or lbw. Hirst and Jackson had occasional successes, but the success of the attack was due mainly to the work of Rhodes and Haigh, backed up by the customary good fielding, wicketkeeping and captaincy.

INTERREGNUM

1903, 1904

1903

Middlesex won the County Championship in 1903, Sussex being runners-up and Yorkshire third. Beginning with wins over Essex and Gloucestershire, Yorkshire lost their chance of retaining the Championship by losing three of the next six matches, three being drawn. Yorkshire were beaten by Sussex (twice), Middlesex, Surrey and Somerset.

Hirst headed the batting and bowling averages, again obtaining a "double" in Championship matches, but the rest of the batting was less reliable, Jackson, Tunnicliffe and Haigh having comparatively poor figures. With five bowlers taking twenty-five or more wickets at costs ranging from Hirst's 12·79 to Jackson's 20·14, not much fault could be found with the attack, only one total exceeding 350 (558 for eight wickets by Sussex) being recorded.

The outstanding performances of the season were as follows:

v. Essex at Sheffield and Gloucestershire at Bristol : In the second innings of these consecutive matches Hirst had the following analyses :

	Overs	Mdns.	Runs	Wkts.
v. Essex	17	5	34	6
v. Gloucestershire	16.2	5	34	6

v. Worcestershire at Worcester : Yorkshire scored 518 (Hirst 123) but were unable to force a win, Worcestershire scoring 278 and 381. Rhodes scored 42 and took fourteen wickets for 211 runs in 83 overs

v. Kent at Leeds : Yorkshire won by an innings and 130 runs, Kent being put out for 66 and 119. Hirst scored 120 and took five wickets for 32 runs and four for 44 in the two Kent innings.

v. Worcestershire at Huddersfield : In their first innings Worcestershire were all out for 24, Hirst (five for 18) and Rhodes (five for 4) doing the damage. Yorkshire scored 76 for one wicket and declared. Before rain caused the final stoppage, Worcestershire had lost six wickets for 27 runs, Rhodes having taken three for 8 in 21 overs (16 maidens).

v. Surrey at the Oval : Hirst and Rhodes bowled unchanged in each Surrey innings (84 and 73), Hirst taking ten wickets for 67 runs and Rhodes ten for 81.

v. Sussex at Brighton : Sussex won a good match by four wickets—Yorkshire 72 and 96 : Sussex 132 and 37 for six wickets. Of the last fourteen wickets that fell, thirteen were bowled and one run out.

73

Hirst headed the batting averages with 1,367 runs (average 44·09) and the bowling averages with 118 wickets for 12·79 runs each.

In all matches during the season Rhodes completed the first of his 16 " doubles "—1,137 runs (average 27·07) and 193 wickets (average 14·57).

1904

Yorkshire were runners-up to Lancashire in 1904, the traditional enemy having a percentage of 100·00 to Yorkshire's 63·63.

After their first four matches had ended in draws, Yorkshire were beaten by Middlesex at Lord's at the beginning of June, and lost by 6 runs to Warwickshire two months later. A record of 9 wins, 2 defeats and 16 drawn games suggests that something was lacking, and for once Yorkshire lacked match-winning bowling. Eight batsmen averaged over 30 runs an innings, but the best bowling average was Rhodes's 19·90. In county matches 17 totals of 300 or more were scored by Yorkshire and 13 by their opponents ; while the Yorkshiremen scored 70 individual innings over 50 to their opponents' 52.

The highlights of the season follow :

v. Middlesex at Lord's : Yorkshire's first defeat of the season was due mainly to good Middlesex bowling and poor batting. In Yorkshire's first innings Trott took four wickets for 7 runs in 32 balls, and in the match J. T. Hearne had ten for 85.

v. Sussex at Sheffield : Scoring 440 for nine wickets declared (C. B. Fry 177, K. S. Ranjitsinhji 148), Sussex put themselves out of danger of defeat, and when the game ended in a draw, Yorkshire were still 2 runs behind with eight wickets to fall.

v. Hampshire at Leeds : Yorkshire won by 370 runs—one of the few occasions in 1904 when the Yorkshire bowling was at its peak. Rhodes (ten for 39) and Haigh (ten for 49) bowled unchanged, Hampshire being all out for 62 and 36.

v. Lancashire at Leeds : Hirst's Benefit, £3,703. The beneficiaire scored 65 and took six wickets for 42 runs in Lancashire's first innings.

v. Warwickshire at Huddersfield : A low-scoring match was won by Warwickshire by 6 runs.

Hirst and Rhodes both completed " doubles " in county matches, the former heading the batting averages with 1,848 runs (average 51·33), and Rhodes being first bowler with 104 wickets for 19·90 runs each.

Twenty-one players appeared, including J. T. Brown, sen., who played in one match, and died later in the year.

SEVENTH CHAMPIONSHIP

1905

Captain : Lord Hawke

After a hard fight with Lancashire the Championship was won by Yorkshire, who were the better finishers. Both counties lost three matches, but Yorkshire won 18 to Lancashire's 12. Yorkshire's defeats came early in the season—one at Derby when Jackson, Hirst, Rhodes and Haigh were required for the Lord's Test match, but this handicap was cancelled out when four Lancastrians were commandeered for the Oval Test. Apart altogether from such vicissitudes, there was little doubt that Yorkshire were the better side, their bowling being much stronger.

THE FIRST SIX

	Played	Won	Lost	Tied	Drawn	Points	Percent.
Yorkshire	28	18	3	—	7	15	71·42
Lancashire	25	12	3	—	10	9	60·00
Sussex	28	13	4	—	11	9	52·94
Surrey	27	14	6	1	6	8	40·00
Leicestershire	22	8	5	—	9	3	23·07
Kent	22	10	7	1	4	3	17·64

METHOD OF SCORING : As in 1896.

MATCH SCORES AND RESULTS

Yorkshire v.	Ground	Yorkshire 1st Inns.	Yorkshire 2nd Inns.	Opponents 1st Inns.	Opponents 2nd Inns.	Result
Somerset	Taunton	*549(9)	—	98	227	Y, inns. and 244 runs
Gloucestershire	Bristol	338	—	96	187	Y, inns. and 55 runs
Worcestershire	Worcester	225	232	97	295	Y, 65 runs
Derbyshire	Bradford	289	—	108	120	Y, inns. and 61 runs
Leicestershire	Leicester	515	—	419	121 (7)	Draw
Warwickshire	Birmingham	361	—	313	238(4)	Draw
Worcestershire	Leeds	323	157	119	158	Y, 203 runs
Middlesex	Lord's	275	103(3)	145	232	Y, 7 wickets
Lancashire	Manchester	133	214	399	—	L, inns. and 52 runs
Derbyshire	Derby	123	161	190	96 (1)	D, 9 wickets
Nottinghamshire	Sheffield	61	227	122	39	Y, 127 runs
Warwickshire	Dewsbury	153	108	138	57	Y, 66 runs
Sussex	Leeds	295	*243 (7)	294	77 (3)	Draw
Kent	Hull	77	162	124	116 (4)	K, 6 wickets
Somerset	Harrogate	474	—	125	200	Y, inns. and 149 runs
Kent	Tunbridge Wells	239	81 (2)	142	174	Y, 8 wickets
Hampshire	Bournemouth	491	—	172	152	Y, inns. and 167 runs
Surrey	Oval	442	—	116	218	Y, inns. and 108 runs
Leicestershire	Sheffield	261	*295 (8)	137	174	Y, 245 runs
Nottinghamshire	Nottingham	343	—	114	174	Y, inns. and 55 runs
Gloucestershire	Bradford	*504 (7)	—	245	141	Y, inns. and 118 runs
Hampshire	Hull	*303 (4)	—	88 (3)	—	Draw
Lancashire	Sheffield	76	285	177	140	Y, 44 runs
Surrey	Leeds	231	33 (5)	171	91	Y, 5 wickets
Essex	Huddersfield	*423 (6)	—	172	58	Y, inns. and 193 runs
Middlesex	Bradford	281	59 (0)	285	87	Draw
Essex	Leyton	98	227 (7)	521	—	Draw
Sussex	Brighton	203	*154 (5)	137	119 (1)	Draw

* Innings declared closed.

75

Yorkshire beat Gloucestershire, Nottinghamshire, Somerset, Surrey, Worcestershire twice; and Derbyshire, Essex, Hampshire, Kent, Lancashire, Leicestershire, Middlesex, Warwickshire once.

Yorkshire were beaten by Derbyshire, Kent, Lancashire.

Yorkshire drew with Sussex twice; and Essex, Hampshire, Leicestershire, Middlesex, Warwickshire once.

SUMMARY

	Yorkshire	Opponents
Runs scored	10827	8955
Average per wicket	28·26	18·54
Hundreds	16	9
Other innings over 50	55	29
Ten wickets in match	6	2
Five wickets in innings	31	22
Highest total	549 (9) dec. v. Somerset	521 (Essex)
Lowest total	61 v. Nottinghamshire	39 (Nottinghamshire)
Totals over 400	7	2
Totals under 100	4	8

PRINCIPAL AVERAGES

	Inns.	Not Out	Runs	Highest Inns.	100's	50's	Aver.
G. H. Hirst	35	7	1713	341	4	8	61·17
D. Denton	43	1	1963	172	7	8	46·73
W. Rhodes	35	4	1117	201	2	9	36·03
Hon. F. S. Jackson	18	—	530	111	1	2	29·44
J. Tunnicliffe	38	5	913	102	1	5	27·66
J. W. Rothery	30	2	738	118	1	7	26·35

	Balls	Balls per Wkt.	Runs	Wkts.	5 Wkts. in Inns.	Aver.
S. Haigh	3732	38·47	1429	97	8	14·73
W. Rhodes	5057	40·13	1986	126	10	15·76
G. H. Hirst	3597	40·87	1618	88	4	18·38
H. Myers	2377	38·33	1209	62	3	19·50
W. Ringrose	2307	38·45	1206	60	5	20·10

NOTES

In the first match of the season, v. Somerset at Taunton, Yorkshire scored 549 for nine wickets declared, Rhodes making 201 and taking seven wickets for 101 runs in the match.

Hirst and Myers bowled unchanged in Worcestershire's first innings at Worcester.

C. J. B. Wood carried his bat through Leicestershire's first innings at Leicester for 160 not out, Leicestershire scoring 419. Yorkshire beat this total by 96, Hirst scoring 341 (a six and 53 fours).

Lancashire's fast bowling won at Old Trafford—Brearley eight for 123 and Kermode nine for 121.

In Notts' second innings at Sheffield (39), Rhodes (four for 15) and Haigh (six for 21) bowled unchanged. Haigh took twelve wickets for 55 runs in the match. In the next match, *v.* Warwickshire at Dewsbury, Rhodes and Haigh again bowled unchanged in the second innings, each taking five wickets for 26 runs.

When Kent won by six wickets at Hull, Blythe took eleven wickets for 89 runs, A. P. Day scoring 54 and 58 not out.

Against Surrey at the Oval, Hirst scored 232 not out, and took five wickets for 43 runs in Surrey's first innings (116).

Yorkshire beat Lancashire at Sheffield by 44 runs after being put out for 76 in the first innings. Jackson scored 30 in Yorkshire's first innings and took four wickets for 15 runs when Lancashire batted. In the match, Brearley took thirteen wickets for 157 runs.

When Yorkshire beat Surrey by five wickets at Leeds, Rhodes scored 59 in the first innings and took ten wickets for 115 runs in the match. J. N. Crawford, who had just left school, was top scorer for Surrey and took seven wickets for 90 in Yorkshire's first innings. In the second innings, N. A. Knox took all the wickets that fell for 21 runs in 5 overs.

Rhodes took six Essex wickets for 9 runs in 50 balls in the second innings (58) at Huddersfield.

The return match *v.* Essex at Leyton provided a sensation. Essex scored 521 and skittled Yorkshire out for 98, J. W. H. T. Douglas taking five wickets for 3 runs in his first 18 balls. Yorkshire followed on 423 behind, and had to draw the match to make the Championship safe. They succeeded, thanks to some stolid stonewalling by Tunnicliffe and Hirst, and a gem of an innings—under the circumstances—by E. Smith, who stayed in for the last hour without scoring.

HOW IT WAS DONE

	100's	50's	10 Wkts. in Match	5 Wkts. in Inns.	50 Runs & 5 Wkts. in Match
D. Denton	7	8	–	–	–
G. Deyes	–	–	–	1	–
C. H. Grimshaw	–	1	–	–	–
S. Haigh	–	4	2	8	–
Lord Hawke	–	1	–	–	–
G. H. Hirst	4	8	1	4	5
Hon. F. S. Jackson	1	2	–	–	1
H. Myers	–	4	–	3	1
W. Rhodes	2	9	3	10	4
W. Ringrose	–	–	–	5	–
J. W. Rothery	1	7	–	–	–
J. Tunnicliffe	1	5	–	–	–
H. Wilkinson	–	4	–	–	–
W. H. Wilkinson	–	2	–	–	–
Total	16	55	6	31	11

FIELDING (192 Catches)

No. of Catches		No. of Catches	
35	W. Rhodes	4	Lord Hawke
30	D. Denton	4	H. Wilkinson
22	J. Tunnicliffe	3	J. W. Rothery
17	S. Haigh	3	W. H. Wilkinson
17	G. H. Hirst	2	H. Rudston
16	C. H. Grimshaw	2	W. Wainwright
14	H. Myers	2	" Sub."
7	Hon. F. S. Jackson	1	F. Crowther
6	E. Smith	1	G. Deyes
5	W. Ringrose	1	J. E. Elms

WICKETKEEPING

	Stumped	Caught	Total
D. Hunter	16	47	63
A. Dolphin	1	2	3
J. Higgins	1	1	2
Total	18	50	68

TOTALS

400 Runs and Over

Yorkshire (7)

549 (9)* *v.* Somerset, Taunton

515 *v.* Leicestershire, Leicester

504 (7)* *v.* Gloucestershire, Bradford

491 *v.* Hampshire, Bournemouth

474 *v.* Somerset, Harrogate

442 *v.* Surrey, Oval

423 (6)* *v.* Essex, Huddersfield

Opponents (2)

521, Essex, Leyton

419, Leicestershire, Leicester

* Innings declared closed.

Under 100 Runs

Yorkshire (4)

61 *v.* Nottinghamshire, Sheffield

76 *v.* Lancashire, Sheffield

77 *v.* Kent, Hull

98 *v.* Essex, Leyton

Opponents (8)

39, Nottinghamshire, Sheffield

57, Warwickshire, Dewsbury

58, Essex, Huddersfield

87, Middlesex, Bradford

91, Surrey, Leeds

96, Gloucestershire, Bristol

97, Worcestershire, Worcester

98, Somerset, Taunton

FIRST WICKET PARTNERSHIP

Score	Partners	Against	Ground
144	C. H. Grimshaw, H. Wilkinson	Somerset	Harrogate

50 RUNS AND 5 WICKETS

Scores	Analyses	Player	Against	Ground
201	3-42, 4-59	W. Rhodes	Somerset	Taunton
86	3-29, 2-40	G. H. Hirst	Gloucestershire	Bristol
108,* 59	3-44, 2-78	G. H. Hirst	Worcestershire	Worcester
54, 7	5-48, 5-26	W. Rhodes	Warwickshire	Dewsbury
54	4-32, 5-48	H. Myers	Hampshire	Bournemouth
232	5-46, 1-6	G. H. Hirst	Surrey	Oval
64	4-105, 2-42	G. H. Hirst	Gloucestershire	Bradford
30, 45	4-15, 1-29	Hon. F. S. Jackson	Lancashire	Sheffield
59,* 0	6-73, 4-42	W. Rhodes	Surrey	Leeds
80	1-58, 4-44	G. H. Hirst	Essex	Huddersfield
66	0-6, 6-9	W. Rhodes	Essex	Huddersfield

* Not out.

MATCHES OF THE SEASON

Yorkshire v. *Leicestershire*

Leicester, May 18, 19, 20

Draw

In spite of a fine first innings by Leicestershire, Yorkshire very nearly won this match, in which 1,055 runs were scored for the loss of twenty-seven wickets.

A big first wicket partnership by C. E. de Trafford and C. J. B. Wood, who carried his bat through the innings for 160, followed by others by Wood and Coe and Wood and Whitehead, resulted in a total of 419, and Leicestershire appeared to be safe.

But Yorkshire, especially Hirst, were not dismayed, and proceeded to pile up a total of 515—a lead of 96. To this total Hirst contributed 341, still a record individual innings in a county match. Hirst went in when three wickets had been lost for 22 runs, and seven hours later was last man out, after scoring 341 of the 495 runs scored from the bat—68 per cent. His hits included a six and 53 fours.

When Leicestershire went in again, it was quite another story. Seven wickets were lost for 121 runs in the available time, and as King and Knight were injured and Davis missed at the wicket, Leicestershire narrowly escaped being beaten.

In Leicestershire's innings, Hunter allowed no byes.

Leicestershire

C. E. de Trafford c Grimshaw b Ringrose	58	c Wilkinson b Rhodes	11
C. J. B. Wood not out	160	c Grimshaw b Ringrose	24
J. H. King retired hurt	0		
A. E. Knight c Tunnicliffe b Rhodes	6		
V. F. S. Crawford c Hunter b Ringrose	7	lbw, b Rhodes	12
H. Whitehead c Hirst b Ringrose	56	b Ringrose	12
S. Coe c Hunter b Ringrose	100	c Myers b Haigh	8
R. J. Crawford c Myers b Ringrose	16	b Rhodes	1
G. Gill st. Hunter b Rhodes	0	b Haigh	1
A. E. Davis c Tunnicliffe b Rhodes	1	not out	21
W. W. Odell st. Hunter b Rhodes	6	not out	27
Extras	9	Extras	4
	419		**121**

Yorkshire

H. Wilkinson c Davis b Gill	14
C. H. Grimshaw c Davis b Gill	2
D. Denton lbw, b R. T. Crawford	6
J. Tunnicliffe c Whitehead b Gill	0
G. H. Hirst c Whitehead b R. T. Crawford	341
W. Rhodes c Davis b Gill	11
S. Haigh c sub. b Gill	31
H. Myers c sub. b Coe	57
Lord Hawke c and b R. T. Crawford	17
W. Ringrose c Davis b Gill	8
D. Hunter not out	9
Extras	20
	515

Yorkshire Bowling

	Overs	Mdns.	Runs	Wkts.		Overs	Mdns.	Runs	Wkts.
Hirst	18	2	70	0					
Myers	22	4	82	0	...	6	0	34	0
Ringrose	41	10	104	5	...	15	0	53	2
Rhodes	41.2	16	82	4	...	23	13	22	3
Haigh	12	0	43	0	...	11	5	8	2
Grimshaw	5	2	9	0					
Denton	3	0	20	0					

Leicestershire Bowling

	Overs	Mdns.	Runs	Wkts.
Gill	52	11	172	6
Crawford (R. T.)	47.5	18	117	2
Odell	26	7	61	0
Coe	28	5	100	1
Whitehead	12	1	29	0
Crawford (V. F. S.)	2	0	16	0

Yorkshire v. *Lancashire*

Sheffield, August 7, 8, 9

Yorkshire won by 44 runs

The August Bank Holiday match between Yorkshire and Lancashire was, perhaps, the most important of the season. Lancashire had won the match at Old Trafford easily, and at this stage were above Yorkshire in the Championship table with 12 wins and 1 loss to 16 wins and 3 losses. It was vital for Yorkshire to win, and they began badly, Brearley and Cook getting the whole side out for 76, of which Jackson scored 30 and Tunnicliffe 17. With seven wickets for 35 runs in 14 overs, Brearley gave his side a fine start.

The Lancastrian batsmen scarcely took full advantage of Yorkshire's collapse. MacLaren, Spooner and Tyldesley batted well, but when they were out the Yorkshire bowlers got on top, Jackson taking four of the last five wickets cheaply, and the Lancashire total only reached 177— a lead of 101.

Yorkshire fought back well in their second innings. Tunnicliffe and Rothery were soon out, but Denton and Jackson added 143 invaluable runs, and, later, Rhodes hit out at the rather sparse Lancashire bowling. When the last wicket fell Yorkshire had scored 285 and Lancashire required 184 runs.

Hirst, Rhodes, Haigh and Jackson were too good a combination to allow such a result. The first four Lancashire batsmen made useful contributions, but nobody stayed long enough to become a menace, and the innings closed for 140.

Apart from Brearley (thirteen for 157) and Cook (seven for 86), Lancashire were disappointing, the batting on a difficult wicket being uninspired and the attack short of reserves.

Denton, Jackson and Rhodes were the match-winners for Yorkshire. Denton was lucky but brilliant, Jackson scored 75 runs and took five wickets for 44 runs in the match, and Rhodes, in addition to a dashing second innings, took nine wickets for 115.

Yorkshire

J. Tunnicliffe c MacLaren b Cook	17	b Brearley		9
J. W. Rothery b Brearley	3	b Brearley		6
D. Denton b Brearley	0	c MacLaren b Cook		96
Hon. F. S. Jackson b Cook	30	c Poidevin b Brearley		45
G. H. Hirst b Cook	6	b Brearley		6
W. Rhodes c Garnett b Brearley	2	c MacLaren b Brearley		74
E. Smith c Kermode b Brearley	0	b Cook		18
S. Haigh c Hornby b Brearley	6	c Brearley b Cook		3
H. Myers c Garnett b Brearley	3	c Brearley b Cook		10
D. Hunter not out	3	b Brearley		0
W. Ringrose b Brearley	0	not out		0
Extras	6	Extras		18
	76			285

Lancashire

A. C. MacLaren st. Hunter b Rhodes	51	b Jackson	14
R. H. Spooner b Rhodes	42	b Haigh	18
J. T. Tyldesley c Hirst b Rhodes	33	b Haigh	26
L. O. S. Poidevin c Denton b Haigh	1	st. Hunter b Rhodes	40
H. G. Garnett lbw, b Rhodes	19	c and b Rhodes	0
J. Sharp b Jackson	7	b Hirst	7
A. H. Hornby b Jackson	0	b Haigh	0
J. Hallows not out	16	c and b Rhodes	4
W. Cook c Tunnicliffe b Jackson	0	not out	20
A. Kermode b Rhodes	2	run out	0
W. Brearley b Jackson	3	c Smith b Rhodes	0
Extras	3	Extras	11
	177		140

Lancashire Bowling

	Overs	Mdns.	Runs	Wkts.		Overs	Mdns.	Runs	Wkts.
Brearley	14	4	35	7	...	26.3	2	122	6
Cook	13	3	35	3	...	15	2	51	4
Kermode						16	0	75	0
Hallows						7	0	19	0

Yorkshire Bowling

	Overs	Mdns.	Runs	Wkts.		Overs	Mdns.	Runs	Wkts.
Hirst	8	2	23	0	...	13	3	29	1
Ringrose	6	2	19	0					
Rhodes	22	3	66	5	...	21.4	6	49	4
Myers	9	1	26	0					
Haigh	4	0	25	1	...	20	10	22	3
Jackson	9.2	4	15	4	...	14	4	29	1

Yorkshire v. *Essex*

Leyton, August 24, 25, 26

Draw

In their last home match at Leyton, Essex collared the Yorkshire bowling, and in scoring 521 treated it more roughly than any other county in 1905.

Scoring 404 for six wickets on the first day, Essex added 117 on the next morning and then set about the serious business of getting Yorkshire out. This proved less serious than could have been anticipated. Apart from Denton and Lord Hawke, the resistance offered to Buckenham, Tremlin and Douglas was very unYorkshire-like, seven wickets being down for 42, and the whole side out for 98. Douglas bowled sensationally during the innings. In his first three overs he took five wickets for 3 runs, doing the hat-trick at the expense of Rhodes, Haigh and Myers. In fact, he obtained five wickets in 8 balls without conceding a run.

Faced with a deficit of 423, Yorkshire's back was definitely to the wall, and never was the traditional ability to struggle out of a tight corner better shown.

Going in late on the second afternoon, Yorkshire lost Rothery with 15 on the board, but next day Tunnicliffe and Hirst stayed together for 3½ hours, taking no risks but wearing down the bowling. Hirst's 90 in 290 minutes may not have been exhilarating but was certainly invaluable, and then, just when it looked as if Essex might win, E. Smith stayed in for the last hour without scoring. At close of play, Yorkshire 196 runs behind with three wickets in hand. Smith's stubborn stonewalling had saved the match—and the Championship.

Of the 150 overs sent down in Yorkshire's second innings, 79 were maidens.

Essex

F. L. Fane c Myers b Smith	106
H. Carpenter run out	69
F. H. Gillingham st. Dolphin b Smith	82
C. McGahey b Rhodes	105
S. A. Trick c Hirst b Smith	0
W. Reeves c Rhodes b Myers	71
J. W. H. T. Douglas b Myers	2
C. Benham b Ringrose	42
E. Russell b Rhodes	17
C. P. Buckenham b Haigh	3
B. Tremlin not out	3
Extras	21
	521

Yorkshire

J. Tunnicliffe b Douglas	11	c McGahey b Benham	59
R. W. Rothery b Buckenham	0	c McGahey b Buckenham	0
D. Denton c Carpenter b Tremlin	40	b Douglas	17
G. H. Hirst b Douglas	0	b Reeves	90
W. Rhodes b Douglas	2	b Buckenham	6
S. Haigh b Douglas	0	c Russell b Reeves	12
H. Myers b Douglas	0	lbw, b Douglas	9
E. Smith b Buckenham	2	not out	0
Lord Hawke b Tremlin	36	not out	9
W. Ringrose b Tremlin	5		
A. Dolphin not out	0		
Extras	2	Extras	25
	98		227

Yorkshire Bowling

	Overs	Mdns.	Runs	Wkts.
Hirst	32	2	111	0
Ringrose	19	1	84	1
Rhodes	29.4	2	107	2
Haigh	23	8	53	1
Myers	15	5	38	2
Smith	20	1	107	3

Essex Bowling

	Overs	Mdns.	Runs	Wkts.		Overs	Mdns.	Runs	Wkts.
Buckenham	12	2	47	2	...	32	15	49	2
Tremlin	6.4	3	16	3	...	21	10	24	0
Douglas	10	1	31	5	...	26	13	49	2
Reeves	2	0	2	0	...	36	24	37	2
McGahey						7	2	8	0
Benham						25	14	29	1
Carpenter						3	1	6	0

APPEARANCES

The following 24 cricketers appeared for Yorkishire in Championship matches—the number of appearances being in parentheses :

F. Crowther (1)	H. Myers (28)
D. Denton (28)	C. Oyston (3)
G. Deyes (1)	W. Rhodes (25)
A. Dolphin (3)	W. Ringrose (14)
J. E. Elms (1)	J. W. Rothery (19)
C. H. Grimshaw (15)	H. Rudston (4)
S. Haigh (27)	E. Smith (8)
Lord Hawke (21)	G. Tattersall (1)
J. Higgins (1)	J. Tunnicliffe (21)
G. H. Hirst (24)	W. Wainwright (2)
D. Hunter (24)	H. Wilkinson (12)
Hon. F. S. Jackson (11)	W. H. Wilkinson (7)

POST MORTEM

For the first time since 1893 Yorkshire had three great bowlers all in form simultaneously, Haigh (14·73), Rhodes (15·76) and Hirst (18·38) being first, second and third in the averages. And to back them up were Myers and Ringrose, each of whom took sixty wickets. The strength of this attack may be judged from the fact that in the season's averages the five Yorkshiremen were in the first fifteen bowlers who took forty or more wickets.

Yorkshire's batting was less outstanding but, with occasional exceptions, adequate. Hirst had an aggregate of 1,713 runs and an average of 61·17, Denton scored 1,963 runs (average 46·73), Rhodes completed a " double " in Championship matches, and there were seven other members of the side with averages in the twenties.

Fine bowling, adequate batting, keen fielding and astute captaincy form a combination capable of winning the Championship five times out of six.

INTERREGNUM

1906, 1907

1906

An exciting struggle for the Championship ended in favour of Kent with a percentage of 77·77, Yorkshire being second with 70·00, and Surrey third with 63·63. Each side had 14 points, but though Kent won fewer matches than Yorkshire and Surrey they also lost fewer.

The outstanding performances of 1906 were as follows :

v. Leicestershire at Leeds : In their first innings Leicestershire were dismissed for 34, Hirst (seven for 18) and Rhodes (three for 16) bowling unchanged.

v. Nottinghamshire at Nottingham : Rhodes, going in first, scored 83 and took six wickets for 95 when Nottinghamshire batted. Denton scored 107 and 100 not out.

v. Nottinghamshire at Dewsbury : Yorkshire lost by 25 runs. Hirst took fourteen wickets for 97 runs (seven in each innings). Wass and Hallam bowled unchanged in Yorkshire's second innings (68).

v. Worcestershire at Hull : In their first innings Worcestershire were all out for 25, the individual scores being two 5's, six 2's, one 1 and two 0's. There were also two extras. Hirst took five wickets for 15 runs and H. Sedgwick, making his début, five for 8 in 9 overs.

v. Gloucestershire at Bristol : A terrific struggle ended in a win for Gloucestershire by one run. Scores : Gloucestershire, 164, 228 ; Yorkshire, 159, 232. Board was top scorer in the match with 57. Had Yorkshire won this match they would have been Champions in 1906.

v. Somerset at Bath : In this match Hirst completed the all-rounder's perfect feat—a hundred in each innings and five wickets in each Somerset innings. His figures were : 111 and 117 not out, six wickets for 70 runs and five for 45. No other cricketer has equalled this performance.

Haigh (138 wickets, average 13·53) and Hirst (182 wickets, average 14·84) bowled well, but Rhodes had, for him, a poor season, taking 91 wickets for 22·37 runs each. The batting, too, was scarcely strong enough, depending mainly on Hirst, Denton, Rhodes and Tunnicliffe.

85

.1907

Nottinghamshire won the Championship with 100 per cent., winning 15 matches out of 19. Yorkshire and Worcestershire tied for second place with 60 per cent.

The outstanding performances of 1907 were as follows :

v. Leicestershire at Leicester : Yorkshire's innings (515) was a curiosity, the individual scores being—50, 112, 30, 43, 65, 27, 31, 27, 42, 22, 36, extras 30.

v. Warwickshire at Sheffield : In the match Haigh took thirteen wickets for 40 runs (six for 27 and seven for 13), bowling unchanged with Hirst in Warwickshire's second innings.

v. Derbyshire at Glossop : An easy win for Yorkshire (246), Derbyshire scoring 44 and 72. Hirst (eleven for 44) and Rhodes (eight for 71) bowling unchanged in both innings.

v. Leicestershire at Hull : Although Yorkshire scored only 115 runs, they won by ten wickets, Leicestershire's totals being 60 and 54. Hirst took fifteen wickets for 63 runs, all his seven wickets in the second innings being bowled.

v. Middlesex at Sheffield : In the second innings of Middlesex (91), Hirst took nine wickets for 45 runs, seven being bowled. Yorkshire won by seven wickets.

v. Worcestershire at Bradford : Yorkshire lost by 30 runs after a Worcestershire second innings of 28 (J. T. Newstead seven for 10). Arnold (seven for 66) and Cuffe (thirteen for 76) bowled unchanged throughout the match.

Yorkshire's batting was not, perhaps, as strong and reliable as usual, only Hirst, Tunnicliffe, Rhodes and Denton scoring over 800 runs, and only the first three averaging over 25 runs an innings. The bowling, too, depended mainly on Haigh, Hirst and Rhodes, who took 78 wickets (average 11·51), 140 (15·21) and 141 (16·41) respectively. J. T. Newstead (21 wickets for 13·23 runs each) gave promise for the future which was fulfilled in 1908. The Hon. F. S. Jackson made his last appearance for Yorkshire.

EIGHTH CHAMPIONSHIP

1908

Captain : Lord Hawke

Somewhat unexpectedly, Yorkshire won the County Championship in 1908 without losing a match. In three fewer matches Kent had 17 wins to Yorkshire's 16, but they lost three times, and had to take second place in the table.

THE FIRST SIX

	Played	Won	Lost	Drawn	Points	Percent.
Yorkshire	28	16	0	12	16	100·00
Kent	25	17	3	5	14	70·00
Surrey	29	13	4	12	9	52·94
Middlesex	19	6	3	10	3	33·33
Sussex	28	6	4	18	2	20·00
Worcestershire	18	6	5	7	1	9·09

METHOD OF SCORING : As in 1896.

MATCH SCORES AND RESULTS

Yorkshire v.	Ground	Yorkshire 1st Inns.	Yorkshire 2nd Inns.	Opponents 1st Inns.	Opponents 2nd Inns.	Result
Northamptonshire	Northampton	*358 (8)	—	27	15	Y, inns. and 314 runs
Kent	Bradford	101	25 (1)	77	46	Y, 9 wickets
Essex	Leyton	188	210 (4)	226	226 (9)	Draw
Surrey	Leeds	113	48 (3)	90	69	Y, 7 wickets
Derbyshire	Chesterfield	190	352 (5)	102	244	Y, 196 runs
Warwickshire	Birmingham	339	—	121	166 (4)	Draw
Worcestershire	Worcester	130	228	197	92	Y, 69 runs
Lancashire	Sheffield	209	210	129	97	Y, 193 runs
Leicestershire	Leicester	437	—	58	58	Y, inns. and 321 runs
Northamptonshire	Huddersfield	347	—	196	—	Draw
Middlesex	Lord's	157	127 (7)	130	153	Y, 3 wickets
Warwickshire	Bradford	239	216 (7)	294	159	Y, 3 wickets
Nottinghamshire	Nottingham	179	374 (6)	207	66 (4)	Draw
Somerset	Dewsbury	240	53 (2)	160	132	Y, 8 wickets
Kent	Dover	401	90 (3)	242	—	Draw
Sussex	Huddersfield	164	—	290	—	Draw
Nottinghamshire	Leeds	189	132	113	68	Y, 140 runs
Essex	Hull	—	—	42 (3)	—	Draw
Gloucestershire	Sheffield	340	—	153	92	Y, inns. and 95 runs
Leicestershire	Harrogate	325	69 (0)	309	—	Draw
Derbyshire	Leeds	*394 (8)	—	127	136	Y, inns. and 131 runs
Lancashire	Manchester	206	243	144	115	Y, 190 runs
Middlesex	Bradford	279	*153 (1)	164	232 (8)	Draw
Surrey	Oval	162	135 (3)	117	177	Y, 7 wickets
Worcestershire	Sheffield	378	—	24 (1)	—	Draw
Gloucestershire	Cheltenham	219	222	83	176	Y, 182 runs
Somerset	Taunton	210	*240 (6)	101	64 (3)	Draw
Sussex	Brighton	111 (3)	—	105	—	Draw

* Innings declared closed.

87

Yorkshire beat Derbyshire, Gloucestershire, Lancashire, Surrey twice; and Kent, Leicestershire, Middlesex, Northamptonshire, Nottinghamshire, Somerset, Warwickshire, Worcestershire once.

Yorkshire drew with Essex, Sussex twice; and Kent, Leicestershire, Middlesex, Northamptonshire, Nottinghamshire, Somerset, Warwickshire, Worcestershire once.

SUMMARY

	Yorkshire		Opponents	
Runs scored	9732		6611	
Average per wicket	27·25		14·62	
Hundreds	8		1	
Other innings over 50	44		9	
Ten wickets in match	6		5	
Five wickets in innings	33		23	
Highest Total	437	v. Leicestershire	309	(Leicestershire)
Lowest total	101	v. Kent	15	(Northamptonshire)
Totals over 400	2		—	
Totals under 100	—		13	

PRINCIPAL AVERAGES

	Inns.	Not Out	Runs	Highest Inns.	100's	50's	Aver.
G. H. Hirst	41	8	1332	128*	1	10	40·36
D. Denton	44	4	1488	110	1	13	37·20
W. Rhodes	43	1	1412	146	3	5	33·61
W. H. Wilkinson	42	3	1111	99	—	7	28·48
C. H. Hardisty	27	4	595	84	—	2	25·86
J. T. Newstead	35	5	733	100*	1	3	24·43

* Not out.

	Balls	Balls per Wkt.	Runs	Wkts.	5 Wkts. in Inns.	Aver.
S. Haigh	2473	34·83	860	71	6	12·11
G. H. Hirst	5379	34·48	1941	156	15	12·44
J. T. Newstead	4828	41·98	1700	115	9	14·78
W. Rhodes	3553	45·55	1295	78	3	16·60

NOTES

In their first county match Yorkshire set up a record which has never been beaten—Northamptonshire's aggregate of 42 for two completed innings is the lowest ever recorded in a county match.

Against Derbyshire at Chesterfield, Hirst scored 58 and 128 not out and took four wickets.

When Yorkshire beat Lancashire at Sheffield, J. T. Tyldesley scored 101 out of 214 runs scored by the Lancashire batsmen. Hirst took eleven wickets for 88 runs.

J. T. Newstead took ten Leicestershire wickets for 29 runs at Leicester—three for 11 and seven for 18.

At Nottingham, Newstead scored 29 and 100 not out, and took seven wickets for 68 in Notts' first innings.

In Gloucestershire's second innings at Sheffield, Haigh took five wickets for 19 runs.

B. B. Wilson scored 109 *v*. Derbyshire at Leeds. This was Wilson's only appearance in Championship matches during the season.

In the Yorkshire–Lancashire match at Old Trafford, Brearley took thirteen Yorkshire wickets—seven for 81 and six for 115.

Newstead took ten wickets for 92 runs *v*. Surrey at the Oval.

Yorkshire had six batsmen who scored 550 or more runs with an average exceeding 24 runs per innings, but it was the bowling that won the matches. In Championship matches, Yorkshire took 433 wickets and 420 were taken by Hirst, Haigh, Rhodes and Newstead. And in addition to their wicket-taking, Rhodes scored 1,412 runs, Hirst 1,332 and Newstead 733. The find of the season was Newstead, whose all-round form was scarcely expected when the season started.

HOW IT WAS DONE

	100's	50's	10 Wkts. in Match	5 Wkts. in Inns.	50 Runs & 5 Wkts. in Match
W. E. Bates	–	1	–	–	–
D. Denton	1	13	–	–	–
S. Haigh	–	1	–	6	–
C. H. Hardisty	–	2	–	–	–
Lord Hawke	–	1	–	–	–
G. H. Hirst	1	10	3	15	9
J. T. Newstead	1	3	3	9	4
W. Rhodes	3	5	–	3	1
J. W. Rothery	1	2	–	–	–
W. H. Wilkinson	–	7	–	–	–
Total	7	44	6	33	14

FIELDING (159 Catches)

No. of Catches		No. of Catches	
23	W. H. Wilkinson	6	S. Haigh
21	G. H. Hirst	6	Lord Hawke
21	J. T. Newstead	5	W. Rhodes
15	W. E. Bates	4	H. S. Kaye
14	D. Denton	2	J. W. Rothery
13	H. Myers	1	M. W. Booth
10	C. H. Grimshaw	1	A. W. Lupton
9	C. H. Hardisty	1	B. B. Wilson
7	" Sub."		

WICKETKEEPING

	Stumped	Caught	Total
D. Hunter	4	43	47
H. Watson	1	18	19
Total	5	61	66

TOTALS

400 Runs and Over

Yorkshire (2)

437 *v.* Leicestershire, Leicester   401 *v.* Kent, Dover

Opponents (0)
None

Under 100 Runs

Yorkshire (0)
None

Opponents (12)

27 and 15, Northamptonshire, Northampton   83, Gloucestershire, Cheltenham
77 and 46, Kent, Bradford   92, Gloucestershire, Sheffield
58 and 58, Leicestershire, Leicester   92, Worcestershire, Worcester
68, Nottinghamshire, Leeds   97, Lancashire, Sheffield
90 and 69, Surrey, Leeds

FIRST WICKET PARTNERSHIPS
None

50 RUNS AND 5 WICKETS

Scores	Analyses	Player	Against	Ground
74, 41*	5-69, 3-57	G. H. Hirst	Essex	Leyton
62	4-42, 1-11	G. H. Hirst	Warwickshire	Birmingham
35,* 61*	4-49, 1-16	J. T. Newstead	Lancashire	Sheffield
50	6-17, 2-20	W. Rhodes	Leicestershire	Leicester
50, 0	2-32, 6-54	G. H. Hirst	Middlesex	Lord's
52, 2	3-80, 3-48	J. T. Newstead	Warwickshire	Bradford
29, 100*	7-68, 0-3	J. T. Newstead	Nottinghamshire	Nottingham
58	6-53, 2-23	G. H. Hirst	Somerset	Dewsbury
72	5-102	G. H. Hirst	Leicestershire	Harrogate
56	6-43, 3-43	J. T. Newstead	Derbyshire	Leeds
46,* 22	2-38, 4-60	G. H. Hirst	Lancashire	Manchester
96	3-42, 3-65	G. H. Hirst	Middlesex	Bradford
32, 19*	5-58, 2-58	G. H. Hirst	Surrey	Oval
46 24	5-21, 2-27	G. H. Hirst	Somerset	Taunton

* Not out.

MATCHES OF THE SEASON

Yorkshire v. Northamptonshire
Northampton, May 7, 8

Yorkshire won by an innings and 314 runs

In their first match against Yorkshire since their promotion to the ranks of the first-class counties Northamptonshire were annihilated, but certain contributory reasons for such a crushing defeat may be mentioned : C. J. T. Pool, L. T. Driffield and East were unable to play, G. J. Thompson owing to illness was unable to bat, and after Yorkshire had batted on a good wicket, Northants went in on a wicket made difficult by rain.

After Yorkshire had scored 356 for eight wickets and declared, the home county were dismissed twice in the space of 135 minutes for totals of 27 and 15, the aggregate of 43, including 4 extras and a top score of 8. This record has never been approached in county cricket, and may be added to the very small number of unbeatable records.

Bowling unchanged in each innings, Hirst took twelve wickets for 19 runs in 121 balls and Haigh six for 19 in 114 balls.

Yorkshire

W. Rhodes b Hawtin (R.)	40
J. W. Rothery b Hawtin (R.)	27
D. Denton b Wells	110
W. H. Wilkinson c Thompson (A.) b Hawtin (R.)	36
G. H. Hirst c Thompson (A.) b Hawtin (R.)	44
W. E. Bates b Cox	12
H. S. Kaye c Hawtin (A.) b Hawtin (R.)	15
S. Haigh b Falconer	13
H. Myers not out	14
J. T. Newstead not out	19
D. Hunter did not bat	
Extras	26
	356*

* Innings declared closed.

Northamptonshire

W. H. Kingston b Hirst	8	b Hirst	3
M. Cox b Hirst	0	b Hirst	2
A. P. R. Hawtin lbw, b Hirst	2	lbw, b Hirst	0
G. A. T. Vials b Haigh	0	c Myers b Hirst	5
R. W. R. Hawtin b Hirst	1	lbw, b Haigh	2
A. R. Thompson b Haigh	1	b Haigh	1
T. E. Manning b Hirst	0	lbw, b Haigh	2
W. A. Buswell b Haigh	4	b Haigh	0
W. Wells not out	5	not out	0
R. Falconer b Hirst	2	b Hirst	0
G. J. Thompson absent ill		absent ill	
Extras	4		
	27		15

Northamptonshire Bowling

	Overs	Mdns.	Runs	Wkts.
Thompson (G.)	26	6	77	0
Wells	31	10	86	1
Hawtin (R.)	25	3	78	5
Falconer	21	4	62	1
Cox	18	5	27	1

Yorkshire Bowling

	Overs	Mdns.	Runs	Wkts.		Overs	Mdns.	Runs	Wkts.
Hirst	8.5	4	12	6	...	11.2	8	7	6
Haigh	8	1	11	3	...	11	6	8	3

Yorkshire v. *Kent*

Bradford, May 18, 19

Yorkshire won by nine wickets

Played on a bowler's wicket, the match against Kent at Bradford was another fine demonstration of Yorkshire's strength as a team, the bowling and fielding being as good as in any of their Championship seasons.

In two hours on the first day Hirst, Haigh, Newstead and Rhodes got Kent out for 77, of which A. P. Day and C. H. B. Marsham scored 45.

Next morning the Yorkshiremen found the wicket equally allergic to run-getting, and, in spite of a good innings of 45 by Rhodes, were all out for 101.

Kent's second innings (46) was a collapse, only K. L. Hutchings reaching double figures : Hirst and Haigh bowled unchanged, there were no extras, and smart fielding ran out two men of Kent. With only 23 runs required, Yorkshire had won by five o'clock on the second afternoon.

Kent

H. T. W. Hardinge b Hirst	6	run out	1
E. Humphreys lbw, b Hirst	6	c Hunter b Haigh	7
Jas. Seymour c Hunter b Haigh	2	lbw, b Haigh	1
K. L. Hutchings c Myers b Haigh	0	b Hirst	16
F. E. Woolley run out	3	b Hirst	0
A. P. Day c Hunter b Newstead	16	run out	6
C. H. B. Marsham b Rhodes	29	b Haigh	1
F. H. Huish b Newstead	3	c Hunter b Hirst	8
W. J. Fairservice c Hunter b Newstead	4	c Hunter b Haigh	6
C. Blythe run out	0	not out	0
A. Fielder not out	0	c Hirst b Haigh	0
Extras	8		
	77		46

Yorkshire

W. Rhodes b Fairservice	45	c Seymour b Blythe	6
J. W. Rothery b Blythe	8	not out	15
D. Denton c Huish b Fielder	10	not out	3
W. H. Wilkinson c Fielder b Humphreys	13		
G. H. Hirst c Huish b Fairservice	1		
W. E. Bates st. Huish b Blythe	5		
J. T. Newstead b Fairservice	2		
S. Haigh c and b Blythe	0		
H. Myers lbw, b Fairservice	5		
Lord Hawke c Day b Blythe	0		
D. Hunter not out	0		
Extras	12	Extras	1
	101		25

Yorkshire Bowling

	Overs	Mdns.	Runs	Wkts.		Overs	Mdns.	Runs	Wkts.
Hirst	15	7	20	2	...	13	6	22	3
Haigh	14	4	22	2	...	13	4	24	5
Newstead	6.4	4	11	3					
Rhodes	6	3	16	1					

Kent Bowling

	Overs	Mdns.	Runs	Wkts.		Overs	Mdns.	Runs	Wkts.
Fielder	10	2	32	1					
Blythe	19	10	24	4	...	8	6	7	1
Fairservice	17.3	11	27	4	...	5	3	10	0
Humphreys	8	4	6	1					
Marsham						2.2	1	7	0

Yorkshire v. *Surrey*
Leeds, May 25, 26

Yorkshire won by seven wickets

A week after winning the match against Kent at Bradford, Yorkshire took another step towards the Championship by beating Surrey at Leeds. The game was played on a soft wicket, Surrey having slightly better batting conditions than Yorkshire.

Winning the toss, Surrey failed badly against Hirst and Haigh, the latter taking six wickets for 13 runs. E. G. Hayes, top scorer in each Surrey innings, scored 58 out of 78, but when the last wicket fell only 90 runs were on the board.

Yorkshire also found run-getting difficult, but Myers, Rhodes and Grimshaw played useful innings, and a lead of 23 runs was not unacceptable.

Surrey's second innings was even more disastrous than the first, only Hayward, Hayes and Marshal reaching double figures and the last six wickets adding only 14. Hirst took six wickets for 23, and bowled unchanged with Haigh.

Yorkshire obtained the 47 runs needed without much difficulty.

Surrey

T. Hayward b Hirst		14	b Hirst	10
J. B. Hobbs c and b Newstead		5	b Hirst	5
E. G. Hayes c Hirst b Haigh		58	c Hunter b Hirst	24
A. Marshal b Hirst		0	b Haigh	13
J. N. Crawford b Haigh		3	b Haigh	5
Lord Dalmeny b Hirst		0	b Hirst	0
F. C. Holland c Bates b Haigh		1	run out	0
H. G. Bush lbw, b Haigh		0	b Hirst	1
W. Lees b Haigh		3	not out	6
W. C. Smith b Haigh		3	b Hirst	1
H. Strudwick not out		1	b Haigh	2
	Extras	2	Extras	2
		90		69

Yorkshire

W. Rhodes b Smith		12	b Crawford	11
H. Myers c Crawford b Marshal		35	b Smith	7
D. Denton b Smith		9	c and b Crawford	0
W. H. Wilkinson c Hayes b Marshal		1	not out	9
C. H. Grimshaw c Dalmeny b Marshal		24		
G. H. Hirst b Smith		0	not out	20
W. E. Bates c Hayward b Smith		0		
S. Haigh c Hayward b Smith		2		
J. T. Newstead run out		7		
Lord Hawke not out		6		
D. Hunter b Crawford		10		
	Extras	7	Extras	1
		113		48

Yorkshire Bowling

	Overs	Mdns.	Runs	Wkts.		Overs	Mdns.	Runs	Wkts.
Hirst	18	1	58	3	...	17	6	23	6
Newstead	8	0	17	1	...	1	0	1	0
Haigh	9.2	3	13	6	...	15.3	1	43	3

Surrey Bowling

	Overs	Mdns.	Runs	Wkts.		Overs	Mdns.	Runs	Wkts.
Smith	31	11	46	5	...	13	3	24	1
Crawford	16.1	2	41	1	...	12.4	3	23	2
Marshal	14	8	19	3					

APPEARANCES

The following 18 cricketers appeared for Yorkshire in Championship matches, the number of appearances being in parentheses :

W. E. Bates (26)
M. W. Booth (1)
D. Denton (28)
C. H. Grimshaw (6)
S. Haigh (21)
C. H. Hardisty (18)
Lord Hawke (19)
G. H. Hirst (28)
D. Hunter (22)

H. S. Kaye (4)
A. W. Lupton (1)
H. Myers (19)
J. T. Newstead (28)
W. Rhodes (27)
J. W. Rothery (25)
H. Watson (6)
W. H. Wilkinson (28)
B. B. Wilson (1)

POST MORTEM

At the beginning of the season few optimists in Yorkshire could have imagined that the available team would win the Championship without losing a match. The side was in process of re-building. Most of the stalwarts who had helped to win Championships since 1900 had retired ; Rhodes had become primarily a batsman and No. 1 in the batting order, but he had no recognised partner ; the remainder of the run-getting depended on Denton, Hirst and a number of promising but comparatively inexperienced aspirants. But there were, as it proved, two factors which made success possible—it was a wet season, when bowlers were more important than batsmen, and J. T. Newstead suddenly developed into a top-rank all-rounder. A glance at the averages and all-round performances will show that Hirst, Haigh, Newstead and Rhodes never failed as bowlers, and that Hirst and Newstead were match-winning all-rounders. A third asset was the fielding. With a side composed mainly of young players, the fielding was as fine as has been seen from any Champion county.

That this diagnosis is correct is shown by the fact that in 28 matches only Leicestershire succeeded in scoring 300 (309 at Harrogate) against the Yorkshire attack, and the average completed innings of Yorkshire's opponents was 138 ; on thirteen occasions they were dismissed for fewer than 100 runs. In May, the Yorkshire bowlers were in tremendous form. In the first 4 matches Hirst took 34 wickets for 7·88 runs each and Haigh 26 for 8·07—and 42 of these 60 wickets were clean-bowled.

INTERREGNUM

1909, 1910, 1911

1909

Yorkshire finished third in the Championship in 1909, Kent being first with 77·77 per cent., Lancashire second with 55·55, Yorkshire having 50·00 per cent. During the season Yorkshire were beaten by Worcestershire (twice), Kent and Surrey, and won 12 matches compared with 16 in 1908.

The principal performances of the season were as follows :

v. Worcestershire at Worcester : Yorkshire lost by 12 runs in a match in which 856 runs were scored.

v. Lancashire at Manchester : In a low-scoring match, Yorkshire beat Lancashire by 65 runs, Denton's 48 being the top score. Brearley took nine for 80 in Yorkshire's first innings and Huddleston eight for 24 in the second. For Yorkshire, Haigh, seven for 25 (first innings), and Hirst, six for 23 (second innings), were the successful bowlers.

v. Kent at Huddersfield : Fielder took thirteen wickets for 164 runs, Kent winning by seven wickets. Yorkshire were all out for 69 in their first innings.

v. Surrey at Sheffield : On a difficult wicket, Yorkshire scored 125 and 91 and Surrey 62 and 103. Hirst took six wickets for 20 runs and Haigh four for 11 in Surrey's first innings.

v. Lancashire at Bradford : Rhodes, going in first, scored 24 and 25 and took thirteen wickets for 108 runs in Haigh's Benefit match.

v. Middlesex at Leeds : Middlesex led by 226, Yorkshire being 5 for no wicket (second innings) when rain stopped play. A new recruit, A. Drake, took six Middlesex wickets for 34 runs in the second innings.

v. Surrey at the Oval : Yorkshire were all out for 26 in their second innings, Drake being top scorer with 6. Rushby (five for 9) and W. C. Smith (five for 12) bowled unchanged. This is the lowest total scored by Yorkshire.

v. Sussex at Brighton : Rhodes scored 199 and 84 in this drawn match.

The cause of the Yorkshire decline after their fine win in 1908 is easily explained. Instead of taking 156 wickets for 12·44 each, Hirst took 84 for 19·51, and Newstead was even less successful— 426 runs and 62 wickets compared with 733 runs and 115 wickets in 1908. Rhodes scored 1,351 runs with an average of 35·55 and took 107 wickets for 15·28 runs each, and Haigh again headed the bowlers with 111 wickets (average 16·67). Denton, with 1,544 runs (average 35·65) was top of the batting averages.

1910

Yorkshire had a disappointing season in 1910, being eighth in the Championship, Kent, Surrey, Middlesex, Lancashire, Nottinghamshire, Hampshire and Sussex being above them. Of their 25 matches, 10 were won and 9 lost.

A new method of reckoning percentages was introduced at the beginning of the season in place of the system used from 1895 to 1909.

The following were the highlights of one of Yorkshire's least successful seasons :

v. Lancashire at Leeds : In Lancashire's second innings (61) Hirst took nine wickets for 23 runs, eight clean-bowled. His match record was thirteen for 78.

v. Kent at Dewsbury : Fielder (six for 46) and Blythe (three for 30) bowled unchanged in Yorkshire's first innings.

v. Worcestershire at Leeds : Haigh took three wickets for 8 runs in Worcestershire's second innings and nine for 38 in the match.

v. Surrey at Bradford : Rhodes scored 2 and 88 not out and took eleven wickets for 72 runs.

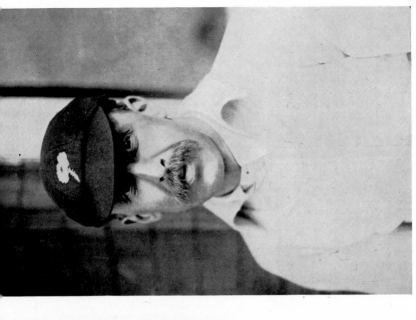

J. T. BROWN

J. TUNNICLIFFE

Photos: Topical Press

v. Kent at Maidstone : Blythe (eleven for 95) and Woolley (eight for 91) bowled unchanged in each innings.

v. Derbyshire at Bradford : Rhodes took five wickets for 5 runs in 28 balls in Derbyshire's second innings.

v. Lancashire at Manchester : R. H. Spooner scored 200 not out in the Lancashire innings (395 for five wickets declared).

v. Middlesex at Sheffield : In the first innings of Middlesex (72), Hirst and Booth bowled unchanged. J. T. Hearne took six wickets for 20 runs in Yorkshire's second innings (61) and twelve for 65 in the match.

v. Hampshire at Portsmouth : Yorkshire won by 6 runs. Scores : Yorkshire, 116, 256 ; Hampshire, 133, 233.

Hirst headed both the batting and bowling averages with 1,425 runs (average 32·38) and 134 wickets (average 15·05). Denton and Rhodes each scored 1,000 runs in county matches, but the bowling was below the normal Yorkshire standard. Rhodes took 77 wickets and Haigh 68, but Newstead took only 27 wickets for 23·48 runs each. The most promising recruits were Drake and Booth.

1911

Showing slightly improved form in 1911, Yorkshire finished seventh in the Championship table with 14 wins and 8 losses, Warwickshire, Kent, Middlesex, Lancashire, Surrey and Essex being the first six. Another new method of reckoning the percentage was evolved : " Five points shall be scored for a win in a completed match. Should a match not be completed the side leading on the first innings shall score three points and its opponents one point."

The principal performances of the season were as follows :

v. Derbyshire at Sheffield : Haigh took three wickets for 4 runs in 21 balls in Derbyshire's first innings (61).

v. Worcestershire at Worcester : M. W. Booth scored 210 in Yorkshire's first innings.

v. Derbyshire at Chesterfield : Drake scored 147 not out and Rhodes took seven Derbyshire wickets for 20 runs in the second innings.

v. Lancashire at Manchester : Drake scored 85 in Yorkshire's second innings and took six wickets for 57 runs in Lancashire's.

v. Warwickshire at Birmingham : F. R. Foster scored 105 and 18 and took twelve Yorkshire wickets for 202 runs—nine for 118 in the first innings.

v. Leicestershire at Bradford : C. J. B. Wood scored a hundred in each Leicestershire innings and carried his bat through the innings on each occasion (107 not out and 117 not out).

G

v. Surrey at Leeds : W. C. Smith took eleven wickets for 96 runs for Surrey and Rhodes eleven for 83 for Yorkshire, who lost by four wickets.

v. Hampshire at Huddersfield : C. P. Mead carried his bat through Hampshire's second innings for 120.

v. Northamptonshire at Northampton : Rhodes took fourteen wickets for 139 runs. Yorkshire lost by 44 runs.

v. Sussex at Leeds : Haigh took seven Sussex wickets for 20 runs in the second innings.

v. Leicestershire at Leicester : Yorkshire lost by an innings and 20 runs, scoring 153 and 47. J. H. King took eight Yorkshire wickets for 17 runs in the second innings.

v. Kent at Canterbury : Yorkshire were all out for 75 and 79, Blythe taking five wickets for 35 runs and six for 28. Kent won by ten wickets.

v. Sussex at Hastings : Hirst scored 218, and Drake 115 in addition to taking eight wickets for 83 runs. Yorkshire won by an innings and 32 runs.

Six Yorkshire batsmen scored 1,000 runs in county matches—Denton, Rhodes, Hirst, Drake, Wilson (B. B.) and Booth. Hirst again completed a " double," taking 119 wickets, and Haigh, Drake, Rhodes and Booth all took over 60 wickets.

NINTH CHAMPIONSHIP

1912

Captain : Sir A. W. White

In a very wet summer Yorkshire won their ninth Championship by a narrow margin from Northamptonshire, whose success provided one of the major surprises of the season. Middlesex beat Yorkshire at Lord's, but in several of the drawn games Yorkshire was in a winning position when bad weather intervened. Rhodes played in the six Test matches of the Triangular Tournament and Haigh in one.

THE FIRST SIX

	Plyd.	Won	Lost	1st Inns. Won	1st Inns. Lost	No Res.	Points Poss.	Points Obtd.	Per-cent.
Yorkshire	28	13	1	7	4	3	125	90	72·00
Northamptonshire	18	10	1	2	4	1	85	60	70·58
Kent	26	14	5	3	3	1	125	82	65·60
Lancashire	22	8	2	4	3	5	85	55	64·70
Middlesex	20	7	4	5	2	2	90	52	57·77
Hampshire	24	7	3	4	4	6	90	51	56·66

METHOD OF SCORING : 5 points for a win ; 3 points for first innings lead, the side behind on the first innings taking 1 point. Championship decided by greatest proportionate number of points obtained to points possible.

MATCH SCORES AND RESULTS

Yorkshire v.	Ground	Yorkshire 1st Inns.	Yorkshire 2nd Inns.	Opponents 1st Inns.	Opponents 2nd Inns.	Result
Leicestershire	Leicester	344	117 (1)	143	317	Y, 9 wickets
Hampshire	Sheffield	471	—	80	260 (4)	Draw
Kent	Leeds	96	—	103 (2)	—	Draw
Lancashire	Bradford	226	17 (0)	76	165	Y, 10 wickets
Somerset	Dewsbury	146	*111(8)	73	45 (3)	Draw
Surrey	Sheffield		Abandoned			
Essex	Huddersfield	242	—	103	—	Draw
Middlesex	Lord's	157	166	185	139 (6)	M, 4 wickets
Gloucestershire	Leeds	82	170	68	110	Y, 74 runs
Nottinghamshire	Nottingham	145	249 (5)	261	132	Y, 5 wickets
Northamptonshire	Bradford	*241 (9)	—	74	24 (7)	Draw
Warwickshire	Birmingham	*451 (4)	—	183	63 (3)	Draw
Worcestershire	Dewsbury	129	*345 (9)	85	175	Y, 214 runs
Gloucestershire	Bristol	134	*411 (9)	132	166	Y, 247 runs
Kent	Tunbridge Wells	543	—	310	188	Y, inns. and 45 runs
Leicestershire	Sheffield	350	115 (2)	140	324	Y, 8 wickets
Northamptonshire	Northampton	330	27 (0)	233	—	Draw
Surrey	Oval	233	*229 (6)	267	93 (1)	Draw
Hampshire	Southampton	492	45 (1)	441	95	Y, 9 wickets
Sussex	Bradford	178	—	28 (2)	—	Draw
Warwickshire	Hull	88	—	59	64 (3)	Draw
Lancashire	Manchester	103	105 (7)	347	—	Draw
Essex	Leyton	278	40 (0)	129	187	Y, 10 wickets
Middlesex	Leeds	92	215	110	90	Y, 107 runs
Nottinghamshire	Harrogate	389	—	161	126	Y, inns. and 102 runs
Worcestershire	Worcester	—	—	134	—	Draw
Somerset	Taunton	330	—	69	125	Y, inns. and 136 runs
Sussex	Brighton	141	—	154 (8)	—	Draw

* Innings declared closed.

99

Yorkshire beat Gloucestershire, Leicestershire, Nottinghamshire twice; and Essex, Hampshire, Kent, Lancashire, Middlesex, Somerset, Worcestershire once.

Yorkshire were beaten by Middlesex once.

Yorkshire drew with Northamptonshire, Sussex, Warwickshire twice; and Essex, Hampshire, Kent, Lancashire, Somerset, Surrey, Worcestershire once.

SUMMARY

	Yorkshire	Opponents	
Runs scored	8773	7236	
Average per wicket	26·50	17·69	
Hundreds	10	5	
Other innings over 50	32	18	
Ten wickets in match	6	2	
Five wickets in innings	24	20	
Highest total	543 v. Kent	441	(Hampshire)
Lowest total	82 v. Gloucestershire	59	(Warwickshire)
Totals over 400	5	1	
Totals under 100	4	10	

PRINCIPAL AVERAGES

	Inns.	Not Out	Runs	Highest Inns.	100's	50's	Aver.
D. Denton	38	4	1831	221	6	4	53·85
W. Rhodes	32	4	965	176	2	3	34·46
B. B. Wilson	41	3	1086	150	1	3	28·57
G. H. Hirst	32	–	880	109	1	5	27·50
R. Kilner	24	5	489	83*	–	2	25·73

* Not out.

	Balls	Balls per Wkt.	Runs	Wkts.	5 Wkts. in Inns.	Aver.
S. Haigh	3695	38·48	1101	96	8	11·46
A. Drake	2969	44·60	1110	67	6	16·56
M. W. Booth	3362	39·55	1525	85	6	17·94
G. H. Hirst	3975	50·96	1492	78	3	19·12
W. Rhodes	1757	47·48	808	37	1	21·83

NOTES

In Somerset's first innings at Bradford, Haigh took five wickets for 14 runs. In Yorkshire's two innings, E. Robson took ten for 103.

The match against Surrey at Sheffield was abandoned without a ball being bowled owing to rain.

Against Gloucestershire at Leeds, Haigh took nine for 25 and five for 40—fourteen wickets for 65 runs in the match, ten being bowled.

Rhodes scored 176 and took five Nottinghamshire wickets for 68 runs in the first innings. Drake scored 53 and took six for 24 in the second innings of Nottinghamshire.

Yorkshire scored 543 v. Kent at Tunbridge Wells, Denton making 221. In seven consecutive innings Denton had scored 784 runs.

Yorkshire had a narrow escape at Manchester, being 139 behind with seven second innings wickets down when the match ended. Spooner and Makepeace scored 181 for Lancashire's first wicket, and Dean and Huddleston bowled finely.

Denton scored 200 not out *v.* Warwickshire at Birmingham and B. B. Wilson 150.

Hirst took twelve wickets for 67 runs against Somerset at Taunton, Denton (82) being top scorer for Yorkshire.

HOW IT WAS DONE

	100's	50's	10 Wkts. in Match	5 Wkts. in Inns.	50 Runs & 5 Wkts. in Match
W. E. Bates	–	2	–	–	–
M. W. Booth	–	4	2	6	2
D. Denton	6	4	–	–	–
A. Drake	–	4	–	6	1
S. Haigh	–	1	2	8	1
G. H. Hirst	1	5	2	3	–
R. Kilner	–	2	–	–	–
E. Oldroyd	–	2	–	–	–
W. Rhodes	2	3	–	1	1
J. Tasker	–	2	–	–	–
Sir A. W. White	–	1	–	–	–
B. B. Wilson	1	3	–	–	–
Total	10	32	6	24	5

FIELDING (123 Catches)

No. of Catches		No. of Catches	
18	A. Drake	7	J. Tasker
18	G. H. Hirst	5	D. Denton
17	W. Rhodes	5	E. Oldroyd
14	S. Haigh	2	W. E. Bates
12	M. W. Booth	2	B. B. Wilson
11	R. Kilner	1	G. Bayes
10	Sir A. W. White	1	J. P. Wilson

WICKETKEEPING

	Stumped	Caught	Total
A. Dolphin	10	27	37
H. Watson	—	6	6
Total	10	33	43

TOTALS

400 Runs and Over

Yorkshire (5)

543 *v.* Kent, Tunbridge Wells
492 *v.* Hampshire, Southampton
471 *v.* Hampshire, Sheffield

451 (4)* *v.* Warwickshire, Birmingham
411 *v.* Gloucestershire, Bristol

* Innings declared closed.

Opponents (1)

441, Hampshire, Southampton

Under 100 Runs

Yorkshire (4)

82 v. Gloucestershire, Leeds   92 v. Middlesex, Leeds
82 v. Warwickshire, Hull   96 v. Kent, Leeds

Opponents (10)

59, Warwickshire, Hull   76, Lancashire, Bradford
68, Gloucestershire, Leeds   80, Hampshire, Sheffield
69, Somerset, Taunton   85, Worcestershire, Dewsbury
73, Somerset, Dewsbury   90, Middlesex, Leeds
74, Northamptonshire, Bradford   95, Hampshire, Southampton

FIRST WICKET PARTNERSHIPS

None.

50 RUNS AND 5 WICKETS

Scores	Analyses	Player	Against	Ground
56	6-31, 0-42	M. W. Booth	Hampshire	Sheffield
71	8-52, 3-91	W. M. Booth	Leicestershire	Sheffield
176	5-68, 0-7	W. Rhodes	Nottinghamshire	Harrogate
0, 83*	4-66, 1-26	R. Kilner	Nottinghamshire	Nottingham
15, 61	6-46, 3-23	S. Haigh	Gloucestershire	Bristol

* Not out.

MATCHES OF THE SEASON

Yorkshire v. Lancashire

Bradford, May 27, 28

Yorkshire won by ten wickets

On a wicket in favour of the bowlers a splendid innings by Rhodes, who opened the innings for Yorkshire, was the deciding factor in the Whitsuntide " Roses " match at Bradford. Rhodes scored 107 out of a total of 226 in 200 minutes off bowling that was always accurate, and the value of his fine batting is shown by the fact that the next best score in the Yorkshire innings was Booth's 29.

Sunshine on a drying wicket made batting conditions more difficult on the second day, and in spite of a good innings by J. T. Tyldesley, Lancashire were all out for 76 and just failed to save the follow on, Hirst and Drake taking every advantage of the state of the pitch.

When Lancashire followed on, Haigh came into the picture, and the last wicket falling at 165, Yorkshire won easily by ten wickets.

Yorkshire

W. Rhodes c Fairclough b Huddleston	107	not out		2
B. B. Wilson c Brooke b Fairclough	10	not out		8
D. Denton b Dean	1			
A. Drake b Dean	9			
G. H. Hirst b Fairclough	15			
J. Tasker c Spooner b Huddleston	4			
M. W. Booth lbw, b Huddleston	29			
S. Haigh c Makepeace b Huddleston	26			
W. E. Bates b Huddleston	19			
Sir A. W. White b Huddleston	0			
A. Dolphin not out	1			
Extras	5	Extras		7
	226			17

Lancashire

R. H. Spooner b Drake	3	lbw, b Haigh		22
H. Makepeace b Hirst	20	b Haigh		10
J. T. Tyldesley c Dolphin b Hirst	43	b Rhodes		5
J. Sharp c Hirst b Drake	1	c Haigh b Rhodes		41
A. Hartley lbw, b Hirst	1	b Haigh		8
E. Tyldesley c Denton b Drake	2	lbw, b Haigh		4
F. R. R. Brooke b Drake	0	b Drake		14
A. H. Hornby c Rhodes b Drake	0	run out		2
W. Huddleston c and b Hirst	2	c Booth b Haigh		37
H. Dean b Drake	1	not out		14
P. M. Fairclough not out	0	c Drake b Booth		7
Extras	3	Extras		1
	76			165

Lancashire Bowling

	Overs	Mdns.	Runs	Wkts.		Overs	Mdns.	Runs	Wkts.
Dean	37	11	67	2	...	1	0	3	0
Huddleston	34.1	11	77	6					
Fairclough	26	9	77	2					
Sharp						1	0	7	0
Hartley						0.3	0	0	0

Yorkshire Bowling

	Overs	Mdns.	Runs	Wkts.		Overs	Mdns.	Runs	Wkts.
Hirst	21.1	6	28	4	...	13	1	35	0
Drake	21	9	33	6	...	17	6	50	1
Rhodes	3	0	8	0	...	18	4	49	2
Haigh	3	0	4	0	...	20	9	25	5
Booth						3.3	1	5	1

1912

Yorkshire v. *Hampshire*
Southampton, July 25, 26, 27

Yorkshire won by nine wickets

Although more than 900 runs were scored in the first two innings at Southampton, Yorkshire, taking full advantage of a change in the state of the wicket, won an interesting match by nine wickets.

Winning the toss, Hampshire had scored 378 when their fourth wicket fell, thanks to splendid batting by Stone, Fry and Barrett, who were given three " lives " by the Yorkshiremen.

Stone and Fry shared a partnership of 109, and when Stone was caught at the wicket, Fry and Barrett added 246 in 210 minutes. Fry was let off twice, but his 186 was invaluable to his side.

Yorkshire's reply was built up round a very fine innings by Denton, who was third out at 319 after scoring 191 in 325 minutes. Oldroyd, Hirst, Booth and " extras " made useful additions to the total, which eventually reached 492, leaving Hampshire 51 runs behind.

When Hampshire began their second innings rain had made the wicket difficult, and the batting collapsed. Hirst and Haigh on such a wicket were not the pleasantest of opponents, and when the last wicket fell Yorkshire needed only 45 runs to win.

Hampshire

A. Bowell lbw, b Hirst	3	c Haigh b Hirst	0
A. Stone c Dolphin b Booth	73	c Kilner b Hirst	16
C. P. Mead lbw, b Hirst	3	b Hirst	19
C. B. Fry c Dolphin b Oldroyd	186	lbw, b Hirst	17
E. I. M. Barrett not out	120	c. Booth b Drake	7
J. Newman c Oldroyd b Rhodes	4	not out	10
W. V. Jephson b Rhodes	2	b Hirst	1
G. Brown b Hirst	18	lbw, b Haigh	8
G. N. Bignell c Kilner b Hirst	0	b Haigh	0
E. M. Sprot c Rhodes b Booth	8	c Rhodes b Hirst	1
A. Kennedy c Denton b Booth	8	c White b Haigh	3
Extras	16	Extras	4
	441		95

Yorkshire

W. Rhodes c Mead b Kennedy	0	not out	18
B. B. Wilson b Brown	74	run out	4
D. Denton c Sprot b Newman	191	not out	23
E. Oldroyd c Barrett b Kennedy	45		
G. H. Hirst b Newman	44		
R. Kilner b Kennedy	19		
A. Drake c Newman b Kennedy	10		
M. W. Booth not out	45		
S. Haigh c Fry b Mead	17		
Sir A. W. White c sub. b Kennedy	0		
A. Dolphin c. Stone b Kennedy	13		
Extras	34		
	492		45

Yorkshire Bowling

	Overs	Mdns.	Runs	Wkts.		Overs	Mdns.	Runs	Wkts.
Hirst	37	12	91	4	...	18	6	47	6
Booth	39.1	4	129	3	...	4	0	26	0
Drake	25	6	58	0	...	2	1	5	1
Haigh	21	3	68	0	...	16	8	13	3
Rhodes	12	1	48	2					
Kilner	4	1	10	0					
Oldroyd	7	1	21	1					

Hampshire Bowling

	Overs	Mdns.	Runs	Wkts.		Overs	Mdns.	Runs	Wkts.
Brown	23	1	93	1					
Kennedy	54.1	8	181	6	...	7.3	1	32	0
Newman	49	9	131	2					
Bignell	2	1	2	0					
Mead	8	1	28	1	...	6	2	10	0
Bowell	8	2	23	0					
Sprot						1	0	3	0

APPEARANCES

The following 17 cricketers appeared for Yorkshire in Championship matches, the number of appearances being in parentheses :

W. E. Bates (7)
G. Bayes (4)
M. W. Booth (26)
D. Denton (26)
A. Dolphin (23)
A. Drake (26)
S. Haigh (25)
G. H. Hirst (24)
R. Kilner (18)

J. T. Newstead (2)
E. Oldroyd (12)
W. Rhodes (20)
J. Tasker (18)
H. Watson (3)
Sir A. W. White (26)
B. B. Wilson (26)
J. P. Wilson (1)

POST MORTEM

The outstanding features of Yorkshire's win in the County Championship of 1912 were, first, the batting of Denton and, second, the all-round strength of the side.

In any season, a batsman who scores 1,800 runs and averages 53 runs an innings in Championship matches has earned a special bouquet, but when he performs these feats in an unusually wet season he has clearly excelled himself. At the age of 38 David Denton headed the Yorkshire batsmen, scoring 750 runs and averaging nearly 20 runs an innings more than the runner-up.

No bowler in 1912 took 100 wickets in Championship matches, but Rhodes, Hirst, Haigh, Booth and Drake all took 37 or more at costs ranging from 11·46 to 21·83, and each of them except Haigh scored over 600 runs. In addition, Roy Kilner showed promise with both bat and ball.

In winning the Championship, Yorkshire scarcely showed the dominating form of, say, 1900, 1901 and 1902, their winning margin over Northamptonshire being small, but on all kinds of wicket they were clearly the most consistent eleven in the competition, and deserved the success won mainly by Denton and their bevy of batsmen-bowlers and bowler-batsmen.

INTERREGNUM

1913, 1914

1913

Yorkshire were runners-up to Kent in 1913, and in view of the facts that the weather was more favourable to batsmen than in 1912, and that Yorkshire's stronger arm was the ball, this must be considered a satisfactory result. The method of reckoning the percentage was unchanged.

A number of interesting performances materialised during the season :

v. Lancashire at Manchester : In the first county match of the season Yorkshire were crushed by Lancashire, their totals being 74 and 53. In the two Yorkshire innings Heap took eleven wickets for 39 runs—six for 16 and five for 23.

v. Gloucestershire at Bristol : Yorkshire beat Gloucestershire, without G. L. Jessop, rather easily, Rhodes and B. B. Wilson scoring 197 for the first wicket in the second innings.

v. Nottinghamshire at Nottingham : G. Gunn scored 132 and 109 not out and Denton 148 in a match which always looked like a draw.

v. Middlesex at Lord's : Booth scored 107 not out and 30 not out and took eight wickets for 136 runs in another drawn game in which Dolphin stumped one and caught five Middlesex batsmen.

v. Northamptonshire at Leeds : Northamptonshire won an exciting match by 20 runs, G. J. Thompson taking eleven wickets for 142 runs, and Rhodes and Booth seven in the two Northants innings. R. Kilner scored 91 in Yorkshire's second innings.

v. Gloucestershire at Sheffield : Yorkshire lost by 2 runs, G. L. Jessop bowling the last two Yorkshiremen for 3 runs in 25 balls, in addition to scoring 67 and 40. Drake scored 45 not out in Yorkshire's second innings (107) and in Gloucestershire's second innings took eight wickets for 59 runs.

v. Surrey at the Oval : Yorkshire scored 409 for nine wickets declared, and got Surrey out for 177 and 213. Hirst (112 not out), Rhodes (90) and B. B. Wilson (51) were top scorers for Yorkshire. E. R. Wilson took three wickets for 18 in Surrey's first innings.

v. Essex at Bradford : E. R. Wilson (No. 9) scored 104 not out when Yorkshire scored 512 for nine wickets declared at Bradford, four other Yorkshiremen scoring over 50.

Six Yorkshire batsmen scored 1,000 runs in county matches in 1913—Hirst, Rhodes, R. Kilner, Booth, B. B. Wilson and Denton, their averages ranging from 43·21 to 28·20. In addition to scoring 1,000 runs, Booth (158 wickets), Hirst and Rhodes took over 60 wickets, while Drake scored 875 runs and took 102 wickets. Six regular members of the side were all-rounders, not counting E. R. Wilson.

1914

Yorkshire's drop to fourth place in the Championship, below Surrey, Middlesex and Kent, was due mainly to less successful batting, the bowling showing better figures than in 1913. In each season Yorkshire lost 4 matches, but in 1914 won 14 compared with 16 in the previous summer. In spite of the outbreak of the First World War in August, the county programme was completed except for 3 matches abandoned.

Some fine performances were recorded during the last pre-war season :

v. Essex at Leyton : Booth took fourteen wickets for 160 runs in the match—six for 96 and eight for 64.

v. Surrey at Bradford : Surrey won a close match by 28 runs, Hobbs scoring 100 and 74 and Hayes 125. For Yorkshire, Rhodes scored 89 in the first innings and took eleven wickets for 165 runs.

v. Derbyshire at Leeds : Rhodes took seven Derbyshire wickets for 19 in the second innings.

v. Kent at Tonbridge : Kent won by an innings and 149 runs, scoring 493. A. P. Day, in addition to scoring 49 runs, took three wickets for 37 and six for 36 in the Yorkshire innings.

v. Kent at Sheffield : Yorkshire lost by five wickets, Blythe taking ten wickets for 77 runs, and Booth ten for 79 for Yorkshire. Kilner (50 out of 101) and Woolley (41) were top scorers.

v. Derbyshire at Chesterfield : Morton scored 50 out of 68 (8 extras) in Derbyshire's second innings, Drake taking five wickets for 6 runs in 18 balls and Rhodes four for 12.

v. Surrey at the Oval : Scoring 549 for six wickets declared, Surrey won by an innings and 30 runs. Each of the first three Surrey batsmen scored a hundred—Hayward 116, Hobbs 202, Hayes 134.

v. Gloucestershire at Bristol : Yorkshire won by an innings and 227 runs, Booth (twelve for 89) and Drake (eight for 81) bowling unchanged. Dolphin stumped one and caught four in Gloucestershire's second innings (84).

v. Somerset at Weston-super-Mare : For the second time in consecutive matches, Booth and Drake bowled unchanged throughout the match, Somerset scoring 44 and 90.   Their analyses were : Booth five for 77 and Drake fifteen for 51.   In the first innings Drake took five for 16 and in the second all ten wickets for 35. He also scored 51 in Yorkshire's first innings.

During the county season, Hirst, Denton, B. B. Wilson, Kilner and Rhodes scored 1,000 runs, Drake, Rhodes and Booth each taking 100 wickets for fewer than 19 runs each.   Hirst was top of the batting averages but took only 41 wickets.

FIRST WORLD WAR, 1914-1918

TENTH CHAMPIONSHIP

1919

Captain : D. C. F. Burton

With matches experimentally limited to two days and all county sides in process of rebuilding, the Championship in 1919 was more open than usual. Yorkshire's backbone of seasoned players—Hirst, Denton, Rhodes, R. Kilner, Dolphin and Holmes, plus three recruits, Sutcliffe, Waddington and Emmott Robinson—enabled them to settle down sooner than most of their opponents. The surprising revival of Rhodes as a bowler and the fine form of Waddington in his first season compensated in some measure for the loss of Booth and Drake.

For this season only one point was given for each win, the positions in the table being decided by the percentage of points to matches played.

THE FIRST SIX

	Played	Won	Lost	Drawn	Percentage.
Yorkshire	26	12	3	11	46·15
Kent	14	6	1	7	42·85
Nottinghamshire	14	5	1	8	35·71
Surrey	20	7	3	10	35·00
Lancashire	24	8	4	12	33·33
Somerset	12	4	3	5*	33·33

* Includes a tie with Sussex.

METHOD OF SCORING : Percentage of wins to matches played.

MATCH SCORES AND RESULTS

Yorkshire v.	Ground	Yorkshire 1st Inns.	Yorkshire 2nd Inns.	Opponents 1st Inns.	Opponents 2nd Inns.	Result
Gloucestershire	Gloucester	279	—	125	89	Y, inns. and 63 runs
Essex	Leyton	348	—	354	55 (1)	Draw
Lancashire	Manchester	232	153	319	206 (9)	L, 140 runs
Warwickshire	Birmingham	*371 (8)	—	115	193	Y, inns. and 63 runs
Derbyshire	Bradford	221	26 (0)	74	172	Y, 10 wickets
Nottinghamshire	Sheffield	112	238	236	117 (6)	N, 6 wickets
Kent	Leeds	64	8 (0)	169	—	Draw
Derbyshire	Chesterfield	251 (6)	—	87	—	Draw
Nottinghamshire	Nottingham	232	—	197	74 (4)	Draw
Essex	Hull	241	—	106	77	Y, inns. and 58 runs
Hampshire	Dewsbury	*401 (8)	—	82	176	Y, inns. and 143 runs
Northamptonshire	Sheffield	85	273	149	135	Y, 74 runs
Leicestershire	Huddersfield	215	314 (6)	223	127 (4)	Draw
Surrey	Bradford	264	25 (0)	143	145	Y, 10 wickets
Northamptonshire	Northampton	*380 (3)	—	72	112	Y, inns. and 196 runs
Gloucestershire	Leeds	*448 (4)	—	121	202	Y, inns. and 126 runs
Sussex	Harrogate	187	228	271	145 (5)	S, 5 wickets
Lancashire	Sheffield	317 (5)	—	124	271 (6)	Draw
Leicestershire	Leicester	423	—	161	136	Y, inns. and 126 runs
Surrey	Oval	243	110 (4)	324	189 (8)	Draw
Middlesex	Leeds	190	358 (8)	208	153	Y, 187 runs
Warwickshire	Bradford	381	—	183	107	Y, inns. and 91 runs
Middlesex	Lord's	187	279 (3)	128	234 (8)	Draw
Kent	Dover	375 (8)	—	168	78 (2)	Draw
Hampshire	Southampton	242 (3)	—	201	—	Draw
Sussex	Brighton	187 (6)	—	100	38 (2)	Draw

* Innings declared closed.

Yorkshire beat Gloucestershire, Northamptonshire, Warwickshire twice; and Derbyshire, Essex, Hampshire, Leicestershire, Middlesex, Surrey once.

Yorkshire were beaten by·Lancashire, Nottinghamshire, Sussex once.

Yorkshire drew with Kent twice; and Derbyshire, Essex, Hampshire, Lancashire, Leicestershire, Middlesex, Nottinghamshire, Surrey, Sussex once.

SUMMARY

	Yorkshire	Opponents
Runs scored	8888	7671
Average per wicket	31·29	17·62
Hundreds	20	5
Other innings over 50	37	32
Ten wickets in match	6	3
Five wickets in innings	26	11
Highest total	448 (4) dec.	354 (Essex)
	v. Gloucestershire	
Lowest total	64 *v.* Kent	72 (Northamptonshire)
Totals over 400	3	–
Totals under 100	2	6

PRINCIPAL AVERAGES

	Inns.	Not Out	Runs	Highest Inns.	100's	50's	Aver.
H. Sutcliffe	36	3	1601	174	5	6	48·51
P. Holmes	37	3	1471	140	5	4	43·26
D. Denton	32	2	1070	122	4	5	35·66
W. Rhodes	34	8	891	135	1	6	34·26
R. Kilner	34	4	955	115	2	6	31·89
G. H. Hirst	29	2	829	120	2	4	30·70

	Balls	Balls per Wkt.	Runs	Wkts.	5 Wkts. in Inns.	Aver.
W. Rhodes	4785	33·69	1764	142	11	12·42
R. Kilner	1643	43·23	573	38	–	15·07
E. R. Wilson	1277	49·11	417	26	1	16·03
A. Waddington	3975	41·84	1676	95	8	17·64
A. C. Williams	962	38·48	472	25	2	18·88
W. E. Blackburne	1074	35·80	596	30	2	19·86

NOTES

In the first county match of the Yorkshire season Rhodes went in first and scored 72. He then took seven Gloucestershire wickets for 47 runs, including four for 5 in 21 balls.

Makepeace scored 105 and 78 in the first post-war Lancashire–Yorkshire match at Manchester. Sutcliffe, going in No. 7, scored 26 and 53. Parkin took fourteen wickets for 123 runs. Lancashire won by 140 runs.

Against Derbyshire at Bradford, Dolphin stumped one and caught eight batsmen. W. E. Blackburne took five wickets for 17 runs in Derbyshire's first innings.

The Holmes–Sutcliffe combination opened Yorkshire's innings for the first time *v.* Kent at Leeds on June 30. Holmes was out for 0, but Sutcliffe was top scorer with 20 out of a total of 64. For Kent, Hardinge carried his bat through the innings for 79.

A. C. Williams took nine Hampshire wickets, eight bowled, for 29 runs in the first innings (82) at Dewsbury.

Holmes (145) and Sutcliffe (133) had their first century first-wicket partnership *v.* Northamptonshire at Northampton, the total being 279 before they were parted.

At Sheffield, Holmes (123) and Sutcliffe (132) registered their first big stand against Lancashire. Four Tyldesleys—J. T., E., J., and R.—appeared for Lancashire.

D. J. Knight scored 114 and 101 for Surrey at the Oval, J. N. Crawford scoring 92 and 11 not out and taking five wickets for 82 runs in the match.

In Warwickshire's second innings at Bradford, Rhodes took the last eight wickets for 44 runs after scoring 56 in Yorkshire's innings.

HOW IT WAS DONE

	100's	50's	10 Wkts. in Match	5 Wkts. in Inns.	50 Runs & 5 Wkts. in Match
W. E. Blackburne	–	–	–	2	–
D. C. F. Burton	1	1	–	–	–
D. Denton	4	5	–	–	–
G. H. Hirst	2	4	–	–	–
P. Holmes	5	4	–	–	–
R. Kilner	2	6	–	–	1
W. Rhodes	1	6	4	11	4
E. Robinson	–	1	–	2	–
H. Sutcliffe	5	6	–	–	–
A. Waddington	–	–	1	8	–
A. C. Williams	–	–	1	2	–
E. R. Wilson	–	1	–	1	–
G. Wilson	–	2	–	–	–
Total	20	37	6	26	5

FIELDING (175 Catches)

No. of Catches		No. of Catches	
30	P. Holmes	8	D. Denton
24	W. Rhodes	4	A. C. Williams
22	R. Kilner	4	E. R. Wilson
19	H. Sutcliffe	3	E. Smith
18	G. H. Hirst	2	N. Kilner
10	E. Robinson	2	G. Wilson
10	A. Waddington	1	H. M. Claughton
9	D. C. F. Burton	1	T. J. Birtles
8	W. E. Blackburne		

WICKETKEEPING

	Stumped	Caught	Total
A. Dolphin	23	42	65
T. H. Hoyle	1	—	1
Total	24	42	66

TOTALS

400 Runs and Over

Yorkshire (3)

448 (4)* v. Gloucestershire, Leeds   401 (8)* v. Hampshire, Dewsbury
423 v. Leicestershire, Leicester

Opponents (0)

None.

* Innings declared closed.

Under 100 Runs

Yorkshire (2)

64 v. Kent, Leeds   85 v. Northamptonshire, Sheffield

Opponents (6)

72, Northamptonshire, Northampton   82, Hampshire, Dewsbury
74, Derbyshire, Bradford   87, Derbyshire, Chesterfield
77, Essex, Hull   89, Gloucestershire, Gloucester

FIRST WICKET PARTNERSHIPS

Score	Partners	Against	Ground
279	P. Holmes, H. Sutcliffe	Northamptonshire	Northampton
253	P. Holmes, H. Sutcliffe	Lancashire	Sheffield
197	P. Holmes, H. Sutcliffe	Leicestershire	Leicester
159	P. Holmes, H. Sutcliffe	Middlesex	Lord's
106	P. Holmes, H. Sutcliffe	Warwickshire	Bradford

50 RUNS AND 5 WICKETS

Scores	Analyses	Player	Against	Ground
72	7-47, 4-5	W. Rhodes	Gloucestershire	Gloucester
135	6-66	W. Rhodes	Hampshire	Dewsbury
58*	1-4, 4-12	R. Kilner	Northamptonshire	Northampton
65, 8	5-46, 0-19	W. Rhodes	Sussex	Harrogate
56	2-31, 8-44	W. Rhodes	Warwickshire	Bradford

* Not out.

GEORGE MACAULAY, ARTHUR DOLPHIN AND MAURICE LEYLAND

[Photo: Overena Press Agency

THE YORKSHIRE TEAM OF 1923

MATCHES OF THE SEASON

Yorkshire v. *Hampshire*
Dewsbury, July 11, 12

Yorkshire won by an innings and 143 runs

Yorkshire beat Hampshire by a big margin at Dewsbury, but the match was outstanding for a number of individual performances—a maiden hundred in county cricket by D. C. F. Burton, a fine all-round display by Rhodes, and a wonderful bit of bowling by A. C. Williams, who had previously played in two matches in 1911 without taking a wicket.

Winning the toss, Yorkshire scored runs so quickly that soon after the tea interval they were able to declare with a total of 401 for eight wickets. Principal credit for this result was due to Rhodes and Burton, who shared a partnership of 254, Rhodes scoring his only hundred of the season and Burton a maiden hundred in county matches. During the Yorkshire innings ten of the Hampshire side bowled.

In the short time remaining for play, Hampshire were skittled out for 82 runs by Williams, whose bowling was sensational. He clean-bowled the first four batsmen, had the fifth caught by Kilner and bowled the next four, Kilner taking the remaining wicket. Williams took his nine wickets for 29 runs in 77 balls, but as the other sixteen wickets he took during the season cost 27·68 runs each, it must be inferred that on this occasion he bowled well above his form.

In Hampshire's second innings, Rhodes followed up his hundred with six wickets for 66 runs, Hampshire being all out before two o'clock, the only serious resistance offered being by Newcombe and Tennyson.

Yorkshire

P. Holmes b Kennedy	9
H. Sutcliffe lbw, b Jameson	46
D. Denton c and b Melle	36
R. Kilner b Jameson	0
W. Rhodes c Kennedy b Newcombe	135
G. H. Hirst c Kennedy b Melle	0
E. Robinson lbw, b Kennedy	12
D. C. F. Burton not out	142
A. Waddington b Jameson	1
A. Dolphin did not bat	
A. C. Williams did not bat	
Extras	20
	401*

* Innings declared closed.

H

Hampshire

B. G. Melle b Williams	24	c Waddington b Rhodes	34
G. Brown b Williams	1	b Rhodes	16
G. Newcombe b Williams	1	c Robinson b Waddington	50
C. P. Mead b Williams	23	c and b Waddington	1
Hon. L. H. Tennyson c Kilner b Williams	5	st. Dolphin b Rhodes	41
M. McGibbon b Williams	0	not out	1
A. S. Kennedy b Williams	5	st. Dolphin b Rhodes	0
T. O. Jameson b Williams	6	c Robinson b Rhodes	6
L. G. Black b Williams	0	c Denton b Rhodes	0
S. G. A. Maartensz c Holmes b Kilner	4	b Williams	21
F. Ryan not out	5	b Waddington	0
Extras	8	Extras	6
	82		**176**

Hampshire Bowling

	Overs	Mdns.	Runs	Wkts.
Brown	11	2	32	0
Kennedy	26	3	109	2
Tennyson	2	0	17	0
Ryan	11	1	44	0
Melle	20	6	42	2
Jameson	21.4	4	82	3
McGibbon	1	0	10	0
Black	5	0	26	0
Mead	2	0	9	0
Newcombe	2	0	10	1

Yorkshire Bowling

	Overs	Mdns.	Runs	Wkts.		Overs	Mdns.	Runs	Wkts.
Waddington	8	1	25	0	...	21	4	50	3
Williams	12.5	4	29	9	...	14.3	4	37	1
Kilner	5	1	20	1					
Rhodes						24	4	66	6
Robinson						5	0	17	0

APPEARANCES

The following 21 cricketers appeared for Yorkshire in Championship matches, the number of appearances being in parentheses :

W. E. Blackburne (6)
T. J. Birtles (4)
D. C. F. Burton (22)
K. Chichester-Constable (1)
H. M. Claughton (3)
D. Denton (24)
A. Dolphin (25)
G. H. Hirst (25)
P. Holmes (26)
T. H. Hoyle (1)
N. Kilner (3)

R. Kilner (26)
G. Render (1)
W. Rhodes (26)
E. Robinson (17)
E. Smith (8)
H. Sutcliffe (26)
A. Waddington (18)
A. C. Williams (9)
E. R. Wilson (8)
G. Wilson (7)

POST MORTEM

The first season after World War No. 1 was a time of team-building for most counties, and Yorkshire were faced with the necessity of finding a new XI. during the next two or three seasons. Hirst, Denton and Rhodes were veterans on the verge of retirement; Booth had been killed and Drake had died during the war. When the season started it was not easy to choose an attack out of the bowlers available. But the emergency produced the men.

Rhodes, after playing himself into the position of Hobbs's Test partner, went back to bowling as a duck takes to water, and had a wonderfully successful season, both as bowler and all-rounder; a young batsman named Sutcliffe, who had played in the Second XI. in 1914, was an immediate success, and by the end of June had worked his way up the batting order to No. 2 and headed the season's batting averages; Waddington, and in a lesser degree Emmott Robinson, soon became regular members of the side, the former being Rhodes's principal collaborator in dismissing opposing XI.'s. Quite soon, indeed, the veterans and recruits, plus a number of aspirants on trial, settled down into a serviceable side—not one of Yorkshire's best teams, but a side capable of winning the Championship and providing a solid foundation for the future.

Put in a nutshell, Yorkshire's success in 1919 may be ascribed to the excellent opening partnerships of Holmes and Sutcliffe in the last half of the season, the steady backing provided by Denton, Hirst, Kilner and Rhodes, and the match-winning bowling of Rhodes and Waddington.

INTERREGNUM

1920, 1921

1920

Middlesex won the County Championship in 1920, Lancashire being second, Surrey third and Yorkshire fourth. A new method of reckoning the percentages, like most such systems, was not free from anomalies, but on the whole produced a fair representation of facts and form.

The season produced some interesting discoveries and performances :

v. Derbyshire at Sheffield : In the first county match, R. Kilner scored 206 not out and took two wickets for 3 runs in 10 balls in Derbyshire's first innings, and G. G. Macaulay made his first appearance for Yorkshire.

v. Lancashire at Bradford : Yorkshire won by 22 runs, Robinson taking nine wickets for 36 runs in Lancashire's second innings.

v. Worcestershire at Worcester : Denton scored 209 not out for Yorkshire (472 for three wickets declared), and Macaulay took six wickets for 47 runs in Worcestershire's first innings.

v. Essex at Dewsbury : Rhodes scored 12 and 66 and took three for 27 and five for 20 in the two Essex innings.

v. Surrey at Sheffield : Surrey won by 204 runs, Hobbs scoring 112 and 70, and Rhodes taking ten Surrey wickets for 136 runs.

v. Leicestershire at Hull : Waddington took twelve wickets for 74 runs (five for 49 and seven for 25) in Leicestershire's two innings (119 and 69).

v. Hampshire at Leeds : Yorkshire lost by an innings and 72 runs, Hampshire scoring 456 for two wickets declared—G. Brown 232 not out and C. P. Mead 122 not out. Kennedy took ten Yorkshire wickets for 135 runs.

v. Northamptonshire at Bradford : Yorkshire won by 228 runs, Northamptonshire scoring 67 and 51. Waddington took eleven wickets for 54 runs and Rhodes eight for 27 (three for 11 and five for 16).

v. Northamptonshire at Northampton : Waddington (thirteen for 48) and Robinson (six for 34) bowled unchanged in each innings. Holmes carried his bat through the Yorkshire innings (270) for 147.

v. Lancashire at Manchester : Holmes scored 126 and 111 not out

v. Middlesex at Bradford : Middlesex won by 4 runs, Dolphin (52) being top scorer for Yorkshire. F. T. Mann obtained " spectacles." Rhodes (ten for 151) and E. R. Wilson (nine for 92) were the most successful bowlers.

v. Surrey at the Oval : Surrey won by 31 runs. Sutcliffe scored 62 and 59 for Yorkshire, and Hirst 81 in the first innings. E. R. Wilson took five wickets for 29 runs in Surrey's second innings (110).

v. Hampshire at Portsmouth : Yorkshire won by an innings and 235 runs after scoring 585 for three wickets declared. Holmes (302 not out) and Sutcliffe (131) scored 347 for the first wicket, Rhodes made 63 not out and took eleven wickets for 129 runs, and in Hampshire's first innings (131) E. R. Wilson took five for 20 in 25.1 overs (18 maidens).

Holmes had a great season in 1920, scoring 2,029 runs, including 7 hundreds, in Championship matches, and having an average of 54·83. Rhodes scored over 900 runs and again headed the bowlers with 143 wickets for 12·90 runs each, Waddington with 137 wickets (average 16·43) being his principal assistant. In August, E. R. Wilson reinforced the attack and took 39 wickets for 15·48 runs each, nearly half of his overs being maidens. During the season two cricketers destined to play prominent parts in Yorkshire cricket made first appearances—Macaulay and Leyland.

1921

After a fine struggle Middlesex retained the Championship won i. 1920, Surrey being second with a percentage of 70·43 compared with the winners' 78·94, and Yorkshire third with 70·40.

In a season favourable to batsmen it was surprising to find the Yorkshire bowling stronger and with better figures than in 1920.

Among the outstanding performances are the following :

v. Hampshire at Southampton : In a drawn match Yorkshire included a new batsman, C. Tyson, whose début remained a record until beaten by A. Morris of New South Wales in 1940-41. In Yorkshire's two innings he scored 100 not out and 80 not out. After playing five innings for the county, Tyson dropped out of the side.

v. Warwickshire at Birmingham : In Warwickshire's first innings, Macaulay took six wickets for 10 runs.

v. Derbyshire at Hull : Robinson scored 100 in the Yorkshire innings (240), and Macaulay took seven wickets for 12 runs (one for 9 and six for 3). Derbyshire scored 105 and 23 (two absent ill).

v. Leicestershire at Leeds : Yorkshire won by an innings, Rhodes scoring 267 not out and taking seven wickets for 66 runs in the match.

v. Derbyshire at Chesterfield : For the second time in a season Derbyshire were dismissed by Yorkshire without a batsman reaching double figures in a first innings of 37.

v. Nottinghamshire at Nottingham : Yorkshire scored 438 for 9 wickets declared, their first eight batsmen making 183 and the " tail " 230—Macaulay 125 not out, Waddington 44, Allen 41.

v. Northamptonshire at Harrogate : After Yorkshire had scored 548 for four wickets declared (Holmes 277 not out), Robinson (ten for 70) and Waddington (nine for 61) bowled unchanged throughout the match.

v. Essex at Bradford : In the first innings of Essex (66), E. R. Wilson took four wickets for 4 runs.

Yorkshire were strong in all departments in 1921. Six batsmen scored 1,000 runs in Championship matches (Oldroyd, Rhodes, Holmes, Robinson, Sutcliffe, R. Kilner), and thirteen averaged over 20 runs an innings. Moreover, six Yorkshire bowlers took 40 or more wickets at costs ranging from E. R. Wilson's 11·34 to Robinson's 19·93. After playing for Yorkshire since 1889, Hirst retired at the end of the season, having scored more than 32,000 runs and taken over 2,500 wickets in Yorkshire matches.

ELEVENTH CHAMPIONSHIP

1922

Captain : G. Wilson

Yorkshire had a great tussle with Nottinghamshire for the Championship of 1922, each side beating its rival once, the final percentages being 73·79 and 71·53 respectively. That Yorkshire deserved to win there can be little doubt, for they won two matches more than Notts and lost three fewer.

THE FIRST SIX

	Plyd.	Won	Lost	1st Inns. Won	1st Inns. Lost	Pts.	Poss. Pts.	Per-cent.
Yorkshire	29	19	2	6	2	107	145	73·79
Nottinghamshire	26	17	5	4	0	93	130	71·53
Surrey	23	13	1	6	3	77	115	66·95
Kent	27	16	3	3	5	86	135	63·70
Lancashire	28	15	7	2	4	79	140	56·42
Hampshire	26	13	6	3	4	71	130	54·61

METHOD OF SCORING : 5 points for a win ; 2 points for first innings lead. Championship decided by percentage of points obtained to points possible. " No result " matches ignored.

MATCH SCORES AND RESULTS

Yorkshire v.	Ground	Yorkshire 1st Inns.	Yorkshire 2nd Inns.	Opponents 1st Inns.	Opponents 2nd Inns.	Result
Northamptonshire	Northampton	112	12(0)	81	42	Y, 10 wickets
Glamorgan	Cardiff	*404 (2)	—	78	68	Y, inns. and 258 runs
Worcestershire	Dudley	421	—	111	90	Y, inns. and 220 runs
Derbyshire	Derby	147	*314 (4)	130	80	Y, 251 runs
Northamptonshire	Leeds	342	—	69	88	Y, inns. and 185 runs
Leicestershire	Leicester	283	—	298	180 (6)	Draw
Lancashire	Sheffield	306	148 (4)	307	144	Y, 6 wickets
Warwickshire	Birmingham	*453 (2)	—	123	178	Y, inns. and 152 runs
Surrey	Bradford	283	—	317	133 (2)	Draw
Middlesex	Lord's	*339 (7)	—	138	180	Y, inns. and 21 runs
Nottinghamshire	Sheffield	140	138	353	—	N, inns. and 75 runs
Warwickshire	Huddersfield	*495 (5)	—	99	125	Y, inns. and 271 runs
Kent	Leeds	*273 (9)	24(0)	163	131	Y, 10 wickets
Glamorgan	Leeds	*429 (7)	—	161	165	Y, inns. and 103 runs
Derbyshire	Sheffield	*202 (6)	—	99	69 (3)	Draw
Sussex	Hull	125	—	95	20	Y, inns. and 10 runs
Worcestershire	Bradford	*214 (4)	—	116	149 (7)	Draw
Essex	Harrogate	*314 (7)	—	105	149 (9)	Draw
Kent	Maidstone	344	228	259	147	Y, 166 runs
Nottinghamshire	Nottingham	222	110 (5)	257	74	Y, 5 wickets
Gloucestershire	Dewsbury	228	—	134	87	Y, inns. and 7 runs
Leicestershire	Sheffield	410	—	97	114	Y, inns. and 199 runs
Lancashire	Manchester	122	129 (8)	118	135	Draw
Gloucestershire	Bristol	66	167 (4)	172	58	Y, 6 wickets
Hampshire	Bradford	56	116	113	60 (5)	H, 5 wickets
Middlesex	Leeds	266	*144 (5)	170	85 (2)	Draw
Surrey	Oval	*539 (5)	—	339	165 (2)	Draw
Hampshire	Bournemouth	293	25(0)	272	44	Y, 10 wickets
Sussex	Brighton	42	228	95	83	Y, 92 runs
Essex	Leyton	—	—	5 (1)	—	Draw

* Innings declared closed.

Yorkshire beat Glamorgan, Gloucestershire, Kent, Northamptonshire, Sussex, Warwickshire twice ; and Derbyshire, Hampshire, Lancashire, Leicestershire, Middlesex, Nottinghamshire, Worcestershire once.

Yorkshire were beaten by Hampshire, Nottinghamshire.

Yorkshire drew with Essex, Surrey twice ; and Derbyshire, Lancashire, Leicestershire, Middlesex, Worcestershire once.

SUMMARY

	Yorkshire	Opponents
Runs scored	9653	7921
Average per wicket	30·93	15·05
Hundreds	19	1
Other innings over 50	35	29
Ten wickets in match	6	3
Five wickets in innings	30	12
Highest total	539 (5) dec. v. Surrey	353 (Nottinghamshire)
Lowest total	42 v. Sussex	20 (Sussex)
Totals over 400	7	—
Totals under 100	3	19

PRINCIPAL AVERAGES

	Inns.	Not Out	Runs	Highest Inns.	100's	50's	Aver.
E. Oldroyd	39	5	1534	151*	5	7	45·11
H. Sutcliffe	41	3	1674	232	2	11	44·05
W. Rhodes	36	6	1181	110	4	4	39·36
P. Holmes	41	3	1489	220*	5	3	39·18
R. Kilner	38	2	1085	124	2	6	30·13

* Not out.

	Balls	Balls per Wkt.	Runs	Wkts.	5 Wkts. in Inns.	Aver.
W. Rhodes	3634	43·26	1068	84	5	12·71
G. G. Macaulay	4330	36·08	1598	120	8	13·31
R. Kilner	5497	54·42	1454	101	5	14·39
A. Waddington	5032	39·62	1956	127	9	15·40
E. R. Wilson	1207	75·43	281	16	1	17·56
E. Robinson	3083	60·44	941	51	2	18·45

NOTES

In the first match of the season Yorkshire, although scoring only 124 runs, beat Northamptonshire (81 and 42) easily. In the first innings Macaulay took six wickets for 8 runs and in the second Rhodes had four for 6. Macaulay took eleven wickets for 31 runs in the match.

Glamorgan (78 and 68) had an even unhappier experience at Cardiff in Yorkshire's second county match, being overwhelmed by an innings and 258 runs before four o'clock on the second day. Holmes and Oldroyd scored hundreds, Macaulay taking seven wickets for 27 runs and Kilner seven for 26 in the two innings.

1922

Against Derbyshire at Derby, Waddington took eleven wickets for 57 runs.

In the return against Northamptonshire at Leeds, Waddington took eight wickets for 34 in the first innings and Macaulay four for 11 in the second.

P. Holmes scored 209 against Warwickshire at Birmingham, Rhodes taking nine wickets for 59 runs (five for 12 and four for 47). Holmes scored a second double hundred against Warwickshire at Huddersfield (220 not out), Yorkshire declaring at 495 for five wickets. Macaulay took three wickets for 4 runs in 6 balls in Warwickshire's first innings.

Waddington took eleven wickets for 72 runs against Kent at Leeds.

At Hull, Yorkshire won by an innings and 10 runs after scoring 125, A. E. R. Gilligan taking six for 20. In their second innings Sussex were all out for 20, Waddington taking seven wickets for 6 runs and bowling unchanged with Kilner (three for 13).

When Yorkshire beat Notts at Nottingham, Robinson took five for 20 and Kilner five for 14 in the second innings.

Sutcliffe scored 232 and Yorkshire 539 for five wickets declared against Surrey at the Oval.

Yorkshire were all out for 42 against Sussex at Brighton, Tate and Roberts bowling unchanged and each taking five wickets for 20 runs.

HOW IT WAS DONE

	100's	50's	10 Wkts. in Match	5 Wkts. in Inns.	50 Runs & 5 Wkts. in Match
P. Holmes	5	3	–	–	–
R. Kilner	2	6	2	5	1
N. Kilner	–	2	–	–	–
G. G. Macaulay	1	–	2	8	–
E. Oldroyd	5	7	–	–	–
W. Rhodes	4	4	–	5	1
E. Robinson	–	2	–	2	–
H. Sutcliffe	2	11	–	–	–
A. Waddington	–	–	2	9	–
E. R. Wilson	–	–	–	1	–
Total	**19**	**35**	**6**	**30**	**2**

FIELDING (205 Catches)

No. of Catches		No. of Catches	
38	A. Waddington	17	H. Sutcliffe
30	E. Robinson	10	P. Holmes
27	G. G. Macaulay	7	G. Wilson
25	W. Rhodes	6	M. Leyland
22	R. Kilner	4	N. Kilner
18	E. Oldroyd	1	A. Mitchell

WICKETKEEPING

	Stumped	Caught	Total
A. Dolphin	13	36	49
W. R. Allen	—	4	4
Total	13	40	53

TOTALS

400 Runs and Over

Yorkshire (7)

539 (5)* v. Surrey, Oval
495 (5)* v. Warwickshire, Huddersfield
453 (2)* v. Warwickshire, Birmingham
429 (7)* v. Glamorgan, Leeds

421 v. Worcestershire, Dudley
410 v. Leicestershire, Sheffield
404 (2)* v. Glamorgan, Cardiff

Opponents (0)

None.

* Innings declared closed.

Under 100 Runs

Yorkshire (3)

42 v. Sussex, Brighton
56 v. Hampshire, Bradford

66 v. Gloucestershire, Bristol

Opponents (19)

95 and 20, Sussex, Hull
81 and 42, Northamptonshire, Northampton
44, Hampshire, Bournemouth
58, Gloucestershire, Bristol
69 and 88, Northamptonshire, Leeds
74, Nottinghamshire, Nottingham
78 and 68, Glamorgan, Cardiff

80, Derbyshire, Derby
95 and 83, Sussex, Brighton
87, Gloucestershire, Dewsbury
90, Worcestershire, Dudley
97, Leicestershire, Sheffield
99, Derbyshire, Sheffield
99, Warwickshire, Huddersfield

FIRST WICKET PARTNERSHIPS

Score	Partners	Against	Ground
145	P. Holmes, H. Sutcliffe	Warwickshire	Huddersfield
143	P. Holmes, H. Sutcliffe	Kent	Maidstone
100	P. Holmes, H. Sutcliffe	Middlesex	Lord's

50 RUNS AND 5 WICKETS

Scores	Analyses	Player	Against	Ground
2, 90	4-31, 2-19	R. Kilner	Derbyshire	Derby
108*	4-43, 3-43	W. Rhodes	Essex	Harrogate

* Not out.

THE MATCHES OF SEASON

Yorkshire v. *Northamptonshire*

Northampton, May 6, 8, 9

Yorkshire won by ten wickets

In their first county match of the season Northamptonshire had the unusual experience of being beaten by ten wickets after their opponents had accumulated a modest total of 112 runs.

Two remarkable bowling spells by Macaulay and Rhodes were responsible for the double collapse of Northamptonshire. In the first innings the former took six wickets for 8 runs and followed it up with five for 25 in the second innings—eleven wickets for 33 in the match.

Rhodes came into the picture in the second innings of Northants when he took four wickets for 6 runs. In this innings the top scorer for Northamptonshire was "Extras" with 8.

In the Yorkshire innings Murdin bowled well, taking six wickets for 38.

Northamptonshire

C. N. Woolley b Rhodes	34	b Macaulay	4
N. P. Andrews lbw, b Robinson	1	c Waddington b Kilner (R.)	4
C. Baker st. Dolphin b Waddington	0	c Kilner (R.) b Rhodes	7
F. Walden c Rhodes b Macaulay	12	b Macaulay	5
W. Wells c Rhodes b Macaulay	0	st. Dolphin b Rhodes	7
J. Wright b Macaulay	1	b Rhodes	0
B. Bellamy lbw, b Macaulay	6	b Macaulay	0
T. E. Manning b Macaulay	1	lbw, b Rhodes	1
A. E. Thomas not out	15	b Macaulay	3
V. Murdin c Sutcliffe b Rhodes	8	not out	3
R. S. Venes lbw, b Macaulay	0	b Macaulay	0
Extras	3	Extras	8
	81		42

Yorkshire

P. Holmes b Murdin	2	not out	6
H. Sutcliffe c and b Murdin	12	not out	6
E. Oldroyd c and b Wells	34		
R. Kilner b Woolley	12		
W. Rhodes c Bellamy b Wells	14		
E. Robinson b Thomas	1		
N. Kilner b Murdin	16		
G. Wilson b Murdin	7		
G. G. Macaulay b Murdin	3		
A. Dolphin b Murdin	4		
A. Waddington not out	0		
Extras	7		
	112		12

Yorkshire Bowling

	Overs	Mdns.	Runs	Wkts.		Overs	Mdns.	Runs	Wkts.
Robinson	8	5	12	1					
Waddington	7	0	19	1	...	2	2	0	0
Macaulay	11.3	8	8	6	...	16.5	8	23	5
Rhodes	11	2	39	2	...	12	7	6	4
R. Kilner						6	4	5	1

Northamptonshire Bowling

	Overs	Mdns.	Runs	Wkts.		Overs	Mdns.	Runs	Wkts.
Wells	9	2	22	2					
Murdin	21.1	9	38	6	...	3	.1	6	0
Thomas	11	3	27	1	...	0.4	0	3	0
Woolley	15	8	18	1					
Venes						4	1	3	0

Yorkshire v. *Sussex*

Hull, July 8, 10, 11

Yorkshire won by an innings and 10 runs

The wicket at Hull had been made extremely difficult by rain, which caused frequent interruptions during the match, which lasted only five hours and ended with a Sussex collapse on the third morning.

When each side had completed an innings, Yorkshire had the useful, but by no means intimidating, lead of 30 runs. Anyone daring, or foolish, enough to bet that Yorkshire would win by an innings would have been thought a suitable subject for certification—and would have won.

Waddington bowled in devastating fashion. Before a run had been scored off him he had taken four wickets, and he clean-bowled three of the last four Sussex batsmen without any of them scoring. Sussex were all out for 20, and Waddington had taken seven wickets for 6 runs in 42 balls.

In the Yorkshire innings, A. E. R. Gilligan with six wickets for 20 runs was almost equally deadly.

Sussex

E. H. Bowley c and b Kilner (R.)	18	c Holmes b Waddington	3
G. Street c and b Rhodes	22	b Waddington	10
M. W. Tate c Sutcliffe b Rhodes	18	c Wilson b Waddington	1
H. E. Roberts c Sutcliffe b Rhodes	0	c Dolphin b Waddington	0
A. H. H. Gilligan c Robinson b Rhodes	7	c Robinson b Kilner (R.)	3
T. Cook c Sutcliffe b Rhodes	6	b Kilner (R.)	0
G. R. Cox b Kilner (R.)	1	not out	2
A. C. Watson c Oldroyd b Rhodes	19	b Waddington	0
A. E. R. Gilligan not out	4	b Waddington	0
G. Stannard b Kilner (R.)	0	b Waddington	0
A. F. Wensley c Holmes b Kilner (R.)	0	c Rhodes b Kilner (R.)	0
		Extras	1
	95		20

Yorkshire

P. Holmes c Gilligan (A. E. R.) b Cox	32
H. Sutcliffe c Wensley b Bowley	5
E. Oldroyd c Gilligan (A. E. R.) b Cox	6
E. Robinson c Street b Gilligan (A. E. R.)	26
R. Kilner c and b Gilligan (A. E. R.)	11
W. Rhodes b Gilligan (A. E. R.)	2
N. Kilner c Wensley b Cox	12
G. Wilson c Street b Gilligan (A. E. R.)	9
G. G. Macaulay c Street b Gilligan (A. E. R.)	5
A. Dolphin not out	12
A. Waddington b Gilligan (A. E. R.)	0
Extras	5
	125

Yorkshire Bowling

	Overs	Mdns.	Runs	Wkts.		Overs	Mdns.	Runs	Wkts.
Kilner (R.)	21	11	19	4	...	7.4	2	13	3
Waddington	9	4	15	0	...	7	4	6	7
Macaulay	9	3	18	0					
Rhodes	12	1	43	6					

Sussex Bowling

	Overs	Mdns.	Runs	Wkts.
Tate	3	1	8	0
Bowley	14	1	38	1
Cox	22	9	54	3
Gilligan (A. E. R.)	15	5	20	6

Yorkshire v. *Lancashire*

Manchester, August 5, 7, 8

Draw

The Bank Holiday " Battle of the Roses " at Manchester was nearly ruined by rain, not a ball being bowled on the Monday. But in a terrific finish in almost total darkness on the third afternoon, close of play found Yorkshire's last two men still requiring 3 runs to win.

On a wicket which was slow rather than difficult, Lancashire scored slowly on the first day, the Yorkshire bowling being very accurate. E. Tyldesley saved his side from collapse by scoring 45 runs in 165 minutes, but at the fall of the last wicket Lancashire had scored only 118. When stumps were drawn on Saturday, Yorkshire had scored 108 for six wickets.

The Bank Holiday deluge did not improve the wicket, and Yorkshire had considerable difficulty in obtaining a modest first innings lead of 4 runs.

Lancashire's second innings was slightly more successful than their first, thanks to J. Tyldesley, who put up 55 not out, Yorkshire being left with the task of getting 132 runs on a bad wicket.

Things went badly for Yorkshire. Holmes scored 21, but Sutcliffe, Oldroyd and Kilner were soon out. Then came a stand by Rhodes and Robinson, but when the latter was lbw to Parkin the Yorkshire tail failed to wag until E. R. Wilson joined Rhodes at 6.30, when the two veterans, taking no risks, came very near to snatching the match out of the fire. When time ran out Yorkshire still needed 3 runs.

Yorkshire's Captain, Geoffrey Wilson, was unable to bat in the second innings, being in hospital after an appendicitis operation.

Lancashire

H. Makepeace run out	11	b Robinson		8
C. Hallows c and b Macaulay	18	b Waddington		1
E. Tyldesley c Waddington b Macaulay	45	lbw, b Robinson		14
J. R. Barnes b Wilson (E. R.)	8	c Dolphin b Macaulay		28
V. Norbury c Holmes b Kilner (R.)	1	b Robinson		9
J. Tyldesley lbw, b Kilner (R.)	1	not out		55
R. Tyldesley c Macaulay b Wilson (E. R.)	14	b Rhodes		0
C. H. Parkin run out	0	b Macaulay		6
M. N. Kenyon lbw, b Wilson (E. R.)	5	run out		0
L. Cook c Rhodes b Macaulay	2	lbw, b Macaulay		5
B. Blomley not out	5	c Dolphin b Macaulay		0
Extras	8	Extras		9
	118			135

Yorkshire

P. Holmes c Tyldesley (R.) b Tyldesley (J.)	0	c Blomley b Norbury		21
H. Sutcliffe b Norbury	38	c Barnes b Parkin		1
E. Oldroyd c and b Tyldesley (J.)	5	run out		9
R. Kilner b Cook	4	b Norbury		1
W. Rhodes lbw, b Norbury	26	not out		48
E. Robinson b Parkin	19	lbw, b Parkin		20
G. Wilson lbw, b Tyldesley (R.)	2	absent ill		0
G. G. Macaulay c Blomley b Cook	22	c Barnes b Parkin		1
A. Dolphin lbw, b Parkin	0	c Tyldesley (R.) b Norbury		8
E. R. Wilson b Cook	1	not out		2
A. Waddington not out	4	run out		1
Extras	1	Extras		17
	122			129

Yorkshire Bowling

	Overs	Mdns.	Runs	Wkts.		Overs	Mdns.	Runs	Wkts.
Robinson	10	3	14	0	...	18	10	25	3
Waddington	5	1	16	0	...	5	0	11	1
Kilner (R.)	24	13	27	2	...	8	3	16	0
Macaulay	15.3	5	25	3	...	10	3	16	4
Wilson (E. R.)	23	9	28	3	...	7	1	21	0
Rhodes						11	1	37	1

Lancashire Bowling

	Overs	Mdns.	Runs	Wkts.		Overs	Mdns.	Runs	Wkts.
Tyldesley (J.)	7	0	20	2					
Cook	17	3	40	3	...	18	4	25	0
Parkin	11	3	15	2	...	20	11	28	3
Tyldesley (R.)	10	3	21	1	...	10	2	23	0
Norbury	9	2	25	2	...	15	5	36	3

1922

Yorkshire v. *Sussex*

Brighton, August 26, 28, 29

Yorkshire won by 92 runs

The return match with Sussex opened with a sensation—in the first 90 minutes Tate and Roberts, bowling unchanged, had Yorkshire back in the pavilion for a total of 42, each bowler taking five wickets for 4 runs each.

Sussex with 95 did a little better, but Holmes and Sutcliffe wiped out the lead and scored 75 together, Kilner, Robinson and Macaulay played useful innings, and in the end Sussex had to get 176 to win.

Vine and Bowley scored 34 for the first wicket, but Rhodes, who had not bowled in the first innings, then took six wickets for 13 runs in 6 overs, the last three wickets falling in the last over, and Yorkshire had staged another fine recovery.

Yorkshire

P. Holmes c Roberts b Tate	6	c Street b Gilligan (A. E. R.)	37
H. Sutcliffe c Street b Roberts	12	c Roberts b Tate	48
E. Oldroyd b Roberts	2	c Gilligan (A. E. R.) b Gilligan (A. H. H.)	9
R. Kilner c Street b Roberts	1	c Street b Gilligan (A. E. R.)	41
W. Rhodes lbw, b Tate	0	c Higgs b Gilligan (A. E. R.)	6
E. Robinson lbw, b Tate	2	run out	37
M. Leyland c Bowley b Tate	2	c Higgs b Bowley	1
G. G. Macaulay c Street b Roberts	4	not out	35
A. Dolphin b Tate	7	b Roberts	2
A. Waddington b Roberts	4	b Tate	0
E. R. Wilson not out	0	lbw, b Tate	1
Extras	2	Extras	11
	42		228

Sussex

J. Vine c and b Macaulay	13	st. Dolphin b Waddington	13
E. H. Bowley b Waddington	19	c Kilner b Macaulay	31
K. A. Higgs lbw, b Kilner	0	b Waddington	7
T. Cook c Waddington b Kilner	3	c Dolphin b Rhodes	3
G. Street c and b Macaulay	7	b Rhodes	8
A. C. Watson c Leyland b Kilner	4	c Waddington b Rhodes	0
M. W. Tate c Dolphin b Kilner	5	not out	2
A. E. R. Gilligan b Macaulay	14	c Waddington b Kilner	6
A. H. H. Gilligan c Robinson b Macaulay	4	st. Dolphin b Rhodes	0
H. E. Roberts st. Dolphin b Waddington	12	lbw, b Rhodes	6
G. Stannard not out	4	c and b Rhodes	0
Extras	10	Extras	7
	95		83

Sussex Bowling

	Overs	Mdns.	Runs	Wkts.		Overs	Mdns.	Runs	Wkts.
Tate	13.5	6	20	5	...	32.5	5	69	3
Roberts	13	5	20	5	...	14	2	36	1
Gilligan (A. E. R.)						28	4	77	3
Bowley						8	2	16	1
Gilligan (A. H. H.)						6	0	19	1

Yorkshire Bowling

	Overs	Mdns.	Runs	Wkts.		Overs	Mdns.	Runs	Wkts.
Waddington	9.3	5	16	2	...	14	4	28	2
Robinson	4	1	10	0					
Kilner	16	4	30	4	...	14	3	26	1
Macaulay	11	1	29	4	...	3	1	9	1
Rhodes						6	3	13	6
Wilson (E. R.)						2	2	0	0

APPEARANCES

The following 16 cricketers appeared for Yorkshire in Championship matches, the number of appearances being in parentheses :

W. R. Allen (2)	A. Mitchell (2)
A. Dolphin (28)	E. Oldroyd (30)
H. D. Badger (1)	W. Rhodes (30)
P. Holmes (30)	E. Robinson (30)
R. Kilner (30)	H. Sutcliffe (30)
N. Kilner (15)	A. Waddington (30)
M. Leyland (12)	E. R. Wilson (8)
G. G. Macaulay (29)	G. Wilson (23)

POST MORTEM

Team work, fine bowling and typical Yorkshire all-roundness in the field won the Championship in 1922.

Throughout May and June the side was unchanged, and during the season only 16 players appeared in the team. The batting was adequate without being spectacular, but the bowling was the winning factor. Rhodes, Macaulay, Kilner, Waddington, E. R. Wilson and Robinson took 499 of the 500 wickets taken by Yorkshire, Sutcliffe taking the 500th, and took them at an average of 14·62 runs each.

Two other points may be noted : 205 catches were made, and on 18 occasions Yorkshire's opponents failed to score 100 in an innings.

TWELFTH CHAMPIONSHIP

1923

Captain : G. Wilson

Losing only one match, as against two in the previous season, Yorkshire had little difficulty in retaining the Championship won in 1922, their percentage, in spite of a points system by no means perfect, being well ahead of their nearest rivals, Nottinghamshire and Lancashire. This result was again due to adequate and consistent batting, very strong and varied bowling and fine fielding.

THE FIRST SIX

			1st Inns.		Points		Per-
	Plyd.	Won	Lost	Won	Lost	Obtd.	Poss.	cent.
Yorkshire	31	25	1	4	1	133	155	85·80
Nottinghamshire	25	15	3	5	2	85	125	68·00
Lancashire	29	15	2	6	6	87	145	60·00
Surrey	23	11	2	6	4	67	115	58·26
Kent	27	15	9	0	3	75	135	55·55
Sussex	30	15	8	2	5	79	150	52·66

METHOD OF SCORING : As in 1922.

MATCH SCORES AND RESULTS

Yorkshire v.	Ground	Yorkshire 1st Inns.	Yorkshire 2nd Inns.	Opponents 1st Inns.	Opponents 2nd Inns.	Result
Glamorgan	Cardiff	93	83 (1)	63	112	Y, 9 wickets
Worcestershire	Worcester	358	—	76	169	Y, inns. and 113 runs
Middlesex	Bradford	*411 (9)	—	122	60	Y, inns. and 229 runs
Lancashire	Manchester	126 (5)	—	108	—	Draw
Warwickshire	Birmingham	113	*162(6)	110	81	Y, 85 runs
Kent	Sheffield	*180 (6)	—	136	48 (5)	Draw
Derbyshire	Derby	*302 (9)	—	104	72	Y, inns. and 126 runs
Nottinghamshire	Leeds	134	158	200	95	N, 3 runs
Middlesex	Lord's	168	225 (4)	289	102	Y, 6 wickets
Northamptonshire	Northampton	308	—	50	198	Y, inns. and 60 runs
Surrey	Sheffield	278	129	224	158	Y, 25 runs
Kent	Tonbridge	255	239	130	244	Y, 120 runs
Essex	Leyton	152	164(3)	251	64	Y, 7 wickets
Northamptonshire	Bradford	312	—	78	79	Y, inns. and 155 runs
Sussex	Leeds	412	—	182	197	Y, inns. and 33 runs
Warwickshire	Hull	170	*311 (8)	249	136	Y, 96 runs
Somerset	Hull	*446 (6)	—	226	90	Y, inns. and 130 runs
Essex	Dewsbury	195	*332(6)	96	151	Y, 280 runs
Leicestershire	Huddersfield	376	—	71	132	Y, inns. and 173 runs
Gloucestershire	Sheffield	*280 (3)	38 (0)	183	133	Y, 10 wickets
Gloucestershire	Bristol	*352 (9)	—	95	239	Y, inns. and 18 runs
Nottinghamshire	Nottingham	216	—	131	50 (5)	Draw
Worcestershire	Harrogate	*242(2)	—	42	163	Y, inns. and 37 runs
Lancashire	Bradford	213	51 (2)	188	73	Y, 8 wickets
Leicestershire	Leicester	311	—	129	108	Y, inns. and 74 runs
Derbyshire	Bradford	196	124 (2)	197	121	Y, 8 wickets
Hampshire	Leeds	246	*206 (5)	327	—	Draw
Glamorgan	Sheffield	233	—	110	89	Y, inns. and 34 runs
Surrey	Oval	88 (2)	—	360	—	Draw
Hampshire	Portsmouth	206	—	66	52	Y, inns. and 88 runs
Sussex	Brighton	135	*170 (5)	129	48 (5)	Draw
Somerset	Taunton	180	81 (3)	134	124	Y, 7 wickets

* Innings declared closed.

Yorkshire beat Derbyshire, Essex, Glamorgan, Gloucestershire, Leicestershire, Middlesex, Northamptonshire, Somerset, Warwickshire, Worcestershire twice; and Hampshire, Kent, Lancashire, Surrey, Sussex once.

Yorkshire were beaten by Nottinghamshire once.

Yorkshire drew with Hampshire, Kent, Lancashire, Nottinghamshire, Surrey, Sussex once.

SUMMARY

	Yorkshire	Opponents
Runs scored	10160	8244
Average per wicket	28·53	13·93
Hundreds	7	3
Other innings over 50	49	17
Ten wickets in match	7	1
Five wickets in innings	30	15
Highest total	446 (6) dec. v. Somerset	360 (Surrey)
Lowest total	93 v. Glamorgan	42 (Worcestershire)
Totals over 400	3	—
Totals under 100	1	19

PRINCIPAL AVERAGES

	Inns.	Not Out	Runs	Highest Inns.	100's	50's	Aver.
H. Sutcliffe	42	2	1453	139	1	9	36·32
P. Holmes	44	1	1546	199	2	8	35·95
R. Kilner	38	6	1126	79	—	6	35·18
W. Rhodes	38	5	1023	126	2	3	31·00
E. Oldroyd	45	4	1237	194	1	7	30·17
M. Leyland	46	11	1006	89	—	7	28·74

	Balls	Balls per Wkt.	Runs	Wkts.	5 Wkts. in Inns.	Aver.
W. Rhodes	5002	41·68	1353	120	8	11·27
R. Kilner	6429	46·25	1586	139	7	11·41
G. G. Macaulay	5637	37·83	1989	149	11	13·34
E. Robinson	4161	43·80	1343	95	2	14·13
A. Waddington	2821	47·73	1110	57	2	19·47

NOTES

In their first county match, Yorkshire recorded their lowest total of the season (93 v. Glamorgan at Cardiff), but Macaulay's seven wickets for 13 runs in the first innings and R. Kilner's eight for 26 brought about a win by nine wickets.

At Bradford, Middlesex were easily beaten, Rhodes with 126 and five wickets for 29 runs in the first innings, Holmes and Sutcliffe with a century first wicket partnership, and Kilner with six wickets for 14 runs in the second Middlesex innings, being chiefly responsible.

After a terrific struggle, Notts won by 3 runs at Leeds, S. J. Staples taking ten wickets for 82 runs and Rhodes nine for 93.

I

In the return match with Middlesex at Lord's, J. W. Hearne scored 175 not out—60 per cent. of the Middlesex first innings total. But consistent bowling by Yorkshire's five bowlers—each of them took four wickets in the match—and a century stand by Holmes and Sutcliffe won the match by six wickets.

Surrey had a good chance of winning at Sheffield, until R. Kilner took the last five wickets for 15 runs.

Macaulay took five wickets for 21 runs at Tonbridge and Robinson seven for 26 in the second innings. A fine innings (139) by Woolley in Kent's second innings failed to save the match.

In the second innings of Essex at Leyton, Rhodes took five wickets for 8 runs in 41 balls.

Northants were easily beaten at Bradford, Macaulay (three for 11 and six for 18) doing most of the damage.

A first wicket partnership of 274 by Holmes and Sutcliffe at Hull and good work by the bowlers were too much for Somerset, who lost by an innings and 130 runs.

Going in No. 9 against Gloucestershire at Bristol, N. Kilner scored 102 not out, and Macaulay (No. 10) 60. Rhodes took eleven wickets for 77 runs, including seven for 15 in the first innings of Gloucestershire, for whom Hammond scored 96.

Macaulay took eleven wickets for 69 runs (five for 11 and five for 58) v. Worcestershire at Harrogate.

Yorkshire beat Lancashire at Bradford in spite of fine bowling by R. Tyldesley—seven for 71.

Hampshire collapsed twice at Portsmouth (66 and 52). Macaulay took eleven wickets for 52 runs, and R. Kilner, in addition to being Yorkshire's top scorer with 77, took two wickets for 5 runs in Hampshire's first innings and three for 7 in the second.

No batsman scored an innings of 50 or more against the Yorkshire bowlers until J. W. Hearne scored 175 not out at Lord's on June 9.

HOW IT WAS DONE

	100's	50's	10 Wkts. in Match	5 Wkts. in Inns.	50 Runs & 5 Wkts. in Match
J. T. Bell	–	1	–	–	–
P. Holmes	2	8	–	–	–
N. Kilner	1	1	–	–	–
R. Kilner	–	6	1	7	2
M. Leyland	–	7	–	–	–
G. G. Macaulay	–	1	3	11	1
E. Oldroyd	1	7	–	–	–
W. Rhodes	2	3	1	8	3
E. Robinson	–	4	1	2	1
H. Sutcliffe	1	9	–	–	–
A. Waddington	–	1	1	2	–
G. Wilson	–	1	–	–	–
Total	7	49	7	30	7

FIELDING (226 Catches)

No. of Catches		No. of Catches	
33	E. Robinson	11	M. Leyland
30	A. Waddington	10	N. Kilner
26	G. G. Macaulay	6	G. Wilson
26	W. Rhodes	2	J. Drake
20	P. Holmes	2	J. S. Stephenson
20	R. Kilner	1	E. R. Wilson
19	E. Oldroyd	1	" Sub."
19	H. Sutcliffe		

WICKETKEEPING

	Stumped	Caught	Total
A. Dolphin	23	45	68
W. R. Allen	—	1	1
Total	23	46	69

TOTALS

400 Runs and Over

Yorkshire (3)

446 (6)* v. Somerset, Hull   411 (9)* v. Middlesex, Bradford
412 v. Sussex, Leeds

Opponents (0)

None.

* Innings declared closed.

Under 100 Runs

Yorkshire (1)

93 v. Glamorgan, Cardiff

Opponents (19)

42, Worcestershire, Harrogate
50, Northamptonshire, Northampton
66 and 52, Hampshire, Portsmouth
60, Middlesex, Bradford
63, Glamorgan, Cardiff
64, Essex, Leyton
71, Leicestershire, Huddersfield
72, Derbyshire, Derby
73, Lancashire, Bradford

76, Worcestershire, Worcester
78 and 79, Northamptonshire, Bradford
81, Warwickshire, Birmingham
89, Glamorgan, Sheffield
90, Somerset, Hull
95, Gloucestershire, Bristol
95, Nottinghamshire, Leeds
96, Essex, Dewsbury

1923

FIRST WICKET PARTNERSHIPS

Score	Partners	Against	Ground
274	P. Holmes, H. Sutcliffe	Somerset	Hull
127	P. Holmes, H. Sutcliffe	Middlesex	Bradford
119	P. Holmes, H. Sutcliffe	Middlesex	Lord's
117	J. T. Bell, N. Kilner	Essex	Leyton
110	P. Holmes, H. Sutcliffe	Warwickshire	Hull
104	P. Holmes, H. Sutcliffe	Kent	Tonbridge

50 RUNS AND 5 WICKETS

Scores	Analyses	Player	Against	Ground
126	5-29	W. Rhodes	Middlesex	Bradford
6, 60	3-30, 3-8	R. Kilner	Warwickshire	Birmingham
88	4-31, 4-29	W. Rhodes	Sussex	Leeds
23, 41*	4-27, 4-22	E. Robinson	Essex	Dewsbury
60	1-30, 4-69	G. G. Macaulay	Gloucestershire	Bristol
57*	3-37, 5-26	W. Rhodes	Glamorgan	Sheffield
77	2-5, 3-7	R. Kilner	Hampshire	Portsmouth

* Not out.

MATCHES OF THE SEASON

Yorkshire v. *Nottinghamshire*

Leeds, June 2, 4, 5

Nottinghamshire won by 3 runs

The cause of Yorkshire's only defeat in 1923 was the unexpected collapse of the " tail " in the second innings, after fine bowling by Rhodes and Kilner in the second Notts innings had swung the game round in Yorkshire's favour.

On the first day the Notts batting was very slow and cautious. G. Gunn and Whysall scored 85 for the first wicket, but after they were out the rest of the side took 200 minutes to add 112 runs. Yorkshire's reply was poor, only Holmes and Leyland offering much resistance, and the last wicket falling at 134. A lead of 66 seemed to put Notts in a comfortable position, but in their second innings the Yorkshire bowling machine got to work so effectively that when the last man was out only 95 runs were on the board.

The task of scoring 162 runs did not appear to be a particularly heavy one for a side like Yorkshire, and when five wickets were down with only 29 runs needed, the match seemed as good as won. Then came the collapse, for which Staples was mainly responsible. Robinson, Wilson and Dolphin were out before they had scored; Waddington could produce only a single; Macaulay was 17 not out; and Notts had won in a desperate finish by 3 runs.

Matthews in the first innings and Staples in both innings (five for 45 and five for 37) were the organisers of victory ; Rhodes with six wickets for 23 runs having the best innings analysis.

Nottinghamshire

G. Gunn c Robinson b Macaulay	47	c Holmes b Robinson	2
W. Whysall lbw, b Rhodes	40	c Rhodes b Kilner (R.)	34
J. Gunn c Dolphin b Macaulay	14	b Kilner (R.)	19
A. W. Carr c Dolphin b Kilner (R.)	27	b Rhodes	0
J. Hardstaff not out	21	c Waddington b Rhodes	1
W. Payton c Dolphin b Rhodes	23	st. Dolphin b Rhodes	7
S. J. Staples lbw, b Kilner (R.)	3	c Macaulay b Kilner (R.)	10
T. Oates st. Dolphin b Rhodes	6	b Rhodes	7
F. Barratt c Waddington b Kilner (R.)	9	c Sutcliffe b Rhodes	7
T. L. Richmond b Waddington	3	c Holmes b Rhodes	4
F. C. Matthews lbw, b Waddington	0	not out	1
Extras	7	Extras	3
	200		95

Yorkshire

P. Holmes c and b Staples	46	hit wkt, b Matthews	0
H. Sutcliffe b Matthews	2	lbw, b Richmond	24
E. Oldroyd c Oates b Matthews	2	lbw, b Staples	24
M. Leyland c Carr b Staples	27	b Matthews	12
W. Rhodes c Whysall b Matthews	5	b Staples	36
R. Kilner c Payton b Matthews	10	c Matthews b Richmond	30
E. Robinson c Oates b Matthews	17	c Gunn (G.) b Richmond	0
G. Wilson lbw, b Staples	0	c Carr b Staples	0
G. G. Macaulay b Staples	5	not out	17
A. Waddington not out	4	c Hardstaff b Staples	1
A. Dolphin c Matthews b Staples	1	b Staples	0
Extras	15	Extras	14
	134		158

Yorkshire Bowling

	Overs	Mdns.	Runs	Wkts.		Overs	Mdns.	Runs	Wkts.
Waddington	15.5	4	34	2	...	10	6	11	0
Robinson	7	2	9	0	...	8	5	9	1
Macaulay	24	9	33	2	...	10	3	19	0
Kilner (R.)	42	20	47	3	...	20	8	30	3
Rhodes	44	19	70	3	...	12.5	2	23	6

Nottinghamshire Bowling

	Overs	Mdns.	Runs	Wkts.		Overs	Mdns.	Runs	Wkts.
Barratt	13	9	9	0					
Matthews	21	8	46	5	...	10	2	35	2
Staples	21.5	7	45	5	...	20.5	6	37	5
Richmond	5	0	19	0	...	22	2	72	3

Yorkshire v. *Surrey*
Sheffield, June 16, 18, 19

Yorkshire won by 25 runs

A fortnight after the Notts disaster at Leeds, a somewhat similar situation materialised at Sheffield when Surrey were beaten by 25 runs.

Yorkshire started badly, only Leyland of the earlier batsmen facing the Surrey bowlers with any confidence. It was left to Wilson, Macaulay and Waddington to save the situation. Runs were always to be expected from Wilson and Macaulay, but 64 from Waddington surprised everybody, including the batsman. As a result of this tail-end enterprise the Yorkshire total reached quite respectable proportions.

Surrey had a less offensive tail. After Hobbs had scored 78, Shepherd 41 and Fender a quick 32, the Surrey batting surrendered rather easily to Yorkshire's five bowlers, and the home county started their second innings with a lead of 54, which was badly needed as Fender, Shepherd and Abel skittled the Yorkshiremen out for 129.

Requiring only 184 to win, Surrey made a good start, and at the tea interval on the last afternoon had scored 127 for three wickets. Then came the collapse. Robinson took two quick wickets and Kilner did the rest, taking the last five wickets for 15 runs. Yorkshire had snatched a win out of the fire.

Yorkshire

P. Holmes b Peach	3	c Hobbs b Shepherd	37
H. Sutcliffe c Strudwick b Hitch	2	c Strudwick b Lowe	19
E. Oldroyd c Shepherd b Peach	11	c Shepherd b Fender	4
M. Leyland c and b Fender	50	b Fender	8
W. Rhodes c Shepherd b Fender	6	c Ducat b Fender	26
R. Kilner b Peach	25	c Hitch b Shepherd	12
E. Robinson b Fender	4	b Abel	9
G. Wilson c Fender b Abel	57	b Abel	2
G. G. Macaulay c Strudwick b Shepherd	30	b Shepherd	3
A. Waddington not out	64	lbw, b Shepherd	0
A. Dolphin b Abel	6	not out	4
Extras	20	Extras	5
	278		**129**

Surrey

J. B. Hobbs c Dolphin b Kilner (R.)	78	b Macaulay	10
A. Sandham b Waddington	0	b Robinson	49
A. Ducat c Macaulay b Robinson	5	c Dolphin b Kilner (R.)	2
T. F. Shepherd c Waddington b Kilner (R.)	41	c Sutcliffe b Robinson	61
H. S. Harrison c Waddington b Kilner (R.)	18	c Waddington b Robinson	1
W. J. Abel st. Dolphin b Rhodes	9	not out	14
P. G. H. Fender c Robinson b Macaulay	32	b Kilner (R.)	6
W. Hitch c Rhodes b Kilner (R.)	2	c Dolphin b Kilner (R.)	0
H. A. Peach c Waddington b Rhodes	5	b Kilner (R.)	0
H. Strudwick c Oldroyd b Macaulay	15	b Kilner (R.)	0
R. F. Lowe not out	0	lbw, b Kilner (R.)	2
Extras	19	Extras	4
	224		**158**

Surrey Bowling

	Overs	Mdns.	Runs	Wkts.		Overs	Mdns.	Runs	Wkts.
Hitch	25	6	66	1	...	1	0	5	0
Peach	36	13	62	3	...	12	1	28	0
Fender	32	9	64	3	...	18	7	18	3
Shepherd	11	0	31	1	...	7.5	2	12	4
Lowe	4	2	13	0	...	16	3	47	1
Abel	7.3	1	22	2	...	8	4	14	2

Yorkshire Bowling

	Overs	Mdns.	Runs	Wkts.		Overs	Mdns.	Runs	Wkts.
Waddington	11	1	33	1	...	9	1	38	0
Robinson	7	2	20	1	...	15	8	21	3
Kilner (R.)	32	6	78	4	...	25.2	15	22	6
Macaulay	14.4	0	35	2	...	23	7	46	1
Rhodes	18	4	39	2	...	13	4	27	0

APPEARANCES

The following 18 cricketers appeared for Yorkshire in Championship matches, the number of appearances being in parentheses :

W. R. Allen (1)
J. T. Bell (5)
J. W. Brooke (1)
A. Dolphin (31)
J. Drake (2)
P. Holmes (31)
N. Kilner (15)
R. Kilner (29)
M. Leyland (32)

G. G. Macaulay (31)
E. Oldroyd (32)
W. Rhodes (31)
E. Robinson (32)
H. Sutcliffe (29)
J. S. Stephenson (2)
A. Waddington (20)
E. R. Wilson (7)
G. Wilson (21)

POST MORTEM

Once again bowling strength backed up by fine fielding and consistent batting was the deciding factor in deciding the destination of he Championship.

Rhodes, R. Kilner and Macaulay each took over 100 wickets for less than 14 runs each, Robinson had 95 wickets for just over 14 runs each, and Waddington, who was out of the side for some weeks through injury, took 57 wickets for 19·47. With such skill and variety in the attack, it is not surprising that Yorkshire won 25 of their 32 county matches, 13 of their wins being by an innings. In 1923 Yorkshire had no change bowlers. Each of the five cricketers mentioned would have been regarded as a " star " in any other side. And this hostile attack was backed up by splendid fielding and an astute placing of the field that saved many runs.

The batting was consistent without reaching the high standard of the bowling. Six batsmen scored 1,000 runs in county matches, nine of the regular players averaged over 19 runs an innings. Rhodes and R. Kilner completed " doubles," and such sound cricketers as N. Kilner and J. T. Bell were unable to obtain regular places in the XI.

A wonderful season for Yorkshire.

THIRTEENTH CHAMPIONSHIP

1924

Captain : G. Wilson

Although Yorkshire lost three matches, they retained the Championship for the third consecutive season without much difficulty, having a percentage of 76·52 compared with Middlesex's 69·00. Once again their quintette of bowlers and the fielding were mainly responsible, the batting being consistent without being outstanding.

THE FIRST SIX

	Plyd.	Won	Lost	1st Inns. Won	1st Inns. Lost	Points Obtd.	Points Poss.	Per-cent.
Yorkshire	30	16	3	2	2	88	115	76·52
Middlesex	22	11	3	4	2	69	100	69·00
Surrey	26	9	1	6	4	67	100	67·00
Lancashire	30	11	2	6	6	79	125	63·20
Kent	28	12	4	6*	4	81	130	62·30
Gloucestershire	26	9	7	6	1	64	115	55·65

* Kent and Somerset tied on first innings.

METHOD OF SCORING : As in 1923, except that first innings lead counts 3 points, the side behind on the first innings taking 1 point.

MATCH SCORES AND RESULTS

Yorkshire v.	Ground	Yorkshire 1st Inns.	Yorkshire 2nd Inns.	Opponents 1st Inns.	Opponents 2nd Inns.	Result
Glamorgan	Cardiff	275	—	48	50	Y, inns. and 177 runs
Gloucestershire	Gloucester	98	14 (2)	68	42	Y, 8 wickets
Surrey	Leeds	262	—	169 (7)	—	Draw
Northamptonshire	Northampton	159	49 (5)	84	123	Y, 5 wickets
Nottinghamshire	Bradford	161	79 (7)	147	92	Y, 3 wickets
Middlesex	Lord's	192	121	*465 (8)	—	M, inns. and 152 runs
Kent	Hull	257	—	128 (9)	—	Draw
Lancashire	Leeds	130	33	113	74	L, 24 runs
Warwickshire	Birmingham	139	—	120 (3)	—	Draw
Derbyshire	Chesterfield	169	205	74	163	Y, 137 runs
Somerset	Dewsbury	*434 (8)	—	132	100	Y, inns. and 202 runs
Sussex	Sheffield	200	*343 (3)	192	125	Y, 226 runs
Essex	Hull	299	111	248	68 (6)	Draw
Middlesex	Sheffield	334	43 (0)	358	268	Draw
Essex	Southend	*471 (5)	—	132	208	Y, inns. and 131 runs
Kent	Maidstone	205	196 (3)	230	273	Draw
Somerset	Weston-super-Mare	342	—	174	127	Y, inns. and 41 runs
Nottinghamshire	Nottingham	206 (9)	—	216	—	Draw
Glamorgan	Bradford	*248 (3)	—	116	106	Y, inns. and 26 runs
Gloucestershire	Leeds	137 (2)	—	—	—	Draw
Derbyshire	Huddersfield	300 (7)	—	111	78 (8)	Draw
Lancashire	Manchester	359	—	78 (2)	—	Draw
Leicestershire	Leicester	228	53 (2)	114	166 (9)	Y, 8 wickets
Warwickshire	Sheffield	275	4 (0)	170	107	Y, 10 wickets
Northamptonshire	Dewsbury	328	23 (0)	163	187	Y, 10 wickets
Leicestershire	Bradford	119	203	71	159	Y, 92 runs
Hampshire	Harrogate	*291 (2)	—	137 (7)	—	Draw
Surrey	Oval	100	202	209	202	S, 109 runs
Hampshire	Portsmouth	136	38 (0)	74	97	Y, 10 wickets
Sussex	Brighton	*253 (9)	—	60	83	Y, inns. and 110 runs

* Innings declared closed.

136

Yorkshire beat Glamorgan, Leicestershire, Northamptonshire, Somerset, Sussex twice ; and Derbyshire, Essex, Gloucestershire, Hampshire, Nottinghamshire, Warwickshire once.

Yorkshire were beaten by Lancashire, Middlesex, Surrey once.

Yorkshire drew with Kent twice ; and Derbyshire, Essex, Gloucestershire, Hampshire, Lancashire, Middlesex, Nottinghamshire, Surrey, Warwickshire once.

SUMMARY

	Yorkshire	Opponents
Runs scored	8824	7295
Average per wicket	25·42	15·26
Hundreds	13	4
Other innings over 50	33	23
Ten wickets in match	7	2
Five wickets in innings	30	18
Highest total	471 (5) dec. v. Essex	465 (8) dec. (Middlesex)
Lowest totals	33 v. Lancashire	42 (Gloucestershire)
Totals over 400	2	1
Totals under 100	2	13

PRINCIPAL AVERAGES

	Inns.	Not Out	Runs	Highest Inns.	100's	50's	Aver.
H. Sutcliffe	33	4	1342	255*	3	7	46·27
E. Oldroyd	42	5	1373	138	3	5	37·10
P. Holmes	41	5	1308	118*	4	7	36·33
M. Leyland	41	7	1138	133*	2	5	33·47
W. Rhodes	37	5	826	100	1	4	25·81

* Not out.

	Balls	Balls per Wkt.	Runs	Wkts.	5 Wkts. in Inns.	Aver.
G. G. Macaulay	5700	35·84	1866	159	11	11·73
R. Kilner	5208	46·08	1370	113	10	12·12
W. Rhodes	3309	40·85	1085	81	4	13·39
E. Robinson	3010	54·72	1084	55	3	19·70
A. Waddington	2702	51·96	1067	52	2	20·51

NOTES

In the first two county matches of the season Yorkshire's opponents, Glamorgan and Gloucestershire, scored only 208 runs for the loss of forty wickets. In the two games Macaulay took nineteen wickets for 67 runs and R. Kilner fifteen for 83.

Yorkshire were beaten by Middlesex at Lord's by an innings and 152 runs, H. L. Dales (113) and G. T. S. Stevens (114) scoring hundreds for Middlesex, and Durston taking four wickets for 11 runs in Yorkshire's second innings (121).

Lancashire won the Whitsuntide match by 24 runs, Yorkshire being all out for 33 in their second innings, R. Tyldesley taking six wickets for 18 runs. In the match, Macaulay took ten wickets for 59 runs.

Sutcliffe scored 213 *v.* Somerset at Dewsbury and 160 in the next match *v.* Sussex at Sheffield. In the latter Tate scored 102 not out in the first innings of Sussex (192).

J. W. H. T. Douglas took eleven Yorkshire wickets for 146 runs for Essex at Hull.

On two occasions Sutcliffe scored more than half his side's runs from the bat—213 out of 407 *v.* Somerset at Dewsbury and 255 out of 459 *v.* Essex at Southend.

P. Holmes scored three hundreds in four consecutive innings against Notts (112) at Nottingham, Glamorgan (118 not out) at Bradford, and Derbyshire (107) at Huddersfield.

Against Somerset at Weston-super-Mare, Rhodes scored 100 in the Yorkshire innings, and took four for 49 and five for 28 when Somerset batted.

Surrey won at the Oval by 109 runs. Sandham scored 72 and 60 and Sadler took ten wickets for 71 runs. For Yorkshire, Rhodes scored 51 not out in the second innings and took six wickets for 65 runs, R. Kilner taking ten for 153.

In the last county match of the season at Brighton, R. Kilner took twelve Sussex wickets for 55 runs.

During the season Macaulay, Kilner, Rhodes, Robinson and Waddington took 460 wickets in county matches for 13·93 runs each

HOW IT WAS DONE

	100's	50's	10 Wkts. in Match	5 Wkts. in Inns.	50 Runs & 5 Wkts. in Match
P. Holmes	4	7	–	–	–
R. Kilner	–	1	3	10	1
M. Leyland	2	5	–	–	–
G. G. Macaulay	–	–	4	11	–
E. Oldroyd	3	5	–	–	–
W. Rhodes	1	4	–	4	3
E. Robinson	–	4	–	3	1
H. Sutcliffe	3	7	–	–	–
A. Waddington	–	–	–	2	–
Total	13	33	7	30	5

FIELDING (191 Catches)

No. of Catches		No. of Catches	
30	E. Robinson	11	H. Sutcliffe
25	G. G. Macaulay	11	G. Wilson
25	A. Waddington	2	L. Ryder
19	W. Rhodes	2	I. Turner
18	R. Kilner	1	C. E. Anson
18	E. Oldroyd	1	J. S. Stephenson
14	P. Holmes	1	H. Taylor
12	M. Leyland	1	" Sub."

WICKETKEEPING

	Stumped	Caught	Total
A. Dolphin	25	24	49

TOTALS

400 Runs and Over

Yorkshire (2)

471 (5)* *v.* Essex, Southend   434 (8)* *v.* Somerset, Dewsbury

Opponents (1)

465 (8),* Middlesex, Lord's

* Innings declared closed.

Under 100 Runs

Yorkshire (2)

33 *v.* Lancashire, Leeds   98 *v.* Gloucestershire, Gloucester

Opponents (13)

68 and 42, Gloucestershire, Gloucester   74 and 97, Hampshire, Portsmouth
48 and 50, Glamorgan, Cardiff   74, Lancashire, Leeds
60 and 83, Sussex, Brighton   84, Northamptonshire, Northampton
71, Leicestershire, Bradford   92, Nottinghamshire, Bradford
74, Derbyshire, Chesterfield

FIRST WICKET PARTNERSHIPS

Score	Partners	Against	Ground
195	P. Holmes, H. Sutcliffe	Sussex	Sheffield
122	P. Holmes, M. Leyland	Kent	Maidstone
110	P. Holmes, H. Sutcliffe	Warwickshire	Birmingham
107	P. Holmes, H. Sutcliffe	Glamorgan	Bradford

50 RUNS AND 5 WICKETS

Scores	Analyses	Player	Against	Ground
63	4-62, 2-63	E. Robinson	Somerset	Weston-super-Mare
100	4-49, 5-28	W. Rhodes	Somerset	Weston-super-Mare
51	3-41, 3-27	W. Rhodes	Warwickshire	Sheffield
17, 41	5-58, 5-95	R. Kilner	Surrey	Oval
51*	2-43, 4-27	W. Rhodes	Surrey	Oval

* Not out.

MATCHES OF THE SEASON

Yorkshire v. *Lancashire*

Leeds, June 7, 9, 10

Lancashire won by 24 runs

The Whitsuntide resumption of "the Wars of the Roses" provided one of the major sensations of the season, but the play on the first day was more productive of yawns than thrills. Taking first innings Lancashire, between the showers, batted with such ultra-caution that only 113 runs were scored in the 225 minutes that the innings lasted. The Yorkshire bowling was good, but not superlative enough to warrant such respect from the Lancastrians. At close of play Yorkshire had scored 3 runs for the loss of Sutcliffe's wicket.

On Whit-Monday the Yorkshiremen consolidated their position—they not only gained a first innings lead of 17 runs, but got Lancashire out a second time for 74, Macaulay and Kilner each taking four wickets for 19 and 13 runs respectively. On the third morning therefore, Yorkshire were faced with the apparently easy task of scoring 57 runs to win.

But Parkin and R. Tyldesley took a different view of the situation. The wicket gave them a good deal of help, and the two Lancashire bowlers took every advantage of it. The first five Yorkshire batsmen scored 0, 3, 3, 0, 7; Kilner was top scorer with 13 not out; the last five batsmen scored 2, 1, 4, 0, 0; there were no extras; Yorkshire were all out in 65 minutes for 33 runs; and Lancashire had snatched a brand from the burning by 24 runs.

The sensations packed into the last hour's play were some compensation for the tedium suffered on the first day.

Lancashire

H. Makepeace b Rhodes		17	c Robinson b Kilner	9
C. Hallows lbw, b Macaulay		5	lbw, b Rhodes	0
E. Tyldesley lbw, b Macaulay		29	c Waddington b Kilner	2
F. Watson c Waddington b Rhodes		13	lbw, b Kilner	21
A. W. Pewtress b Macaulay		20	b Macaulay	5
J. Sharp b Kilner		12	c and b Kilner	14
J. Iddon b Macaulay		6	b Rhodes	4
A. Rhodes c Oldroyd b Macaulay		1	b Macaulay	6
R. Tyldesley c Holmes b Kilner		3	b Macaulay	0
C. H. Parkin lbw, b Macaulay		0	not out	2
G. Duckworth not out		0	c Robinson b Macaulay	0
Extras		7	Extras	11
		113		74

Yorkshire

P. Holmes b Parkin		10	lbw, b Tyldesley	0
H. Sutcliffe c Tyldesley (R.) b Parkin		0	lbw, b Parkin	3
E. Oldroyd b Tyldesley (R.)		37	b Parkin	3
M. Leyland run out		21	c and b Tyldesley (R.)	0
W. Rhodes lbw, b Parkin		18	c Makepeace b Tyldesley (R.)	7
R. Kilner b Parkin		35	not out	13
E. Robinson c and b Parkin		1	run out	2
I. Turner lbw, b Tyldesley (R.)		2	b Tyldesley (R.)	1
G. G. Macaulay c and b Tyldesley (R.)		0	b Parkin	4
A. Waddington b Tyldesley (R.)		0	b Tyldesley (R.)	0
A. Dolphin not out		0	st. Duckworth b Tyldesley (R.)	0
	Extras	6	Extras	0
		130		33

Yorkshire Bowling

	Overs	Mdns.	Runs	Wkts.		Overs	Mdns.	Runs	Wkts.
Robinson	11	7	10	0	...	2	1	3	0
Macaulay	33	14	40	6	...	16.2	7	19	4
Kilner	26.2	12	28	2	...	23	16	13	4
Rhodes	20	7	28	2	...	15	5	28	2

Lancashire Bowling

	Overs	Mdns.	Runs	Wkts.		Overs	Mdns.	Runs	Wkts.
Parkin	27.2	9	46	5	...	12	7	15	3
Tyldesley (R.)	27	9	69	4	...	11.5	6	18	6
Watson	7	2	9	0					

Yorkshire v. *Sussex*

Brighton, August 31, September 1, 2

Yorkshire won by an innings and 110 runs

On a drying wicket at Brighton, Sussex began badly against Yorkshire in the last match of their county programme, being all out for 60 in 90 minutes. Kilner (five wickets for 18 runs) and Rhodes (three for 10) proved practically unplayable.

Before stumps were drawn Yorkshire had scored 50 for the loss of Sutcliffe, and, on the Monday, Holmes and Oldroyd stayed together until 107 had been added for the second wicket. With Rhodes scoring 35 not out, the Yorkshire innings was declared closed when the total reached 253 for nine wickets.

Going in 193 runs behind, Sussex found Kilner and Rhodes almost as difficult as in the first innings, the former taking seven wickets for 37, making his figures twelve for 55 in the match, and Rhodes three for 20.

Sussex

J. E. Frazer c Wilson b Macaulay	1	b Kilner	8
E. H. Bowley c Holmes b Kilner	17	c Holmes b Kilner	2
R. A. Young lbw, b Macaulay	6	st. Dolphin b Kilner	27
M. W. Tate c Leyland b Rhodes	25	c Wilson b Kilner	6
H. L. Wilson st. Dolphin b Rhodes	3	c Holmes b Kilner	2
G. S. Grimston c Macaulay b Kilner	3	c sub. b Rhodes	13
A. E. R. Gilligan c Wilson b Kilner	0	c Robinson b Kilner	0
N. J. Holloway b Rhodes	0	lbw, b Rhodes	4
T. Cook lbw, b Kilner	1	not out	17
A. F. Wensley lbw, b Kilner	3	c Sutcliffe b Rhodes	1
W. Cornford not out	0	c Macaulay b Kilner	0
Extras	1	Extras	3
	60		83

Yorkshire

P. Holmes c Cornford b Wilson	88
H. Sutcliffe lbw, b Bowley	28
E. Oldroyd lbw, b Wilson	42
R. Kilner lbw, b Wilson	8
W. Rhodes not out	35
E. Robinson c Tate b Bowley	3
G. G. Macaulay c Tate b Gilligan	12
J. S. Stephenson b Gilligan	9
G. Wilson st. Cornford b Bowley	8
A. Dolphin c Wensley b Bowley	3
M. Leyland absent hurt	0
Extras	17
	283*

* Innings declared closed.

Yorkshire Bowling

	Overs	Mdns.	Runs	Wkts.		Overs	Mdns.	Runs	Wkts.
Macaulay	10	3	31	2	...	10	3	23	0
Kilner	16.4	7	18	5	...	19.4	8	37	7
Rhodes	7	1	10	3	...	10	3	20	3

Sussex Bowling

	Overs	Mdns.	Runs	Wkts.
Gilligan	18	4	45	2
Tate	22	9	30	0
Bowley	29.4	4	78	4
Holloway	17	4	33	0
Wensley	6	2	13	0
Wilson	10	0	37	3

APPEARANCES

The following 20 cricketers appeared for Yorkshire in Championship matches, the number of appearances being in parentheses :

S. Allen (1)
C. E. Anson (1)
T. J. Birtles (1)
J. Drake (1)
A. Dolphin (30)
P. Holmes (28)
R. Kilner (24)
M. Leyland (30)
G. G. Macaulay (27)
A. Mitchell (1)

E. Oldroyd (30)
W. Rhodes (30)
E. Robinson (30)
L. Ryder (2)
J. S. Stephenson (5)
H. Sutcliffe (23)
H. Taylor (5)
I. Turner (5)
A. Waddington (26)
G. Wilson (29)

POST MORTEM

With the batting scarcely as reliable and consistent as it was in 1923, Yorkshire were beaten three times in Championship matches by Middlesex, Lancashire and Surrey, but on most occasions the bowling proved equal to neutralising any batting breakdowns.

Four batsmen, Sutcliffe, Oldroyd, Holmes and Leyland, scored 1,000 runs with averages ranging from Sutcliffe's 46·27 to Leyland's 33·47 ; Rhodes, Robinson and Kilner, the best all-rounders, all did good work with both bat and ball ; but the real strength of the XI. was the attack backed up by good fielding.

Macaulay headed the bowlers with 159 wickets for 11·73 runs each, Kilner took 113 wickets for 12·12 runs each, and good backing when necessary was provided by Rhodes, Robinson and Waddington. During the season these five bowlers took 460 wickets at a cost of 14·06 runs each, a very fine performance which deserved to win the Championship.

FOURTEENTH CHAMPIONSHIP

1925

Captain : Major A. W. Lupton

For the fourth time in consecutive seasons Yorkshire won the Championship, a feat which had not been repeated since Nottinghamshire won in 1883-84-85-86. In the previous three seasons the bowling had been the deciding factor in Yorkshire's success, but in 1925 the batsmen came right into the limelight, and had a wonderful season.

THE FIRST SIX

	Plyd.	Won	Lost	1st Inns. Won	1st Inns. Lost	Points Obtd.	Points Poss.	Per-cent.
Yorkshire	32	21	0	3	3	117	135	86·66
Surrey	26	14	2	4	2	84	110	76·36
Lancashire	32	19	4	7	1	117	155	75·48
Nottinghamshire	26	15	3	1	6	84	125	67·20
Kent	28	15	7	1	1	79	120	65·83
Middlesex	24	12	3	2	5	71	110	64·54

METHOD OF SCORING : As in 1924.

MATCH SCORES AND RESULTS

Yorkshire v.	Ground	Yorkshire 1st Inns.	Yorkshire 2nd Inns.	Opponents 1st Inns.	Opponents 2nd Inns.	Result
Glamorgan	Cardiff	134 (1)	—	—	—	Draw
Gloucestershire	Bristol	166	* 77 (4)	82	42	Y, 119 runs
Worcestershire	Worcester	295	—	213	65	Y, inns. and 17 runs
Northamptonshire	Sheffield	412	—	148	127	Y, inns. and 137 runs
Derbyshire	Chesterfield	*330 (7)	—	61	109	Y, inns. and 160 runs
Kent	Leeds	39 (0)	—	—	—	Draw
Lancashire	Manchester	232	186 (6)	265	—	Draw
Warwickshire	Birmingham	265	*275 (3)	195	203	Y, 142 runs
Middlesex	Lord's	*538 (6)	—	118	271	Y, inns. and 149 runs
Gloucestershire	Bradford	365	4 (0)	137	229	Y, 10 wickets
Nottinghamshire	Sheffield	157	148 (5)	139	165	Y, 5 wickets
Glamorgan	Huddersfield	*579 (6)	—	246	197	Y, inns. and 136 runs
Leicestershire	Hull	*451 (3)	—	85	206	Y, inns. and 160 runs
Hampshire	Hull	408	—	139	153	Y, inns. and 116 runs
Surrey	Bradford	233	49 (0)	105	175	Y, 10 wickets
Derbyshire	Leeds	*423 (9)	—	128	136	Y, inns. and 159 runs
Somerset	Harrogate	*414 (9)	—	148	116	Y, inns. and 150 runs
Worcestershire	Harrogate	438	14 (0)	215	235	Y, 10 wickets
Kent	Maidstone	196	333	259	160	Y, 110 runs
Essex	Sheffield	303	68 (2)	250	182	Draw
Nottinghamshire	Nottingham	386	*142 (4)	312	103 (9)	Draw
Northamptonshire	Kettering	*259 (4)	—	107	42	Y, inns. and 110 runs
Middlesex	Leeds	*528 (6)	—	184	149 (4)	Draw
Lancashire	Sheffield	277	—	320	74 (6)	Draw
Leicestershire	Leicester	197	—	222	195 (5)	Draw
Warwickshire	Dewsbury	507 (8)	—	323	128	Y, inns. and 56 runs
Essex	Leyton	80 (1)	—	*218 (3)	—	Draw
Sussex	Bradford	119	230	87	239	Y, 23 runs
Hampshire	Southampton	264	—	114 (4)	—	Draw
Surrey	Oval	82 (0)	—	*246 (8)	—	Draw
Sussex	Brighton	305	89 (1)	156	237	Y, 9 wickets
Somerset	Taunton	362	22 (0)	235	147	Y, 10 wickets

* Innings declared closed.

Yorkshire beat Derbyshire, Gloucestershire, Northamptonshire, Somerset, Sussex, Warwickshire, Worcestershire twice; and Glamorgan, Hampshire, Kent, Leicestershire, Middlesex, Nottinghamshire, Surrey once.

Yorkshire drew with Essex, Lancashire twice; and Glamorgan, Hampshire, Kent, Leicestershire, Middlesex, Nottinghamshire, Surrey once.

SUMMARY

	Yorkshire	Opponents
Runs scored	11381	9542
Average per wicket	38·57	18·03
Hundreds	19	3
Other innings over 50	54	32
Ten wickets in match	4	—
Five wickets in innings	26	8
Highest total	579 (6) dec. *v.* Glamorgan	323 (Warwickshire)
Lowest total	119 *v.* Sussex	42 (Gloucestershire and Northants.)
Totals over 400	10	—
Totals under 100	—	7

PRINCIPAL AVERAGES

	Inns.	Not Out	Runs	Highest Inns.	100's	50's	Aver.
P. Holmes	41	7	2123	315*	5	9	62·44
H. Sutcliffe	40	5	1787	235	5	8	51·05
M. Leyland	35	4	1391	138	3	9	44·87
W. Rhodes	35	7	1234	157	2	9	44·07
E. Oldroyd	39	8	1228	109*	1	9	39·61
E. Robinson	30	8	791	112*	2	2	35·95

* Not out.

	Balls	Balls per Wkt.	Runs	Wkts.	5 Wkts. in Inns.	Aver.
G. G. Macaulay	6646	37·76	2678	176	15	15·21
R. Kilner	6218	53·60	1891	116	5	16·30
W. Rhodes	2686	51·65	928	52	—	17·84
A. Waddington	4342	47·71	1786	91	3	19·62
E. Robinson	3957	57·34	1528	69	3	22·14

NOTES

In Gloucestershire's second innings at Bristol, Kilner took four wickets for 10 runs.

Against Worcestershire at Worcester, Macaulay took nine wickets for 39 runs—two for 19 and seven for 20. Holmes and Sutcliffe scored 118 for Yorkshire's first wicket.

Robinson scored 112 not out and took five wickets for 44 runs in Northants' second innings at Sheffield.

During Yorkshire's second innings at Manchester (186 for six wickets), every member of the Lancashire side except Duckworth went on to bowl.

K

In the match against Middlesex at Lord's, P. Holmes scored 315 not out, beating the previous record for the ground of 278 by William Ward, which had stood for 105 years. (In 1926, J. B. Hobbs scored 316 not out for Surrey v. Middlesex at Lord's.)

Holmes and Sutcliffe scored 221 for the first wicket v. Glamorgan at Huddersfield, the Yorkshire innings being declared when 579 had been scored for the loss of six wickets.

In Yorkshire's next match at Hull, Holmes and Sutcliffe scored 272 for the first wicket v. Leicestershire.

In the Somerset–Yorkshire match at Harrogate, the first four Somerset batsmen scored 5, 0, 0, 1 in the first innings and 5, 2, 4, 3 in the second.

F. E. Woolley scored 81 and 52 v. Yorkshire at Maidstone.

In their second innings at Kettering, Northants scored 42, of which R. L. Wright scored 20 and " extras " 2. Macaulay (six for 19) and Kilner (four for 21) bowled unchanged.

Sutcliffe and Leyland scored 218 for Yorkshire's first wicket v. Middlesex at Leeds. When Middlesex scored 149 for four wickets in their second innings, nine Yorkshiremen had bowled. This was Kilner's Benefit match.

Kilner took five wickets for 14 runs in Lancashire's unfinished second innings at Sheffield, and five for 14 against Sussex at Bradford.

Sutcliffe scored 206 against Warwickshire at Dewsbury, the Yorkshire total being 507 for eight wickets declared.

At Bradford, F. B. R. Browne took ten Yorkshire wickets for 79 runs— three for 17 and seven for 62.

During the season, Yorkshire recorded ten innings totals exceeding 400 runs, four being over 500.

In all Yorkshire matches, both Holmes and Sutcliffe scored over 2,000 runs with averages exceeding 55, Macaulay took 200 wickets, and Kilner completed a " double."

HOW IT WAS DONE

	100's	50's	10 Wkts. in Match	5 Wkts. in Inns.	50 Runs & 5 Wkts. in Match
W. R. Allen	–	1	–	–	–
P. Holmes	5	9	–	–	–
R. Kilner	1	4	–	5	2
M. Leyland	3	9	–	–	–
G. G. Macaulay	–	2	4	15	2
E. Oldroyd	1	9	–	–	–
W. Rhodes	2	9	–	–	–
E. Robinson	2	2	–	3	1
H. Sutcliffe	5	8	–	–	–
A. Waddington	–	–	–	3	–
Total	19	54	4	26	5

FIELDING (189 Catches)

No. of Catches		No. of Catches	
28	P. Holmes	15	W. Rhodes
26	E. Robinson	12	R. Kilner
26	H. Sutcliffe	8	A. W. Lupton
23	E. Oldroyd	7	M. Leyland
21	G. G. Macaulay	4	" Sub."
19	A. Waddington		

WICKETKEEPING

	Stumped	Caught	Total
A. Dolphin	18	30	48
W. R. Allen	2	8	10
Total	20	38	58

TOTALS

400 Runs and Over

Yorkshire (10)

579 (6)* v. Glamorgan, Huddersfield
538 (6)* v. Middlesex, Lord's
528 (6)* v. Middlesex, Leeds
507 (8)* v. Warwickshire, Dewsbury
451 (3)* v. Leicestershire, Hull

438 v. Worcestershire, Harrogate
423 (9)* v. Derbyshire, Leeds
414 (9)* v. Somerset, Harrogate
412 v. Northamptonshire, Sheffield
408 v. Hampshire, Hull

Opponents (o)

None.

* Innings declared closed.

Under 100 Runs

Yorkshire (o)

None.

Opponents (7)

42, Northamptonshire, Kettering
82 and 42, Gloucestershire, Bristol
61, Derbyshire, Chesterfield

65, Worcestershire, Worcester
85, Leicestershire, Hull
87, Sussex, Bradford

FIRST WICKET PARTNERSHIPS

Score	Partners	Against	Ground
272	P. Holmes, H. Sutcliffe	Leicestershire	Hull
221	P. Holmes, H. Sutcliffe	Glamorgan	Huddersfield
218	H. Sutcliffe, M. Leyland	Middlesex	Leeds
199	P. Holmes, H. Sutcliffe	Warwickshire	Birmingham
153	P. Holmes, H. Sutcliffe	Middlesex	Lord's
118	P. Holmes, H. Sutcliffe	Worcestershire	Worcester

50 RUNS AND 5 WICKETS

Scores	Analyses	Player	Against	Ground
112*	0-8, 5-44	E. Robinson	Northamptonshire	Sheffield
87	4-32, 2-5	R. Kilner	Derbyshire	Leeds
71	1-60, 7-81	G. G. Macaulay	Glamorgan	Huddersfield
63	4-40, 6-73	G. G. Macaulay	Hampshire	Hull
124	4-108, 2-44	R. Kilner	Warwickshire	Dewsbury

* Not out.

MATCHES OF THE SEASON

Yorkshire v. *Middlesex*
Lord's, June 6, 8, 9

Yorkshire won by an innings and 149 runs

Yorkshire were in wonderful form when they appeared at Lord's for the first of the season's matches against Middlesex. The Londoners were overplayed in every department of a game which they lost by an innings and 149 runs.

Taking first innings on a good wicket Robinson, Macaulay and Waddington soon had them back in the pavilion for 118 runs.

Holmes and Sutcliffe then put on 140 for the first wicket, and in the rest of the Yorkshire innings all the limelight was cornered by Holmes, who scored 315 not out in 410 minutes, hitting 38 fours, and breaking the record of 278 set up 105 years earlier by William Ward. Holmes batted brilliantly and, in addition to his stand with Sutcliffe, added 166 when partnered by Leyland. When the Yorkshire total reached 538 for six wickets the innings was declared closed, Middlesex requiring 420 to save the innings defeat.

G. T. S. Stevens and Hearne batted well in the second innings of Middlesex, but were only able to postpone the inevitable.

Middlesex

G. T. S. Stevens c Sutcliffe b Robinson	10	b Macaulay	65
H. L. Dales b Robinson	27	b Macaulay	0
J. W. Hearne b Macaulay	1	b Macaulay	91
E. Hendren lbw, b Robinson	15	c Robinson b Macaulay	7
Hon. C. N. Bruce b Robinson	5	not out	42
G. O. Allen c Kilner b Macaulay	7	c and b Kilner	2
F. T. Mann b Robinson	5	c sub. b Robinson	7
N. Haig b Macaulay	5	b Waddington	32
H. W. Lee c Macaulay b Waddington	5	b Kilner	0
H. R. Murrell not out	8	b Robinson	4
T. J. Durston c Robinson b Waddington	2	lbw, b Robinson	4
Extras	8	Extras	17
	118		**271**

Yorkshire

P. Holmes not out	315
H. Sutcliffe c Murrell b Stevens	58
E. Oldroyd b Allen	8
M. Leyland c Mann b Haig	61
W. Rhodes c Murrell b Durston	0
R. Kilner c Hendren b Stevens	37
E. Robinson c Murrell b Allen	6
G. G. Macaulay not out	21
Major A. W. Lupton did not bat	
A. Waddington did not bat	
A. Dolphin did not bat	
Extras	32
	538*

* Innings declared closed.

Yorkshire Bowling

	Overs	Mdns.	Runs	Wkts.		Overs	Mdns.	Runs	Wkts.
Macaulay	24	7	54	3	...	27	3	94	4
Robinson	27	6	52	5	...	21	1	64	3
Waddington	2.5	0	4	2	...	11	2	33	1
Kilner						33	15	56	2
Rhodes						5	1	7	0

Middlesex Bowling

	Overs	Mdns.	Runs	Wkts.
Haig	43	11	93	1
Durston	30	6	97	1
Allen	23	2	106	2
Stevens	26	3	89	2
Hearne	31	3	100	0
Lee	2	0	21	0

Yorkshire v. *Sussex*

Bradford, August 15, 17, 18

Yorkshire won by 23 runs

Yorkshire's last county match in Yorkshire ended sensationally, a magnificent spell of bowling by Macaulay snatching a win when the game seemed lost.

Good bowling by Tate, Wensley and Browne kept Yorkshire's first innings to very modest dimensions, 119 being on the board when the last wicket fell, but Robinson, Macaulay and Kilner, especially Kilner, proceeded to give their side a first innings lead of 32 runs.

Encouraged by this somewhat unexpected advantage, Sutcliffe, Oldroyd, Robinson and Macaulay batted efficiently against fine bowling by Browne, and when the innings closed Sussex required 263 runs to win, a task which could scarcely be described as impossible.

When the lunch interval arrived on the third day, Sussex, with six wickets in hand, were within 40 runs of their objective, and the possibility of a win had become a probability, Bowley being chiefly responsible for the metamorphosis.

But Macaulay, one of the most hostile bowlers in cricket history, had different ideas regarding the result. In each of his first three overs after lunch he took a wicket, another in his fifth over, and a fifth in his sixth—at which point Yorkshire, thanks to Macaulay, had won by 23 runs.

In his wonderful post-lunch spell the Yorkshireman took five wickets for 8 runs in 33 balls.

Yorkshire

P. Holmes b Wensley	10	c Cox b Wensley	7
H. Sutcliffe c Wensley b Tate	9	c Cox b Browne	38
E. Oldroyd c Cook b Wensley	19	c Wensley b Cox	77
M. Leyland lbw, b Browne	18	c Bowley b Browne	1
W. Rhodes c Bowley b Wensley	15	b Browne	3
R. Kilner c Bowley b Cox	3	c Bowley b Browne	0
E. Robinson b Browne	17	c Gilligan b Bowley	54
G. G. Macaulay c Cornford b Tate	0	c Parks b Browne	39
A. Waddington not out	19	b Browne	2
Major A. W. Lupton c Cox b Browne	0	not out	0
A. Dolphin b Wensley	0	b Browne	0
Extras	9	Extras	9
	119		230

Sussex

E. H. Bowley lbw, b Robinson	8	c Dolphin b Macaulay	'105
M. W. Tate c Dolphin b Robinson	9	b Kilner	39
R. A. Young c Holmes b Robinson	26	c Oldroyd b Macaulay	11
T. Cook run out	1	b Waddington	42
G. R. Cox lbw, b Kilner	4	b Macaulay	16
R. L. Holdsworth c Oldroyd b Kilner	11	b Macaulay	2
J. H. Parks c Holmes b Kilner	7	b Macaulay	3
A. E. R. Gilligan c Waddington b Kilner	7	c Robinson b Macaulay	3
A. F. Wensley lbw, b Macaulay	6	lbw, b Kilner	2
W. Cornford not out	1	c Waddington b Macaulay	0
F. B. R. Browne b Kilner	0	not out	0
Extras	7	Extras	16
	87		239

Sussex Bowling

	Overs	Mdns.	Runs	Wkts.		Overs	Mdns.	Runs	Wkts.
Tate	24	8	36	2	...	23	6	35	0
Wensley	20.1	6	44	4	...	22	3	52	1
Cox	11	6	13	1	...	17	9	25	1
Browne	8	3	17	3	...	27.5	4	62	7
Bowley						5	2	17	1
Parks						2	0	10	0

Yorkshire Bowling

	Overs	Mdns.	Runs	Wkts.		Overs	Mdns.	Runs	Wkts.
Robinson	18	5	38	3	...	22	9	59	0
Macaulay	12	7	21	1	...	22.3	1	67	7
Kilner	15.2	9	14	5	...	32	13	35	2
Waddington	3	1	7	0	...	15	3	42	1
Rhodes						11	3	20	0

APPEARANCES

The following 17 cricketers appeared for Yorkshire in Championship matches, the number of appearances being in parentheses :

W. R. Allen (7)
G. H. Crawford (1)
A. Dolphin (25)
S. Douglas (1)
P. Holmes (31)
R. Kilner (31)
M. Leyland (31)
Major A. W. Lupton (32)
G. G. Macaulay (30)

A. Mitchell (2)
E. Oldroyd (32)
W. Rhodes (32)
E. Robinson (31)
H. Sutcliffe (30)
H. Taylor (3)
C. Turner (1)
A. Waddington (32)

POST MORTEM

With a record at least as fine as that of 1923, Yorkshire could look back on the summer of 1925 with even greater satisfaction, for their latest Championship was the reward for splendid batting backed up by equally fine bowling and fielding, whereas in 1923 the bowling was undoubtedly the decisive factor.

The fine form of Holmes and Sutcliffe, particularly the former, who scored over 2,000 runs in county matches, ensured a good start for most Yorkshire innings, and they received consistent support from Leyland, Rhodes, Oldroyd, Robinson, Macaulay and Kilner.

With wickets more favourable to batsmen than in 1923 the bowling figures were naturally higher, but the well-tried quintette (Macaulay, Kilner, Rhodes, Waddington and Robinson) took 504 of the 509 wickets that fell in county matches at a communal cost of 17·48 runs each.

Note.—Have any five bowlers ever had a period of consistent success in Championship matches comparable with the record of Rhodes, Kilner, Waddington, Macaulay and Robinson in 1922, 1923, 1924 and 1925 ? In these four seasons Yorkshire bowlers took 2,031 wickets in county matches, and the five bowlers mentioned took 2,007 of them at a cost of 14·24 runs each. The individual contributions to this amazing " bag " were as follows : G. G. Macaulay, 604 wickets (average 13·46) ; R. Kilner, 469 (13·43) ; W. Rhodes, 337 (13·15) ; A. Waddington, 327 (18·10) ; E. Robinson, 270 (18·13).

INTERREGNUM

1926, 1927, 1928, 1929, 1930

1926

Lancashire won the County Championship by a very short head, their percentage being 75·71 to Yorkshire's 74·28. The discrepancy may have been caused by one of Yorkshire's matches being abandoned without a ball being bowled, and also to the calls made on Yorkshire for Test cricketers, Sutcliffe, Rhodes, Kilner and Macaulay all appearing in England sides against Australia.

The principal events of the season were as follows :

v. Leicestershire at Leeds : Yorkshire won easily, Macaulay taking eleven wickets for 37 runs (six for 22 and five for 15).

v. Lancashire at Bradford : Another easy win by an innings and 94 runs. R. Kilner scored 85 and took three for 40 and four for 19 when Lancashire batted. Every Lancashire batsman was caught in the second innings (73), Holmes making 4 catches.

v. Glamorgan at Hull : Macaulay took twelve wickets for 71, bowling unchanged with Robinson in the first innings. Glamorgan scored 52 and 95.

v. Surrey at Sheffield : Yorkshire won by an innings, Leyland and Mitchell scoring 192 for the first wicket. D. R. Jardine scored 82 and 63 for Surrey, who were without Hobbs. Holmes, Sutcliffe, Kilner and Macaulay were Yorkshire absentees.

v. Middlesex at Bradford : Yorkshire won by ten wickets. Kilner scored 44 and took ten wickets for 117 runs—eight for 40 in the second innings (80).

v. Gloucestershire at Bristol : Macaulay took fourteen wickets for 92 runs, and Yorkshire won by an innings and 41 runs.

v. Glamorgan at Swansea : Leyland scored 191 in Yorkshire's first innings (420 for six wickets declared) and Robinson 124 not out.

In 1926 the Yorkshire batting was very strong, five batsmen averaging over 40 an innings, two others over 30, and six from 14 to 21 runs an innings. The attack, consisting of Rhodes (13·88), Macaulay (15·79), Kilner (18·74), Waddington (22·88) and Robinson (24·20), was perhaps the best in the country.

1927

Yorkshire were third in the Championship, Lancashire and Notts being first and second. In a very wet season a high proportion of the matches ended as draws, Lancashire having definite results in only 11 out of 28 matches.

Most of the highlights of 1927 were provided by the bowlers, especially during the last three months :

v. Gloucestershire at Gloucester : Holmes and Sutcliffe scored 274 in 210 minutes for Yorkshire's first wicket.

v. Glamorgan at Cardiff : Macaulay scored 57 in the Yorkshire innings and took eleven wickets for 71 runs.

v. Worcestershire at Leeds : Macaulay (twelve for 50) and Robinson (eight for 65) bowled unchanged in the two Worcestershire innings (46 and 81). When Yorkshire batted, Macaulay (67) and Waddington (114) added 163 in 85 minutes for the seventh wicket.

v. Lancashire at Manchester : Yorkshire lost by eight wickets, Macdonald taking eleven wickets for 135 runs.

v. Hampshire at Portsmouth : In a drawn match, Hampshire scored 521 for eight wickets declared, G. Brown making 204 and Mead 183.

v. Middlesex at Sheffield : Leyland scored 204 not out and Yorkshire declared after scoring 490 for nine wickets. Hendren scored 127 and 62 not out for Middlesex. A draw, ten Yorkshiremen having bowled in the second innings.

v. Northamptonshire at Northampton : In Yorkshire's first innings Holmes, Sutcliffe and Extras scored 60 of the total of 67, V. W. C. Jupp having seven wickets for 21 runs. In the two innings, Holmes and Sutcliffe scored 188 of the 242 runs from the bat. Yorkshire won by five wickets.

v. Lancashire at Leeds : A draw, Sutcliffe scoring 95 and 135 and E. Tyldesley 165.

v. Sussex at Brighton : Kilner scored 91 not out and took eight wickets for 66 in the match, Yorkshire winning by nine wickets.

For once the Yorkshire bowlers were less successful than might have been expected in a wet season, only Macaulay (118 wickets for 17·98 runs each) taking wickets for fewer than 20 runs. As six batsmen had averages ranging from Sutcliffe's 52·41 to Macaulay's 32·35, no fault could be found with the batting.

As a matter of interest, it may be noted that a young bowler named Verity appeared in one match for Yorkshire Second XI., and took four wickets for 71 runs.

1928

Although Yorkshire went through the season without losing a match, they won only 8 and finished fourth in the Championship table, below Lancashire, Kent and Nottinghamshire. The batting was strong, six batsmen averaging over 40 runs an innings and five others from 22 to 28 runs an innings, but the bowling was too expensive to win matches, only Rhodes taking wickets for less than 20 runs each. The fact that Rhodes, Macaulay and Robinson required 63 balls for each of the 306 wickets they took is a sufficient explanation of Yorkshire's 18 drawn games.

Here are the outstanding events of the season :

v. Worcestershire at Worcester : Yorkshire scored 560 for six wickets declared, Leyland making 247 and Rhodes 100 not out.

v. Essex at Leyton : In the second county match of the season Yorkshire made 514 for six wickets declared, Holmes (136), Sutcliffe (129) and Leyland (133 not out) all scoring hundreds.

v. Surrey at Bradford : A match in which both sides scored over 400 in their first innings produced two fine bowling performances, P. G. H. Fender taking six wickets for 116 runs in 47 overs, and Macaulay five for 104 in 51 overs.

v. Nottinghamshire at Nottingham : Holmes (83 and 101 not out) and Sutcliffe (111 and 100 not out) shared century first wicket partnerships in each innings.

v. Essex at Sheffield : Yorkshire scored 512 for nine wickets, and when Essex batted, Rhodes took four wickets for 26 and four for 10.

v. Middlesex at Leeds : When Yorkshire (303) followed on after Middlesex had scored 488, Holmes (179 not out) and Sutcliffe (104) scored 290 before the latter was bowled.

v. Warwickshire at Bradford : Holmes scored 275 of Yorkshire's total of 540 for seven wickets declared.

During the season, Yorkshire scored over 500 five times and between 400 and 500 eight times. Sutcliffe scored 2,137 runs (average 85·48), Leyland and Holmes averaged over 60, and Mitchell and Oldroyd over 50. Each of the 370 wickets taken by Yorkshire cost 25 runs.

1929

Yorkshire and Lancashire were joint runners-up to Nottinghamshire in the Championship, Gloucestershire and Sussex being fourth and fifth.

During the season the following were Yorkshire's principal performances :

v. Essex at Leyton : In the first county match of the season, Rhodes (in his 52nd year) took twelve wickets for 80 runs, including nine for 39 in the second innings (67).

v. Nottinghamshire at Sheffield : For their defeat of the season's champions by five wickets, Yorkshire were mainly indebted to Rhodes, who took eleven wickets for 85 runs.

v. Nottinghamshire at Nottingham : The return match at Nottingham was ruined by rain, but Yorkshire had time to score 498 runs, of which Holmes made 285.

v. Surrey at the Oval : After being 104 behind on the first innings, Yorkshire scored 315 for one wicket, Holmes (142) and Sutcliffe (123 not out) making 265 of them.

Six of the Yorkshiremen averaged over 30 runs an innings, Sutcliffe with 54·44 being at the top of the list, but the bowling was, perhaps, less effective than usual. Rhodes led with 85 wickets for 17·22 runs each, Dennis (76 wickets), Macaulay (95) and Robinson (72) all averaged fewer than 25 runs per wicket. One of the most interesting features of the season was the appearance occasionally of W. E. Bowes, who took 40 wickets for 17·77 runs each, and was runner-up to Rhodes.

1930

In 1930, Lancashire won the Championship without losing a match, Gloucestershire were second and Yorkshire third. The season was notable in Yorkshire history for two events—the retirement of Rhodes after a career extending over 29 seasons, and the appearance of his successor, Hedley Verity. During the summer two successive matches against Derbyshire and Northamptonshire were abandoned unstarted owing to bad weather.

Here are the highlights of the season :

v. Leicestershire at Hull : The début of Verity coincided with an easy win over Leicestershire, who were dismissed for 113 and 43. Macaulay took ten wickets for 59 runs (six for 11 in the second innings) and Verity four for 45 and four for 15.

v. Lancashire at Leeds : In a drawn match, Leyland scored 211 not out and took four Lancashire wickets for 49.

v. Middlesex at Sheffield : Yorkshire won a narrow victory by 29 runs after declaring their second innings when 329 ahead. Leyland scored 172 in Yorkshire's first innings and took five wickets for 82 when Middlesex scored 300 in their second innings, J. W. Hearne making 158.

v. Gloucestershire at Bristol : Yorkshire won by an innings and 187 runs, Gloucestershire being put out for 125 and 150 after Yorkshire had scored 462. Verity took five wickets for 18 in the first innings.

v. Glamorgan at Sheffield : In Glamorgan's second innings, W. E. Bates and Dyson scored 233 for the first wicket, after Holmes and Sutcliffe had shared in their 62nd first wicket partnership, scoring 235 in 160 minutes. All four players were Yorkshire-born.

v. Hampshire at Bournemouth : Yorkshire won by ten wickets, Verity taking thirteen wickets for 83 runs, and Holmes and Sutcliffe winning the match with an unfinished stand of 116.

Leyland (66·95), Sutcliffe, Oldroyd, A. Mitchell and Holmes all averaged over 40 runs an innings. Verity finished top of the bowlers with 52 wickets for 11·44 runs each, and was followed by Bowes with 76 for 17·32, but Rhodes, Macaulay and Robinson all averaged over 20.

In his last season, Rhodes scored 337 runs (average 22·46) and took 42 wickets (average 20·42). In all Yorkshire matches during his 29 seasons, Rhodes scored 31,156 runs (average 30·10) and took 3,608 wickets (average 16·00).

FIFTEENTH CHAMPIONSHIP

1931

Captain : F. E. Greenwood

After a lapse of five seasons Yorkshire resumed their Championship-winning habit in 1931, and finished 68 points above Gloucestershire, who lost four matches to Yorkshire's solitary defeat in a freak match at Sheffield. It can scarcely be maintained that the Yorkshire bowling was as dominating or varied as in the period 1922 to 1925, but Verity and Bowes were a more dangerous pair of bowlers than any other county could produce, and Sutcliffe, in spite of unfavourable batting conditions, was in tremendous form right through the summer. As Yorkshire won more and lost fewer matches than any of their rivals, they undoubtedly deserved to finish first.

THE FIRST SIX

	Played	Won	Lost	1st Inns. Won	1st Inns. Lost	No Result	Points
Yorkshire	28	16	1	4	1	6	287
Gloucestershire	28	11	4	7	5	1	219
Kent	28	12	7	3	3	3	216
Sussex	28	10	6	8	1	3	205
Nottinghamshire	28	9	3	9	6	1	202
Lancashire	28	7	4	7	6	4	174

METHOD OF SCORING : Each county to play 28 matches. 15 points for a win ; in drawn games, 5 points for a first innings lead, the side behind taking 3 points ; each side takes 4 points when a match is unfinished, when there is no play, or when there is no first innings result.

MATCH SCORES AND RESULTS

Yorkshire v.	Ground	Yorkshire 1st Inns.	Yorkshire 2nd Inns.	Opponents 1st Inns.	Opponents 2nd Inns.	Result
Essex	Leyton	*329 (8)	—	106	215	Y, inns. and 8 runs
Warwickshire	Leeds	298	—	201	72	Y, inns. and 25 runs
Lancashire	Manchester	231	76 (2)	128	—	Draw
Warwickshire	Birmingham	*468 (8)	—	64 (6)	—	Draw
Kent	Bradford	—	—	296 (4)	—	Draw
Gloucestershire	Sheffield	*4 (0)	124	*4 (0)	171	G, 47 runs
Sussex	Hull		Abandoned			
Leicestershire	Sheffield	263	*167 (2)	157	29(1)	Draw
Hampshire	Hull	135	—	—	—	Draw
Middlesex	Lord's	302	—	111	126	Y, inns. and 65 runs
Hampshire	Portsmouth	*387 (8)	—	136	180	Y, inns. and 71 runs
Kent	Folkestone	*467 (9)	—	167	188	Y, inns. and 112 runs
Somerset	Dewsbury	*451 (9)	—	309	107	Y, inns. and 35 runs
Surrey	Bradford	*281 (4)	—	165	61	Y, inns. and 55 runs
Nottinghamshire	Sheffield	313	—	288	1 (0)	Draw
Essex	Leeds	109	119 (0)	108	119	Y, 10 wickets
Nottinghamshire	Nottingham	*204 (6)	93 (1)	201	95	Y, 9 wickets
Glamorgan	Swansea	*178 (8)	—	62	91	Y, inns. and 25 runs
Gloucestershire	Bristol	*118 (9)	137 (1)	*182 (9)	70	Y, 9 wickets
Somerset	Taunton	314	43 (0)	176	177	Y, 10 wickets
Lancashire	Sheffield	*484 (7)	—	221	165 (2)	Draw
Leicestershire	Leicester	*447 (4)	—	241	181	Y, inns. and 25 runs
Northamptonshire	Bradford	*4 (0)	88 (5)	*4 (0)	86	Y, 5 wickets
Glamorgan	Scarborough	378	—	105	153	Y, inns. and 120 runs
Middlesex	Leeds	141 (3)	—	*190 (5)	—	Draw
Northamptonshire	Northampton	38 (0)	—	163	—	Draw
Surrey	Oval	233	178 (4)	300	—	Draw
Sussex	Brighton	148	124 (1)	106	165	Y, 9 wickets

* Innings declared closed.

Yorkshire beat Essex, Glamorgan, Somerset twice; and Gloucester-shire, Hampshire, Kent, Leicestershire, Middlesex, Northamptonshire, Nottinghamshire, Surrey, Sussex, Warwickshire once.

Yorkshire were beaten by Gloucestershire once.

Yorkshire drew with Lancashire twice; and Hampshire, Kent, Leicestershire, Middlesex, Northamptonshire, Nottinghamshire, Surrey, Warwickshire once.

The match between Yorkshire and Sussex at Hull was abandoned.

SUMMARY

	Yorkshire	Opponents
Runs scored	7874	6563
Average per wicket	35˙95	16˙53
Hundreds	13	3
Other innings over 50	32	13
Ten wickets in match	6	—
Five wickets in innings	30	10
Highest total	484 (7) dec. v. Lancashire	309 (Somerset)
Lowest total	109 v. Essex	61 (Surrey)
Totals over 400	5	—
Totals under 100	—	6

PRINCIPAL AVERAGES

	Inns.	Not Out	Runs	Highest Inns.	100's	50's	Aver.
H. Sutcliffe	27	6	2049	230	8	9	97˙57
P. Holmes	34	3	1211	250	3	5	39˙06
A. Mitchell	23	4	681	134	1	3	35˙84
M. Leyland	28	4	823	124	1	5	34˙29
E. Oldroyd	23	2	707	93	—	5	33˙66

	Balls	Balls per Wkt.	Runs	Wkts.	5 Wkts. in Inns.	Aver.
H. Verity	4736	34˙31	1703	138	12	12˙34
W. E. Bowes	4389	40˙26	1667	109	12	15˙29
G. G. Macaulay	4355	57˙30	1170	76	4	15˙39
E. Robinson	3421	79˙55	1050	43	1	24˙41

NOTES

In his fourteenth county match Verity took all ten Warwickshire wickets for 36 runs in their second innings at Leeds.

Holmes (250) and Sutcliffe (129) scored 309 for Yorkshire's first wicket v. Warwickshire at Birmingham.

F. E. Woolley scored 188 out of Kent's 296 for four wickets at Bradford.

The match between Yorkshire and Sussex at Hull was abandoned without a ball being bowled.

Bowes took eleven wickets for 102 runs v. Middlesex at Lord's, nine of his wickets being bowled or lbw.

Yorkshire scored 467 for nine wickets declared v. Kent at Folkestone, Sutcliffe scoring 230, and Freeman taking five wickets for 189 runs in 53 overs.

At Dewsbury *v.* Somerset, Sutcliffe scored his fourth hundred in successive innings : 120 *v.* Middlesex, 107 *v.* Hampshire, 230 *v.* Kent, 183 *v.* Somerset.

In Surrey's second innings (61) at Bradford (Macaulay's Benefit), Verity took six wickets for 11 runs.

Verity took fourteen wickets for 54 runs *v.* Glamorgan (62 and 91) at Swansea.

Holmes (125) and Sutcliffe (195) scored 323 for Yorkshire's first wicket against Lancashire at Sheffield.

For Surrey, at the Oval, J. B. Hobbs carried his bat through the Surrey innings for 133.

In county matches during the season, Sutcliffe's average (97·57) was 58·51 runs per innings higher than that of the second Yorkshire batsman. His consecutive innings were :

> May—18, 67, 75, 11, 129.
> June—27, 75, 72,* 4, 120, 107, 230.
> July—183, 42, 4, 38,* 9, 58, 78.*
> August—195, 187, 62, 44, 26, 101,* 15, 72.*
> * Not out.

In August he scored 702 runs in 7 matches and averaged 117·00 per innings.

HOW IT WAS DONE

	100's	50's	10 Wkts. in Match	5 Wkts. in Inns.	50 Runs & 5 Wkts. in Match
W. Barber	–	3	–	–	–
W. E. Bowes	–	–	3	12	–
F. E. Greenwood	–	1	–	–	–
P. Holmes	3	5	–	–	–
T. A. Jacques	–	–	–	1	–
M. Leyland	1	5	–	–	–
G. G. Macaulay	–	–	–	4	–
A. Mitchell	1	3	–	–	–
E. Oldroyd	–	5	–	–	–
E. Robinson	–	2	–	1	–
H. Sutcliffe	8	9	–	–	–
H. Verity	–	–	3	12	–
A. Wood	–	1	–	–	–
Total	13	32	6	30	–

FIELDING (147 Catches)

No. of Catches		No. of Catches	
31	A. Mitchell	8	P. Holmes
20	F. E. Greenwood	7	E. Oldroyd
16	E. Robinson	6	W. E. Bowes
13	M. Leyland	3	W. Barber
13	G. G. Macaulay	1	T. A. Jacques
12	H. Verity	1	" Sub."

WICKETKEEPING

	Stumped	Caught	Total
A. Wood	18	39	57

TOTALS

400 Runs and Over

Yorkshire (5)

484 (7)* v. Lancashire, Sheffield
468 (8)* v. Warwickshire, Birmingham
467 (9)* v. Kent, Folkstone

451 (9)* v. Somerset, Dewsbury
447 (4)* v. Leicestershire, Leicester

Opponents (0)
None.

* Innings declared closed.

Under 100 Runs

Yorkshire (0)
None.

Opponents (7)

61, Surrey, Bradford
62 and 91, Glamorgan, Swansea
70, Gloucestershire, Bristol

72, Warwickshire, Leeds
86, Northamptonshire, Bradford
95, Nottinghamshire, Nottingham

FIRST WICKET PARTNERSHIPS

Score	Partners	Against	Ground
323	P. Holmes, H. Sutcliffe	Lancashire	Sheffield
309	P. Holmes, H. Sutcliffe	Warwickshire	Birmingham
140	P. Holmes, H. Sutcliffe	Leicestershire	Sheffield
130	P. Holmes, H. Sutcliffe	Somerset	Dewsbury
120	P. Holmes, H. Sutcliffe	Warwickshire	Leeds
119*	P. Holmes, A. Mitchell	Essex	Leeds
112	P. Holmes, H. Sutcliffe	Leicestershire	Leicester

* Unfinished.

In 1932 no player scored 50 runs and took 5 wickets in the same match for Yorkshire.

MATCHES OF THE SEASON

Yorkshire v. Warwickshire
Leeds, May 16, 18, 19

Yorkshire won by an innings and 25 runs

In the second county match of the season, and the fourteenth county match in which he played, Verity ensured immortality in *Wisden's* records by taking all ten Warwickshire wickets in their second innings. Only one Yorkshire bowler had previously performed this feat in a first-class match—A. Drake *v.* Somerset at Weston-super-Mare in 1914.

Winning the toss, Warwickshire put together a modest total of 201 runs, Croom, Bates and Parsons being the principal contributors. All the bowlers tried during the innings took wickets, but no outstanding analysis was recorded.

Holmes and Sutcliffe scored 120 for Yorkshire's first wicket, Oldroyd played a bright innings of 67, and Wood was 40 not out when the innings closed for 298, Yorkshire having a lead of 97 runs.

Warwickshire's second innings was a triumph for Verity, who, ably assisted by his fielders, dismissed the whole side for 36 runs. During this rout he took four wickets in one over without doing the hat-trick.

Warwickshire

R. E. S. Wyatt b Macaulay	13	c Holmes b Verity	23
A. J. Croom c Wood b Robinson	46	c Greenwood b Verity	7
L. A. Bates c Mitchell b Bowes	54	c Mitchell b Verity	19
N. Kilner lbw, b Macaulay	9	c Mitchell b Verity	0
J. H. Parsons lbw, b Macaulay	48	c Leyland b Verity	9
A. W. Hill lbw, b Bowes	0	c Wood b Verity	8
J. Smart b Verity	6	c Mitchell b Verity	0
D. G. Foster b Macaulay	5	st. Wood b Verity	0
C. F. Tate lbw, b Verity	8	lbw, b Verity	0
G. A. E. Paine b Verity	6	c and b Verity	0
J. H. Mayer not out	2	not out	6
Extras	4	Extras	0
	201		**72**

Yorkshire

P. Holmes b Mayer	58
H. Sutcliffe c Croom b Tate	67
M. Leyland c Kilner b Mayer	2
E. Oldroyd lbw, b Mayer	67
A. Mitchell b Wyatt	12
F. E. Greenwood c Smart b Mayer	30
E. Robinson run out	2
A. Wood not out	40
G. G. Macaulay b Mayer	0
H. Verity b Mayer	7
W. E. Bowes c Kilner b Paine	0
Extras	13
	298

Yorkshire Bowling

	Overs	Mdns.	Runs	Wkts.		Overs	Mdns.	Runs	Wkts.
Bowes	14	5	25	2	...	5	1	7	0
Robinson	20	8	50	1	...	4	1	9	0
Macaulay	35	14	61	4	...	18	11	20	0
Verity	32.3	11	61	3	...	18.4	6	36	10

HEADINGLEY CRICKET AND FOOTBALL GROUND, LEEDS, FROM THE AIR

Warwickshire Bowling

	Overs	Mdns.	Runs	Wkts.
Mayer	30	8	76	6
Foster	17	2	58	0
Wyatt	8	3	12	1
Paine	17.3	3	45	1
Tate	25	6	94	1

Yorkshire v. *Gloucestershire*

Sheffield, June 3, 4, 5

Gloucestershire won by 47 runs

In the previous match against Kent at Bradford the second and third days had been blank owing to rain, and when the first and second days at Sheffield resulted in similar inactivity, the enterprising captains of Yorkshire and Gloucestershire went into a huddle and evolved a little plan calculated to circumvent the anomalies of the points system.

It was agreed that each side should declare after the first ball in each innings had been allowed to go for four byes. Thereafter normal cricket would be resumed, and if a winner materialised, 15 points instead of 8 would be the reward of ingenuity.

Yorkshire won the toss and sent Gloucestershire in to bat. When the innings ended Yorkshire had 150 minutes in which to score 172 runs. Sutcliffe, Leyland and Greenwood did as well as could reasonably be expected, but Goddard was too effective for the rest of the side, Gloucestershire winning by 47 runs.

This novel and not unamusing idea, after a second trial run at Bradford, two months later withered away under the frown of Authority.

Gloucestershire

A. E. Dipper	not out	0	c Leyland b Bowes	0
R. A. Sinfield	not out	0	c Verity b Macaulay	24
W. R. Hammond			c Robinson b Verity	6
B. H. Lyon			c Bowes b Verity	31
H. Smith			b Verity	30
W. L. Neale			c Macaulay b Verity	9
C. C. Dacre			b Verity	21
C. J. Barnett			st. Wood b Verity	26
A. Rogers			b Verity	0
C. W. L. Parker			not out	6
T. W. Goddard			c Greenwood b Leyland	13
	Extras	4	Extras	5
		4*		171

* Innings declared closed.

L

Yorkshire

P. Holmes	not out	0	c Smith b Hammond	2
A. Wood	not out	0	run out	1
H. Sutcliffe			lbw, b Goddard	27
E. Oldroyd			b Goddard	1
M. Leyland			c Dacre b Goddard	35
A. Mitchell			lbw, b Goddard	6
F. E. Greenwood			not out	33
E. Robinson			lbw, b Goddard	0
G. G. Macaulay			c Lyon b Parker	4
H. Verity			c Hammond b Parker	0
W. E. Bowes			run out	0
	Extras	4	Extras	15
		—		—
		4*		124

* Innings declared closed.

Yorkshire Bowling

	Overs	Mdns.	Runs	Wkts.		Overs	Mdns.	Runs	Wkts.
Robinson	1	0	0	0	...	6	1	19	0
Bowes						15	5	38	1
Verity						25	5	64	7
Macaulay						13	3	28	1
Leyland						9.5	3	17	1

Gloucestershire Bowling

	Overs	Mdns.	Runs	Wkts.		Overs	Mdns.	Runs	Wkts.
Hammond	1	0	0	0	...	6	2	18	1
Rogers						4	0	18	0
Goddard						13	4	21	5
Parker						11	0	52	2

Yorkshire v. *Surrey*

Bradford, July 4, 6, 7

Yorkshire won by an innings and 55 runs

In Macaulay's Benefit match Surrey were heavily defeated, putting together a moderate total for a strong batting side in the first innings and collapsing in the second.

On the first day Surrey occupied the wicket all the time that play was in progress, rain preventing the start of Yorkshire's innings. The rate of scoring was unduly sedate, 260 minutes being required to score 165. Ducat, who was top scorer, was in over three hours for his 42, and the later batsmen quite failed to cope with Yorkshire's bowling, Bowes taking six wickets for 93 runs.

Yorkshire's innings was declared when a lead of 116 runs had been obtained, Leyland and Oldroyd adding 103 and Leyland and Greenwood 129 unfinished.

The effect of a hot sun on a damp wicket proved disastrous to Surrey.
Bowes and Verity appeared to be almost unplayable, and only Hobbs
offered any serious resistance. Verity, with six wickets for 11 runs in
14 overs, was a particularly painful thorn in the Surrey flesh.

Macaulay, the beneficiaire, had little chance of distinguishing himself,
but made 5 catches in the two innings.

Surrey

J. B. Hobbs c and b Macaulay	26	lbw, b Verity	24
A. Sandham c Greenwood b Bowes	2	c Wood b Bowes	3
A. Ducat b Bowes	42	c Macaulay b Verity	9
T. F. Shepherd lbw, b Verity	40	c Wood b Bowes	4
T. H. Barling c Robinson b Bowes	4	b Verity	5
H. S. Squires c Leyland b Verity	28	c Leyland b Verity	7
P. G. H. Fender c and b Bowes	11	c Macaulay b Bowes	3
R. J. Gregory c Macaulay b Bowes	6	c Greenwood b Verity	0
E. W. Brooks c Macaulay b Verity	0	not out	0
A. R. Gover not out	2	c Holmes b Verity	1
H. Lock c Leyland b Bowes	1	hit wkt, b Bowes	1
Extras	3	Extras	4
	165		61

Yorkshire

P. Holmes c and b Gregory	21
A. Mitchell c Gregory b Gover	17
E. Oldroyd b Squires	66
M. Leyland c and b Lock	124
F. E. Greenwood not out	44
W. Barber did not bat	
E. Robinson did not bat	
A. Wood did not bat	
G. G. Macaulay did not bat	
H. Verity did not bat	
W. E. Bowes did not bat	
Extras	9
	281*

* Innings declared closed.

Yorkshire Bowling

	Overs	Mdns.	Runs	Wkts.		Overs	Mdns.	Runs	Wkts.
Bowes	37.3	11	93	6	...	15.1	2	32	4
Robinson	9	5	15	0	...	5	1	13	0
Macaulay	18	11	11	1	...	4	3	1	0
Verity	28	12	43	3	...	14	7	11	6

Surrey Bowling

	Overs	Mdns.	Runs	Wkts.
Gover	23	2	88	1
Lock	21.4	2	69	1
Gregory	18	3	43	1
Fender	11	1	42	0
Squires	10	1	30	1

APPEARANCES

The following 18 cricketers appeared for Yorkshire in Championship matches, the number of appearances being in parentheses :

W. Barber (14)
A. Booth (2)
W. E. Bowes (24)
F. Dennis (1)
H. Fisher (1)
F. E. Greenwood (27)
C. H. Hall (1)
P. Holmes (27)
T. A. Jacques (1)

M. Leyland (27)
G. G. Macaulay (27)
A. Mitchell (22)
E. Oldroyd (21)
E. Robinson (27)
H. Sutcliffe (23)
C. Turner (1)
H. Verity (24)
A. Wood (27)

POST MORTEM

Cricket history repeated itself in 1931. When Peel dropped out of the side in 1897, Yorkshire produced a ready-made genius (Rhodes) to take his place in 1898. At the end of the 1930 campaign Rhodes retired, and in the following season his successor (Verity) took 138 wickets for 12·34 runs each in his first full season.

From the figures it is clear that Sutcliffe, Verity and Bowes were the stars of 1931. In a season of wickets unfavourable to batsmen Sutcliffe had a wonderfully successful time, scoring over 2,000 runs with a record average of 97·57. In match after match he scored his 50 or 100, and his record would probably have been even more amazing if he had not been kept out of one match by a strain.

The bowling of Verity and Bowes, and in a lesser degree Macaulay, was equally match-winning, and as usual the fielding and field-setting gave splendid assistance to the bowlers. If there was a flaw in the composition of the Yorkshire side it was the lack of all-rounders, but in a wet season this was less noticeable than it might otherwise have been.

SIXTEENTH CHAMPIONSHIP

1932

Captain : F. E. Greenwood

Yorkshire won their sixteenth Championship as easily as they had won their fifteenth in 1931, being 53 points ahead of Sussex, the runners-up. The method of scoring remained unchanged in spite of the obvious flaws revealed in the previous season.

THE FIRST SIX

	Played	Won	Lost	1st Inns. Won	1st Inns. Lost	No Result	Points
Yorkshire	28	19	2	3	1	3	315
Sussex	28	14	1	4	4	5	262
Kent	28	14	3	1	7	3	248
Nottinghamshire	28	13	4	6	4	1	241
Surrey	28	9	2	10	3	4	210
Lancashire	28	8	6	7	4	3	179

METHOD OF SCORING : As in 1931.

MATCH SCORES AND RESULTS

Yorkshire v.	Ground	Yorkshire 1st Inns.	Yorkshire 2nd Inns.	Opponents 1st Inns.	Opponents 2nd Inns.	Result
Lancashire	Bradford	46	167	263	—	L, inns. and 50 runs
Warwickshire	Birmingham	*403 (5)	—	17 (0)	—	Draw
Derbyshire	Chesterfield		Aban	doned		
Somerset	Bath	115	58 (1)	78	94	Y, 9 wickets
Kent	Sheffield		Aban	doned		
Hampshire	Leeds	183	170	199	203	H, 49 runs
Warwickshire	Hull	229	*326 (6)	285	54 (1)	Draw
Gloucestershire	Bristol	418	—	173	158	Y, inns. and 95 runs
Kent	Tonbridge	207	67 (6)	196	75	Y, 4 wickets
Essex	Leyton	*555 (1)	—	78	164	Y, inns. and 313 runs
Middlesex	Lord's	254	34 (1)	152	134	Y, 10 wickets
Sussex	Leeds	*500 (8)	—	259	258 (4)	Draw
Middlesex	Sheffield	*481 (7)	—	340	196 (5)	Draw
Northamptonshire	Northampton	*251 (6)	—	89	113	Y, inns. and 49 runs
Surrey	Sheffield	241	160	126	97	Y, 178 runs
Gloucestershire	Bradford	*472 (7)	*240 (6)	404	175	Y, 133 runs
Nottinghamshire	Leeds	*163 (9)	139 (0)	234	67	Y, 10 wickets
Northamptonshire	Huddersfield	*384 (9)	—	161	207	Y, inns. and 16 runs
Nottinghamshire	Nottingham	169 (6)	—	168	—	Draw
Lancashire	Manchester	*362 (9)	—	170	187	Y, inns. and 5 runs
Leicestershire	Leicester	365	—	155	141	Y, inns. and 69 runs
Derbyshire	Leeds	*416 (7)	—	78	249	Y, inns. and 89 runs
Essex	Scarborough	*476 (9)	—	325	143	Y, inns. and 8 runs
Leicestershire	Bradford	*467 (7)	—	111	72	Y, inns. and 284 runs
Somerset	Sheffield	*357 (8)	—	93	171	Y, inns. and 93 runs
Surrey	Oval	215	135 (7)	231	118	Y, 3 wickets
Hampshire	Bournemouth	307	*199 (5)	174	160	Y, 172 runs
Sussex	Brighton	258	*225 (3)	166	150	Y, 167 runs

* Innings declared closed.

165

Yorkshire beat Essex, Gloucestershire, Leicestershire, Northampton-shire, Somerset, Surrey twice; and Derbyshire, Hampshire, Kent, Lancashire, Middlesex, Nottinghamshire, Sussex once.

Yorkshire were beaten by Hampshire, Lancashire once.

Yorkshire drew with Warwickshire twice; and Middlesex, Notting-hamshire, Sussex once.

The matches between Yorkshire and Derbyshire at Chesterfield and Kent at Sheffield were abandoned.

SUMMARY

	Yorkshire	Opponents
Runs scored	10214	8111
Average per wicket	36·09	17·67
Hundreds	24	9
Other innings over 50	35	25
Ten wickets in match	8	3
Five wickets in innings	34	15
Highest total	551 (1) dec. v. Essex	404 (Gloucestershire)
Lowest total	46 v. Lancashire	67 Nottinghamshire)
Totals over 400	9	1
Totals under 100	1	10

PRINCIPAL AVERAGES

	Inns.	Not Out	Runs	Highest Inns.	100's	50's	Aver.
H. Sutcliffe	35	5	2624	313	12	7	87·46
M. Leyland	29	2	1624	189	5	7	60·11
P. Holmes	23	3	946	224*	2	6	47·30
W. Barber	34	2	932	162	3	2	29·12
A. Mitchell	35	3	929	177*	2	3	29·03
A. B. Sellers	29	4	672	85	—	6	26·88

* Not out.

	Balls	Balls per Wkt.	Runs	Wkts.	5 Wkts. in Inns.	Aver.
H. Verity	5689	42·14	1856	135	11	13·74
W. E. Bowes	5953	37·20	2364	160	13	14·77
G. G. Macaulay	4503	68·22	1323	66	4	20·45

NOTES

In their first innings in a county match, v. Lancashire at Bradford, Yorkshire's total was 46, of which Sutcliffe scored 27. Sibbles took seven wickets for 10 runs in the innings and fifteen for 68 in the match.

At Leeds, Sutcliffe carried his bat through the second innings (170) v. Hampshire for 104. Hampshire won by 49 runs, Kennedy taking ten wickets for 139 runs.

Bowes (four for 26) and A. C. Rhodes (six for 48) bowled unchanged in Kent's second innings (75) at Tonbridge.

Holmes (224 not out) and Sutcliffe (313) set up a new first wicket record v. Essex at Leyton, who lost by an innings and 313 runs.

Sutcliffe scored 270 v. Sussex at Leeds.

Barber (162) and Leyland (189) set up a new second wicket record for Yorkshire by scoring 346 against Middlesex at Sheffield.

In the Yorkshire-Gloucestershire match at Bradford, Sutcliffe scored 83 and 132, and Hammond 147 and 71 not out.

For the second successive season Verity took all ten wickets in an innings—ten for 10 runs in the second innings of Notts (67) at Leeds. In the first innings Leyland took four wickets for 14 runs.

In consecutive innings v. Lancashire, Leicestershire, Derbyshire, Essex, Leicestershire and Somerset, Sutcliffe scored 135, 60, 182, 194, 47, 136—754 runs (average 125·66). Against Essex during the season he scored 507 runs in two innings.

At Scarborough v. Essex, Sutcliffe and Leyland added 149 runs in 55 minutes, six successive overs from Farnes, O'Connor and Nicholls producing 102. Sutcliffe scored his 50 in 75 minutes, his 100 in 125 minutes, and his last 94 runs in 40 minutes—194 in 165 minutes.

In successive matches, H. Fisher took six wickets for 11 runs v. Leicestershire (first innings), and five for 12 v. Somerset (first innings). Against Somerset he did a record hat-trick, each of the batsmen being lbw.

In Championship matches, Sutcliffe scored 2,624 runs—a record aggregate for Yorkshire—and averaged 87·46. In two consecutive seasons (1931 and 1932) he had the following figures:

Runs	Highest Inns.	100's	50's	Average
4673	313	18	16	91·62

Nearly 55 per cent. of his innings in Championship matches exceeded 50.

Yorkshire's Maytime in 1932 was less " merrie " than usual, 1 match being lost, 1 drawn, 2 abandoned without a ball being bowled, and 1 won. Then followed 1 defeat, 18 wins, and 3 draws.

HOW IT WAS DONE

	100's	50's	10 Wkts. in Match	5 Wkts. in Inns.	50 Runs & 5 Wkts. in Match
W. Barber	3	2	—	—	—
W. E. Bowes	—	—	4	13	—
H. Fisher	—	1	—	2	1
F. E. Greenwood	—	1	—	—	—
C. H. Hall	—	—	—	2	—
P. Holmes	2	6	—	—	—
M. Leyland	5	7	—	—	—
G. G. Macaulay	—	—	—	4	—
A. Mitchell	2	3	—	—	—
A. C. Rhodes	—	1	—	2	1
A. B. Sellers	—	6	—	—	—
H. Sutcliffe	12	7	—	—	—
H. Verity	—	—	4	11	—
A. Wood	—	1	—	—	—
Total	24	35	8	34	2

FIELDING (180 Catches)

No. of Catches		No. of Catches	
34	A. Mitchell	8	W. E. Bowes
25	G. G. Macaulay	8	P. Holmes
20	H. Sutcliffe	5	C. H. Hall
19	H. Verity	4	F. Dennis
13	W. Barber	3	H. Fisher
13	A. C. Rhodes	3	" Sub."
13	A. B. Sellers	2	F. E. Greenwood
9	M. Leyland	1	T. F. Smailes

WICKETKEEPING

	Stumped	Caught	Total
A. Wood	9	55	64

TOTALS

400 Runs and Over

Yorkshire (9)

555 (1)* v. Essex, Leyton
500 (8)* v. Sussex, Leeds
481 (7)* v. Middlesex, Sheffield
476 (8)* v. Essex, Scarborough
472 (7)* v. Gloucestershire, Bradford

467 (7)* v. Leicestershire, Bradford
418 v. Gloucestershire, Bristol
416 (7)* v. Derbyshire, Leeds
403 (5)* v. Warwickshire, Birmingham

Opponents (1)

404, Gloucestershire, Bradford

* Innings declared closed.

Under 100 Runs

Yorkshire (1)

46 v. Lancashire, Bradford

Opponents (10)

67, Nottinghamshire, Leeds
72, Leicestershire, Bradford
75, Kent, Tonbridge
78, Derbyshire, Leeds
78 and 94, Somerset, Bath

78, Essex, Leyton
89, Northamptonshire, Northampton
93, Somerset, Sheffield
97, Surrey, Sheffield

FIRST WICKET PARTNERSHIPS

Score	Partners	Against	Ground
555	P. Holmes, H. Sutcliffe	Essex	Leyton
169	H. Sutcliffe, M. Leyland	Derbyshire	Leeds
161	P. Holmes, H. Sutcliffe	Gloucestershire	Bradford
161	P. Holmes, H. Sutcliffe	Northamptonshire	Huddersfield
139*	P. Holmes, H. Sutcliffe	Nottinghamshire	Leeds
120	H. Sutcliffe, W. Barber	Warwickshire	Hull

* Unfinished.

50 RUNS AND 5 WICKETS

Scores	Analyses	Player	Against	Ground
53, 1	3-45, 2-33	A. C. Rhodes	Hampshire	Leeds
76*	5-12, 0-14	H. Fisher	Somerset	Sheffield

* Not out.

MATCHES OF THE SEASON

Yorkshire v. *Lancashire*

Bradford, May 14, 16, 17

Lancashire won by an innings and 50 runs

Yorkshire started the season of 1932 with a heavy defeat from Lancashire. The start was delayed owing to rain, but as soon as play began Paynter showed that run-getting was not impossible. In 30 minutes he scored 50 runs and in 210 minutes 152, including 5 sixes and 17 fours. Watson, Tyldesley and Parkinson gave modest assistance, but the Lancashire total (263) was by no means overpowering.

Yorkshire, however, found Sibbles decidedly overpowering. Sutcliffe scored a stubborn 27 in 80 minutes, but no other batsman scored more than 6. Sibbles and Hopwood bowled unchanged, the former having the very fine figures of seven wickets for 10 runs in 124 balls.

Following on, Yorkshire showed some improvement, but not enough. Sutcliffe again batted well, and Leyland scored 43 quick runs, but the end arrived with only 167 on the board.

In the match, Sibbles took twelve wickets for 68 runs.

Lancashire

F. Watson c Holmes b Verity	19
E. Paynter st. Wood b Verity	152
E. Tyldesley lbw, b Verity	20
J. Iddon c Sutcliffe b Verity	2
C. Hallows c Smailes b Verity	0
J. L. Hopwood c Mitchell b Verity	2
L. Parkinson c and b Bowes	39
R. Parkin c Mitchell b Verity	13
P. T. Eckersley b Verity	5
F. M. Sibbles not out	3
G. Duckworth c Sutcliffe b Bowes	2
Extras	6
	263

Yorkshire

P. Holmes c Tyldesley b Sibbles	0	lbw, b Parkin	7
H. Sutcliffe c Sibbles b Hopwood	27	c Tyldesley b Sibbles	61
A. Mitchell b Sibbles	1	lbw, b Hopwood	13
M. Leyland c Parkin b Sibbles	6	c Eckersley b Hopwood	43
W. Barber c Hallows b Sibbles	3	b Hopwood	2
F. E. Greenwood c Watson b Hopwood	3	st. Duckworth b Sibbles	9
T. F. Smailes b Hopwood	0	b Parkin	7
A. Wood lbw, b Sibbles	0	b Sibbles	11
G. G. Macaulay c Watson b Sibbles	0	not out	1
H. Verity not out	4	c Iddon b Sibbles	8
W. E. Bowes c Watson b Sibbles	0	c Watson b Sibbles	0
Extras	2	Extras	5
	46		167

Yorkshire Bowling

	Overs	Mdns.	Runs	Wkts.
Bowes	10.5	5	16	2
Smailes	13	4	30	0
Macaulay	29	10	65	0
Verity	39	13	107	8
Leyland	11	3	39	0

Lancashire Bowling

	Overs	Mdns.	Runs	Wkts.		Overs	Mdns.	Runs	Wkts.
Sibbles	20.4	13	10	7	...	27	8	58	5
Hopwood	20	6	34	3	...	25	3	52	3
Iddon						10	2	18	0
Parkin						12	4	32	2
Parkinson						1	0	2	0

Yorkshire v. *Essex*

Leyton, June 15, 16, 17

Yorkshire won by an innings and 313 runs

Yorkshire's appearance at Leyton put another major record into *Wisden*, Holmes and Sutcliffe beating the 34-year-old first wicket record of J. T. Brown and Tunnicliffe by 1 run, scoring 555 in 445 minutes.

Everything else in the match was, of course, dwarfed by this mass run-getting. Yorkshire's famous opening pair scored 100 runs in 105 minutes, 200 in 200 minutes, 400 in 325 minutes, and throughout the long innings averaged 75 runs an hour.

In his 313, Sutcliffe hit a six and 33 fours, Holmes having 19 fours in his 224 not out. This was their seventieth three-figure first wicket partnership.

When Essex batted, Verity and Bowes showed very little mercy, the former taking ten wickets for 53 runs (five for 8 and five for 45), and Bowes nine for 85.

Yorkshire

P. Holmes not out	224
H. Sutcliffe b Eastman	313
A. Mitchell did not bat	
M. Leyland did not bat	
W. Barber did not bat	
A. B. Sellers did not bat	
A. C. Rhodes did not bat	
A. Wood did not bat	
H. Verity did not bat	
G. G. Macaulay did not bat	
W. E. Bowes did not bat	
Extras	18
	555*

* Innings declared closed.

Essex

L. G. Crawley b Bowes	0	c Sutcliffe b Bowes	27
D. F. Pope c Rhodes b Bowes	6	c Mitchell b Bowes	9
J. O'Connor b Bowes	20	c Rhodes b Bowes	7
J. A. Cutmore lbw, b Bowes	0	b Verity	1
M. S. Nichols b Verity	25	not out	59
L. C. Eastman c Sutcliffe b Macaulay	16	c Barber b Verity	19
C. Bray c and b Verity	1	st. Wood b Verity	6
R. H. Taylor c Macaulay b Verity	5	c Macaulay b Verity	13
J. R. Sheffield c and b Verity	0	c Sutcliffe b Verity	5
A. G. Daer c and b Verity	0	c Verity b Bowes	0
P. Smith not out	2	c Rhodes b Bowes	0
Extras	3	Extras	18
	78		164

Essex Bowling

	Overs	Mdns.	Runs	Wkts.
Nichols	31	4	105	0
Daer	40	8	106	0
Smith	46	10	128	0
O'Connor	23	5	73	0
Eastman	22.4	2	97	1
Crawley	3	0	7	0
Taylor	4	0	14	0
Bray	1	0	7	0

Yorkshire Bowling

	Overs	Mdns.	Runs	Wkts.		Overs	Mdns.	Runs	Wkts.
Bowes	12	1	38	4	...	23.4	5	47	5
Rhodes	10	5	15	0	...	9	5	23	0
Macaulay	7.1	2	14	1	...	16	5	31	0
Verity	7	3	8	5	...	30	12	45	5

Yorkshire v. *Nottinghamshire*
Leeds, July 9, 11, 12

Yorkshire won by ten wickets

Yorkshire had a fine win against Nottinghamshire at Leeds, in the course of which Verity made cricket history.

In the first innings Notts were only moderately successful, scoring 234—a total which might have been more imposing had not Leyland taken four wickets for 14 runs.

Yorkshire were even less successful, Holmes scoring 65 before he was bowled by Larwood, but the total was 163 for nine wickets when a thunderstorm put an end to play on the second day.

With a lead of 71, Notts appeared to be in a comfortable position, but after the first three batsmen had scored 53 runs the last eight scored 10, and six of them did not score. In the course of this rout Verity took all ten wickets for 10 runs—the most amazing analysis in the history of cricket—doing the hat-trick and in two successive overs taking two wickets with consecutive balls.

To complete the picture, Holmes and Sutcliffe then scored the required runs (139) in 90 minutes.

Nottinghamshire

W. W. Keeton	b Rhodes	9	c Macaulay b Verity	21
F. W. Shipstone	b Macaulay	8	c Wood b Verity	21
W. Walker	c Barber b Bowes	36	c Macaulay b Verity	11
A. W. Carr	c Barber b Verity	0	c Barber b Verity	0
A. Staples	b Macaulay	3	c Macaulay b Verity	7
C. B. Harris	lbw, b Leyland	35	c Holmes b Verity	0
G. V. Gunn	b Verity	31	lbw, b Verity	0
B. Lilley	not out	46	not out	3
H. Larwood	b Leyland	48	c Sutcliffe b Verity	0
W. Voce	b Leyland	0	c Holmes b Verity	0
S. J. Staples	b Leyland	0	st. Wood b Verity	0
	Extras	18	Extras	4
		234		67

Yorkshire

P. Holmes	b Larwood	65	not out	77
H. Sutcliffe	c Voce b Larwood	0	not out	54
A. Mitchell	run out	24		
M. Leyland	b Voce	5		
W. Barber	c and b Larwood	34		
A. B. Sellers	b Staples (A.)	0		
A. Wood	b Larwood	1		
A. C. Rhodes	c Staples (A.) b Voce	3		
H. Verity	b Larwood	12		
G. G. Macaulay	not out	8		
W. E. Bowes	not out	1		
	Extras	10	Extras	8
		163*		139

* Innings declared closed.

Yorkshire Bowling

	Overs	Mdns.	Runs	Wkts.		Overs	Mdns.	Runs	Wkts.
Bowes	31	9	55	1	...	5	0	19	0
Rhodes	28	8	49	1					
Verity	41	13	64	2	...	19.4	16	10	10
Macaulay	24	10	34	2	...	23	9	34	0
Leyland	8.2	3	14	4					

Nottinghamshire Bowling

	Overs	Mdns.	Runs	Wkts.		Overs	Mdns.	Runs	Wkts.
Larwood	22	4	73	5	...	3	0	14	0
Voce	22	2	52	2	....	10	0	43	0
Staples (S. J.)	7	2	8	0	...	18.4	5	37	0
Staples (A.)	11	3	20	1	...	6	1	25	0
Harris						3	0	12	0

Yorkshire v. *Essex*

Scarborough, August 10, 11, 12

Yorkshire won by an innings and 8 runs

Scarborough air is bracing, but the most partisan Yorkshireman could scarcely anticipate that it would suffice to move the Yorkshire XI. in general, and Sutcliffe in particular, to indulge in a Jessopian frenzy at the expense of the unfortunate Essex attack.

Taking first innings, Essex produced the respectable total of 325, assisted by an unusual epidemic of missed catches by the Yorkshiremen. In spite of these lapses, Bowes took nine wickets for 121. And then the fun started.

Mitchell scored 80 and Sutcliffe, accelerating slightly, reached his 100 in 125 minutes. About this time he was joined by Leyland, and the pace was increased. Four overs from Farnes provided 75 runs, and in six successive overs 102 runs were added. The Sutcliffe-Leyland partnership produced 149 runs in 55 minutes, and when Sutcliffe was caught for 194, he had actually scored his last 94 runs in 40 minutes. No wonder Essex lost by an innings and 8 runs.

Essex

J. A. Cutmore c Fisher b Bowes	45	c Wood b Bowes	11
D. F. Pope c Barber b Bowes	0	lbw, b Fisher	11
D. R. Wilcox b Bowes	1	c Mitchell b Verity	29
J. O'Connor c Sutcliffe b Fisher	29	c Verity b Bowes	11
M. S. Nichols b Bowes	105	c Wood b Leyland	23
L. C. Eastman c Barber b Bowes	4	absent ill	0
R. H. Taylor c Leyland b Bowes	106	c Mitchell b Verity	10
T. H. Wade lbw, b Bowes	1	b Verity	7
J. R. Sheffield c Verity b Bowes	2	b Bowes	8
G. R. Brown b Bowes	9	c Wood b Bowes	16
K. Farnes not out	3	not out	0
Extras	20	Extras	17
	325		143

Yorkshire

A. Mitchell c Farnes b Nichols	80
H. Verity c Nichols b Farnes	6
H. Fisher c Nichols b Farnes	38
H. Sutcliffe c Pope b O'Connor	194
M. Leyland c Wilcox b O'Connor	45
W. Barber c Farnes b O'Connor	2
F. Dennis not out	34
A. B. Sellers b Brown	21
A. Wood st. Sheffield b Brown	27
A. C. Rhodes b Brown	8
Bowes did not bat	

Extras   21

476*

* Innings declared closed.

Yorkshire Bowling

	Overs	Mdns.	Runs	Wkts.		Overs	Mdns.	Runs	Wkts.
Bowes	44.1	7	121	9	...	22.1	3	62	4
Rhodes	14	5	33	0					
Dennis	2	0	9	0					
Fisher	27	7	79	1	...	13	6	21	1
Verity	15	2	49	0	...	11	2	23	3
Leyland	6	0	14	0	...	2	0	20	1

Essex Bowling

	Overs	Mdns.	Runs	Wkts.
Farnes	24	3	135	2
Nichols	25	6	80	1
Eastman	5	1	14	0
O'Connor	39	9	126	3
Brown	28.4	3	100	3

APPEARANCES

The following 18 cricketers appeared for Yorkshire in Championship matches, the number of appearances being in parentheses :

W. Barber (26)	G. G. Macaulay (23)
W. E. Bowes (24)	A. Mitchell (26)
F. Dennis (8)	A. C. Rhodes (21)
H. Fisher (6)	A. B. Sellers (23)
F. E. Greenwood (6)	T. F. Smailes (1)
C. H. Hall (6)	H. Sutcliffe (24)
W. E. Harbord (1)	C. Turner (1)
P. Holmes (16)	H. Verity (26)
M. Leyland (22)	A. Wood (26)

POST MORTEM

Yorkshire began the season badly by losing 2 of the first 5 county matches played, their record on June 8 being 1 match won, 2 lost, 2 drawn and 2 abandoned. But from this point their fortunes changed, and of the remaining 21 matches 3 were drawn and 18 won—10 with an innings to spare.

Sutcliffe had another wonderful season, scoring 2,624 runs and averaging 87·46 runs an innings, and was well supported by Leyland (60·11) and Holmes (47·30), while Barber and Mitchell both scored over 900 runs with averages of 29.

The bowling depended mainly on Verity and Bowes, with useful support from Macaulay, but in quantity, variety and quality was scarcely up to the standard of the early nineteen-twenties.

F. E. Greenwood, the official captain, played in 6 matches only, the vice-captain, A. B. Sellers, leading the side in 20 of the Championship fixtures.

Two major records were set up during the season : the great first wicket partnership of Holmes and Sutcliffe (555) at Leyton, and Verity's wonderful bowling—ten wickets for 10 runs in the second innings of Notts at Leeds.

SEVENTEENTH CHAMPIONSHIP

1933

Captain : A. B. Sellers

Yorkshire started well in 1933, winning 11 of their first 12 matches and remaining unbeaten until the end of June. Sussex, the runners-up, beat them twice, and Kent also won at Dover, but with 19 wins, Yorkshire managed to neutralise these rebuffs, and finished at the top of the table, in spite of a percentage system which contrived to place Derbyshire with 11 losses above Warwickshire with 5, and only just below Lancashire, who lost only 1 match.

THE FIRST SIX

	Plyd.	Won	Lost	1st Inns. Won	1st Inns. Lost	No Res.	Points Obtd.	Points Poss.	Per-cent.
Yorkshire	30	19	3	3	5	0	315	450	70·00
Sussex	32	18	5	7	2	0	311	480	64·79
Kent	30	15	8	3	3	1	253	450	56·22
Essex	28	13	8	4	3	0	224	420	53·38
Lancashire	28	9	1	10	7	1	210	420	50·00
Derbyshire	28	11	11	3	3	0	189	420	45·00

METHOD OF SCORING : Each county to play 24 matches. Counties allowed to arrange more matches, but all must count in the competition. System of points as in 1931, but the county obtaining the greatest proportionate number of points on a percentage basis to be Champions.

MATCH SCORES AND RESULTS

Yorkshire v.	Ground	Yorkshire 1st Inns.	Yorkshire 2nd Inns.	Opponents 1st Inns.	Opponents 2nd Inns.	Result
Derbyshire	Hull	96	35 (4)	51	78	Y, 6 wickets
Essex	Dewsbury	*128 (4)	5 (0)	64	68	Y, 10 wickets
Leicestershire	Bradford	*250 (7)	—	65	39	Y, inns. and 146 runs
Glamorgan	Cardiff	299	*236 (3)	208	166	Y, 166 runs
Kent	Leeds	286	—	90	172	Y, inns. and 24 runs
Gloucestershire	Sheffield	369	25 (0)	245	148	Y, 10 wickets
Lancashire	Manchester	341	—	93	92	Y, inns. and 156 runs
Warwickshire	Birmingham	*591 (6)	—	319	127 (4)	Draw
Worcestershire	Sheffield	*500 (9)	—	231	104	Y, inns. and 165 runs
Northamptonshire	Kettering	301	—	27	68	Y, inns. and 206 runs
Gloucestershire	Gloucester	227	153	144	135	Y, 101 runs
Warwickshire	Leeds	229	—	63	101	Y, inns. and 65 runs
Nottinghamshire	Nottingham	155	176 (4)	241	*199 (8)	Draw
Sussex	Hull	131	263	378	17 (0)	S, 10 wickets
Surrey	Sheffield	253	195	134	252	Y, 62 runs
Northamptonshire	Leeds	*349 (7)	—	63	135	Y, inns. and 151 runs
Essex	Leyton	340	—	104	64	Y, inns. and 172 runs
Middlesex	Bradford	367	53 (0)	305	114	Y, 10 wickets
Hampshire	Bournemouth	255	58 (3)	177	*330 (8)	Draw
Middlesex	Lord's	302	28 (0)	136	192	Y, 10 wickets
Hampshire	Sheffield	338	—	268	68 (2)	Draw
Glamorgan	Scarborough	308	4 (0)	157	154	Y, 10 wickets
Lancashire	Leeds	296	153 (3)	431	—	Draw
Leicestershire	Leicester	550	—	154	145	Y, inns. and 251 runs
Derbyshire	Chesterfield	218	137 (2)	245	*330 (8)	Draw
Nottinghamshire	Bradford	515	12 (0)	324	202	Y, 10 wickets
Kent	Dover	*333 (6)	88	332	133	K, 44 runs
Surrey	Oval	233	219 (5)	*560 (6)	—	Draw
Sussex	Brighton	115	114	249	—	S, inns. and 20 runs
Worcestershire	Worcester	223	421 (3)	420	—	Draw

* Innings declared closed.

HOLMES AND SUTCLIFFE, IN FRONT OF THE SCOREBOARD AT LEYTON
IN 1932, AFTER THEIR RECORD FIRST-WICKET PARTNERSHIP

Yorkshire beat Essex, Glamorgan, Gloucestershire, Leicestershire, Middlesex, Northamptonshire twice; and Derbyshire, Kent, Lancashire, Nottinghamshire, Surrey, Warwickshire, Worcestershire once.

Yorkshire were beaten by Sussex twice; and Kent once.

Yorkshire drew with Hampshire twice; and Derbyshire, Lancashire, Nottinghamshire, Surrey, Warwickshire, Worcestershire once.

SUMMARY

	Yorkshire	Opponents
Runs scored	11273	9911
Average per wicket	31·75	18·84
Hundreds	19	11
Other innings over 50	38	25
Ten wickets in match	14	—
Five wickets in innings	36	14
Highest total	591 (6) dec.	560 (6) dec. (Surrey)
	v. Warwickshire	
Lowest total	88 v. Kent	27 (Northamptonshire)
Totals over 400	4	3
Totals under 100	2	14

PRINCIPAL AVERAGES

	Inns.	Not Out	Runs	Highest Inns.	100's	50's	Aver.
M. Leyland	39	4	1969	210*	6	9	56·25
A. Mitchell	40	8	1547	150*	5	5	48·34
H. Sutcliffe	40	3	1635	205	4	5	44·19
W. Barber	42	4	1477	124	4	8	38·86
A. Wood	38	8	791	85	—	4	26·36

* Not out.

	Balls	Balls per Wkt.	Runs	Wkts.	5 Wkts. in Inns.	Aver.
H. Verity	5548	36·26	1826	153	14	11·93
G. G. Macaulay	5486	47·70	1761	115	8	15·31
W. E. Bowes	4668	37·95	2139	123	11	17·39

NOTES

In their first three county matches Yorkshire dismissed Derbyshire, Essex and Leicestershire for 51 and 78, 64 and 68, 65 and 39 respectively—an average innings of just under 61. In these three matches Verity took 29 wickets for 5·85 runs each and Macaulay 24 for 5·83.

W. E. Bowes took twelve wickets for 117 runs v. Kent at Leeds.

When Essex scored 64 v. Yorkshire at Dewsbury, J. A. Cutmore carried his bat through the innings for 31.

A. Mitchell scored 123 v. Lancashire at Manchester, Macaulay taking twelve wickets for 49 runs (seven for 28 and five for 21).

Sutcliffe scored 205 at Birmingham when Yorkshire scored 591 for six wickets against Warwickshire, Mitchell, Leyland, Barber and Verity also scoring over 50. For Warwickshire, N. Kilner scored 197 out of 319 in the first innings.

M

At Kettering, Northamptonshire were all out for 27 in their first innings, Macaulay taking seven wickets for 9 runs in 14 overs.

D. R. Jardine scored 105 in Surrey's second innings at Sheffield, Bowes taking twelve wickets for 140 in the match.

When Yorkshire beat Essex by an innings and 172 runs at Leyton, A. B. Sellers made 7 catches, including 5 in the first innings. Verity took seventeen wickets for 91 runs on the last day of the match.

M. Leyland took ten Leicestershire wickets for 94 runs at Leicester—four for 48 and six for 46.

When Kent beat Yorkshire by 44 runs at Dover, Leyland scored 210 not out in Yorkshire's first innings and took five wickets for 88 runs in the two Kent innings.

Surrey scored 560 for six wickets declared at the Oval, Squires scoring 178 and Barling 112. For Yorkshire, Leyland scored 77 and 74 not out. The match aggregate of 1,012 runs included 105 extras, of which 14 were wides and 24 no-balls.

During the season 44 three-figure partnerships were recorded for Yorkshire, the following batsmen being responsible : Leyland 12 times, Mitchell 12, Sutcliffe 8, Barber 7, Verity 2, and Davidson, Holmes, Sellers 1 each.

HOW IT WAS DONE

	100's	50's	10 Wkts. in Match	5 Wkts. in Inns.	50 Runs & 5 Wkts. in Match
W. Barber	4	8	–	–	–
W. E. Bowes	–	–	4	11	–
P. Holmes	1	1	–	–	–
M. Leyland	6	9	1	2	2
G. G. Macaulay	–	–	3	8	–
A. Mitchell	5	5	–	–	–
A. C. Rhodes	–	1	–	1	–
A. B. Sellers	–	1	–	–	–
H. Sutcliffe	4	5	–	–	–
C. Turner	–	1	–	–	–
H. Verity	–	3	6	14	–
A. Wood	–	4	–	–	–
Total	19	38	14	36	2

FIELDING (216 Catches)

No. of Catches		No. of Catches	
29	A. B. Sellers	6	W. E. Bowes
28	A. Mitchell	6	S. Douglas
28	H. Sutcliffe	4	F. Dennis
24	A. C. Rhodes	3	C. Turner
20	G. G. Macaulay	2	K. R. Davidson
17	W. Barber	2	W. E. Harbord
17	H. Verity	2	" Sub."
14	M. Leyland	1	C. H. Hall
13	P. Holmes		

WICKETKEEPING

	Stumped	Caught	Total
A. Wood	19	43	62

TOTALS

400 Runs and Over

Yorkshire (5)

591 (6)* v. Warwickshire, Birmingham   500 (9)* v. Worcestershire, Sheffield
550 v. Leicestershire, Leicester   421 (3) v. Worcestershire, Worcester
515 v. Notinghamshire, Bradford

Opponents (3)

560 (6),* Surrey, Oval   420, Worcestershire, Worcester
431, Lancashire, Leeds

* Innings declared closed.

Under 100 Runs

Yorkshire (2)

†88 v. Kent, Dover   96 v. Derbyshire, Hull

† One man short.

Opponents (13)

27 and 68, Northamptonshire, Kettering   64, Essex, Leyton
‡65 and 39, Leicestershire, Bradford   ‡64 and 68, Essex, Dewsbury
‡51 and 78, Derbyshire, Hull   90, Kent, Leeds
63, Northamptonshire, Leeds   93 and 92, Lancashire, Manchester
63, Warwickshire, Leeds

‡ Consecutive matches.

FIRST WICKET PARTNERSHIPS

Score	Partners	Against	Ground
141	P. Holmes, H. Sutcliffe	Nottinghamshire	Bradford

50 RUNS AND 5 WICKETS

Scores	Analyses	Player	Against	Ground
50, 25	5-67	M. Leyland	Sussex	Hull
210,* 10	4-56, 1-28	M. Leyland	Kent	Dover

* Not out

MATCHES OF THE SEASON
Yorkshire v. *Northamptonshire*
Kettering June 14, 15, 16
Yorkshire won by an innings and 206 runs

Batting first on a wicket made difficult by sunshine after rain, Northamptonshire, for the second time in their history, were put out by Yorkshire for 27.

After only one over, Bowes made way for Verity, who took the first wicket when 12 runs had been scored. The remainder of the side scored 13 runs, Macaulay being particularly deadly with seven wickets for 9 runs in 14 overs.

Yorkshire began badly, Holmes and Mitchell being out with only 4 on the board. But after Leyland had been given a life in the slips, he and Sutcliffe settled down, and when Jupp came on scored freely. When the total reached 181, Sutcliffe was caught at the wicket off Thomas after scoring 113, including 10 sixes, from pulls over a short leg boundary. Jupp took the last five wickets for 12 runs.

Thanks to their last two men, Northamptonshire did a little better in the second innings, but Bowes and Macaulay were always on top, the latter's match record being eleven wickets for 34 runs.

Northamptonshire

A. H. Bakewell lbw, b Verity	4	c Verity b Bowes	6
A. W. Snowden b Macaulay	10	b Bowes	0
B. Bellamy c Macaulay b Verity	0	c Verity b Macaulay	12
J. E. Timms st. Wood b Verity	1	c Barber b Macaulay	1
V. W. C. Jupp b Macaulay	0	c Rhodes b Bowes	3
A. L. Cox b Macaulay	1	c Wood b Macaulay	4
A. G. Liddell b Macaulay	6	run out	0
A. D. G. Matthews c Rhodes b Macaulay	0	lbw, b Macaulay	8
W. C. Brown c Verity b Macaulay	0	c Rhodes b Bowes	1
R. J. Partridge b Macaulay	0	not out	14
A. E. Thomas not out	3	b Verity	10
Extras	2	Extras	9
	27		68

Yorkshire

P. Homes run out	0
H. Sutcliffe c Bellamy b Thomas	113
A. Mitchell c Patridge b Matthews	1
M. Leyland c Partridge b Jupp	36
W. Barber c Bakewell b Partridge	69
A. B. Sellars c Brown b Jupp	49
H. Verity c Brown b Jupp	0
A. Wood lbw, b Jupp	6
A. C. Rhodes lbw, b Jupp	14
G. G. Macaulay not out	4
W. E. Bowes c Matthews b Jupp	0
Extras	9
	301

Yorkshire Bowling

	Overs	Mdns.	Runs	Wkts.		Overs	Mdns.	Runs	Wkts.
Bowes	1	0	1	0	...	18	8	20	4
Macaulay	14	7	9	7	...	23	10	25	4
Verity	13	8	15	3	...	5.3	2	14	1

Northamptonshire Bowling

	Overs	Mdns.	Runs	Wkts.
Matthews	23	5	67	1
Thomas	18	2	38	1
Jupp	17	0	99	6
Partridge	19	4	54	1
Cox	9	0	34	0

Yorkshire v. *Kent*

Dover, August 19, 21, 22

Kent won by 44 runs

The last home county match of the Kent season resulted in an unexpected win by 44 runs, Yorkshire being all out in the last innings of the match for their lowest total of the summer.

In Kent's first innings the outstanding features were the batting of Woolley, Valentine and Ashdown, Leyland being the most successful Yorkshire bowler with four wickets for 56.

When Yorkshire batted, Leyland was the shining light, scoring 210 not out before Sellers declared as soon as the Kent total had been passed. Leyland scored his 210 out of 289 in 220 minutes, and hit 1 six and 28 fours.

When Kent went in again, rain on the previous evening had made the wicket difficult, and only F. G. H. Chalk made any prolonged stand, Verity taking nine wickets for 59 runs.

The task of scoring 133 runs, even on a difficult wicket, did not seem an impossible objective, but Freeman and Marriott, bowling unchanged, had the last Yorkshireman back in the pavilion with only 88 on the board. An interesting match and a fine win for Kent.

Kent

W. H. Ashdown c Wood b Verity	59	c Sellers b Verity	0
L. J. Todd c Verity b Bowes	11	lbw, b Verity	10
F. E. Woolley c Bowes b Macaulay	86	c Mitchell b Verity	8
L. E. G. Ames b Bowes	12	c and b Verity	15
B. H. Valentine lbw, b Leyland	90	c Rhodes b Verity	8
F. G. H. Chalk c Wood b Verity	20	c Sutcliffe b Verity	39
C. H. Knott b Leyland	19	c and b Verity	4
H. T. W. Hardinge c and b Leyland	0	hit wkt, b Leyland	19
A. E. Watt c Sellers b Verity	23	c Macaulay b Verity	4
A. P. Freeman not out	0	not out	7
C. S. Marriott b Leyland	0	st. Wood b Verity	9
Extras	12	Extras	10
	332		133

Yorkshire

P. Holmes c Valentine b Freeman	19	c Ashdown b Marriott	10
H. Sutcliffe run out	17	b Freeman	11
H. Verity c Ames b Freeman	2	c Chalk b Freeman	0
A. Mitchell lbw, b Freeman	13	lbw, b Freeman	0
M. Leyland not out	210	c Woolley b Freeman	10
W. Barber c Freeman b Ashdown	40	c Ashdown b Marriott	25
A. Wood lbw, b Marriott	15	c Knott b Freeman	19
A. B. Sellers not out	2	b Freeman	4
A. C. Rhodes did not bat		not out	3
G. G. Macaulay did not bat		c Watt b Marriott	4
W. E. Bowes absent hurt		absent hurt	0
Extras	15	Extras	1
	333*		88

* Innings declared closed.

Yorkshire Bowling

	Overs	Mdns.	Runs	Wkts.		Overs	Mdns.	Runs	Wkts.
Bowes	19	3	70	2					
Macaulay	17	3	39	1	...	14	5	26	0
Rhodes	13	0	57	0	...	3	1	10	0
Verity	29	8	78	3	...	30	10	59	9
Sellers	4	0	20	0					
Leyland	12.1	3	56	4	...	12	1	28	1

Kent Bowling

	Overs	Mdns.	Runs	Wkts.		Overs	Mdns.	Runs	Wkts.
Watt	22	3	71	0					
Freeman	46.4	16	100	3	...	23	8	51	6
Marriott	43	10	113	1	...	22.4	8	36	3
Ashdown	9	1	34	1					

APPEARANCES

The following 19 cricketers appeared for Yorkshire in Championship matches, the number of appearances being in parentheses:

W. Barber (30)	G. G. Macaulay (26)
W. E. Bowes (22)	A. Mitchell (28)
K. R. Davidson (3)	A. C. Rhodes (28)
F. Dennis (7)	A. B. Sellers (30)
S. Douglas (4)	T. F. Smailes (1)
C. H. Hall (4)	H. Sutcliffe (27)
W. E. Harbord (2)	C. Turner (5)
P. Holmes (28)	H. Verity (26)
T. A. Jacques (1)	A. Wood (30)
M. Leyland (28)	

POST MORTEM

In 1933, Yorkshire were indebted to the batting of Leyland, Mitchell, Sutcliffe and Barber and the bowling of Verity, Macaulay and Bowes for their seventeenth Championship. Sutcliffe could scarcely be expected to repeat his phenomenal scoring of the two previous seasons, and his aggregate dropped from 2,624 runs to 1,636, with an average just over half that of 1932. But, by way of compensation, Leyland, Mitchell and Barber all increased their aggregates ; Holmes not only scored fewer runs but averaged fewer than 20 per innings.

The bowling, however, was certainly stronger than in 1932, Verity, Macaulay and Bowes all taking 100 wickets in county matches, with Leyland lending a very useful hand on occasion.

Not one of Yorkshire's more notable Championships, perhaps, but well up to the average of such events.

INTERREGNUM

1934

Yorkshire were lower in the table in 1934 than in any season since 1911. Lancashire won the Championship, Yorkshire being sixth, Sussex, Derbyshire, Warwickshire and Kent being above them. Sutcliffe, Leyland, Verity and Bowes were frequently absent owing to Test match requirements, and this undoubtedly had its effect on the county's programme.

The following were the outstanding events of the season :

v. Derbyshire at Chesterfield : Verity had remarkable figures in the two Derbyshire innings—29 overs, 20 maidens, 18 runs, 5 wickets.

v. Middlesex at Lord's : Yorkshire lost by two wickets at Lord's, Hulme scoring 116 and I. A. R. Peebles taking twelve wickets for 153 runs. In the second innings of Middlesex (51 for eight wickets), Bowes took six wickets for 17 runs.

v. Hampshire at Bradford : Leyland scored 87 in the Yorkshire innings, and took four wickets for 16 runs in Hampshire's second innings.

v. Sussex at Sheffield : Yorkshire lost by an innings and 116 runs, Sutcliffe, Leyland, Bowes and Verity being absentees. In the second Yorkshire innings (115) James Langridge took nine wickets for 34 runs.

v. Northamptonshire at Northampton : In the two Northants innings (85 and 84) Bowes took ten wickets for 47 runs and Macaulay seven for 37.

v. Gloucestershire at Bristol : Yorkshire lost by nine wickets, Sinfield scoring 70 and taking nine wickets for 141.

v. Warwickshire at Scarborough : Yorkshire lost by one wicket after Warwickshire had scored 45 in their first innings. Paine took ten Yorkshire wickets for 121 runs, and J. H. Parsons scored 94 in Warwickshire's second innings.

v. Worcestershire at Worcester : Yorkshire won by ten wickets, Hutton scoring 196—his maiden hundred—in the first innings (416), and Bowes taking ten wickets for 126 runs.

v. Essex at Southend : Scoring 441 for eight wickets declared, Essex won by an innings and 46 runs, K. Farnes taking eleven wickets for 131 runs—four for 72 and seven for 59.

A. Mitchell headed the batting averages with 55·06 (1,652 runs), and Sutcliffe, Barber, Davidson and Turner all scored over 1,000 runs with averages exceeding 30 runs per innings ; but the bowling figures were below the usual Yorkshire standard. Verity and Bowes took 79 and 97 wickets respectively for 15 runs each, but no one else averaged under 21 runs per wicket.

EIGHTEENTH CHAMPIONSHIP

1935

Captain : A. B. Sellers

Yorkshire's eighteenth success in the County Championship might be termed comfortable, although the system of percentages contained possibilities of exotic and Gilbertian mathematical results. At the end of the season Yorkshire's percentage was 71·33 compared with Derbyshire's 63·33, a difference which may seem inadequate when it is noted that the winners had three more wins and five fewer defeats than the runners-up. In the end, however, even a points system fruitful of anomalies could not prevent the best team of the season from finishing at the top of the table.

THE FIRST SIX

	Plyd.	Won	Lost	1st Inns. Won	1st Inns. Lost	No Res.	Points Obtd.	Points Poss.	Per-cent.
Yorkshire	30	19	1	3	7	0	321	450	71·33
Derbyshire	28	16	6	4	2	0	266	420	63·33
Middlesex	24	11	5	6	1	1	202	360	56·11
Lancashire	28	12	6	8	1	1	227	420	54·04
Nottinghamshire	28	10	3	8	5	2	213	420	50·71
Leicestershire	24	11	9	2	2	0	181	360	50·27

METHOD OF SCORING : As in 1933.

MATCH SCORES AND RESULTS

Yorkshire v.	Ground	Yorkshire 1st Inns.	Yorkshire 2nd Inns.	Opponents 1st Inns.	Opponents 2nd Inns.	Result
Glamorgan	Neath	262	72 (3)	270	*211 (4)	Draw
Derbyshire	Chesterfield	328	102 (4)	382	*211 (6)	Draw
Gloucestershire	Gloucester	166	79 (2)	128	116	Y, 8 wickets
Sussex	Leeds	421	—	86	212	Y, inns. and 123 runs
Worcestershire	Sheffield	*445 (5)	—	92	189	Y, inns. and 164 runs
Kent	Bradford	131	192 (8)	182	140	Y, 2 wickets
Hampshire	Hull	*315 (5)	—	63	117	Y, inns. and 135 runs
Lancashire	Manchester	140	—	153	80 (0)	Draw
Warwickshire	Birmingham	161	225 (3)	254	221	Draw
Middlesex	Lord's	307 (6)	—	108	—	Draw
Leicestershire	Leeds	93	75 (2)	153	55	Draw
Glamorgan	Bradford	*423 (7)	—	178	145	Y, inns. and 100 runs
Northamptonshire	Kettering	280	—	62	52	Y, inns. and 166 runs
Essex	Colchester	253	*228 (5)	150	105	Y, 226 runs
Surrey	Sheffield	*582 (7)	—	206	256	Y, inns. and 120 runs
Kent	Tonbridge	326	245	171	247	Y, 153 runs
Northamptonshire	Harrogate	*459 (8)	—	289	94	Y, inns. and 76 run
Nottinghamshire	Nottingham	268	20 (1)	402	—	Draw
Gloucestershire	Hull	260	*294 (9)	203	154	Y, 197 runs
Nottinghamshire	Sheffield	421	—	232	286 (8)	Draw
Essex	Huddersfield	31	99	334	—	E, 204 runs
Lancashire	Bradford	225	181 (3)	53	352	Y, 7 wickets
Leicestershire	Leicester	393	15 (0)	274	130	Y, 10 wickets
Warwickshire	Bradford	354	4 (0)	105	250	Y, 10 wickets
Derbyshire	Scarborough	304	5 (0)	133	174	Y, 10 wickets
Middlesex	Leeds	367	—	183	102	Y, inns. and 82 runs
Worcestershire	Worcester	358	—	154	144	Y, inns. and 60 runs
Surrey	Oval	*299 (8)	—	44	26 (3)	Draw
Sussex	Hove	221	28 (1)	274	121	Draw
Hampshire	Portsmouth	*309 (8)	—	99	94	Y, inns. and 116 runs

* Innings declared closed.

185

Yorkshire beat Gloucestershire, Hampshire, Kent, Northamptonshire, Worcestershire twice; and Derbyshire, Essex, Glamorgan, Lancashire, Leicestershire, Middlesex, Surrey, Sussex, Warwickshire once.

Yorkshire were beaten by Essex once.

Yorkshire drew with Nottinghamshire twice; and Derbyshire, Glamorgan, Lancashire, Leicestershire, Middlesex, Surrey, Sussex, Warwickshire once.

SUMMARY

	Yorkshire	Opponents
Runs scored	10766	9701
Average per wicket	32·13	18·23
Hundreds	15	7
Other innings over 50	49	35
Ten wickets in match	11	2
Five wickets in innings	34	11
Highest total	582 (7) dec. *v.* Surrey	402 (Nottinghamshire)
Lowest total	31 *v.* Essex	44 (Surrey)
Totals over 400	6	1
Totals under 100	3	11

PRINCIPAL AVERAGES

	Inns.	Not Out	Runs	Highest Inns.	100's	50's	Aver.
H. Sutcliffe	36	3	1966	212	8	6	59·57
W. Barber	36	3	1678	255	4	8	50·88
A. Mitchell	36	3	1239	98	—	10	37·54
A. Wood	41	11	1087	123*	1	7	36·23
M. Leyland	31	2	915	95	—	7	31·55

* Not out.

	Balls	Balls per Wkt.	Runs	Wkts.	5 Wkts. in Inns.	Aver.
H. Verity	5439	33·78	2196	161	18	13·63
W. E. Bowes	4866	39·55	1819	138	12	15·18
T. F. Smailes	3350	47·85	1453	70	2	20·75

NOTES

In the first county match of the season (*v.* Glamorgan at Neath), Sutcliffe carried his bat through the innings for 135.

Against Worcestershire at Sheffield, Sutcliffe (200 not out) and Wood (123 not out) shared an unbroken partnership of 217 for the sixth wicket, and Bowes took thirteen wickets for 88 in the two Worcester innings.

For Hampshire at Hull, C. P. Mead was not out in each innings, scoring 25 and 18, and in the second innings J. Arnold made 70 of the 110 runs scored from the bat. Verity took fourteen wickets for 78 runs (seven for 31 and seven for 47).

When Middlesex scored 108 at Lord's, J. Smith (No. 10) made 57 in 30 minutes. Smailes took five wickets—all bowled—for 23.

Verity took eight Leicestershire wickets for 28 runs in the second innings at Leeds.

At Kettering, Bowes took sixteen wickets for 35 runs *v.* Northampton-shire (eight for 18 and eight for 17).

W. Barber scored 255 *v.* Surrey at Sheffield, Leyland taking nine wickets for 125 and scoring 80.

Against Nottinghamshire at Sheffield, P. A. Gibb scored 157 not out.

On successive days Yorkshire were dismissed before lunch for 31 and 99 by Essex at Huddersfield.

Bowes (six for 16) and Rawlin (three for 28) bowled unchanged in Lancashire's first innings (53) at Bradford.

Sutcliffe scored 212 out of Yorkshire's 393 at Leicester.

Yorkshire beat Middlesex by an innings at Leeds, Hutton scoring 131 and Verity taking eleven wickets for 73 (six for 53 and five for 20).

During the season, eight Yorkshire bowlers took 18 or more wickets at costs ranging from 15·18 to 24·26 runs per wicket.

In 1935, A. Wood scored over 1,000 runs and dismissed 60 opposing batsmen at the wicket.

HOW IT WAS DONE

	100's	50's	10 Wkts. in Match	5 Wkts. in Inns.	50 Runs & 5 Wkts. in Match
W. Barber	4	8	–	–	–
W. E. Bowes	–	–	5	12	–
P. A. Gibb	1	1	–	–	–
L. Hutton	1	–	–	–	–
M. Leyland	–	7	–	1	1
G. G. Macaulay	–	–	–	1	–
A. Mitchell	–	10	–	–	–
A. B. Sellers	–	3	–	–	–
T. F. Smailes	–	3	1	2	1
H. Sutcliffe	8	6	–	–	–
C. Turner	–	4	–	1	–
H. Verity	–	–	5	18	–
A. Wood	1	7	–	–	–
Total	15	49	11	34	2

FIELDING (196 Catches)

No. of Catches		No. of Catches	
26	A. B. Sellers	6	P. A. Gibb
24	C. Turner	6	L. Hutton
22	H. Verity	4	W. E. Hardbord
20	A. Mitchell	4	G. G. Macaulay
14	H. Sutcliffe	4	E. P. Robinson
13	W. E. Bowes	4	" Sub."
13	T. F. Smailes	2	K. R. Davidson
12	B. Barber	2	E. R. Rawlin
10	H. Fisher	1	T. Bottomley
8	M. Leyland	1	T. A. Jacques

1935

WICKETKEEPING

	Stumped	Caught	Total
A. Wood	17	43	60
P. A. Gibb	—	3	3
Total	17	46	63

TOTALS

400 Runs and Over

Yorkshire (6)

582 (7)* *v.* Surrey, Sheffield
459 (8)* *v.* Northamptonshire, Harrogate
445 (5)* *v.* Worcestershire, Sheffield

423 (7)* *v.* Glamorgan, Bradford
421 *v.* Essex, Leeds
421* *v.* Nottinghamshire, Sheffield

Opponents (1)

402, Nottinghamshire, Nottingham

* Innings declared closed.

Under 100 Runs

Yorkshire (3)

31 and 39 *v.* Essex, Huddersfield   93 *v.* Leicestershire, Leeds

Opponents (11)

44, Surrey, Oval
62 and 52, Northamptonshire, Kettering
53, Lancashire, Bradford
55, Leicestershire, Leeds
63, Hampshire, Hull

86, Sussex, Leeds
92, Worcestershire, Sheffield
94, Northamptonshire, Harrogate
99 and 94, Hampshire, Portsmouth

FIRST WICKET PARTNERSHIPS

Score	Partners	Against	Ground
207	A. Mitchell, W. Barber	Middlesex	Lord's
147	H. Sutcliffe, A. Mitchell	Worcestershire	Worcester
138	A. Mitchell, W. Barber	Surrey	Sheffield
111	H. Sutcliffe, L. Hutton	Hampshire	Hull
109	H. Sutcliffe, A. Mitchell	Hampshire	Portsmouth
106	A. Mitchell, W. Barber	Kent	Tonbridge

50 RUNS AND 5 WICKETS

Score	Analyses	Player	Against	Ground
89	2-8, 4-69	T. F. Smailes	Sussex	Leeds
80	5-46, 4-79	M. Leyland	Surrey	Sheffield

MATCHES OF THE SEASON

Yorkshire v. *Kent*

Bradford, June 1, 3, 4

Yorkshire won by two wickets

After an exciting and fluctuating struggle with Kent at Bradford, Yorkshire won by two. wickets.

Useful innings by Woolley, Todd and Valentine took Kent's first innings total to 182 ; but after Sutcliffe and Hutton had scored 70 for Yorkshire's first wicket, the remaining batsmen added only 41 (Freeman six for 47), and Kent resumed with a lead of 41.

Ashdown and Woolley made a promising start, putting on 107 for the first wicket, but the other nine wickets went down for 33 runs, Verity having a deadly spell when he took five wickets for 15.

Yorkshire obtained the 192 runs required for the loss of eight wickets, but this achievement was mainly due to Sutcliffe, who scored an invaluable 110, and at the critical moment shared a seventh wicket partnership of 65 with Sellers.

In the two innings, Freeman took thirteen wickets for 155 runs, only Sutcliffe playing him with any confidence.

Kent

W. H. Ashdown b Bowes	8	c Sellers b Verity	44
A. Fagg b Smailes	0	lbw, b Macaulay	0
F. E. Woolley lbw, b Macaulay	33	b Macaulay	73
L. E. G. Ames b Bowes	11	b Macaulay	0
L. J. Todd not out	63	c and b Macaulay	5
B. H. Valentine st. Wood b Verity	35	c Mitchell b Verity	3
A. P. F. Chapman c Bowes b Macaulay	1	c Macaulay b Verity	0
W. H. V. Levett c Sellers b Verity	0	lbw, b Macaulay	1
D. V. P. Wright st. Wood b Verity	6	st. Wood b Verity	0
A. P. Freeman c and b Verity	6	st. Wood b Verity	7
C. Lewis c Sutcliffe b Leyland	3	not out	0
Extras	16	Extras	7
	182		140

Yorkshire

H. Sutcliffe c Woolley b Freeman	44	lbw, b Freeman	110
L. Hutton hit wkt, b Freeman	42	lbw, b Lewis	5
A. Mitchell st. Ames b Lewis	1	lbw, b Freeman	10
M. Leyland b Lewis	15	c Chapman b Freeman	15
W. Barber lbw, b Freeman	0	c Valentine b Freeman	3
A. B. Sellers c Valentine b Freeman	16	not out	34
A. Wood not out	5	b Freeman	11
H. Verity lbw, b Freeman	0	b Freeman	0
T. F. Smailes lbw, b Lewis	5	c Fagg b Freeman	0
G. G. Macaulay st. Ames b Lewis	0	not out	1
W. E. Bowes st. Ames b Freeman	3		
Extras	0	Extras	3
	131		192

Yorkshire Bowling

	Overs	Mdns.	Runs	Wkts.		Overs	Mdns.	Runs	Wkts.
Bowes	15	2	38	2	...	6	0	28	0
Smailes	9	0	36	1	...	3	2	13	0
Macaulay	19	6	44	2	...	12	2	40	5
Verity	18	4	47	4	...	12.3	1	52	5
Leyland	1	0	1	1					

Kent Bowling

	Overs	Mdns.	Runs	Wkts.		Overs	Mdns.	Runs	Wkts.
Ashdown	5	4	8	0					
Todd	3	0	13	0	...	3	1	8	0
Wright	4	0	18	0	...	2	0	7	0
Freeman	23.2	8	47	6	...	39.1	11	108	7
Lewis	20	6	45	4	...	34	7	66	1

Yorkshire v. *Essex*

Huddersfield, July 31, August 1, 2

Essex won by an innings and 204 runs

The first of Yorkshire's matches with Essex provided the sensation of the season and a crushing defeat for the prospective Champions.

On the opening day Yorkshire's first innings ended before half-past twelve for 31 runs, the lowest total by a Yorkshire side for 26 years. The debacle was caused by fine fast bowling by Read (six for 11) and Nichols (four for 17), who bowled unchanged and got rid of the whole side in 76 balls.

When Essex batted, five wickets fell for 65 runs, and then Nichols and Belle came to the rescue with a partnership of 174 in three hours, Nichols scoring 146 before he was caught by Hutton off Bowes. His splendid innings included 2 sixes and 16 fours. The Essex innings ended with a total of 334 just before close of play, and Yorkshire had two days in which to save the match.

When play restarted on the second day, it was soon seen that the Nichols-Read offensive was still in being, and before one o'clock the match was over, Essex winning by an innings and 204 runs. With the exception of three overs from Eastman, Read and Nichols bowled unchanged.

Nichols' performance in the match was the best of his career—146 and eleven wickets for 54 (four for 17 and seven for 37) in 130 balls.

Of Yorkshire's 130 runs, Wood (37) and Bowes (23) scored 60.

Yorkshire

H. Sutcliffe c Sheffield b Nichols	4	c Eastman b Nichols	1
W. Barber c Wilcox b Read	1	b Nichols	18
A. B. Sellers c Wilcox b Read	2	lbw, b Nichols	2
M. Leyland b Read	0	b Read	2
P. A. Gibb c Rist b Read	0	lbw, b Nichols	11
C. Turner c Sheffield b Read	4	b Nichols	13
L. Hutton b Nichols	0	lbw, b Nichols	0
A. Wood c Read b Nichols	13	b Nichols	24
H. Fisher b Read	0	c Rist b Read	2
H. Verity not out	0	c Smith (P.) b Read	6
W. E. Bowes c Rist b Nichols	4	not out	19
Extras	3	Extras	1
	31		**99**

Essex

J. R. Sheffield b Verity	5
F. Rist c Gibb b Verity	35
D. R. Wilcox c Wood b Turner	2
J. A. Cutmore c Wood b Fisher	2
J. O'Connor b Fisher	0
M. S. Nichols c Hutton b Bowes	146
B. H. Belle c Verity b Leyland	63
L. C. Eastman c Gibb b Bowes	23
P. Smith b Bowes	5
R. Smith not out	16
H. D. Read st. Wood b Verity	0
Extras	37
	334

Essex Bowling

	Overs	Mdns.	Runs	Wkts.		Overs	Mdns.	Runs	Wkts.
Nichols	6.4	2	17	4	...	15	3	37	7
Read	6	1	11	6	...	14.4	2	51	3
Eastman						3	0	10	0

Yorkshire Bowling

	Overs	Mdns.	Runs	Wkts.
Bowes	37	8	77	3
Turner	16	2	41	1
Verity	24.2	4	79	3
Fisher	25	5	62	2
Leyland	5	1	38	1

APPEARANCES

The following 21 cricketers appeared for Yorkshire in Championship matches, the number of appearances being in parentheses :

W. Barber (26)
T. Bottomley (1)
W. E. Bowes (25)
K. R. Davidson (2)
H. Fisher (23)
P. A. Gibb (6)
W. E. Harbord (5)
L. Hutton (14)
T. A. Jacques (1)
M. Leyland (23)
G. G. Macaulay (8)

A. Mitchell (26)
J. H. Pearson (1)
E. R. Rawlin (5)
E. P. Robinson (9)
A. B. Sellers (29)
T. F. Smailes (25).
H. Sutcliffe (26)
C. Turner (19)
H. Verity (27)
A. Wood (29)

POST MORTEM

Apart from the fantastic collapses against Essex at Huddersfield, Yorkshire's batting was solid and reliable, nine of the regular members of the side averaging over 22 runs an innings. But the bowling was less satisfactory. Verity and Bowes each took well over 100 wickets at low cost, but their only regular support came from Smailes, whose 70 wickets cost 20·75 runs each. During the season ten bowlers took wickets in Championship matches, but the task of getting the other sides out really depended on the efforts of Verity, Bowes and Smailes. Fortunately for Yorkshire, the Verity-Bowes combination rarely failed.

INTERREGNUM

1936

For the first time since 1874 Derbyshire won the County Championship, Middlesex being second and Yorkshire third. Some of the percentages and positions in the table suggested that the points system was rather apt to produce anomalies.

The highlights of the season were as follows :

v. Essex at Hull : In the first county match of the season Leyland scored 263 of the Yorkshire total (454).

v. Worcestershire at Stourbridge : Yorkshire lost by 11 runs, Howorth taking five wickets for 21 runs in the second innings. Verity took thirteen wickets for 88 runs (five for 48 and eight for 40).

v. Kent at Sheffield : Deadly bowling by Verity was mainly responsible for Kent's dismissal for 107 and 39, his analysis being six wickets for 26 runs and nine for 12 in 39 balls.

v. Essex at Westcliff : Verity took fifteen wickets for 100 runs (nine for 48 in the second innings) and also scored 59 not out in Yorkshire's second innings. Yorkshire won by 137 runs.

v. Surrey at Leeds : A good opening partnership by Sutcliffe (129) and Hutton (163), followed by 163 not out by Leyland, enabled Yorkshire to declare with the score 519 for six wickets. Good bowling by Bowes in the first innings and Smailes in the second got rid of Surrey for 127 and 207.

v. Nottinghamshire at Bradford : Curtailed by rain into a draw, Verity was the central figure of yet another match, taking eleven wickets for 90 runs.

v. Middlesex at Scarborough : Yorkshire won by an innings and 170 runs, Sutcliffe scoring 202, Leyland 107, and all the bowlers doing well. In the second innings of Middlesex, Hutton made 4 catches.

v. Leicestershire at Scarborough : Bowes took thirteen wickets for 96 runs (eight for 56 and five for 40).

Leyland headed the Yorkshire batsmen in 1936, scoring 1,291 and averaging 46·10. Only Sutcliffe and Hutton also scored 1,000 runs in county games.

The bowling depended mainly on Bowes, Verity and Smailes, who in the majority of matches proved quite capable of doing all that was required. Each took 100 wickets, their figures being: Bowes 109 wickets (average 12·33), Verity 153 (12·69), Smailes 101 (18·94). Leyland was the only other bowler to take 25 wickets.

N

NINETEENTH CHAMPIONSHIP

1937

Captain : A. B. Sellers

After a neck-and-neck race with Middlesex, Yorkshire contrived to win by a short head in 1937—a percentage of 71·90 to 68·33 representing the difference. On paper, the figures suggest that the difference should have been greater, Yorkshire winning 18 matches and losing 2, while Middlesex had 15 wins and 4 defeats, but the percentage system in force in 1937 was capable of playing strange mathematical tricks.

THE FIRST SIX

	Plyd.	Won	Lost	1st Inns. Won	1st Inns. Lost	No Res.	Points Obtd.	Points Poss.	Per-cent.
Yorkshire	28	18	2	4	4	0	302	420	71·90
Middlesex	24	15	4	3	2	0	246	360	68·33
Derbyshire	28	14	6	2	4	2	240	420	57·14
Gloucestershire	30	15	10	2	3	0	244	450	54·22
Sussex	32	13	7	8	4	0	247	480	51·45
Essex	28	13	11	2	1	1	212	420	50·47

METHOD OF SCORING : As in 1933.

MATCH SCORES AND RESULTS

Yorkshire v.	Ground	Yorkshire 1st Inns.	Yorkshire 2nd Inns.	Opponents 1st Inns.	Opponents 2nd Inns.	Result
Lancashire	Manchester	270	35 (0)	106	197	Y, 10 wickets
Warwickshire	Birmingham	*492 (9)	—	496 (8)	—	Draw
Sussex	Sheffield	465	166 (5)	566	—	Draw
Gloucestershire	Leeds	157	147	77	87	Y, 140 runs
Derbyshire	Chesterfield	261	94 (4)	248	106	Y, 6 wickets
Worcestershire	Stourbridge	460	—	190	189	Y, inns. and 81 runs
Kent	Bradford	297	*328 (7)	254	84	Y, 87 runs
Middlesex	Lord's	218	131	371	—	M, inns. and 22 runs
Kent	Tonbridge	*462 (8)	—	141	270	Y, inns. and 51 runs
Derbyshire	Sheffield	*525 (4)	—	145	281	Y, inns. and 99 runs
Leicestershire	Hull	523 (3)	77 (4)	458	—	Draw
Nottinghamshire	Leeds	379	7 (0)	191	346	Draw
Essex	Ilford	440	—	152	80	Y, inns. and 208 runs
Surrey	Bradford	398	199 (7)	187	409	Y, 3 wickets
Middlesex	Sheffield	238	128 (4)	267	—	Draw
Hampshire	Hull	244	119 (6)	180	182	Y, 4 wickets
Nottinghamshire	Nottingham	209	101 (3)	326	*145 (7)	Draw
Glamorgan	Cardiff	255	*103 (4)	150	104 (5)	Draw
Gloucestershire	Bristol	346	*273 (4)	286	214	Y, 119 runs
Essex	Huddersfield	279	69 (0)	184	163	Y, 10 wickets
Lancashire	Sheffield	246	168	324	91 (5)	L, 5 wickets
Leicestershire	Leicester	*333 (9)	*183 (9)	202	185	Y, 129 runs
Warwickshire	Leeds	282	106 (1)	205	180	Y, 9 wickets
Worcestershire	Bradford	*258 (8)	—	120	129	Y, inns. and 9 runs
Glamorgan	Scarborough	356	*171 (7)	243	199	Y, 85 runs
Surrey	Oval	463	—	273	295 (6)	Draw
Sussex	Eastbourne	457	—	198	143	Y, inns. and 116 runs
Hampshire	Bournemouth	191	88 (0)	93	185	Y, 10 wickets

* Innings declared closed.

Yorkshire beat Derbyshire, Essex, Gloucestershire, Hampshire, Kent, Worcestershire twice; and Glamorgan, Lancashire, Leicestershire, Surrey, Sussex, Warwickshire once.

Yorkshire were beaten by Lancashire, Middlesex once.

Yorkshire drew with Nottinghamshire twice; and Glamorgan, Leicestershire, Middlesex, Surrey, Sussex, Warwickshire once.

SUMMARY

	Yorkshire	Opponents
Runs scored	12197	10897
Average per wicket	33·97	22·37
Hundreds	21	13
Other innings over 50	51	37
Ten wickets in match	9	2
Five wickets in innings	30	16
Highest total	525 (4) dec.	556 (Sussex)
	v. Derbyshire	
Lowest total	131 v. Middlesex	77 (Gloucestershire)
Totals over 400	9	4
Totals under 100	—	5

PRINCIPAL AVERAGES

	Inns.	Not Out	Runs	Highest Inns.	100's	50's	Aver.
L. Hutton	36	5	1728	271*	5	7	55·74
H. Sutcliffe	45	5	1822	189	4	9	45·55
N. W. D. Yardley	17	3	616	101	1	3	44·00
W. Barber	37	5	1270	115	3	5	39·68
A. Mitchell	42	6	1286	105	2	7	35·72
M. Leyland	25	1	856	167	3	2	35·66
C. Turner	32	4	861	84	—	6	30·75

* Not out

	Balls	Balls per Wkt.	Runs	Wkts.	5 Wkts. in Inns.	Aver.
H. Verity	6471	41·21	2270	157	16	14·45
W. E. Bowes	3559	53·92	1330	66	4	20·15
E. P. Robinson	3292	49·87	1528	66	3	23·15
T. F. Smailes	5347	57·49	2219	93	4	23·86

NOTES

In the second county match of the season (Yorkshire v. Warwickshire at Birmingham) the first four batsmen on each side each scored over 50; Sutcliffe 70, Hutton 88, Barber 50, Leyland 66 for Yorkshire; and N. Kilner 56, Croom 118, R. E. S. Wyatt 152, Dollery 110 for Warwickshire. Yorkshire lost first innings points after declaring at 492 for nine wickets.

Sussex scored 566 after Yorkshire had made 465 at Sheffield, John Langridge scoring 175.

In the second innings of Kent at Bradford, Smailes took five wickets for 16 runs, Sellers catching three consecutive batsmen off his bowling.

Yorkshire beat Kent at Tonbridge in the last five minutes of the extra half-hour.

W. F. Price made 7 catches at the wicket (a record) in Yorkshire's first innings v. Middlesex at Lord's.

In four consecutive innings for Yorkshire, Hutton scored hundreds : 136 v. Kent at Tonbridge, 271 not out v. Derbyshire at Sheffield, 153 v. Leicestershire at Hull, and 124 v. Essex at Ilford.

Yorkshire scored 523 for three wickets declared v. Leicestershire at Hull, Sutcliffe and Hutton scoring 315 for the first wicket.

Verity took six Essex wickets for 10 runs in the second innings at Ilford.

Lancashire beat Yorkshire by five wickets at Manchester, J. Iddon taking nine wickets for 42 runs in Yorkshire's second innings.

Hutton took ten wickets for 101 runs (four for 25 and six for 76) v. Leicestershire at Leicester.

Against Warwickshire at Leeds, Verity took fourteen wickets for 92 runs—nine for 43 and five for 49.   Sutcliffe and Hutton each scored 75.

At the Oval, Fishlock scored 113 and 105.

Yorkshire beat Sussex at Eastbourne by an innings and 116 runs, five Yorkshiremen scoring over 50 and Verity taking fourteen wickets for 132 runs.

On eleven occasions during the season the Yorkshire innings opened with a century first wicket partnership, Sutcliffe and Hutton each having a share in nine.   In all Yorkshire matches 36 century partnerships were recorded, Hutton being concerned with 20—9 for the first wicket, 5 for the second, 3 for the third, 2 for the fourth and 1 for the fifth.

HOW IT WAS DONE

	100's	50's	10 Wkts. in Match	5 Wkts. in Inns.	50 Runs & 5 Wkts. in Match
W. Barber	3	5	–	–	–
W. E. Bowes	–	–	1	4	–
P. A. Gibb	–	1	–	–	–
L. Hutton	5	7	1	1	–
M. Leyland	3	2	–	–	–
A. Mitchell	2	7	–	–	–
J. A. Richardson	–	1	–	–	–
E. P. Robinson	–	2	1	3	1
A. B. Sellers	2	1	–	–	–
T. F. Smailes	1	2	–	4	1
H. Sutcliffe	4	9	–	–	–
C. Turner	–	6	–	2	1
H. Verity	–	1	6	16	1
A. Wood	–	4	–	–	–
N. W. D. Yardley	1	3	–	–	–
Total	21	51	9	30	4

FIELDING (215 Catches)

No. of Catches		No. of Catches	
38	A. Mitchell	9	W. E. Bowes
27	C. Turner	6	N. W. D. Yardley
24	A. B. Sellers	5	M. Leyland
19	L. Hutton	2	F. Wilkinson
19	T. F. Smailes	2	G. A. Wilson
18	E. P. Robinson	2	" Sub."
18	H. Sutcliffe	1	J. Hampshire
13	W. Barber	1	J. A. Richardson
11	H. Verity		

WICKETKEEPING

	Stumped	Caught	Total
A. Wood	15	36	51
H. Crick	—	4	4
Total	15	40	55

TOTALS

400 Runs and Over

Yorkshire (9)

525 (4)* v. Derbyshire, Sheffield 462 (8)* v. Kent, Tonbridge
523 (3)* v. Leicestershire, Hull 460 v. Worcestershire, Stourbridge
492 (9)* v. Warwickshire, Birmingham 457 v. Sussex, Eastbourne
465 v. Sussex, Sheffield 440 v. Essex, Ilford
463 v. Surrey, Oval

Opponents (4)

566, Sussex, Sheffield 458, Leicestershire, Hull
496 (8), Warwickshire, Birmingham 409, Surrey, Bradford

* Innings declared closed.

Under 100 Runs

Yorkshire (0)
None.

Opponents (5)

77 and 87, Gloucestershire, Leeds 84, Kent, Bradford
80, Essex, Ilford 93, Hampshire, Bournemouth

FIRST WICKET PARTNERSHIPS

Score	Partners	Against	Ground
315	H. Sutcliffe, L. Hutton	Leicestershire	Hull
181	H. Sutcliffe, L. Hutton	Derbyshire	Sheffield
160	H. Sutcliffe, L. Hutton	Warwickshire	Birmingham
158	H. Sutcliffe, A. Mitchell	Sussex	Sheffield
129	H. Sutcliffe, L. Hutton	Warwickshire	Leeds
118	H. Sutcliffe, L. Hutton	Surrey	Bradford
109	H. Sutcliffe, L. Hutton	Essex	Ilford
106	H. Sutcliffe, L. Hutton	Surrey	Oval

50 RUNS AND 5 WICKETS

Scores	Analyses	Player	Against	Ground
65, 80*	3-86, 5-16	T. F. Smailes	Kent	Bradford
81*	5-45	C. Turner	Derbyshire	Sheffield
76, 0*	4-62, 5-113	H. Verity	Surrey	Bradford
61, 8	2-52, 4-52	E. P. Robinson	Glamorgan	Cardiff

* Not out.

MATCHES OF THE SEASON

Yorkshire v. *Derbyshire*

Sheffield, June 19, 21, 22

Yorkshire won by an innings and 99 runs

After Derbyshire's first innings had closed for 145, Turner taking five wickets for 45, Yorkshire piled up their biggest total of the season—525 for four wickets.

Sutcliffe and Hutton started with a partnership of 181 for the first wicket, Sutcliffe scoring 86 before he was caught at the wicket off Townsend. Mitchell and Leyland were soon out, but Hutton and Barber added 105 and Hutton and Turner 191, at which point Sellers declared, Hutton being 271 not out and Turner 81 not out.

In scoring his highest innings, Hutton was batting for seven hours.

Smith played a fine innings of 158 when Derbyshire went in 380 runs behind, but received little assistance. Townsend helped him in a stand of 123, and G. H. Pope scored a useful 30, but when the last wicket fell 99 runs were still needed to save the innings defeat.

Derbyshire

D. Smith c Turner b Robinson	40	lbw, b Robinson	158
A. E. Alderman c Mitchell b Turner	3	st. Wood b Turner	0
C. Elliott c Mitchell b Smailes	11	c Smailes b Turner	0
L. F. Townsend c Robinson b Turner	6	lbw, b Verity	51
E. Carrington c Turner b Smailes	0	c Mitchell b Verity	12
G. H. Pope c Wood b Turner	22	c Leyland b Smailes	30
H. Elliott c Mitchell b Turner	5	b Turner	5
A. V. Pope c Sutcliffe b Verity	31	lbw, b Verity	1
R. H. R. Buckston c Sellers b Verity	18	not out	6
T. B. Mitchell lbw, b Turner	7	c Hutton b Verity	3
W. H. Copson not out	0	c Barber b Robinson	1
Extras	2	Extras	14
	145		281

Yorkshire

H. Sutcliffe c Elliott (H.) b Townsend	86
L. Hutton not out	271
A. Mitchell c Smith b Copson	17
M. Leyland b Pope (A. V.)	8
W. Barber b Copson	39
C. Turner not out	81
A. B. Sellers did not bat	
T. F. Smailes did not bat	
A. Wood did not bat	
E. P. Robinson did not bat	
H. Verity did not bat	

Extras 23

525*

* Innings declared closed.

Yorkshire Bowling

	Overs	Mdns.	Runs	Wkts.		Overs	Mdns.	Runs	Wkts.
Smailes	18	3	60	2	...	21	5	61	1
Turner	31	14	45	5	...	33	14	63	3
Robinson	7	0	27	1	...	25.2	7	44	2
Verity	6.1	1	11	2	...	43	18	86	4
Leyland						2	0	4	0
Hutton						2	0	9	0

Derbyshire Bowling

	Overs	Mdns.	Runs	Wkts.
Copson	37	8	124	2
Pope (A. V.)	37	6	77	1
Mitchell	23	0	115	0
Pope (G. H.)	29	4	97	0
Townsend	15	1	45	1
Smith	6	0	30	0
Elliott (C.)	4	0	14	0

Yorkshire v. *Surrey*

Bradford, July 3, 5, 6

Yorkshire won by three wickets

In his Benefit match at Bradford, Mitchell had the satisfaction of playing a big part in Yorkshire's narrow defeat of Surrey.

Sutcliffe and Hutton gave Yorkshire a good start by scoring 118 for the first wicket, and Sutcliffe continued the good work after Hutton was out until he had scored 138. Mitchell, Turner and Sellers contributed modest but useful scores, and Verity hit well for 76. A total of 398 was eminently comfortable.

Surrey were less successful, finding Verity and Robinson difficult, and found themselves invited to follow on 211 behind at the end of their first innings.

The second Surrey innings was quite another story. Fishlock produced a fine innings of 146, Gregory, Squires, Barling, Holmes and Brown all treated the bowling with considerable and profitable disrespect, and by the time Verity dismissed the last four men at the same total, 199 runs were needed for a Yorkshire win with 108 minutes left for play.

Hutton was run out before he had scored, but Sutcliffe and Mitchell then knocked up 108 in 55 minutes. The remaining 91 runs were then scored in 46 minutes, thanks mainly to the ruthlessness of Leyland and Smailes.

In the match, Verity scored 76 and took nine wickets for 175 runs.

Yorkshire

H. Sutcliffe c Sandham b Squires	138	b Squires	56
L. Hutton c Gregory b Brown	67	run out	0
A. Mitchell st. Brooks b Brown	15	c Squires b Brown	57
M. Leyland run out	7	c Barling b Brown	21
C. Turner c Fishlock b Watts	22	b Brown	2
A. B. Sellers c Brooks b Squires	24	b Brown	3
T. F. Smailes b Brown	7	not out	47
H. Verity c Brooks b Brown	76	not out	0
E. P. Robinson b Walls	16	c Brown b Squires	11
H. Crick lbw, b Gover	2		
W. E. Bowes not out	9		
Extras	15	Extras	2
	398		199

Surrey

A. Sandham c Smailes b Verity	19	lbw, b Bowes	2
L. B. Fishlock c Sellers b Verity	41	c Mitchell b Turner	146
R. J. Gregory lbw, b Robinson	15	c Mitchell b Bowes	73
H. S. Squires c Mitchell b Verity	10	c Smailes b Leyland	50
T. H. Barling c Bowes b Verity	28	c Sellers b Verity	31
J. F. Parker b Robinson	0	c Verity b Bowes	4
E. R. T. Holmes not out	34	c Sutcliffe b Verity	44
F. R. Brown b Robinson	23	c Crick b Verity	51
E. A. Watts b Robinson	4	c Turner b Verity	0
E. W. Brooks lbw, b Robinson	0	not out	0
A. R. Gover c Sellers b Robinson	6	c Crick b Verity	0
Extras	7	Extras	8
	187		409

Surrey Bowling

	Overs	Mdns.	Runs	Wkts.		Overs	Mdns.	Runs	Wkts.
Gover	28	3	66	1	...	7	0	39	0
Watts	21	1	94	2	...	4	0	24	0
Parker	11	2	50	0					
Brown	33.5	4	144	4	...	14.4	0	67	4
Squires	18	7	29	2	...	12	0	67	2

Yorkshire Bowling

	Overs	Mdns.	Runs	Wkts.		Overs	Mdns.	Runs	Wkts.
Bowes	15	4	37	0	...	35	9	91	3
Smailes	15	5	31	0	...	19	3	63	0
Turner	7	0	12	0	...	14	4	34	1
Verity	24	5	62	4	...	38.3	10	113	5
Robinson	11	1	33	6	...	16	3	66	0
Hutton	1	0	5	0					
Leyland						15	6	34	1

APPEARANCES

The following 21 cricketers appeared for Yorkshire in Championship matches, the number of appearances being in parentheses :

W. Barber (25)
W. E. Bowes (17)
H. Brearley (1)
H. Crick (2)
P. A. Gibb (2)
J. Hampshire (3)
H. S. Hargreaves (4)
L. Hutton (22)
M. Leyland (19)
A. Mitchell (26)
J. A. Richardson (4)

E. P. Robinson (18)
A. B. Sellers (25)
T. F. Smailes (26)
H. Sutcliffe (27)
C. Turner (23)
H. Verity (24)
F. Wilkinson (1)
G. A. Wilson (2)
A. Wood (26)
N. W. D. Yardley (11)

POST MORTEM

As a rule the Yorkshire bowling was a deciding factor in the winning of Championships, but in 1937 the batsmen must be given most credit for the success. Hutton, Sutcliffe and Yardley all averaged over 44 runs an innings, four other batsmen averaged over 30, and a further five had averages ranging from 28·33 to 21·38. Of the 21 cricketers who represented the county during the season, all except Hargreaves, who played in only four matches, averaged over 15 runs an innings.

The bowling was less satisfactory. Verity was as consistent as ever with 157 wickets for 14·45 runs each, but no other bowler took his wickets for less than 20 runs each. Owing to a knee injury suffered in the first match of the season at Lord's, Bowes was out of the team for two months. Brilliant fielding helped the bowlers, but the attack was below the normal Yorkshire standard.

At the conclusion of the season an unofficial challenge match was played at the Oval between the two leaders in the Championship, which Yorkshire won by an innings and 115 runs.

TWENTIETH CHAMPIONSHIP

1938

Captain : A. B. Sellers

A new method of scoring in the competition did not deprive Yorkshire of their second Championship in successive seasons, though the latest system was as capable of anomalies as previous inventions. At one time Middlesex threatened danger, but six wins and two draws in August took Yorkshire to safety and success.

THE FIRST SIX

	Plyd.	Won	Lost	Drawn	1st Inns. Lead in Match Lost	1st Inns. Lead in Match Drawn	Pts.	Aver.
Yorkshire	28	20	2	6	0	4	256	9·14
Middlesex	22	15	5	2	0	1	184	8·36
Surrey	25	12	6	7	2	5	172	6·88
Lancashire	28	14	6	8	0	6	192	6·85
Derbyshire	25	11	8	6	3	6	160	6·40
Essex	26	12	11	3	3	2	164	6·30

METHOD OF SCORING : Each county to play a minimum of 24 matches. 12 points for a win ; 4 points for a first innings lead ; a side obtaining first innings lead and then winning the match receives 12 points ; if it loses it retains 4 points. In deciding the Championship the points gained are divided by the number of matches played, the county with the highest average being Champions.

MATCH SCORES AND RESULTS

Yorkshire v.	Ground	Yorkshire 1st Inns.	Yorkshire 2nd Inns.	Opponents 1st Inns.	Opponents 2nd Inns.	Result
Essex	Ilford	289	257 (6)	327	218	Y, 4 wickets
Gloucestershire	Gloucester	266	58 (0)	*428 (9)	—	Draw
Essex	Sheffield	171	177	131	90	Y, 127 runs
Sussex	Leeds	401	—	260	115 (3)	Draw
Kent	Hull	—	—	78(1)	—	Draw
Hampshire	Huddersfield	202	24(3)	188	—	Draw
Lancashire	Bradford	273	98 (2)	232	138	Y, 8 wickets
Warwickshire	Birmingham	415	—	41	232	Y, inns. and 142 runs
Middlesex	Leeds	173	84 (3)	105	148	Y, 7 wickets
Glamorgan	Cardiff	343	*221(4)	250	184	Y, 130 runs
Surrey	Sheffield	416	—	52	162	Y, inns. and 202 runs
Glamorgan	Hull	273	* 68(5)	179	150	Y, 12 runs
Nottinghamshire	Bradford	133	—	87	95 (5)	Draw
Worcestershire	Worcester	*359 (9)	—	118	223	Y, inns. and 18 runs
Worcestershire	Bradford	93 (4)	—	227	—	Draw
Derbyshire	Chesterfield	198	*210(7)	158	87	Y, 163 runs
Northamptonshire	Peterborough	*435 (5)	—	196	177	Y, inns. and 62 runs
Middlesex	Lord's	144	103	205	43 (2)	M, 8 wickets
Hampshire	Bournemouth	254	159 (3)	199	211	Y, 7 wickets
Surrey	Oval	100	285	264	*383 (3)	S, 262 runs
Northamptonshire	Scarborough	311	128(4)	283	155	Y, 6 wickets
Lancashire	Manchester	453	—	133	120	Y, inns. and 200 runs
Leicestershire	Leicester	*440 (6)	—	297	69	Y, inns. and 74 runs
Derbyshire	Sheffield	192	*232 (9)	113	101	Y, 210 runs
Warwickshire	Leeds	324	—	263	14 (1)	Draw
Leicestershire	Bradford	328	—	62	125	Y, inns. and 141 runs
Gloucestershire	Scarborough	346	—	119	147	Y, inns. and 80 runs
Nottinghamshire	Nottingham	320	267 (5)	403	—	Draw
Kent	Dover	*326 (8)	—	168	109	Y, inns. and 49 runs
Sussex	Brighton	*330 (9)	70 (6)	77	322	Y, 4 wickets

* Innings declared closed.

202

Yorkshire beat Derbyshire, Essex, Glamorgan, Lancashire, Leicestershire, Northamptonshire twice; and Gloucestershire, Hampshire, Kent, Middlesex, Surrey, Sussex, Warwickshire, Worcestershire once.

Yorkshire were beaten by Middlesex, Surrey once.

Yorkshire drew with Nottinghamshire twice; and Gloucestershire, Hampshire, Kent, Sussex, Warwickshire, Worcestershire once.

SUMMARY

	Yorkshire	Opponents
Runs scored	10749	9461
Average per wicket	30·21	18·82
Hundreds	17	6
Other innings over 50	45	32
Ten wickets in match	4	—
Five wickets in innings	31	15
Highest total	453 v. Lancashire	429 (9) dec. (Gloucestershire)
Lowest total	100 v. Surrey	41 (Warwickshire)
Totals over 400	6	2
Totals under 100	—	8

PRINCIPAL AVERAGES

	Inns.	Not Out	Runs	Highest Inns.	100's	50's	Aver.
L. Hutton	17	3	631	107	1	3	45·07
M. Leyland	38	4	1441	135	3	8	42·38
H. Sutcliffe	37	2	1451	142	5	6	41·45
P. A. Gibb	11	2	332	78	—	1	36·88
A. Mitchell	33	1	1108	133	3	7	34·62
C. Turner	20	3	581	97	—	5	34·17
W. Barber	40	3	1244	157	3	5	33·62
A. B. Sellers	39	6	999	93*	—	5	30·27

* Not out.

	Balls	Balls per Wkt.	Runs	Wkts.	5 Wkts. in Inns.	Aver.
H. Verity	4476	40·32	1526	111	11	13·74
W. E. Bowes	4517	45·17	1424	100	6	14·24
M. Leyland	1750	36·45	841	48	2	17·52
F. Wilkinson	1332	55·50	471	24	1	19·62
E. P. Robinson	3769	41·87	1788	90	5	19·86
T. F. Smailes	3921	49·01	1689	80	5	21·11

NOTES

Leyland took eight wickets for 63 runs in Hampshire's innings at Huddersfield.

When Warwickshire were all out for 41 at Birmingham, no batsman reached double figures. Bowes took five wickets for 14 runs.

Smailes scored 117 and 56 not out v. Glamorgan at Cardiff. In the next match he made 116 v. Surrey at Sheffield and, bowling unchanged with Bowes in Surrey's first innings (52), took four wickets for 16 runs.

Yorkshire beat Glamorgan by 12 runs at Hull after losing five wickets for 68 in the second innings and declaring.

F. Wilkinson took ten Hampshire wickets for 129 runs at Bournemouth—seven for 68 and three for 61.

Surrey beat Yorkshire by 262 runs at the Oval, E. W. Whitfield scoring 77 and 174 not out. Yorkshire scored 100 in their first innings, of which the last two men, Smailes (36) and Wilkinson (18), scored 54.

In Leicestershire's first innings (62) at Bradford, E. P. Robinson made six catches, five off Verity's bowling and one off his own. He also scored 49 runs and took four wickets for 31 runs.

In Yorkshire's second innings *v.* Middlesex at Lord's, Hutton and Gibb were unable to bat owing to injuries, and Leyland retired hurt.

HOW IT WAS DONE

	100's	50's	10 Wkts. in Match	5 Wkts. in Inns.	50 Runs & 5 Wkts. in Match
W. Barber	3	5	–	–	–
W. E. Bowes	–	–	–	6	–
P. A. Gibb	–	1	–	–	–
L. Hutton	1	3	–	1	–
M. Leyland	3	8	–	2	1
A. Mitchell	3	7	–	–	–
E. P. Robinson	–	1	–	5	1
A. B. Sellers	–	5	–	–	–
T. F. Smailes	2	2	1	5	–
H. Sutcliffe	5	6	–	–	–
C. Turner	–	5	–	–	–
H. Verity	–	–	2	11	–
G. A. Wilson	–	2	–	–	–
F. Wilkinson	–	–	1	1	–
N. W. D. Yardley	–	1	–	–	–
Total	17	45	4	31	2

FIELDING (227 Catches)

No. of Catches		No. of Catches	
38	E. P. Robinson	9	M. Leyland
35	A. Mitchell	9	F. Wilkinson
22	A. B. Sellers	8	H. Sutcliffe
21	C. Turner	7	L. Hutton
15	N. W. D. Yardley	5	" Sub."
14	W. Barber	4	G. A. Wilson
13	T. F. Smailes	2	H. Halliday
13	H. Verity	2	A. Hamer
10	W. E. Bowes		

WICKETKEEPING

	Stumped	Caught	Total
A. Wood	18	28	46
P. A. Gibb	2	3	5
Total	20	31	51

TOTALS

400 Runs and Over

Yorkshire (6)

453 v. Lancashire, Manchester   416 v. Surrey, Sheffield
440 (6)* v. Leicestershire, Leicester   415 v. Warwickshire, Birmingham
435 (5)* v. Northamptonshire, Peterborough   401 v. Sussex, Leeds

Opponents (2)

428 (9)*, Gloucestershire, Gloucester   403, Nottinghamshire, Nottingham

* Innings declared closed.

Under 100 Runs

Yorkshire (0)

None.

Opponents (8)

41, Warwickshire, Birmingham   77, Sussex, Brighton
52, Surrey, Sheffield   87, Derbyshire, Chesterfield
62, Leicestershire, Bradford   87, Nottinghamshire, Bradford
69, Leicestershire, Leicester   90, Essex, Sheffield

FIRST WICKET PARTNERSHIPS

Score	Partners	Against	Ground
153	H. Sutcliffe, L. Hutton	Sussex	Leeds
148	A. Mitchell, W. Barber	Glamorgan	Hull
110	H. Sutcliffe, P. A. Gibb	Nottinghamshire	Nottingham
108	H. Sutcliffe, L. Hutton	Essex	Sheffield

50 RUNS AND 5 WICKETS

Scores	Analyses	Player	Against	Ground
66	5-65	E. P. Robinson	Warwickshire	Birmingham
63*	5-77	M. Leyland	Leicestershire	Leicester

* Not out.

MATCHES OF THE SEASON

Yorkshire v. *Glamorgan*

Hull, June 22, 23, 24

Yorkshire won by 12 runs

Yorkshire were weakened by the absence of Hutton and Verity playing in the second Test match at Lord's when they faced Glamorgan at Hull, but good batting by Mitchell, Barber and Leyland, fine bowling by Smailes and a perfectly-timed declaration by Sellers, combined to get the Champions home by a very short head.

Between showers on the first day, Mitchell and Barber scored 148 for Yorkshire's first wicket, but when play closed on the second evening Glamorgan, with one wicket down, were only 133 behind Yorkshire's first innings total (273).

All the fun and games were reserved for the third day. When Glamorgan resumed, Smailes was in such devastating form that he took six wickets for 17 runs, and Yorkshire found themselves with an unexpected lead of 94. Quick runs were the order of the day when Yorkshire went in, and when 68 had been scored Sellers declared, leaving Glamorgan with a reasonable time to make the 163 runs required for a win.

Brierley and Davies hit hard, but the off-breaks of Smailes were too deadly, and in an exciting finish Yorkshire won by 12 runs.

Smailes took fourteen wickets for 103 runs in the match (six for 35 and eight for 68), all his wickets being taken on the last day at a cost of 85 runs.

Yorkshire

A. Mitchell c Davies (H.) b Smart	69	b Mercer		0
W. Barber c and b Davies (E.)	90	c Dyson b Davies (E.)		10
A. B. Sellers b Jones	7	b Mercer		3
M. Leyland c and b Jones	39	c Davies (E.) b Mercer		21
J. Brumfitt c Dyson b Davies (E.)	9			
T. F. Smailes c Turnbull b Davies (E.)	1	c Turnbull b Jones		7
H. Halliday b Davies (E.)	17			
A. Wood c Davies (H.) b Jones	18	not out		1
E. P. Robinson b Davies (E.)	11	not out		24
F. Wilkinson b Jones	2			
W. E. Bowes not out	0			
Extras	10	Extras		2
	273			***68**

* Innings declared closed.

Glamorgan

A. H. Dyson lbw, b Bowes	34	lbw, b Smailes	15
E. Davies b Smailes	64	b Smailes	13
T. L. Brierley c and b Smailes	40	b Smailes	36
D. Davies b Robinson	0	c and b Smailes	23
R. Duckfield c and b Smailes	7	b Smailes	13
C. Smart c Robinson b Smailes	0	lbw, b Smailes	9
M. J. Turnbull c Bowes b Smailes	2	b Leyland	6
E. C. Jones c Wilkinson b Robinson	0	b Leyland	0
H. Davies c Wilkinson b Robinson	4	not out	19
A. Davies b Smailes	3	b Smailes	0
J. Mercer not out	6	b Smailes	4
Extras	19	Extras	12
	179		**150**

Glamorgan Bowling

	Overs	Mdns.	Runs	Wkts.		Overs	Mdns.	Runs	Wkts.
Mercer	25	7	48	0	...	7	0	31	3
Smart	16	3	31	1					
Davies (E.)	34.1	5	83	5	...	5	0	31	1
Davies (A.)	3	0	10	0					
Jones	26	3	75	4	...	2	0	4	1
Davies (D.)	4	0	16	0					

Yorkshire Bowling

	Overs	Mdns.	Runs	Wkts.		Overs	Mdns.	Runs	Wkts.
Bowes	22	5	43	1	...	1	1	0	0
Smailes	14.1	4	35	6	...	22.5	3	68	8
Wilkinson	11	3	27	0					
Robinson	18	5	49	3	...	11	2	51	0
Leyland	2	1	6	0	...	10	5	19	2

Yorkshire v. *Leicestershire*

Bradford, August 13, 15, 16

Yorkshire won by an innings and 141 runs

Winning the toss, Sellers sent Leicestershire in, but the expected sunshine did not materialise. By way of compensation Verity found a " spot," made the ball play all kinds of tricks, and took seven wickets for 18 runs. Leicestershire were all out for 62 runs, C. S. Dempster, the New Zealand Test cricketer, having carried his bat through the innings for 28 and Robinson having made 6 catches in the slips.

Yorkshire began badly, three wickets being down for 37, but Sutcliffe and Leyland—just the men for such a crisis—then added 140 runs, and with Robinson knocking up 49 in quick time, the total achieved respectable proportions.

Leicestershire second innings numerically was twice as successful as the first, but it still fell short of the target by 141 runs, and Yorkshire won with an innings in hand.

During the match, Robinson made 7 catches, scored 49, and took four wickets for 31 runs—a very satisfying three-days work.

Leicestershire

L. G. Berry c Robinson b Verity	10		lbw, b Bowes	2
C. S. Dempster not out	28		c Robinson b Bowes	18
N. F. Armstrong c Mitchell b Verity	1		b Bowes	0
F. Prentice c Robinson b Verity	0		b Bowes	11
F. Watson c Robinson b Verity	0		b Robinson	24
P. Cherrington b Verity	0		b Smailes	4
G. Dawkes c and b Robinson	4		b Smailes	15
W. E. Astill c Robinson b Verity	3		not out	29
H. A. Smith c Robinson b Verity	0		b Robinson	12
G. Lester b Smailes	5		absent hurt	0
J. Sperry b Smailes	4		c Leyland b Robinson	9
Extras	7		Extras	1
	62			125

Yorkshire

H. Sutcliffe c Dawkes b Sperry	105
L. Hutton b Astill	9
A. Mitchell b Smith	1
P. A. Gibb c Smith b Astill	7
M. Leyland st. Dawkes b Sperry	85
E. P. Robinson b Smith	49
W. Barber b Smith	4
A. B. Sellers c Dawkes b Smith	18
T. F. Smailes c Dempster b Smith	14
H. Verity c Sperry b Smith	19
W. E. Bowes not out	2
Extras	15
	328

Yorkshire Bowling

	Overs	Mdns.	Runs	Wkts.		Overs	Mdns.	Runs	Wkts.
Bowes	11	6	10	0	...	16	2	30	4
Smailes	5.4	2	14	2	...	7	1	36	2
Verity	15	5	18	7	...	11	8	9	0
Robinson	5	2	13	1	...	4.2	0	18	3
Leyland						3	0	19	0
Hutton						4	0	12	0

Leicestershire Bowling

	Overs	Mdns.	Runs	Wkts.
Sperry	25	4	83	2
Smith	37.5	6	132	6
Astill	23	1	63	2
Lester	9	0	20	0
Cherrington	7	3	12	0
Prentice	2	0	3	0

APPEARANCES

The following 22 cricketers appeared for Yorkshire in Championship matches, the number of appearances being in parentheses :

W. Barber (27)
W. E. Bowes (24)
J. Brumfitt (1)
P. A. Gibb (8)
H. Halliday (7)
A. Hamer (2)
H. S. Hargreaves (1)
L. Hutton (13)
J. Johnson (1)
M. Leyland (27)
A. Mitchell (23)

E. P. Robinson (26)
A. B. Sellers (30)
T. F. Smailes (24)
J. Smurthwaite (1)
H. Sutcliffe (25)
C. Turner (17)
H. Verity (20)
G. A. Wilson (6)
F. Wilkinson (11)
A. Wood (25)
N. W. D. Yardley (11)

POST MORTEM

Yorkshire were strong in all departments in 1938 : eight batsmen averaged over 30 runs an innings, six bowlers took their wickets for 21 runs or less, and nine of the side made 10 or more catches. There were, in short, no weak spots, and even when injuries and the demands

[*Photo: Topical Press*

DAVID DENTON

[*Photo: Yorkshire Evening Post*

LEN HUTTON

[*Photo : Yorkshire Evening Post*

GEORGE HIRST DEMONSTRATING SOME OF THE FINER POINTS OF BOWLING TO YOUNG
CRICKETERS AT HEADINGLEY, LEEDS

of Test selectors depleted the XI., reserves were ready to step into the breaches. And the captaincy was equal to and largely responsible for the fine team-work

During the season 20 matches were won, and there were special contributory causes of the two defeats : at Lord's, when Middlesex won by eight wickets, Hutton and Gibb were both injured and unable to bat in the second innings, in which Leyland retired with a fractured thumb after scoring one run ; while when Surrey won at the Oval, Yorkshire, owing to the fourth Test match at Leeds and injuries, were without Hutton, Leyland, Verity, Bowes, Yardley and Gibb. Later in the season Yorkshire's pre-eminence was recognised when five of the side were selected for England in the fifth Test at the Oval.

TWENTY-FIRST CHAMPIONSHIP

1939

Captain : A. B. Sellers

For the third consecutive season Yorkshire and Middlesex were Champions and runners-up respectively, with Gloucestershire, who beat Yorkshire twice, close up third. At the end of the season a number of matches were cancelled owing to the international situation, the Yorkshire-Sussex game at Brighton (J. H. Parks' Benefit) being the last " between-the-wars " match.

THE FIRST SIX

	Plyd.	Won	Lost	Drawn	1st Inns. Lead in Match Lost	Drawn	Pts.	Aver.
Yorkshire	28	20	4	4	2	3	260	9·28
Middlesex	22	14*	6	2	3	1	180	8·18
Gloucestershire	26	15	7	4	1	3	196	7·53
Essex	24	12	10	2	4	2	170†	7·08
Kent	26	14	9	3	2	1	180	6·92
Lancashire	22	10	6	6	3	2	140	6·36

* Includes one win in one-day match (8 points).
† Includes 2 points for tie on first innings in match lost.

METHOD OF SCORING : As in 1938.

MATCH SCORES AND RESULTS

Yorkshire v.	Ground	Yorkshire 1st Inns.	Yorkshire 2nd Inns.	Opponents 1st Inns.	Opponents 2nd Inns.	Result
Kent	Leeds	169	*171 (9)	100	139	Y, 101 runs
Gloucestershire	Bradford	252	*162 (7)	227	190 (4)	G, 6 wickets
Essex	Ilford	141	237 (3)	209	165	Y, 7 wickets
Lancashire	Manchester	*528 (8)	—	300	185	Y, inns. and 43 runs
Warwickshire	Birmingham	417	—	219	144	Y, inns. and 54 runs
Hampshire	Sheffield	*493 (1)	—	174	190	Y, inns. and 129 runs
Leicestershire	Hull	*500 (7)	—	366	104	Y, inns. and 30 runs
Middlesex	Lord's	*430 (5)	—	62	122	Y, inns. and 246 runs
Northamptonshire	Leeds	207 (8)	—	180	—	Draw
Nottinghamshire	Nottingham	244	108	120	3 (4)	Draw
Glamorgan	Bradford	328	—	168	65	Y, inns. and 95 runs
Derbyshire	Sheffield	83	310	20	97	Y, 276 runs
Gloucestershire	Bristol	176	105	168	114 (3)	G, 7 wickets
Surrey	Leeds	406	*199 (6)	290	138	Y, 177 runs
Middlesex	Bradford	171	172 (5)	290	—	Draw
Northamptonshire	Northampton	*502 (4)	—	216	188	Y, inns. and 98 runs
Derbyshire	Chesterfield	—	—	208 (6)	—	Draw
Sussex	Scarborough	386	90 (0)	156	319	Y, 10 wickets
Nottinghamshire	Sheffield	94 (3)	—	200	—	Draw
Worcestershire	Stourbridge	91	113	102	118	W, 16 runs
Surrey	Oval	431	—	219	227 (2)	Draw
Glamorgan	Cardiff	234	*186 (6)	194	140	Y, 86 runs
Lancashire	Leeds	163	147 (5)	217	92	Y, 5 wickets
Leicestershire	Leicester	155	*134 (3)	89	103	Y, 97 runs
Worcestershire	Bradford	171	309	194	197	Y, 89 runs
Warwickshire	Scarborough	403	*171 (4)	158	310	Y, 106 runs
Essex	Sheffield	131	208	343	—	E, inns. and 84 runs
Kent	Dover	338	—	109	215	Y, inns. and 14 runs
Hampshire	Bournemouth	243	—	116	116	Y, inns. and 11 runs
Sussex	Brighton	392	30 (1)	387	33	Y, 9 wickets

* Innings declared closed.

Yorkshire beat Glamorgan, Hampshire, Kent, Lancashire, Leicestershire, Sussex, Warwickshire twice; and Derbyshire, Essex, Middlesex, Northamptonshire, Surrey, Worcestershire once.

Yorkshire were beaten by Gloucestershire twice; and Essex, Worcestershire once.

Yorkshire drew with Nottinghamshire twice; and Derbyshire, Middlesex, Northamptonshire, Surrey once.

SUMMARY

	Yorkshire	Opponents
Runs scored	11131	9517
Average per wicket	30·49	18·37
Hundreds	25	6
Other innings over 50	35	37
Ten wickets in match	6	1
Five wickets in innings	31	20
Highest total	528 (8) dec.	387 (Sussex)
	v. Lancashire	
Lowest total	83 v. Derbyshire	20 (Derbyshire)
Totals over 400	9	—
Totals under 100	2	7

PRINCIPAL AVERAGES

	Inns.	Not Out	Runs	Highest Inns.	100's	50's	Aver.
L. Hutton	40	4	2167	280*	9	6	60·19
H. Sutcliffe	26	2	1230	234*	6	2	51·25
M. Leyland	33	5	1191	180*	3	3	42·53
W. Barber	41	5	1388	141	3	6	38·55

* Not out.

	Balls	Balls per Wkt.	Runs	Wkts.	5 Wkts. in Inns.	Aver.
H. Verity	6382	38·67	2097	165	11	12·70
W. E. Bowes	4399	45·82	1389	96	8	14·46
L. Hutton	1505	40·67	681	37	2	18·40
T. F. Smailes	2158	44·04	931	49	1	19·00
E. P. Robinson	4799	47·04	2039	102	6	19·99

NOTES

In the first county match of the season Robinson did the hat-trick in Kent's second innings at Leeds.

Yorkshire beat Lancashire by an innings and 43 runs at Manchester, scoring 528 for nine wickets before declaring. Bowes took six wickets for 43 in Lancashire's second innings.

Bowes took twelve Warwickshire wickets for 96 runs at Birmingham, Hutton scoring 158.

Against Hampshire at Sheffield, Yorkshire scored 493 for one wicket declared, Sutcliffe scoring 116, Hutton 280 not out and Barber 91 not out. Sutcliffe and Hutton scored 315 for the first wicket.

When Yorkshire scored 500 for seven wickets declared v. Leicestershire at Hull, Sutcliffe carried his bat for 234 not out. Verity took twelve wickets for 114 runs.

Sutcliffe scored his fourth hundred in successive innings *v.* Middlesex at Lord's—165 *v.* Lancashire at Manchester, 116 *v.* Hampshire at Sheffield, 234 not out *v.* Leicestershire at Hull, 175 *v.* Middlesex at Lord's.

Bowes took eight Notts wickets for 29 runs at Nottingham (five for 29 and three for 0 in 30 balls).

Verity took fourteen wickets for 68 *v.* Glamorgan at Bradford (seven for 48 and seven for 20) ; Hutton scored 144.

Derbyshire were all out for 20 runs in their first innings at Sheffield, Smailes taking four wickets for 11 and Smurthwaite five for 7. In the second innings, Smailes took all ten wickets for 47.

Against Surrey at the Oval, Hutton scored 151 and 81, Verity taking four wickets for 17 in Surrey's second innings. For Surrey, F. R. Brown scored 119 and took four wickets for 56 in Yorkshire's second innings.

Hutton scored 177 and 57 not out *v.* Sussex at Scarborough and took four wickets for 80 runs.

Worcestershire beat Yorkshire by 16 runs at Stourbridge.

Robinson took thirteen Lancashire wickets for 115 runs at Leeds.

N. W. D. Yardley scored 108 and 83 not out *v.* Warwickshire at Scarborough.

Essex beat Yorkshire by an innings and 4 runs at Sheffield, P. Smith taking three wickets for 4 runs in 24 balls in the first innings.

Sussex were all out for 33 in their second innings at Hove, Verity taking seven wickets for 9 runs.

In his final season, H. Sutcliffe (1) scored the first hundred of the season and carried his bat through the innings while doing so (125 not out *v.* Oxford University), (2) scored his 50,000th run, (3) scored four hundreds in consecutive innings, (4) averaged 51·25 and finished second in the Yorkshire batting averages in Championship matches. A great finish !

HOW IT WAS DONE

	100's	50's	10 Wkts. in Match	5 Wkts. in Inns.	50 Runs & 5 Wkts. in Match
W. Barber	3	6	–	–	–
W. E. Bowes	–	–	1	8	–
L. Hutton	9	6	–	2	1
J. Johnson	–	–	–	1	–
M. Leyland	3	3	–	1	1
A. Mitchell	2	4	–	–	–
E. P. Robinson	–	1	2	6	–
A. B. Sellers	–	3	–	–	–
T. F. Smailes	–	1	1	1	–
H. Sutcliffe	6	2	–	–	–
J. Smurthwaite	–	–	–	1	–
C. Turner	–	1	–	–	–
H. Verity	–	1	2	11	1
A. Wood	–	2	–	–	–
N. W. D. Yardley	2	5	–	–	–
Total	25	35	6	31	3

FIELDING (237 Catches)

No. of Catches		No. of Catches	
43	A. Mitchell	12	C. Turner
37	E. P. Robinson	7	W. E. Bowes
31	L. Hutton	7	H. Sutcliffe
24	H. Verity	7	" Sub."
16	A. B. Sellers	6	M. Leyland
15	T. F. Smailes	3	J. Smurthwaite
14	W. Barber	1	G. Cawthray
13	N. W. D. Yardley	1	G. A. Wilson

WICKETKEEPING

	Stumped	Caught	Total
A. Wood	27	38	65
K. Fiddling	3	1	4
Total	30	39	69

TOTALS

400 Runs and Over

Yorkshire (9)

528 (8)* v. Lancashire, Manchester
502 (4)* v. Northamptonshire, Northampton
500 (7)* v. Leicestershire, Hull
493 (1)* v. Hampshire, Sheffield
431 v. Surrey, Oval

430 (5)* v. Middlesex, Lord's
417* v. Warwickshire, Birmingham
406 v. Surrey, Leeds
403 v. Warwickshire, Scarborough

Opponents (0)

None.

* Innings declared closed.

Under 100 Runs

Yorkshire (2)

83 v. Derbyshire, Sheffield

91 v. Worcestershire, Stourbridge

Opponents (7)

20 and 97, Derbyshire, Sheffield
33, Sussex, Brighton
62, Middlesex, Lord's

65, Glamorgan, Bradford
89, Leicestershire, Leicester
92, Lancashire, Leeds

FIRST WICKET PARTNERSHIPS

Score	Partners	Against	Ground
315	H. Sutcliffe, L. Hutton	Hampshire	Sheffield
142	L. Hutton, N. W. D. Yardley	Northamptonshire	Northampton

50 RUNS AND 5 WICKETS

Scores	Analysis	Player	Against	Ground
31, 38	5-74, 1-42	M. Leyland	Essex	Ilford
1, 54	4-48, 2-38	H. Verity	Worcestershire	Bradford
14, 109	2-19, 5-58	L. Hutton	Worcestershire	Bradford

MATCHES OF THE SEASON

Yorkshire v. *Hampshire*
Sheffield, June 3, 5, 6

Yorkshire won by an innings and 129 runs

A remarkable game in which Yorkshire declared after scoring nearly 500 runs for the loss of Sutcliffe's wicket, must have been particularly gratifying to Hutton, who scored his highest innings for the county and finished off Hampshire's second innings by taking four wickets for 40 runs.

As usual, Sutcliffe and Hutton opened the Yorkshire innings after Hampshire had put together a very moderate 174, and before they were parted 315 runs had been scored in 4½ hours. When he was 12 Sutcliffe gave a chance, and added a further 104 before Heath bowled him. But that was not the end of Hampshire's troubles. Hutton and Barber continued the assault on the Hampshire bowlers, and when Sellers declared at 493 had added 178 for the second wicket.

Hutton scored his 280 in 375 minutes, hitting 36 fours, Barber, whose share of the stand was 91, having 15 boundaries.

Hampshire's second innings closely resembled their first. Bailey batted stubbornly and Arnold indulged in a little hitting, but the bowlers and fielders were always on top, and the end came when Hutton took the last three wickets. In this innings nine of the Hampshire batsmen were caught and the tenth stumped.

Hampshire

J. Bailey c Yardley b Bowes	45	st. Wood b Hutton	27
N. McCorkell c Verity b Turner	18	c Yardley b Turner	4
A. Holt b Yardley	13	c Wood b Smailes	26
W. L. Creese c Turner b Smailes	27	c Bowes b Turner	13
J. Arnold b Turner	6	c Wood b Verity	52
D. F. Walker lbw, b Smailes	5	c Turner b Smailes	5
G. Hill c and b Smailes	0	c Wood b Bowes	16
G. S. Boyes c Wood b Bowes	22	c Smailes b Hutton	27
G. R. Taylor c Smailes b Leyland	4	c Barber b Hutton	4
R. C. Court b Smailes	9	c Sellers b Hutton	5
G. E. M. Heath not out	15	not out	1
Extras	10	Extras	10
	174		**190**

Yorkshire

H. Sutcliffe b Heath	116
L. Hutton not out	280
W. Barber not out	91
M. Leyland did not bat	
N. W. D. Yardley did not bat	
C. Turner did not bat	
A. B. Sellers did not bat	
T. F. Smailes did not bat	
A. Wood did not bat	
H. Verity did not bat	
W. E. Bowes did not bat	

Extras   6

493*

* Innings declared closed.

Yorkshire Bowling

	Overs	Mdns.	Runs	Wkts.		Overs	Mdns.	Runs	Wkts.
Bowes	19.4	5	35	2	...	15	2	38	1
Smailes	15	2	41	4	...	8	0	27	1
Turner	13	1	42	2	...	7	1	26	3
Yardley	6	1	14	1	...	2	0	5	0
Verity	4	2	5	0	...	8	3	14	1
Leyland	5	0	27	.1	...	6	0	30	0
Hutton						9.1	0	40	4

Hampshire Bowling

	Overs	Mdns.	Runs	Wkts.
Heath	28	2	131	1
Court	20	1	120	0
Bailey	5	1	17	0
Hill	20	1	70	0
Boyes	14	1	66	0
Creese	12	2	51	0
Arnold	3	0	32	0

Yorkshire v. *Middlesex*

Lord's, June 10, 12, 13

Yorkshire won by an innings and 246 runs

At Lord's, Yorkshire inflicted a heavy defeat on Middlesex, whose top-scorer in the two innings was Compton with 25.

After Hutton (29) and Mitchell (1) had been dismissed cheaply, Sutcliffe and Leyland joined forces in a third wicket partnership of 301. Each had a "life" and each took every advantage of the escape. When Sutcliffe was caught by Compton off his own bowling he had scored 175 (17 fours) in his fourth hundred in consecutive innings, a great performance for a cricketer in his forty-fifth year.

Leyland continued to bat well until the total reached 430, when Sellers declared with five wickets in hand. In his 180 Leyland had scored 20 fours.

Middlesex were in and out twice in less than 270 minutes, Bowes and Verity being the destructive agents with eight for 50 and eight for 37 respectively. One curious feature in these innings was the fact that no Middlesex batsman was bowled—one was stumped, two lbw, and seventeen caught.

Yorkshire

H. Sutcliffe c and b Compton	175
L. Hutton b Peebles	29
A. Mitchell lbw, b Gray	1
M. Leyland not out	180
N. W. D. Yardley lbw, b Edrich	7
A. B. Sellers b Compton	14
T. F. Smailes not out	7
A. Wood did not bat	
E. P. Robinson did not bat	
H. Verity did not bat	
W. E. Bowes did not bat	
Extras	17
	430*

* Innings declared closed.

Middlesex

J. D. Robertson c Robinson b Smailes	1	c Sutcliffe b Bowes	19
S. M. Brown c sub. b Bowes	17	c Wood b Bowes	3
W. J. Edrich c Smailes b Bowes	1	c Wood b Bowes	9
D. Compton lbw, b Bowes	25	c and b Verity	18
E. T. Killick c Mitchell b Verity	6	lbw, b Robinson	15
J. Hulme c Sutcliffe b Bowes	0	c Smailes b Robinson	1
W. F. Price c Wood b Verity	2	c sub. b Verity	10
J. M. Sims st. Wood b Verity	1	c Wood b Robinson	21
J. Smith c Mitchell b Bowes	0	c Hutton b Verity	9
I. A. R. Peebles c Hutton b Verity	2	not out	8
L. H. Gray not out	0	c Wood b Verity	1
Extras	7	Extras	8
	62		122

Middlesex Bowling

	Overs	Mdns.	Runs	Wkts.
Smith	21	1	85	0
Gray	21	1	118	1
Edrich	10	5	37	1
Peebles	15	0	70	0
Sims	10	0	62	0
Compton	12	0	40	2

Yorkshire Bowling

	Overs	Mdns.	Runs	Wkts.		Overs	Mdns.	Runs	Wkts.
Bowes	12	3	20	5	...	8	0	30	3
Smailes	2	0	3	1	...	5	1	9	0
Verity	9	5	17	4	...	9.4	5	20	4
Robinson	4	0	15	0	...	9	2	36	3
Yardley						5	0	19	0

Yorkshire v. *Derbyshire*
Sheffield, June 24, 26, 27

Yorkshire won by 276 runs

The match against Derbyshire at Sheffield produced some of the most exciting and sensational cricket of the season.

Taking first innings, Yorkshire were soon back in the pavilion after scoring 83, of which Yardley and Sellers made 52. Two brothers (A. V. and G. H. Pope) engineered this collapse, bowling unchanged throughout the innings.

But Yorkshire were in even deadlier mood when Derbyshire batted, Smailes and Smurthwaite, a recruit playing in his second county match, bowling unchanged for 40 minutes, during which Derbyshire scored 20— their lowest total in 41 years. During this disaster Smailes took four wickets for 11 runs and Smurthwaite five wickets for 7 runs in 40 balls.

Yorkshire's second innings produced 310 runs, thanks mainly to Barber, Mitchell, Sellers, Yardley and not very good fielding, and Derbyshire began their second innings facing a deficit of 373.

The rest of the story is all Smailes, who took all ten Derbyshire wickets for 47 runs, and finished with a match analysis of fourteen wickets for 58 runs. Derbyshire scored 97. Smailes was the third Yorkshire bowler to take all ten wickets in an innings in a Championship match, A. Drake and H. Verity (twice) being the others.

Yorkshire

H. Sutcliffe c Worthington b Pope (A. V.)	0	c Gladwin b Pope (G. H.)	18
A. Mitchell c Rhodes b Pope (G. H.)	14	c Smith b Pope (A. V.)	40
W. Barber c Elliott b Pope (A. V.)	2	c Smith b Pope (A. V.)	100
M. Leyland b Pope (G. H.)	0	c Elliott b Pope (G. H.)	1
N. W. D. Yardley c Gladwin b Pope (A. V.)	21	c and b Rhodes	34
G. A. Wilson b Pope (A. V.)	0	b Mitchell	21
A. B. Sellers c Elliott b Pope (G. H.)	31	run out	43
T. F. Smailes c Pope (A. V.) b Pope (G. H.)	4	b Pope (A. V.)	8
E. P. Robinson b Pope (G. H.)	0	c Hounsfield b Pope (G. H.)	23
J. Smurthwaite b Pope (G. H.)	0	b Pope (A. V.)	1
K. Fiddling not out	0	not out	5
Extras	2	Extras	16
	83		315

Derbyshire

D. Smith b Smurthwaite	5	b Smailes	8
A. E. Alderman c Fiddling b Smailes	1	c Smurthwaite b Smailes	0
T. S. Worthington run out	0	c Mitchell b Smailes	32
L. F. Townsend c Robinson b Smurthwaite	2	b Smailes	0
G. H. Pope c Robinson b Smailes	0	lbw, b Smailes	1
A. Rhodes c Robinson b Smurthwaite	0	b Smailes	18
T. D. Houndsfield c Sutcliffe b Smailes	2	not out	21
A. V. Pope b Smurthwaite	6	b Smailes	4
C. Gladwin c Smailes b Smurthwaite	0	b Smailes	0
H. Elliott not out	2	b Smailes	16
T. B. Mitchell c Leyland b Smailes	0	st. Fiddling b Smailes	6
Extras	1	Extras	1
	—		—
	20		97

Derbyshire Bowling

	Overs	Mdns.	Runs	Wkts.		Overs	Mdns.	Runs	Wkts.
Pope (A. V.)	18	4	37	4	...	25	5	72	4
Pope (G. H.)	17.3	2	44	6	...	24.5	3	90	3
Mitchell						9	0	52	1
Gladwin						8	2	36	0
Rhodes						4	0	16	1
Townsend						5	0	28	0

Yorkshire Bowling

	Overs	Mdns.	Runs	Wkts.		Overs	Mdns.	Runs	Wkts.
Smailes	4.3	0	11	4	...	17.1	5	47	10
Smurthwaite	4	2	7	5	...	14	5	43	0
Yardley						2	0	5	0
Robinson						1	0	1	0

Yorkshire v. *Sussex*

Brighton, August 30, 31, September 1

Yorkshire won by nine wickets

By the end of August most cricket matches had been cancelled, but as the meeting of Sussex and Yorkshire at Brighton was the Benefit match of J. H. Parks, it was decided to play, and as a result the last match of the inter-war seasons synchronised with one of the finest bowling performances of Hedley Verity.

Winning the toss, Sussex made a good start by scoring 387. Cox, who scored 198 of the total in 200 minutes, hit a six and 28 fours.

Yorkshire's retort was 392, Hutton playing a fine innings of 102 and Yardley another of 108. Mitchell and Leyland also added appreciably to the total.

So far the batsmen had held the upper hand, but when Sussex went in again there was a striking change. On a rain-affected wicket the whole side could muster only 33 runs, no batsman reaching double figures.

Verity was the moving spirit in this procession. In the last bowling spell of his short career he took seven wickets for 9 runs in 48 balls, an analysis only excelled by his ten wickets for 10 against Notts in 1932.

Yorkshire obtained the 29 runs required for the loss of Hutton's wicket, and the two sides dispersed to less pleasant and more arduous duties.

Sussex

R. G. Stainton c Wood b Bowes	14	absent hurt		0
John Langridge run out	60	c Sellers b Robinson		3
H. Parks c Wood b Smailes	35	c Hutton b Verity		9
G. Cox c Mitchell b Robinson	198	c Wood b Verity		9
Jas. Langridge c Mitchell b Bowes	17	c Mitchell b Verity		0
J. H. Parks c Robinson b Smailes	2	lbw, b Verity		0
H. T. Bartlett b Robinson	24	b Verity		3
A. J. Holmes b Verity	11	b Verity		4
S. C. Griffith c Smailes b Verity	17	b Verity		1
J. Nye not out	2	not out		3
D. J. Wood lbw, b Robinson	0	run out		0
Extras	7	Extras		1
	387			33

Yorkshire

L. Hutton lbw, b Cox	103	c Griffith b Langridge (Jas.)	1
W. Barber c Griffith b Nye	22	not out	11
A. Mitchell c Langridge (Jas.) b Holmes	67	not out	18
M. Leyland c sub. b Parks (J. H.)	64		
N. W. D. Yardley c and b Langridge (Jas.)	108		
A. B. Sellers c Bartlett b Parks (J. H.)	12		
T. F. Smailes b Parks (J. H.)	0		
A. Wood c Wood b Langridge (Jas.)	2		
E. P. Robinson b Langridge (Jas.)	0		
H. Verity not out	7		
W. E. Bowes c Parks (J. H.) b Langridge (Jas.)	2		
Extras	5		
	392		30

Yorkshire Bowling

	Overs	Mdns.	Runs	Wkts.		Overs	Mdns.	Runs	Wkts.
Bowes	17	0	71	2					
Smailes	12	0	48	2					
Yardley	9	0	48	0					
Verity	18	1	108	2	...	6	1	9	7
Robinson	15	2	87	3	...	5.3	0	23	1
Hutton	4	0	18	0					

Sussex Bowling

	Overs	Mdns.	Runs	Wkts.		Overs	Mdns.	Runs	Wkts.
Nye	19	1	104	1					
Parks (J. H.)	33	3	120	3	...	6.6	1	21	0
Wood	10	1	30	0					
Langridge (Jas.)	20.4	5	84	4	...	6	0	9	1
Cox	10	2	34	1					
Holmes	3	0	15	1					

APPEARANCES

The following 19 cricketers appeared for Yorkshire in Championship matches, the number of appearances being in parentheses :

W. Barber (27)
W. E. Bowes (22)
B. Cawthray (2)
K. Fiddling (3)
L. Hutton (26)
J. Johnson (1)
M. Leyland (24)
A. Mitchell (27)
E. P. Robinson (27)
A. B. Sellers (29)

T. F. Smailes (17)
H. Sutcliffe (19)
J. Smurthwaite (4)
C. Turner (15)
H. Verity (28)
W. Watson (4)
G. A. Wilson (2)
A. Wood (27)
N. W. D. Yardley (26)

POST MORTEM

Yorkshire's twenty-first Championship was won by the usual combination—clever captaincy, sound batting, and bowling that had variety and quality and the backing of splendid fielding. All the regular members of the side except Bowes (9·41) had double-figure averages, eight scored over 500 runs and five over 1,000. Hutton, with 2,167 runs (9 hundreds) and an average of 60·19 in Championship matches, was the outstanding batsman, and in his last season Sutcliffe was not far behind him (further details of his doings will be found under " Notes ").

The bowling was very strong. In Bowes, Verity, Smailes and Robinson, Yorkshire had the best quartette in the competition, and Hutton's leg-breaks proved more useful and economical than in any previous season. Bowling to an attacking field, these five were rarely mastered.

Finally, by winning the Championship five times in seven seasons, A. B. Sellers set up a captaincy record which will be difficult to surpass.

SECOND WORLD WAR, 1939-1945

TWENTY-SECOND CHAMPIONSHIP

1946

Captain : A. B. Sellers

As in 1919, Yorkshire won the first post-war Championship. All the counties were team-building, and during the season Yorkshire tried 23 players, 10 of whom might be classed as recruits. Leyland, Barber and C. Turner had reached veteran age and retired at the end of the summer, but their presence in the side stiffened the batting and was of much greater value than figures may suggest. Middlesex, the runners-up, and Lancashire were close on Yorkshire's heels, but the latter's loss of only one match just made the difference.

THE FIRST SIX

	Played	Won	Lost	Drawn	1st Inns. Lead in Match Lost	Drawn	Points
Yorkshire	26	16	1	6	0	5	216*
Middlesex	26	16	5	5	1	2	204
Lancashire	26	15	4	5	1	4	200
Somerset	26	12	6	7	2	3	166†
Gloucestershire	26	12	6	4	1	3	160
Glamorgan	26	10	8	6	3	3	144
Kent	26	11	8	7	0	3	144

* Includes 8 points for lead on first innings in one-day match.

† Includes 2 points for tie on first innings in match lost.

METHOD OF SCORING : All counties to play 26 matches. 12 points for a win ; 4 points for a losing side obtaining first innings lead ; 4 points for first innings lead in a drawn match.

MATCH SCORES AND RESULTS

Yorkshire v.	Ground	Yorkshire 1st Inns.	Yorkshire 2nd Inns.	Opponents 1st Inns.	Opponents 2nd Inns.	Result
Glamorgan	Cardiff	195	84 (5)	116	162	Y, 5 wickets
Kent	Canterbury	252	—	69	92	Y, inns. and 91 runs
Leicestershire	Leeds	232	37 (0)	203	—	Draw
Kent	Bradford	236	175	106	113	Y, 192 runs
Gloucestershire	Bristol	336 (6)	—	369	—	Draw
Lancashire	Sheffield	*171 (3)	—	127 (4)	—	Draw
Warwickshire	Birmingham	*268 (9)	—	99	91	Y, inns. and 78 runs
Middlesex	Lord's	140	108	74	101	Y, 73 runs
Nottinghamshire	Bradford	*417 (9)	—	209	159	Y, inns. and 49 runs
Glamorgan	Sheffield	83	179 (4)	165	96	Y, 6 wickets
Derbyshire	Chesterfield	173	88 (6)	182	78	Y, 4 wickets
Surrey	Leeds	195	167 (4)	191	—	Y, 6 wickets
Essex	Harrogate	262	168 (4)	170	256	Y, 6 wickets
Worcestershire	Leeds	152	90 (9)	119	121	Y, 1 wicket
Somerset	Taunton	312 (7)	—	508	—	Draw
Surrey	Oval	197	113 (2)	114	194	Y, 8 wickets
Northamptonshire	Hull	344 (5)	—	183	138	Y, inns. and 23 runs
Lancashire	Manchester	180	220 (5)	396	—	Draw
Leicestershire	Leicester	308	*106 (1)	159	125 (9)	Draw
Warwickshire †	Bradford	*104 (7)	—	56	—	Y, 48 runs
Hampshire	Scarborough	168	69	97	84	Y, 56 runs
Middlesex	Sheffield	226	*202 (8)	169	144 (8)	Draw
Gloucestershire	Leeds	188	8 (1)	106	89	Y, 9 wickets
Sussex	Eastbourne	82	115 (4)	91	105	Y, 6 wickets
Hampshire	Bournemouth	135	130	204	64 (0)	H, 10 wickets
Nottinghamshire	Nottingham	301	—	102	161 (5)	Draw

* Innings declared closed.　　　† One-day match.

Yorkshire beat Glamorgan, Kent, Warwickshire, Surrey twice; and Derbyshire, Essex, Gloucestershire, Hampshire, Middlesex, Northamptonshire, Nottinghamshire, Sussex, Worcestershire once.

Yorkshire were beaten by Hampshire.

Yorkshire drew with Lancashire, Leicestershire twice; and Gloucestershire, Middlesex, Nottinghamshire, Somerset once.

SUMMARY

	Yorkshire	Opponents
Runs scored	7716	6924
Average per wicket	23·75	15·88
Hundreds	6	5
Other innings over 50	32	17
Ten wickets in match	2	1
Five wickets in innings	28	19
Highest total	417 (9) dec.	508 (Somerset)
	v. Nottinghamshire	
Lowest total	69 v. Hampshire	56 (Warwickshire)
Totals over 400	1	1
Totals under 100	4	12

PRINCIPAL AVERAGES

	Inns.	Not Out	Runs	Highest Inns.	100's	50's	Aver.
L. Hutton	26	4	1112	171*	3	5	50·54
W. Barber	36	3	1029	113	1	3	31·18
A. B. Sellers	30	6	709	85*	—	7	29·54
P. A. Gibbs	17	1	460	104	1	2	28·75
C. Turner	27	3	597	89*	—	6	24·85
M. Leyland	26	2	543	88	—	3	22·62
N. W. D. Yardley	23	2	470	137	1	1	22·38
T. F. Smailes	32	3	589	67*	—	1	20·31

	Balls	Balls per Wkt.	Runs	Wkts.	5 Wkts. in Inns.	Aver.
A. Booth	4441	52·86	1000	84	2	11·90
W. E. Bowes	2756	49·21	778	56	4	13·89
E. P. Robinson	4996	38·72	1810	129	13	14·03
A. Coxon	3246	51·52	1154	63	3	18·31
T. F. Smailes	3339	52·17	1203	64	4	18·79

NOTES

In the second county match of the season Yorkshire beat Kent with ease at Canterbury, the home side scoring 69 and 92. Five Yorkshire bowlers (Bowes, Smailes, Coxon, Beaumont and Booth) had a hand in this win.

Against Warwickshire at Birmingham, P. A. Gibb scored 104, Booth took nine wickets for 40 in the match, and Leyland, after scoring 52 in Yorkshire's innings, took seven wickets for 36 in Warwickshire's second innings.

J. Young took twelve wickets for 72 and Bowes six for 27 when Yorkshire beat Middlesex at Lord's.

N. W. D. Yardley scored 137 against Nottinghamshire at Bradford.

T. F. Smailes scored 51 and took six wickets for 40 runs in Surrey's first innings at Leeds.

Yorkshire beat Worcestershire by one wicket at Leeds in a low-scoring match. E. P. Robinson (seven for 41 in the first innings) and Coxon (eight for 31 in the second) were mainly responsible.

G. R. L Langdale scored a fine 146 for Somerset at Taunton.

Robinson took thirteen Surrey wickets for 164 runs at the Oval, Hutton (101), Sellers (58) and extras (16) scoring 175 of Yorkshire's first innings total of 197.

When Warwickshire scored 56 at Bradford, Smailes took five wickets for 16 runs and Booth three for 6.

Robinson took twelve wickets for 53 runs against Hampshire at Scarborough.

At Eastbourne, *v.* Sussex, Smailes scored 22 and 67 not out and in the Sussex innings took five for 16 and two for 13. In Yorkshire's first innings (82), C. Oakes took five wickets for 10 runs in 49 balls.

HOW IT WAS DONE

	100's	50's	10 Wkts. in Match	5 Wkts. in Inns.	50 Runs & 5 Wkts. in Match
W. Barber	1	3	–	–	–
H. Beaumont	–	2	–	–	–
A. Booth	–	–	–	2	–
W. E. Bowes	–	–	–	4	–
A. Coxon	–	1	–	3	–
P. A. Gibb	1	2	–	–	–
L. Hutton	3	5	–	–	–
M. Leyland	–	3	–	1	1
E. P. Robinson	–	1	2	13	1
A. B. Sellers	–	7	–	–	–
T. F. Smailes	–	1	–	4	2
C. Turner	–	6	–	1	1
N. W. D. Yardley	1	1	–	–	–
Total	6	32	2	28	5

FIELDING (142 Catches)

No. of Catches		No. of Catches	
21	E. P. Robinson	5	W. Barber
19	A. Coxon	5	W. Watson
18	A. B. Sellers	4	W. E. Bowes
16	T. F. Smailes	4	J. V. Wilson
11	N. W. D. Yardley	2	H. Halliday
9	A. Booth	2	M. Leyland
9	L. Hutton	2	" Sub."
7	H. Beaumont	1	G. A. Smithson
7	C. Turner		

WICKETKEEPING

	Stumped	Caught	Total
K. Fiddling	7	20	27
P. A. Gibb	6	9	15
A. Wood	1	9	10
Total	14	38	52

TOTALS

400 Runs and Over

Yorkshire (1)

417 (9)* v. Nottinghamshire, Bradford

Opponents (1)

508, Somerset, Taunton

* Innings declared closed.

Under 100 Runs

Yorkshire (4)

69 v. Hampshire, Scarborough
82 v. Sussex, Eastbourne

83 v. Glamorgan, Sheffield
90 v. Worcestershire, Leeds

Opponents (11)

56, Warwickshire, Bradford
69 and 92. Kent, Canterbury
74, Middlesex, Lord's
97 and 84, Hampshire, Scarborough

89, Gloucestershire, Leeds
91, Sussex, Eastbourne
99 and 91, Warwickshire, Birmingham
96, Glamorgan, Sheffield

FIRST WICKET PARTNERSHIPS
None.

50 RUNS AND 5 WICKETS

Scores	Analyses	Player	Against	Ground
52	7-36	M. Leyland	Warwickshire	Birmingham
51	6-40, 1-48	T. F. Smailes	Surrey	Leeds
51*	3-45, 6-26	E. P. Robinson	Gloucestershire	Leeds
22, 67*	5-16, 2-13	T. F. Smailes	Sussex	Eastbourne
68	0-10, 5-39	C. Turner	Nottinghamshire	Bradford

* Not out.

[*Photo : Central Press*]

W. E. BOWES

[*Photo : Topical Press*]

HEDLEY VERITY

A B SELLERS

[Photo : Topical Press

N W D YARDLEY

Photo : Central Press

MATCHES OF THE SEASON

Yorkshire v. *Worcestershire*

Leeds, July 20, 22, 23

Yorkshire won by one wicket

After a hard struggle, Yorkshire beat Worcestershire by one wicket at Leeds in a low-scoring match.

In their first innings Worcestershire could score only 119 runs, E. P. Robinson taking seven wickets for 41 runs. Yorkshire did very little better, but obtained a lead of 33 on the first innings, Watson (43) and Coxon (31) being mainly responsible.

When Worcestershire batted a second time all the batsmen, with the possible exception of E. Cooper (38) and M. Young (33), found Coxon difficult, the Yorkshireman having taken eight wickets for 31 runs when the innings closed for 121. Cooper carried his bat through the innings.

Requiring 88 to win, Yorkshire collapsed, Watson (29), the opening batsman, and E. P. Robinson (16), the last man, offering most resistance to the bowling of Jackson, Wyatt and Howarth. In the end, Smailes and Wardle just managed to scramble home.

In the match, P. F. Jackson took nine wickets for 69 runs and E. P. Robinson nine for 76.

Worcestershire

A. P. Singleton c Beaumont b Robinson	12	lbw, b Coxon	15
E. Cooper lbw, b Robinson	14	not out	38
R. Howorth c Beaumont b Robinson	13	c Beaumont b Coxon	6
R. E. S. Wyatt c and b Robinson	15	lbw, b Robinson	12
A. F. T. White c Coxon b Robinson	0	c Wood b Coxon	8
R. E. Bird c Wood b Smailes	36	c Wood b Coxon	1
N. H. Humphries lbw, b Smailes	0	b Robinson	5
M. Young b Robinson	1	c Yardley b Coxon	33
J. S. Buller b Robinson	0	b Coxon	0
R. Perks b Smailes	13	b Coxon	0
P. F. Jackson not out	8	b Coxon	0
Extras	7	Extras	3
	119		121

Yorkshire

W. Watson c Singleton b Howarth	43	b Howarth	29
W. Barber lbw, b Jackson	11	c Bird b Wyatt	2
M. Leyland lbw, b Jackson	8	b Wyatt	0
N. W. D. Yardley b Jackson	4	b Jackson	12
H. Beaumont b Jackson	0	lbw, b Jackson	4
C. Turner b Jackson	21	lbw, b Howorth	1
A. Wood lbw, b Howarth	4	c Buller b Jackson	3
T. F. Smailes run out	10	not out	8
A. Coxon c and b Wyatt	31	lbw, b Jackson	5
J. H. Wardle not out	10	not out	2
E. P. Robinson b Wyatt	0	c Buller b Wyatt	16
Extras	10	Extras	8
	152		90

Yorkshire Bowling

	Overs	Mdns.	Runs	Wkts.		Overs	Mdns.	Runs	Wkts.
Smailes	29.4	13	51	3	...	15	5	28	0
Coxon	11	5	10	0	...	26.1	14	31	8
Robinson	26	9	41	7	...	25	10	35	2
Wardle	3	0	10	0					
Leyland						5	2	24	0

Worcestershire Bowling

	Overs	Mdns.	Runs	Wkts.		Overs	Mdns.	Runs	Wkts.
Perks	20	9	23	0	...	6	3	12	0
Wyatt	10.1	2	21	2	...	8	2	29	3
Jackson	32	12	48	5	...	16	7	21	4
Howorth	19	4	50	2	...	11.3	4	20	2

Yorkshire v. *Surrey*

Oval, July 27, 29, 30

Yorkshire won by eight wickets

A fine bowling performance by E. P. Robinson was mainly responsible for Yorkshire's win at the Oval, but if Hutton and Sellers had not batted stubbornly in Yorkshire's first innings, the result might have been reversed.

When Surrey went in only Squires (44) seemed able to deal with Robinson and Booth. The former took eight wickets for 76 runs, but Booth in the same number of overs took two wickets for 28, and obviously kept one end quiet while Robinson got the wickets.

Yorkshire's batting, apart from Hutton and Sellers, was even less impressive than Surrey's had been. These two cricketers, with the assistance of 16 extras, scored 175 of Yorkshire's 197 runs—88 per cent. of the runs.

Surrey's second innings, thanks to Fishlock's 99, was more successful, but Robinson and Booth again bowled well and kept the Surrey total to economical proportions. When the last wicket fell at 194, Yorkshire required 111 runs.

When Hutton and Yardley were dismissed cheaply, it seemed that Surrey might have a chance, but Barber and Turner soon dissipated such wishful thinking, and were both not out when the end was reached.

In the match, Robinson took thirteen wickets for 154 runs, while Booth bowled 42.5 overs of which 25 were maidens. Gover (seven for 66) bowled well in Yorkshire's first innings.

Surrey

L. B. Fishlock c Sellers b Robinson	9	lbw, b Coxon	99
R. J. Gregory lbw, b Robinson	10	c Yardley b Robinson	11
H. S. Squires c Hutton b Robinson	44	lbw, b Robinson	0
T. H. Barling c Barber b Robinson	17	lbw, b Booth	9
J. F. Parker b Robinson	0	b Robinson	0
A. McIntyre b Robinson	7	c Wood b Smailes	23
G. S. Mobey lbw, b Booth	5	b Coxon	2
N. H. Bennett b Robinson	1	lbw, b Booth	13
E. A. Watts lbw, b Robinson	5	b Robinson	17
A. V. Bedser c Yardley b Booth	12	b Robinson	12
A. R. Gover not out	1	not out	0
Extras	3	Extras	8
	114		194

Yorkshire

L. Hutton c Bennett b Glover	101	c Watts b Bedser	3
W. Watson lbw, b Bedser	3		
W. Barber lbw, b Gover	6	not out	41
N. W. D. Yardley b Gover	2	b Bedser	4
T. F. Smailes b Parker	1		
C. Turner b Gover	1	not out	51
A. B. Sellers c Bennett b Bedser	58		
A. Wood b Gover	0		
A. Coxon c Gregory b Gover	3		
E. P. Robinson b Gover	6		
A. Booth not out	0		
Extras	16	Extras	14
	197		113

Yorkshire Bowling

	Overs	Mdns.	Runs	Wkts.		Overs	Mdns.	Runs	Wkts.
Smailes	4	1	6	0	...	25	9	37	1
Coxon	3	2	1	0	...	17	7	32	2
Robinson	22	5	76	8	...	30.2	5	88	5
Booth	21.5	13	28	2	...	21	12	29	2

Surrey Bowling

	Overs	Mdns.	Runs	Wkts.		Overs	Mdns.	Runs	Wkts.
Gover	28	4	66	7	...	18	3	41	0
Bedser	26	3	58	2	...	12	2	22	2
Parker	12	3	31	1	...	4	0	6	0
Squires	10	6	15	0	...	15	7	17	0
Watts	4	1	11	0					
Gregory						3	0	5	0
Barling						2	0	3	0
Bennett						1.1	0	5	0

APPEARANCES

The following 23 cricketers appeared for Yorkshire in Championship matches, the number of appearances being in parentheses :

W. Barber (22)
H. Beaumont (16)
A. Booth (22)
W. E. Bowes (17)
A. Coxon (23)
K. Fiddling (12)
P. A. Gibb (11)
H. Halliday (4)
L. Hutton (17)
F. Jakeman (1)
E. Lester (1)
M. Leyland (18)

E. P. Robinson (24)
A. B. Sellers (22)
T. F. Smailes (22)
G. A. Smithson (1)
C. Turner (18)
J. H. Wardle (1)
W. Watson (8)
J. P. Whitehead (1)
J. V. Wilson (5)
A. Wood (5)
N. W. D. Yardley (15)

POST MORTEM

Yorkshire were not a strong batting side in 1946, Hutton being the only top-class bat in the XI. But in Robinson, Booth, Bowes, Smailes and Coxon they had five bowlers capable of taking advantage of any help provided by wickets or weather—and 1946 was a very wet season.

Robinson bowled finely throughout the summer, but perhaps the unexpected deadliness of Booth on anything approaching a bowler's wicket was the deciding factor. Making his first appearance in the Yorkshire side in 1931, Booth had to play second fiddle to his great contemporary, Hedley Verity. It was not until he was 43 that he got his chance, and he did not fail to take it. At the end of the summer he had taken 111 wickets for 11·61 runs each and was at the top of the season's bowling averages, a performance never excelled by a cricketer of his age in his first full season.

As so often before, bowling plus astute captaincy and keen fielding won another Championship for Yorkshire.

SUMMARY (22 Seasons)

	Yorkshire	Opponents
Total runs scored	213,850	178,734
Average per wicket	29·73	17·35
Number of hundreds	332	135
Other innings over 50	899	554
Ten wickets in match	151	46
Five wickets in an innings	651	351
Totals over 400	116	28
Totals under 100	41	236

In the 22 seasons, Yorkshire fielders made 4,878 catches and stumped 407 batsmen—a total of 5,285 dismissals by catching and stumping and an average per season of 240.

THE BEST SIDE

An attempt to discover the best side that ever represented Yorkshire in a winning Championship season must always be a direct and immediate incentive to disagreement and argument. As a beginning a mathematical approach might be tried, a system of points being used to crystallize each season's performances. The following allocation of points is suggested :

For winning the Championship	10 points, less 1 point for each defeat
Innings of 50 or more (40)	1 point
5 wickets in an innings (20)	1 point
Aggregates of 2,000 runs	2 points each
Aggregates of 1,000 runs	1 point each
200 wickets in a season	2 points each
100 wickets in a season	1 point each
20 catches	1 point each
40 wicketkeeping dismissals	1 point each
500 runs and 50 wickets	1 point each

Omitting Yorkshire's first Championship win (1893), when only nine counties competed, the results of this classification are as follows :

Season	Points	Season	Points	Season	Points
1923	29	1935	22	1937	20
1925	29	1938	22	1931	19
1922	27	1905	21	1932	19
1908	25	1924	21	1898	18
1900	23	1939	21	1919	18
1901	23	1896	20	1912	17
1933	23	1902	20	1946	17

Clearly, the choice lies between the teams that won the Championship in the first-named seven seasons. The cricketers who played for Yorkshire in these seasons may be divided into four groups, the sides of

1900-01 and those of 1922-23-25 being for all practical purposes in each case identical. Here are the names, the captains being given first :

1900-01.

Lord Hawke, J. T. Brown, J. Tunnicliffe, D. Denton, T. L. Taylor, F. Mitchell, E. Smith, G. H. Hirst, E. Wainwright, S. Haigh, W. Rhodes, D. Hunter.

1908.

Lord Hawke, W. Rhodes, J. W. Rothery, D. Denton, G. H. Hirst, W. H. Wilkinson, W. E. Bates, H. Myers, S. Haigh, J. T. Newstead, D. Hunter.

1922-23-25.

G. Wilson or A. W. Lupton (the former for preference), P. Holmes, H. Sutcliffe, E. Oldroyd, M. Leyland, W. Rhodes, R. Kilner, E. Robinson, N. Kilner, G. G. Macaulay, E. R. Wilson, A. Waddington, A. Dolphin.

1933.

A. B. Sellers, P. Holmes, H. Sutcliffe, A. Mitchell, M. Leyland, W. Barber, T. F. Smailes, H. Verity, A. Wood, G. G. Macaulay, W. E. Bowes.

Now comes the invidious process of elimination. In 1900 and 1901 the twelve cricketers named filled over 90 per cent. of the available places in the sides. F. S. Jackson, after heading the Yorkshire batting averages in 1899, did not appear in the side again until 1902.

Yorkshire's success in 1908 was unexpected, even by confirmed partisans. It was the result, primarily, of the fine bowling and all-round form of Hirst, Newstead, Rhodes and Haigh, particularly of Hirst and Newstead. The batting, however, cannot bear comparison with that of 1900 and 1901 for reliability, and for this reason the 1908 team goes out.

In 1922-23-25 the attack, judging from results and figures, was as strong as any in Yorkshire's history. Rhodes, Macaulay, R. Kilner, Robinson and Waddington, reinforced by E. R. Wilson in August, were equal to any calls made upon them. The batting was also very strong, with a pair of record-breaking opening batsmen in Holmes and Sutcliffe to open the innings, and Oldroyd, Leyland, Rhodes, the two Kilners and Robinson, any one of whom was likely to score a fifty or hundred, to follow. A very fine and well-balanced XI.

The 1933 team was a good one, usually capable of dealing adequately with the opposition it encountered. But Holmes and Macaulay were nearing the end of their careers, the bowling was less varied than that of the other three sides, and there was even the suggestion of a " tail." For these reasons 1933 must join 1908.

The choice has now been narrowed down to two teams or periods, and perhaps the problem may look simpler if " Twelves " of each are put side by side :

	1900-01		1923-25
1	J. T. Brown	1	P. Holmes
2	J. Tunnicliffe	2	H. Sutcliffe
3	D. Denton	3	E. Oldroyd
4	T. L. Taylor	4	M. Leyland
5	F. Mitchell	5	R. Kilner
6	G. H. Hirst	6	W. Rhodes
7	E. Wainwright	7	E. Robinson
8	S. Haigh	8	G. G. Macaulay
9	Lord Hawke	9	G. Wilson
10	W. Rhodes	10	A. Waddington
11	D. Hunter	11	A. Dolphin
12th man : E. Smith		12th man : E. R. Wilson	

When put like this it is difficult to avoid the conclusion that the Yorkshire side of 1901 was a little stronger than the teams that represented the county so splendidly in 1923 and 1925. Holmes and Sutcliffe may have a slight advantage over Brown and Tunnicliffe ; but Denton, Taylor, Mitchell, Lord Hawke, Rhodes and Hunter were surely superior—in the seasons under review—to their opposite numbers in the later sides. The Hirst-Rhodes, Wainwright-Robinson and Haigh-Macaulay comparisons might well be regarded as dead-heats.

Two points demonstrating the strength of the Yorkshire XI. of 1901 may be added : in Championship matches eleven of the twelve players named had batting averages ranging from 49·23 to 21·75, and the twelfth (Hunter) averaged 14·60 ; and in Tunnicliffe, Denton and Hirst Yorkshire had the finest slip, out-field (J. T. Tyldesley barred) and mid-off in the country.

MAKING A YORKSHIRE CRICKETER

It would be an exaggeration, perhaps, to assert that every Yorkshire boy is born with a bat or ball in his hand (preferably the left hand if it is a ball), but it would not be unduly fantastic to suggest that, sooner or later, many young Yorkshiremen harbour ambitions to play cricket for the county. It may be added that, as will appear later, the county authorities do everything possible to aid, abet and assist promising aspirants to realize such ambitions.

Many counties must envy the facility with which Yorkshire produces replacements and reinforcements just when they are required, and wonder how this apparent miracle is contrived. First-class cricketers do not grow on bushes waiting to be plucked, nor can they be produced like rabbits out of a hat. The nearest approach to such a feat of legerdemain in Yorkshire history was the appearance of Rhodes in 1898 to take the place of Peel. Much thought, care, trouble and administrative hard work behind the scenes goes to the grooming of the potential Yorkshire cricketer, and the operative slogan seems to be : " Catch them young ! "

The Secretary of the County Club, Mr J. H. Nash, has been good enough to outline the process from the time a " find " is discovered to his début in the county XI. And in this connection it may be noted that in recent years Yorkshire has been peculiarly fortunate in its coaches. The long list of successes in the County Championship would probably have been considerably shorter but for the hard work and expert guidance of George Hirst, Wilfred Rhodes, Emmott Robinson and Arthur Mitchell, the present occupant of this vital post. It would be difficult to find four cricketers more likely to spot the latent possibilities of the novice, and here is the system followed in developing such possibilities.

At the beginning of each year the county coach visits schools and clubs in January and February and lectures on various aspects of cricket. In this way hundreds of boys and youths are given a lead as to the Yorkshire attitude to cricket.

In February and March, coaching in the Winter Shed at Headingley is given to selected young players who have shown promise with their schools or league clubs during the previous summer and have been recommended for inspection at headquarters. On the average, a hundred of these " possibles " are seen and appraised during the coaching sessions. During April these young players attend the First XI. practices and are given opportunities to test their abilities against the skill of the regular players and senior colts.

For two hours each morning in April coaching is given to schoolboys, each being invited on three or four days. All these boys have to bat *and* bowl—which may account for the traditional inclination towards all-roundness of Yorkshire cricketers.

During the summer, in addition to trying out likely candidates in the Second XI., which competes in the Minor Counties Championship, the work of discovering new stars is continued by the county coach, who visits grounds in every part of the county to watch young players who have been recommended by their clubs. Those who make the grade are noted and invited to Headingley in the following spring.

From the foregoing it will be seen that the business of unearthing recruits is methodical and continuous. Much sifting must be done before the potential Hirst, Rhodes or Sutcliffe is revealed, but such treasures are unlikely to remain undetected for want of sifting.

Yorkshire enjoys two great advantages : it is a big county and has unlimited League cricket, which closely resembles the Grade system in Australia. The experience gained in these League matches is a fine training for any youth who has the ambition and innate ability to become a first-class cricketer. Co-operation between the Leagues and the County Club is close and has done much to ensure the success of Yorkshire cricket.

PART III

YORKSHIRE PROFILES

BY

J. M. KILBURN

LORD HAWKE
1881-1911

For one whose cricketing quality was useful rather than outstanding, Lord Hawke built up for himself a tremendous place in the history of the game. His was perhaps the most significant voice of his time, and that time extended far beyond playing days into a generation with ideas vastly different from those of his own youth. As Yorkshire's captain for twenty-eight years and President from 1898 until his death in 1938, his work can scarcely be overestimated ; he gave a character and purpose to the side, established a Yorkshire " cap " as the qualification for an honourable and assured profession, and constructed the tradition by which a Yorkshire cricketer became a public figure of standing and renown.

His care was at all times for the player, for his county and for the game as a whole. His faults were easily forgiven, for they were the faults of one who loved beyond wisdom, and he had something of the spirit ascribed to W. G. Grace in the saying : " May the best side win ! Certainly—and ain't we the best side ? " No doubt Lord Hawke was uncommonly fond of having his own way, both on the field and in the committee room, but, after all, the way he wanted must have had much merit, for there have been few to deny him the highest of positions as " guide, philosopher and friend." In his pronouncements at Yorkshire annual meetings he spoke his mind, but invariably with kindly encouragement for the young cricketer and sincere affection for the old. Sometimes he laid himself open to misinterpretation, as when he said : " I pray God no professional will ever captain England," and found he had created a world-wide storm by the expression of what was no more than a fervent hope for the preservation of amateur cricket of international standard.

Lord Hawke believed in captaincy by amateurs, but not to a point of bigotry, for he was Yorkshire's President when the county leadership was offered to a professional. In his own captaincy he approached the martinet, but his was a benevolent despotism, winning from the players who served him a true affection and an abiding loyalty. He was not regarded by his team as " one of themselves " ; he was more than that— a man in authority who used the position for the good of those under him, and without self-interest. In his service to others he found his satisfaction, and his memorial is the status of cricket and cricketers in the life of a nation.

R. PEEL
1882-1897

Peate, Peel and Rhodes represented Yorkshire's slow left-hand bowling for a period of over fifty years. Bobby Peel came in the middle of these three, beginning before Peate had finished and ending the season before Rhodes began. The relative merits of the three must remain a matter of opinion ; there is no dispute that all of them were truly great bowlers. Peel's success began immediately upon his introduction to the county side, and season after season he was responsible for outstanding performances in full confirmation of his early promise. Perhaps the most remarkable of all his feats was in the match with Nottinghamshire at Sheffield in 1883, when Nottinghamshire were all out for 24 in their first innings and Peel's return was eight for 12. Yorkshire made 46, to which Peel contributed 13, and then he bowled again to take six for 21 in the Nottinghamshire total of 58. Fourteen wickets for 33 runs all in one match—yet Peel probably gave no sign of elation. He was a most taciturn cricketer, treating triumph and disaster precisely as the poet advised. Under the fiercest punishment he never wilted or lost his length, yet he was certainly no mere mass-production labourer working without thought or imagination.

As his career matured he developed his batting, and though he made 1,000 runs and took 100 wickets in a season only once, in all he scored over 10,000 runs and took more than 1,500 wickets. Of his ten centuries two exceeded the second hundred, and, curiously enough, the ten were made at the expense of only four counties—four against Leicestershire, three against Sussex, two off the Warwickshire bowling, and one against Middlesex.

Peel's first-class career ended prematurely, but he continued as coach and club cricketer for many years, and he was still to be seen as a spectator at Yorkshire matches up to the outbreak of the Second World War.

D. HUNTER
1888-1909

No cricketer ever inspired more quiet affection than did David Hunter, who was Yorkshire's wicketkeeper for twenty-one years. Cricket is character, and Hunter's wicketkeeping was Hunter himself—neat, unostentatious and good-humoured. He never bullied the batsman or threatened of the wrath to come, but gently removed the bails and as like as not offered a word of condolence with the departing. An artist himself, he rejoiced in the artistry of others : " Well bowled," he would say as he took the ball that had beaten batsman and stumps, " Well bowled, honey." A cricket accident brought on deafness in his later years, but he never lost his smile or the twinkle in his eye, and back in his native Scarborough he became the kindliest of coaches to a host of small boys in holiday times.

In earlier days he was a man of many interests. He bred canaries and pigeons, and was a handbell ringer and clog-dancer of considerable skill, all these occupations involving the dexterity and patient application that were his birthright. He was also the best batsman ever to hold a permanent position at No. 11, where he found much scope for his dry humour and not a little honour in many notable fighting actions. His partnership with Lord Hawke of 148 against Kent stands as a Yorkshire record for the last wicket, and this was not his only experience of a century partnership when he went in last.

It was his pride that a lifetime of wicketkeeping left his hands free from serious damage, and the fact says more than volumes of words for the effectiveness of his methods, for he could reasonably claim that no wicketkeeper ever had more difficult bowling to take.

E. WAINWRIGHT
1888-1902

It is the modern fashion for cricketers to speak of each other in meiosis, and high appreciation is implied in the simplicity of " He's a good player." Ted Wainwright would have been placed unhesitatingly in the category of " good player," not only because of what he did but because of the manner of its performance. He was a right-handed, off-spin bowler who turned the ball tremendously, and a batsman of luxurious stroke play, particularly on the off side. Descended, through the immediate link of George Ulyett, from the line of great Sheffield players who virtually established the county club in the early years of the nineteenth century, Wainwright introduced himself to Yorkshire cricket with a century against the Australians in his very first season. In 1890 he took all ten wickets in an innings against Staffordshire, and throughout his career he was one of the outstanding all-rounders of cricket, for his slip fielding ranked of equal status with his batting and bowling.

He was not perhaps the most fortunate of cricketers. His tour of Australia in 1897-98 was spoiled for him by his inability to acclimatise himself in an exceptionally hot summer ; many times he had to miss matches because his method of spinning the ball had torn the skin from his finger ; and at Scarborough in 1893 he very nearly suffered a fatal accident when a ball from Richardson rose sharply, struck him on the temple and left him unconscious, with subsequent grave danger of lockjaw.

These, however, were misfortunes in a career that brought much distinction, twenty-one centuries and many remarkable bowling feats, including a hat-trick in which he clean-bowled all three men. He was indeed " a good player."

G. H. HIRST
1889-1921

If one cricketer alone had to be chosen to represent Yorkshire, there would surely be an almost unanimous vote for George Herbert Hirst. He had every qualification. Among the very finest of all-rounders in the history of the game, he added to his playing skill the unquenchable spirit that knew no situation too desperate for retrieving, no hope too forlorn for continued struggle. " George Hirst to the Rescue " was a newspaper headline that might well have been kept permanently in type for thirty years. No player was ever less interested in personal achievement for its own sake, yet in the course of the duty that was also so obviously his pleasure he attained figures that stagger the imagination. He accomplished perhaps the greatest individual feat in all cricket when, in 1906, he scored over 2,000 runs and took over 200 wickets, and season after season he headed the county averages in batting or bowling or both.

Cricketers loved him not only for what he did, but for how he did it and for what he was. His whole heart and soul went into whatever he was doing. He began his career as a fast left-arm bowler of perhaps more energy than real quality, but the discovery of his famous " swerver," bowled without much loss of pace, took him from the ranks of the striving straight into the company of the renowned. With the development of his bowling came that advance in batting which led him to attack through innings after innings of superb confidence, each characterised by the particular pull shot he used to such effect against all bowling on all types of wicket. In between batting and bowling he stood like a rock at mid-off to stop the fiercest drives.

His cricket, like his personality, was the pure gold of genuine endeavour and unassuming kindliness, and when his first-class career was done he became beloved to another generation for whose benefit he poured out cricketing wisdom in patient, encouraging coaching. Come who may into Yorkshire cricket, George Hirst must stand supreme in Yorkshire cricketing affection.

J. T. BROWN
1889-1904

During the summer of 1904 the Yorkshire committee received a letter announcing the retirement of J. T. Brown. In November of the same year John Thomas Brown of Driffield (thus distinguished from J. T. Brown of Darfield) was dead, and the cricket world was shocked by the sudden end of one of its most prominent characters. Brown and Tunnicliffe knew in their day all the fame that later came to Holmes and Sutcliffe, and their achievements ran closely parallel. Both pairs were record-makers, and both played an incalculable part in the Championship successes of the Yorkshire teams of their time. When Holmes and Sutcliffe were making 555 to set up a world's record first wicket partnership, it was the 554 of Brown and Tunnicliffe, made thirty-four years earlier, that they had to beat.

Jackie Brown was a delightful bat to watch. He was small and neat and quick upon his feet, and his cutting and hooking were famous. He could force the pace whenever it was necessary, and he knew all about placing singles from the last ball of the over when he was particularly anxious to have the bowling. He played much representative cricket, and in 1894-95 he enjoyed a highly successful tour of Australia. He was of solemn countenance, and delivered his jokes, which were many, without the tremor of a smile. Most of them were practical jokes, and perhaps Brown himself included the hat-trick he once did with the bowling that came " dropping slow," and which altogether brought him a surprising number of wickets.

Whilst his batting partner, Tunnicliffe, stood fast-footed in the slips and collected all manner of catches that came within his enormous reach, little Brown scouted round the boundary edge and was a notable out-fielder, with an accurate return and a safe pair of hands.

E. SMITH
1889-1907

Fame comes in curious ways. Ernest Smith earned his cricketing reputation as a mighty hitter and a lively fast bowler, but higher than his centuries or his many notable bowling feats stands in public memory the innings he once played of sixty minutes for o not out.

In the August of 1905, Yorkshire went to Leyton assured of the Championship if they could avoid defeat. For a day and a half they fielded to an Essex total of 521, and by the end of the second day they had been dismissed, mainly by a youngster named J. W. H. T. Douglas, for a first innings of 98 and had lost one second innings wicket for 15 runs. Grim were the hours of the final day as a long partnership by Tunnicliffe and Hirst brought safety within sight. There was almost an hour left for play when the sixth wicket fell and Ernest Smith went out to the middle. He stayed to the end and never scored a single run, thereby suggesting both a tidy mind and a sense of humour.

No doubt, however, he was happier following the natural inclinations which led him to stand fast-footed and drive for all he was worth anything pitched within range. The football stand at Park Avenue, Bradford, was one of his favourite targets, and at Scarborough in 1892 his hitting so dismayed the fieldsmen that they gave him six innings whilst he scored a century in less than two hours.

His bowling had some pace and was not to be regarded with complacency when the wicket gave him any encouragement. His real value to Yorkshire was even greater than could be measured in his figures, for he was a schoolmaster and came into the county side during August, when relief for " full-timers " was very welcome and fast bowlers were glad of employment in short spells.

SIR STANLEY JACKSON

1890-1907

In comparatively few appearances on the cricket field, F. S. Jackson won an undisputed position as one of the greatest players of all time. No one ever came closer to illustration of the complete cricketer, and one glance at him was enough to denote England batsman, England bowler or England fieldsman. He looked a great player, and his performances matched his promise, for to exceptional technical skill he allied a spirit incapable of accepting hopelessness in any situation.

He came into first-class cricket by the dignified gateways of Harrow and Cambridge, and he brought with him the grand manner of success as by divine right. It was not in his nature to consider the possibility of failure, and when the improbable happened there was almost embarrassment, as though a wrong note had been played by the leader of a symphony orchestra. Beauty and utility and self-confidence blended superbly in Jackson's cricket. On bad wickets or on good, in crisis or in comfort, he was as likely as anyone to make a score, and not a score of mere accumulation but in an innings of free driving and skilful forcing shots to leg. In 1900 he came back to first-class cricket after considerable absence in South Africa, and in his very first match at the Scarborough Festival he made a century with all the assurance of a season's practice behind him.

His bowling was faster than medium, with the liveliness born of a smooth action, and he gave unfailing attention to good length. Natural gifts rather than any prolonged practice provided him with accuracy, and when the ball would turn, his off-break could be devastating. Opposing batsmen knew no peace of mind, for there was shrewd judgment in all Jackson's cricket and he was busy every minute of the match.

Scarcely less notable than his playing performances were his services in committee, where, both to M.C.C. and to Yorkshire, his experience and influence were of incalculable value.

J. TUNNICLIFFE

1891-1907

The little township of Pudsey has provided four notable cricketers for Yorkshire, and the first of them was " Long John " Tunnicliffe, who joined the county side in 1891 and left it at the end of the 1907 season, when he accepted a coaching appointment at Clifton College. He brought to his career the comfortable dignity of his times, applying himself industriously to his business and rising in due course to the respectability of senior professional with a clearly defined position in the scheme of things.

He sowed his cricketing wild oats in early youth when he found his excitement in hitting the ball " hard and high and often," one of his most purposeful drives carrying the pavilion roof at Bramall Lane,

Sheffield. Acceptance of the responsibilities of a county cap led to an altogether more staid and reliable method of run-getting, and for seventeen years he opened the Yorkshire innings in lofty calm, his long left leg stretching down the wicket to cope with any ball that might turn or attempt other misbehaviour.

The exact standard of Tunnicliffe's batsmanship may remain open to debate, with 20,000 runs representing an irrefutable point. There are no two opinions about Tunnicliffe's quality as a fieldsman ; it was of the very highest. Normally he spent his time in the slips, where six feet four inches covers a lot of ground, especially when the structure is apparently of elastic. Tunnicliffe took some astonishing catches, many of them with one hand, for he preferred to use his reach and balance rather than move from his position : " c. Tunnicliffe b. Rhodes " was as inevitable as close of play when Yorkshire found a sticky wicket.

His physical characteristics would, of course, have made him prominent in any company, but his talents as a cricketer also gave him an unmistakable place as an important member of a magnificent county team.

D. DENTON
1894-1920

There is a legend that county captains opposing Yorkshire used to say, " Here comes David Denton : who's going to miss him first ? "— the implication being that Denton had more than a fair share of good luck at the wicket. Had any counter been necessary, the batsman could justifiably have retorted that fortune favours the brave. Denton came to his innings with pennant flying and lance set for combat. He accepted challenge from the first ball sent down to him, and in such eager search for adventure he was almost bound to cause some flutterings in the early overs. But to attribute his success mainly to good fortune is to deny the facts, for, with all the luck in the world, no man could score over 33,000 runs in the absence of exceptional skill. Denton was, indeed, among the greatest batsmen of his time, and no doubt Yorkshire would have seen less, and England more, of him had he not been contemporary with J. T. Tyldesley.

Denton's off-driving was one of the major glories of cricket, and found its way into the text-books as a shining example. His small stature gave an altogether false conception of the power in his shots, and so sweet was his timing that he seemed to be merely stroking the ball away with a smooth, unhurried swing of the bat. The illusion was not appreciated by the fieldsmen in the covers. When Denton had finished his innings he offered another glory, for he was without peer in the long field or at third man, where his safe catching, his speed, his picking-up and his throwing were models for all fieldsmen. His methods had the economy of natural grace and notable judgment. With him the spectacular was a rarity, because his anticipation and timing made the spectacular unnecessary. His was the artistry that overcomes difficulties by preventing them from arising.

F. MITCHELL

1894-1904

Frank Mitchell had two distinguished cricketing careers, one as a Yorkshireman and one as a South African by adoption. The careers were rather curiously entwined, for it was after he had made a tour of South Africa with Lord Hawke's team of 1898-99 that Mitchell was invited to play regularly for Yorkshire, and it was on his return to England as captain of the South African touring team of 1904 that he made his four final appearances for the county.

Mitchell was a big man and strong, and played rugby football for England. His batsmanship was characterised by attack, and he was famous for his off-driving and straight driving with his shoulders well over the ball. He was in the Cambridge University XI. for four years and was captain in 1896, but for Yorkshire his principal achievements were confined to the two seasons of 1899 and 1901. In 1899 his was the highest Yorkshire aggregate. In 1900 he was fighting in the Boer War and played no cricket, but in 1901 he came to his greatest success with seven centuries in a total of 1,801 runs and an average of 46. After that, South Africa became his home and had the benefit of his cricket, and in the following generation that of his son, Bruce Mitchell, one of South Africa's finest players.

Frank Mitchell's significance in cricket perhaps exceeded his actual playing achievements, for his influence was important in the stimulation of the game in South Africa, and in Yorkshire his recommendation had much to do with the establishment of Hubert Myers as a bowler.

S. HAIGH

1895-1913

Schofield Haigh represented one of the most difficult propositions a batsman could meet on a turning wicket. In general classification you would write him down as medium pace, but when the judgment had to be made from twenty-two yards away it was necessary to anticipate fast, medium or slow, for Haigh had a wide variation of pace, and of length, and of spin.

His action was unmistakable, with its long final stride, the arm brought from far behind the back, and a prolonged drag of the right foot. His off-break not only turned but jumped, and if the turf gave him any encouragement, he was virtually unplayable. His was the immortal prophecy made on return from inspection of a wicket upon which the sun was shining after rain.

" What is it like, Schofie ? " he was asked.

" Oh," he replied, " they'll deviate somewhat."

When the ball did deviate he often went round the wicket, not so much to bowl to a leg trap under the modern theory as to avoid spinning the ball past bat, stumps, wicketkeeper and all. He took more than two thousand wickets, and a remarkable number of them were clean-bowled.

Quite as dangerous as his off-break was his slow yorker, which left many an experienced batsman with his stroke completed long before the ball had pitched and which became a notorious breaker of threatening partnerships.

Schofield Haigh's was a happy cricketing life because he could find entertainment in everything, including his own misfortunes. Not even Yorkshire defeats could depress him unduly, and his own lack of success was always taken philosophically. He played cricket seriously and whole-heartedly but without dramatisation, and the triumphs of his friends were as welcome to him as any of his own. George Hirst was his hero, the cricket field was his home, and he did honour to the game by his prowess and to himself by the smile that was never absent for long from his pleasant round face.

W. RHODES

1898-1930

The story of Wilfred Rhodes told as a schoolboy romance would stretch credulity to breaking point. No sooner had he entered first-class cricket, at the age of twenty-one, than he placed himself among the great bowlers of all time, and was a batsman in crisis only, making history for England as last man in at the Oval and at Sydney. In his thirties he was England's opening batsman, and with J. B. Hobbs he created a Test-match record on the Melbourne ground during a tour in which he bowled so little that he did not take a single wicket. In his forties Yorkshire had need of his bowling again, so he resumed his collection of 100 wickets and more season upon season, and in his forty-ninth year his fellow-members of the England selection committee persuaded him back to international cricket for a final triumph. At fifty-two he retired, having claimed conquest over more than 4,000 batsmen and made nearly 40,000 runs.

Rhodes bowling was a lovely sight. He illustrated to perfection the slow left-hander, patiently alluring when wickets were good, impossible to counter for long when the ball spun swiftly away to the slips. His three deliberate steps to the wicket, the smooth, economical curve of the arm, the immobile watchfulness as the harassed batsman tried to sum up the problem of flight made one of cricket's imperishable pictures.

Rhodes was a bowler by the light of nature, and he made himself a great bowler by building on natural facility. His batsmanship grew from the accumulated experience and persistent experiment of the wisest cricketer of them all. Eyesight and common-sense and time formed the basis of his run-getting. He got himself into the best position for seeing the ball, he countered the bowler's deceits with his own wisdom, and in due course the runs came to him. His principles were utilitarian. Whenever he could he played back, because back-play reduces risk to a minimum, and Rhodes was concerned with batting as a business proposition. Playing back was the creed of his coaching, and it is because of his efficiency based on back-play that Rhodes counts Bradman first among batsmen. No one has better grounds for expressing an opinion.

Q

T. L. TAYLOR
1899-1906

T. L. Taylor was but briefly a first-class cricketer, yet his quality
was very evident. He came to the Yorkshire side through Cambridge
University, where he was captain in 1899 and where he made a brilliant
century against the Australians, and in his three full seasons for the
county he was twice head of the batting averages. After 1902 business
claimed too much of his time for regular county cricket to be possible
for him, though he was persuaded into some welcome appearances in
1906 when Yorkshire were in difficulties, and his interest always remained
high. The Scarborough Festival knew him as President from 1921 to
1923, and on the death of Sir Stanley Jackson he became President of
the Yorkshire C.C.C.

As a player he enjoyed himself and made the most of a natural talent
for games. He was close upon the England side as a cricketer, he was
an international hockey player, and only untimely and serious injury
prevented distinction as a rugby footballer. All these things must be
discovered from the record books, for in conversation with Taylor
himself you would never derive the least hint that he had ever been
upon a games field as anything but a spectator. In committee and in
appreciation of younger players his judgment is kindly and his help
readily given. His unfailing determination is to encourage the cricket
in the county of his birth and affection.

E. R. WILSON
1899-1923

Rockley Wilson's Yorkshire career stretched over a period of twenty-
four years, but the dates give an altogether false impression of his
appearances, for he played no county cricket between 1902 and 1913,
and his fame rests chiefly on his performances in the early nineteen-
twenties, when he not only made his way to the head of the bowling
averages, but also became a member of the M.C.C. team to Australia
in 1920-21. He was a bowler of wisdom and cunning, a slow, right-
handed spinner with alluring flight and impeccable length, redolent of
the schoolmasterly virtues. In action no one could have appeared more
guileless, for he came rather hesitatingly up to the wicket, brought over
his arm in a manner suggesting that it was not at all the sort of thing
that a middle-aged man should be asked to do, and—bowled superbly.

His duties at Winchester did not permit him to play for full seasons,
but he came to help Yorkshire just when help was most needed, and
he went so patiently and persistently to work that he invariably collected
close upon fifty wickets between the beginning of August and the end of
the season. It says much for his quality that a very strong team could
always find a place for him whenever he was available.

At Cambridge, his batting was as notable as his bowling, and he
actually scored a century against his university before he became a

member of the side which he eventually captained. For Yorkshire he made one century in 1913, and he himself claims as its principal feature a six off Buckenham skied over the wicketkeeper's head.

His great knowledge of bowling and clear exposition make his chapter in the Badminton series perhaps the most notable treatise so far written on the bowler's art.

A. DOLPHIN

1905-1927

Yorkshire cricket extended over fifty years with only three regular wicketkeepers, and Arthur Dolphin, who came in the middle of the three, was not the least distinguished of them. Another great wicket-keeper has said of him that he was " the quickest to the stumps " of all his contemporaries, and certainly his work always left an impression of eager hostility and no offering of second chance to mistakenly peripatetic batsmen.

In some ways Dolphin was among the unlucky cricketers, for not only were important years taken from his career by the 1914-18 war, in which he served with Roy Kilner and Major Booth in the " Leeds Pals," but injuries cost him a good deal of playing time. In 1921 the collapse of a dressing-room chair on which he was standing brought him a broken wrist which ended his cricket for the season and had some effect on his enjoyment, if not his efficiency, in the following year. Again, if international honours were his ambition he chose his time badly, for he was contemporary with Lilley and Strudwick, and though his quality was recognised plainly enough by his selection for the M.C.C. tour of Australia in 1920-21, he had little chance to keep wicket for England at home.

When playing days were done, Dolphin turned to umpiring and soon became of Test-match class. His unmistakable appearance, either in a sun hat or hatless, with grey hair standing up straight above his round, red face and his characteristic attitude at square leg with hands behind him pushing out his umpire's coat like a bustle, made him an inevitable subject for the cartoonists, and he became almost as well known and as popular an umpire as he had been a wicketkeeper. He was only fifty-six when he died suddenly in the autumn of 1942.

R. KILNER

1911-1927

Humanity beamed from Roy Kilner's cricket. When he flashed a speculative bat at the rising ball outside the off stump he knew very well that he should be doing no such thing, but, after all, wasn't life made for fun and wasn't there a boundary line somewhere behind the slips ? Kilner was, of course, far too good a cricketer not to learn by experience, but he was also far too human a being to sacrifice adventure in the quest for knowledge. No doubt he had his mundane worries, but he always played cricket as though he enjoyed it. He was a good man in a crisis with either bat or ball—he put his back to the wall and pulled his cap a little farther to one side with cheerful as distinct from dour determination.

There were some who thought that he dissipated the gifts of nature by frequently bowling, as a slow left-hander, from over the wicket. Perhaps in different circumstances he would have confined himself to the classical principles of attack, but Wilfred Rhodes was a team-mate, and Kilner went over the wicket to introduce even wider variety into a wonderfully varied Yorkshire bowling scheme. In fact, it may fairly be said that he only bowled at all because Yorkshire needed him. He came into the county side as a batsman, he established himself as a batsman, and when Drake and Hirst were gone he learned to become a bowler. So doing he developed into the leading left-hand all-rounder of his day, playing for England at home and abroad and illustrating his popularity with a Benefit match that represented a record for his generation.

How he would have matured there is no guessing. He never did mature ; the adventure, the boyishness, the irrepressible sense of fun remained in his cricket all his life, which came to a tragically early end when he contracted illness in India and died in his thirty-eighth year.

P. HOLMES
1913-1933

When partnerships attain the renown that came to Holmes and Sutcliffe there is danger of inadequate appreciation of the individuals, but the quality of Percy Holmes would surely have been evident in any circumstances. His was most attractive batsmanship ; quick of footwork, assured, enduring, and his association for so long with one first wicket partner gave him the chance to develop clever running between the wickets. He made sixty centuries for Yorkshire alone, six of them counting more than 200, and two of them exceeding 300. Why he never played more than once for England against Australia is beyond the understanding of most cricketers.

He was the apotheosis of self-confidence at the wicket. His precise walk, quick lift of the bat and the little flourish in the stroke labelled him as clearly as the name upon his cricket bag. He was one of the few batsmen of his time to maintain dignity and accomplishment against fast bowling, and his skill was based upon the classical principles of a very straight bat and closeness to the line of the ball. He scored quickly because he had forcing shots for the ball pitched just short of a length, and if he played back more than he played forward that was because the bowling fashion of his day imposed back play upon him.

In the field he was an outstanding member of perhaps the finest fielding side a county ever knew. Either in the country or in the slips his catching was safe, and his ground fielding was as neat and polished as was his batsmanship. Holmes will remain in cricket history as half an imperishable partnership, but he was also an individual worthy of a pedestal to himself.

H. SUTCLIFFE

1919-1939

Herbert Sutcliffe's cricket story is one of unbroken success. From his first appearance in the Yorkshire side he was recognised as a player of uncommon talent, and there were no setbacks to a career that reached the highest peaks of cricketing distinction. His Test match achievements left him with the reputation of a patient, unruffled accumulator of big scores, but such summary provides the injustice of a half-truth, for Sutcliffe's batsmanship for Yorkshire often showed a brilliance that mere run-getting should not be allowed to obscure. It is doubtful, for instance, if any Yorkshireman ever hit more sixes. Ten of them came in one innings at Kettering, and Sutcliffe and Leyland together once made 102 runs in six overs from Farnes and Nichols, Sutcliffe on that memorable Scarborough day taking his own score from 100 to 194 in forty minutes.

In the comparatively brief space of fourteen seasons he had made his hundred centuries and so given comprehensive answer to any question of his technical ability, but Sutcliffe's unique talent lay more in temperament than in technique. Napoleon himself had no greater power of concentration upon the business in hand. At the wicket, Sutcliffe stood completely aloof from troubles past and possible misfortunes to come. He was the last man in the world whom a bowler could hope to worry into dismissal and the last man likely to be driven into anxiety by the importance of an occasion. It is untrue to say that Sutcliffe was not affected by the prospect of going in to bat in a Test match : he was—he was stimulated to the peak of his powers. His amazing performances in special matches or on difficult wickets were based on treating every ball as a separate problem to be solved without reference to what had gone before or what was likely to come next.

Sutcliffe's batting will be remembered for two outstanding features. In defence he was an artist of the dead bat, defeating spin and awkward length and the close-in fieldsmen by " killing " the ball as though it were made of soap. In attack he was a magnificently courageous hooker of fast bowling ; nobody ever saw him flinch, nobody ever wasted more time than fast bowlers bowling " bumpers " to Herbert Sutcliffe.

E. ROBINSON

1919-1931

Charles Dickens should have written on Emmott Robinson, for this notable little Yorkshireman had every attribute of a Dickens character. In the field he was unmistakable ; his flannels wrinkled over the top of his boots, his toes turned in, he walked with a roll, and his demeanour told the exact state of Yorkshire's fortunes. If you came late to the ground and Yorkshire were fielding you did not need the scoreboard to tell you the situation ; you looked at Emmott Robinson and you knew at once whether some unfortunate had dropped a catch or whether wickets had been falling in seemly regularity. Emmott Robinson lived Yorkshire cricket twenty-four hours of every summer's day, and then thought about it all the winter. He was the most completely Yorkshire character—virtues, failings, appearance and all—ever to play for the county, and had he never taken a wicket or made a run or held a catch, he would have been an important factor in psychological warfare. In fact, of course, he made thousands of runs and took hundreds of wickets and catches. He was a new-ball bowler of considerable potency, and through the 1920's his shambling run-up, prefaced by a little kick-off as though he were starting a motor-cycle, marked daily onslaught upon the enemy's opening batsmen. With his sweater on—a wrinkled sweater—he would station himself alarmingly close to the batsman and create catches. As a batsman himself he fought uncompromisingly through all manner of crises. As Yorkshire cricket, he was a perfect illustration.

M. LEYLAND

1920-1946

Maurice Leyland has been much the most successful of all Yorkshire's left-handed batsmen, with his character as strong as his off-drive. Indeed, his triumphs, both for Yorkshire and for England, were founded upon the self-discipline without which technical skill, like patriotism, is not enough. Nobody was ever more satisfied than Leyland with a chosen profession ; he has always enjoyed cricket and the cricketer's life at home and abroad, and whenever there was a tour in prospect he would say : " They can pick me. I'll always go."

Sanguine and unruffled by nature, he schooled himself to the very peaks of what is known as the big-match temperament. Sometimes he failed because the bowling was too good for him, but he never failed through any lack of heart or determination. In his ordinary, everyday innings he was prepared for adventure and could be found committing sins to horrify the purists, but when occasion insisted, his bat was as straight, his method as faultless as the most exigent text-book could demand. It is nonsense to say that a sense of crisis never affected him ; he was as sensible to atmosphere as the next man, but anxiety was a stimulant and not a conqueror. Perhaps equally as remarkable as his personal performance was the inspiration of his colleagues by the calmness of his attitude in time of trouble.

His immense popularity had its basis in his homeliness. He appreciated the delight of spectators in fours and sixes because those were also his delights, and he never forgot his responsibility to those who watch, or lost his sense of fun. He was completely unself-conscious, yet always aware of the crowds, to whom he behaved as a friend and consequently won universal friendship. His great talent and his unfailing appreciation of the appropriate made him the man for every occasion. In county match, Test match or Festival he could be relied upon to strike the mood of the moment and to offer either light-hearted entertainment or the sternest of battle, according to the needs of the day. Maurice Leyland's place is very secure among the great players and personalities of cricket.

G. G. MACAULAY

1920-1935

Hostility as a characteristic of bowling has now become an over-worked and consequently a weakened epithet. It should have been reserved for George Macaulay, whom it fitted like his skin. When Macaulay was bowling he really did hate the batsman immediately opposed to him, and he was at no pains to conceal his feelings. Should that enemy have been so presumptuous as to survive the latest of a series of vicious off-spinners, Macaulay would stand, hands on hips, glaring down the pitch at such defiance of the natural order of things. He expected to take a wicket with every ball, and was not to be soothed before the last man was gone or stumps were drawn for the day. The more impossible the situation before him the more bitterly he attacked. Once Sussex, with six wickets in hand, needed 40 runs for victory at lunch time on the third day at Bradford. In the afternoon Macaulay took five wickets at a current cost of 8 runs and Sussex lost, not so much defeated as devastated.

Sometimes the circumstances were too much for him, or for any bowler, and batsmen took their ease on a docile wicket. Macaulay wiped the sweat from his brow, waited his time, and as likely as not ran somebody out with a passionate throw where a run was being considered rather than definitely attempted. His spirit burned hot all the time he was in the field. One very fine day he bowled a full toss which was thankfully put away to the boundary. " It's a long time since I had one of those from you, Mac," said the batsman. " It'll be a sight longer before you get another," was the grim retort.

Macaulay began his Yorkshire career as a fast-medium bowler of promise but no outstanding quality. He changed himself into a medium-pace off-spinner of rare power, making defence almost impossible when the wicket helped him and the leg-trap held catches. When all he could rely upon was accuracy and endurance, he offered little encourage-ment to easy run-getting, and spoke feelingly on the subject of groundsmen. He was always a factor in every game in which he played.

A. MITCHELL

1922-1939

Arthur Mitchell travelled the hard road to cricketing distinction. For a long time he was the " bag carrier," in and out of the side on those depressingly limited occasions dependent upon injuries or the calls of representative matches, and waiting, waiting for the establishment that

offers a chance to find form and maintain it.   The twelfth man has much
time for study but too little for practice, and his most likely acquisition
is of loyalty.

Mitchell's characteristic became devotion to duty.   His batting was
based on the needs of the situation, and personal fancies were subjugated
always to what was best, or thought to be best, for the side.   He could
hit sixes as well as most people, and when there was urgent call for them
hit sixes he did.   In his own Benefit match he and Sutcliffe made 105
in 55 minutes to set the pace in a victory over Surrey which involved
the collection of 198 runs in an hour and three-quarters in the fourth
innings.   Mainly, however, Mitchell was required to operate upon a
sterner front, and he developed into one of the most trustworthy defensive
batsmen of his time, with a bad-wicket century against Lancashire at
Old Trafford in 1933, generally counted as the very peak of achievement.

Yet his valuable batting scarcely represents his major contribution
to Yorkshire cricket history.   As a batsman Mitchell was good ; as a
fieldsman he was superb.   In the gully when Verity was bowling he did
not so much take catches as create them.   Quite apart from the miss-
hits that went squirming from the edge of the bat, purely defensive
shots, dropping the ball only a yard away, were liable to become fatalities
when Mitchell came diving into " no man's land " on Yorkshire business.
His anticipation bordered upon the uncanny, though in fact it was founded
upon long study and immense concentration.   His acute judgment of
play and players made him the very man for the appointment he holds
with such success as coach to the county club.

A. WOOD

1927-1947

Wicketkeepers are usually the humourists in cricket teams, their
fooling perhaps a natural reaction to the concentration demanded of
them in the ordinary business of the day.   Arthur Wood wore cap and
bells for Yorkshire for twenty years, and the part was not without point
and purpose in the play, for Wood brought cheerfulness to the dressing-
room and entertainment to the crowds.   He was the comic relief to any
over-seriousness with which Yorkshire might be inclined to take its
cricket.

Wood's foolery had in common with that of Grock a basis of
considerable technical skill in the chosen medium ; it was not his
comicality but his cricket prowess that took him eventually into the
England team, and it was not his comicality but his very fine catching
and taking of the ball on the leg side that kept him for so long as
Yorkshire's choice.

He had batting ability, too, and made his 1,000 runs in a season.
For many county sides he would have been high in the list, for when he
was in form his off-driving and cutting brought him quick and handsome
runs.   He had, in fact, a native grace of style that all his self-deprecation

could not quite obscure, and he had the great affection for cricket and the cricketer's life that made him a good companion, a generous opponent and an open admirer of the talents of other people. International honours came to him when he had probably abandoned hope of them, and his first appearance against Australia provided the occasion for one of the most memorable of his witticisms. With England's total at 876 for seven wickets he was caught and bowled off a full toss for 53, and when he returned to the dressing-room he threw down his bat and gloves and said in tones of tragedy : "Just the sort of thing I would do— in a crisis."

W. E. BOWES

1929-1947

Bill Bowes had two publics, and he captivated both. For those satisfied with direct observation of cause and effect he gave season after season of delight by being the fast bowler who shattered the enemy innings in the first overs, and so established another Yorkshire claim towards another Yorkshire Championship. For the more discerning he was an artist, perhaps the best user of a new ball cricket has ever known. The lethargic run-up, the apparently casual delivery, were undramatic introduction to the problems he set with the ball " moving " suddenly and sharply late in its flight, and exercising that fatal fascination for the bat to follow it, where discretion demanded withdrawal.

His great height proved an incalculable asset, for it enabled him to pitch the ball on a length difficult to reach with a forward stroke and to make it come to the batsman at an awkward elevation. When he thought it necessary he exercised the fast bowler's privilege of testing a batsman's physical courage, but never in any other spirit than as a business proposition. Only the best of batsmen could cope with him, and they were glad enough to find no trace of " greenness " in the wicket when they had to meet him. He was a devastator of the " near-good," and probably the most notable deflator of false reputations in his time.

His skill and success, though, were not the absolute basis of his universal popularity. That came from an appreciation of his perseverance. The captain never called on him in vain ; first thing in the morning, in the heat of mid-afternoon, last over of the day, Bill Bowes was always trying. From a personal point of view he was cruelly used, for he had to be spearhead and stock bowler when Championships and Test rubbers were in dispute, and he gave himself unsparingly, probably to the shortening of his own career. His reward is the affection and admiration of cricketers all over the world.

H. VERITY

1930-1939

Hedley Verity brought a student's mind to cricket. His whole appearance and behaviour on the field suggested professorial research, and off the field he was usually talking cricket or thinking about it. When he was otherwise engaged it was with an air of deliberate recreation—for the ultimate good of cricket.

His bowling was full of conscious artistry, and there were times when you felt that he regretted his own conquest because it brought solution to a problem utterly fascinating in itself. The mechanics of bowling no doubt brought occasional weariness to the flesh, but the theories of bowling, the planning in campaigns of attack, gave him endless delight. Thus did he bowl to Bradman and the other great enemies of his time, rejoicing in their challenge and devoting himself to the difficulties of dismissing them with patient application until he won his way. He almost scorned an accident that brought him a wicket before he was ready to take it.

This is not to say that he rejected gifts from the gods in the shape of turning wickets. There is overwhelming evidence of his mastery in circumstances where batsmen plunged towards the pitch of the ball to find it squirming from the bat's edge to waiting slips or gully. No, when the wicket was made for slow left-handers and Verity was bowling, queues formed automatically in the dressing-room. Those were expected triumphs, the inevitable product of technical efficiency and natural skill. His greater achievements were in controlling the situation when the odds were against him, in keeping an end closed up for a critical hour, in enticing a batsman to downfall at 50 where there lay threat of an innings of 200. That was the time to watch his true bowling character; to note the rhythm in his gentle run-up and beautifully controlled action, the complete concentration in the follow-through that ended with poise on one foot, body leaning forward, hands half raised in expectation.

Greatness glowed around Verity, and the years held glorious prospect when war came to take his life away.

A. B. SELLERS

1932-1948

Brian Sellers made himself into one of Yorkshire's most notable captains by the application of experience and cricketing common-sense to an inherently vivid personality. His father had played for Yorkshire before him, but when Brian joined the side he was younger than the majority of his players, he had seen little first-class cricket and played none, and his capacity for leadershp was untried. His first business was to learn and to establish some respect for himself as a player. His limitations in batsmanship were obvious, and to no one more plainly than himself, but he added lesson to lesson and within a year or two had contrived a century against the Australians and had made the record individual score for a Yorkshire amateur. He developed into a very useful stand-by in time of trouble and fought many a gallant rearguard action, particularly when faster bowlers were proving awkward,

High-class batsmanship requires an inborn quality, but anyone of health and strength can turn himself into a high-class fieldsman. Sellers did—into one of the finest fieldsmen of the game, and so doing acquired an important asset for his captaincy. In the field he could, and did, lead his men by example, and there was no position from long-field to leg-trap into which he could not go to demonstrate courage and efficiency. In the covers and in the " silly " positions he took some astonishing catches, and his energy and concentration through the longest days were a notable inspiration to Yorkshire and a formidable obstacle to opponents.

In captaincy he learned to know his own mind and to maintain his authority. He appreciated his purpose and he appreciated his men, keeping his object plainly before him from the first match of the season until the Championship was settled. His own straightforwardness and fair dealing brought him real affection, and his breezy optimism carried welcome balance to the councils of cricket.

T. F. SMAILES

1932-1948

Frank Smailes has played good cricket for Yorkshire. Into his batting and bowling have gone all his heart and energy, and he has enjoyed his triumphs and come philosophically through the dark moments of failure. The county—and the country, too, for he won an England cap —have used him mainly as a bowler, of more than medium pace and with a marked ability to make the new ball " run away," but he is properly to be placed among the all-rounders, with batting powers that would surely have found more profit from greater opportunities. It is difficult to attain any real consistency when your place is well down in the list and you are required to adapt yourself to different needs almost innings by innings. When Smailes is out of form he is usually only briefly at the wicket, for his bent is aggressive, and he does not struggle to play himself into smooth waters. When he is seeing the ball well he looks to be one of the best left-handers in the game, hitting in front of the wicket with rare power. He has made his centuries and his thousand runs in a season and played many a match-winning innings.

As a bowler he has given the considerable service that the wickets taken would suggest, and has represented a notable supporter for Bowes in the opening attack. Like Macaulay, he turned in the later stages of his career from swing to off-spinners and, again like Macaulay, he achieved a palpable air of hostility. In conditions giving him any help he looked, and was, a fine bowler, and he shares with only three other Yorkshiremen the distinction of having taken all ten wickets in an innings.

Though he first came into the Yorkshire side in 1932, it was in 1934 that he really established himself, and he remained a regular member of the team through the very successful years immediately preceding the Second World War.

L. HUTTON

1934-1948

Leonard Hutton was marked out for cricketing honours from very early days, for scarcely had he been seen, a slim boy, in the county nets than Herbert Sutcliffe, for one, pronounced him a great player in the making. He began his first-class experiences at the age of seventeen, and his remarkable technique at once became evident. He had been advised to take his time, to gather the wisdom that can be gained only at the wicket, and he followed the plan laid down for him so resolutely that within two years he was opening the innings for England and within four he had made the world's record score against Australia.

His development was smooth and untroubled. Possessed of an almost faultless method, he has revealed his mastery on all types of wicket in all parts of the world, and with the growth of self-confidence and the physical strength of full manhood he advanced from excellence to brilliance. His tour of South Africa in 1938-39 took him to the heights of stroke play, and when the war interrupted cricket he was perhaps the most attractive batsman playing and one of the most dependable.

Army service brought a serious accident, with a broken arm healing slowly and unsatisfactorily, and of course he missed five years in what should have been the very crown of his career, but when cricket began again he was seen to have lost nothing of his skill, and he delighted everyone with a series of brilliant innings. He extended his experience with a tour of Australia and with a hurried trip to the West Indies, when an M.C.C. team depleted by injuries sent cables for help, and were his career to end without further achievement, he would have earned his place among the very greatest of batsmen in the history of the game.

Hutton is the complete cricketer. There is no stroke in batsmanship that he does not play, and play as a model. His bowling has a quality that would quickly become evident were he allowed to indulge in much bowling, and in the field he is more than useful anywhere from the boundary edge to the slips.

N. W. D. YARDLEY

1936-1948

Norman Yardley's cricketing distinction began in his schooldays, when he proved himself not only an exceptional technician but also a man for the important occasion. His Cambridge " Blue " and some notable innings at Lord's served as an introduction to county cricket, and, without having to struggle unduly hard for the prominence, he found himself in course of time first vice-captain and then captain of England and of his county. There are now no further worlds to conquer, but Yardley is not likely to follow Alexander's example of depression on that account, for he is of cheerful and equable temperament, and will enjoy captaincy and cricket so long as they remain available to him.

His batsmanship, always suggesting an uncommon natural talent, has reached an admirable maturity. Since early days he has been capable of big scores, but their accumulation on any particular occasion appeared at one time to require a basis of mood and fortune. When he made runs he made them well ; when he failed it was usually a failure in adventure. Increasing experience and responsibility brought the prolonged concentration which was all that he needed to take him from the class of attractive and potentially dangerous to the category of really potent force. With the development of strength he lost none of his attractiveness. A Yardley innings is still an exhibition of skilful on-side forcing shots, of neat footwork and of attack. He is a welcome and worthy member of any side.

Rather curiously in so handsome a games player, his bowling is somewhat awkward of action and unconvincing in appearance. Yet it has its uses. He has bowled for England, and Bradman has been among his wickets, and he is rarely to be discovered in neglect of the ancient virtues of length and direction. As a fieldsman he is quite first-class, and as his whole attitude to the game is one of genuine endeavour, with a sense of proportion preserved, it is no wonder that his popularity is high and universal.

PART IV
THE COUNTY CRICKET CHAMPIONSHIP
1893—1946

Season	Played	Won	Lost	Drawn	Position in Championship
1893	16	12	3	1	First
1894	15	12	2	1	2
1895	26	14	7	5	3
1896	26	16	3	7	First
1897	26	13	5	8	4
1898	26	16	3	7	First
1899	28	14	4	10	3
1900	28	16	0	12	First
1901	27	20	1	6	First
1902	25	13	1	11	First
1903	26	13	5	8	3
1904	27	9	2	16	2
1905	28	18	3	7	First
1906	28	17	3	8	2
1907	26	12	3	11	2*
1908	28	16	0	12	First
1909	26	12	4	10	3
1910	27	10	7	10	8
1911	28	14	8	6	7
1912	27	13	1	13	First
1913	28	16	4	8	2
1914	28	14	4	10	4
		First World War			
1919	26	12	3	11	First
1920	28	15	6	7	4
1921	26	16	3	7	3
1922	30	19	2	9	First
1923	32	25	1	6	First
1924	30	16	3	11	First
1925	32	21	0	11	First
1926	31	14	0	7	2
1927	31	10	3	18	3
1928	28	8	0	20	4
1929	28	10	2	16	3
1930	26	11	2	13	3
1931	27	16	1	10	First
1932	26	19	2	5	First
1933	30	19	3	8	First
1934	30	12	7	11	6
1935	30	19	1	10	First
1936	30	10	2	18	3
1937	28	18	2	8	First
1938	28	20	2	6	First
1939	28	20	4	4	First
		Second World War			
1946	26	16	1	9	First
Totals	1201	656	123	422	

* Tied with Worcestershire for second place.
Fifteen matches abandoned are not included.
Average position in 44 seasons—2·22.

Percentage of matches won in 22 Championship seasons—62·80.
Percentage of matches won in 22 non-Championship seasons—46·06.
Percentage of matches lost in 22 Championship seasons—6·61.
Percentage of matches lost in 22 non-Championship seasons—13·90.
Percentage of county matches won in 44 seasons—54·62.
Percentage of county matches lost in 44 seasons—10·24.

In 3 of the 22 seasons, Yorkshire won the Championship without losing a match ; in 7 they suffered a single defeat ; in 4 they were beaten twice ; in 7 they lost three times ; and in 1939 they finished first after losing four matches.

Perhaps the most remarkable season was 1923, when 25 out of 32 matches were won and 1 lost. In the words of *Wisden :* " Yorkshire had a wonderful season. Never since the competition reached its present dimensions has the Championship been won in such overwhelming fashion." How overwhelming the fashion may be realised from a study of the 25 wins :

> Yorkshire won by an innings 13 times,
> by 10, 9 and 6 wickets once each,
> by 8 and 7 wickets twice each,
> and by 280, 120, 96, 84 and 25 runs.

The only defeat occurred when Nottinghamshire won at Leeds by 3 runs.

The responsibility for this "wonderful" season may be divided between the batsmen and bowlers, with a slight trend in favour of the latter. Holmes, Sutcliffe, R. Kilner, Rhodes, Oldroyd and Leyland each scored over 1,000 runs ; and Rhodes (120 wickets), Kilner (139), Macaulay (149), Robinson (95) and Waddington (59) took their wickets at costs ranging from 11·27 to 19·47. Rhodes and Kilner completed " doubles."

YORKSHIRE *v.* THE COUNTIES
1893—1946

Note :—Only Championship Matches played in the 22 seasons under review are included.

Versus	Played	Won	Lost	Drawn	Percentage of Wins	Percentage of Defeats
Derbyshire	36	24	1	11	66·66	2·77
Essex	41	27	3	11	65·85	7·31
Glamorgan	22	19	—	3	86·36	—
Gloucestershire	44	37	3	4	84·09	6·81
Hampshire	38	24	3	11	63·15	7·89
Kent	43	29	3	11	67·44	6·97
Lancashire	44	19	7	18	44·18	16·27
Leicestershire	41	30	—	11	73·17	—
Middlesex	44	25	5	14	58·13	11·62
Northamptonshire	27	22	—	5	81·48	—
Nottinghamshire	44	16	4	24	36·36	9·09
Somerset	29	23	2	4	79·31	6·89
Surrey	42	20	5	17	47·61	12·19
Sussex	42	22	3	17	53·65	7·31
Warwickshire	42	23	—	19	57·50	—
Worcestershire	29	21	1	7	72·41	3·44
Total	608	381	40	187	62·66	6·57

Matches abandoned are not included.

In the 22 seasons Gloucestershire lost 37 matches and won 3. In 16 of the seasons Yorkshire won both home and away matches.

More than half the Yorkshire-Nottinghamshire matches were drawn, and in 6 of the 22 seasons both matches were drawn.

Three counties beat Yorkshire twice in a season—Gloucestershire in 1939, Lancashire in 1893, and Sussex in 1933.

Four of the sixteen counties failed to win a match against Yorkshire in the 22 seasons: Glamorgan, Leicestershire, Northamptonshire and Warwickshire. Lancashire with seven wins was Yorkshire's most successful opponent.

YORKSHIRE v. "THE BIG FIVE"

Versus	Played	Won	Lost	Drawn	Percentage of Wins	Percentage of Defeats
Kent	43	29	3	11	67·44	6·97
Lancashire	44	19	7	18	44·18	16·27
Middlesex	44	25	5	14	58·13	11·62
Nottinghamshire	44	16	4	24	36·36	9·09
Surrey	42	19	5	17	46·34	12·19
Total	217	109	24	84	50·23	11·21

Yorkshire's record against the five strongest counties is particularly impressive—more than half the matches played were won, and four and a half times as many won as were lost.

TEN BATSMEN
who scored 5,000 runs in the 22 Championship seasons

	Inns.	Not Out	Runs	Highest Inns.	100's	50's	Aver.
H. Sutcliffe	438	43	20635	313	60	75	52·24
L. Hutton	138	19	6049	280*	19	21	50·83
G. H. Hirst	329	42	10241	341	18	60	43·21
P. Holmes	302	27	10857	315*	26	43	39·48
M. Leyland	385	47	13036	210*	26	65	38·56
W. Barber	279	27	9282	255	21	38	36·83
D. Denton	343	21	11035	221	21	54	35·36
J. T. Brown sen.	222	19	6600	300	11	29	32·51
J. Tunnicliffe	269	25	7907	243	13	44	32·41
W. Rhodes	404	67	10343	201	17	50	30·68

* Not out.

TEN BOWLERS
who took 350 wickets in the 22 Championship seasons

	Wickets	Runs	5 Wkts. in Inns.	Average
H. Verity	1020	13471	93	13·21
W. Rhodes	1388	18976	106	13·66
R. Kilner	520	7126	27	13·70
S. Haigh	740	10704	58	14·46
G. G. Macaulay	879	12791	62	14·55
W. E. Bowes	857	12910	68	15·06
G. H. Hirst	734	13524	42	18·42
E. P. Robinson	407	7582	27	18·62
E. Robinson	350	6741	13	19·26
T. F. Smailes	356	7526	16	21·70

TEN FIELDERS
who made 100 catches in 5 or more of the 22 Championship seasons

	Number of Championships	Catches	Average
J. Tunnicliffe	7	256	36·57
A. Mitchell	9	230	25·55
A. Waddington	5	122	24·40
E. Robinson	6	143	23·83
E. P. Robinson	5	118	23·60
E. Wainwright	5	107	21·40
A. B. Sellers	7	148	21·14
W. Rhodes	12	211	17·58
R. Kilner	6	105	17·50
H. Sutcliffe	12	203	16·91

THREE WICKETKEEPERS

	Number of Championships	Dismissals			Average for Championship
		Stumped	Caught	Total	
A. Dolphin	6	112	204	316	52·66
D. Hunter	8	127	293	420	52·50
A. Wood	8	124	291	415	51·87

FIFTY RUNS IN EACH INNINGS

Scores	Player	Against	Ground	Season
62, 57	J. T. Brown	Sussex	Brighton	1893
64, 50*	J. T. Brown	Derbyshire	Sheffield	1896
115, 83	F. S. Jackson	Middlesex	Bradford	1896
62, 63*	J. Tunnicliffe	Middlesex	Lord's	1896
203, 81*	J. T. Brown	Middlesex	Lord's	1896
58, 52	F. W. Milligan	Hampshire	Southampton	1896
55, 64	J. Mounsey	Hampshire	Southampton	1896
55, 68	G. H. Hirst	Hampshire	Southampton	1896
111, 92	G. H. Hirst	Gloucestershire	Bradford	1900
76, 91	J. T. Brown	Worcestershire	Worcester	1902
64, 88*	T. L. Taylor	Surrey	Oval	1902
108,* 59*	G. H. Hirst	Worcestershire	Worcester	1905
53, 78	D. Denton	Sussex	Leeds	1905
51, 103*	G. H. Hirst	Sussex	Leeds	1905
60, 57	W. H. Wilkinson	Leicestershire	Sheffield	1905
79, 50	W. Rhodes	Sussex	Brighton	1905
58, 128*	G. H. Hirst	Derbyshire	Chesterfield	1908
63, 51	D. Denton	Lancashire	Manchester	1908
103, 78	H. Sutcliffe	Middlesex	Lord's	1919
59, 105*	P. Holmes	Kent	Maidstone	1924
59, 54*	W. Rhodes	Lancashire	Manchester	1925
75, 72*	H. Sutcliffe	Leicestershire	Sheffield	1931
58, 78*	H. Sutcliffe	Gloucestershire	Bristol	1931
83, 132	H. Sutcliffe	Gloucestershire	Bradford	1932
65, 77*	P. Holmes	Nottinghamshire	Leeds	1932
69, 57	A. B. Sellers	Essex	Colchester	1935
80, 74	W. Barber	Gloucestershire	Hull	1935
65, 80	T. F. Smailes	Kent	Bradford	1937
138, 56*	H. Sutcliffe	Surrey	Bradford	1937
117, 56	T. F. Smailes	Glamorgan	Cardiff	1938
111, 50	W. Barber	Hampshire	Bournemouth	1938
95, 60*	M. Leyland	Surrey	Leeds	1938
85, 53	A. B. Sellers	Middlesex	Sheffield	1946

* Not out.

No. of Times			No. of Times	
5	G. H. Hirst		2	T. F. Smailes
5	H. Sutcliffe		1	F. S. Jackson
4	J. T. Brown		1	M. Leyland
2	W. Barber		1	F. W. Milligan
2	D. Denton		1	J. Mounsey
2	P. Holmes		1	T. L. Taylor
2	W. Rhodes		1	J. Tunnicliffe
2	A. B. Sellers		1	W. H. Wilkinson

Yorkshire's opponents performed the feat on 28 occasions.

FIVE WICKETS IN EACH INNINGS

Analyses	Player	Against	Ground	Season
6-43, 8-34	E. Wainwright	Essex	Bradford	1896
6-43, 6-70	S. Haigh	Derbyshire	Sheffield	1896
7-24, 6-21	W. Rhodes	Somerset	Bath	1898
8-21, 6-22	S. Haigh	Hampshire	Southampton	1898
5-46, 7-24	W. Rhodes	Surrey	Bradford	1898
5-31, 7-54	E. Wainwright	Leicestershire	Dewsbury	1898
6-43, 8-23	W. Rhodes	Hampshire	Hull	1900
8-72, 6-120	W. Rhodes	Gloucestershire	Bradford	1900
6-40, 8-28	W. Rhodes	Essex	Harrogate	1900
6-61, 7-33	S. Haigh	Middlesex	Leeds	1900
6-36, 7-67	W. Rhodes	Gloucestershire	Cheltenham	1900
7-78, 7-63	W. Rhodes	Gloucestershire	Bristol	1901
6-115, 6-67	W. Rhodes	Somerset	Taunton	1901
5-54, 7-23	G. H. Hirst	Lancashire	Manchester	1901
6-41, 7-55	W. Rhodes	Leicestershire	Leicester	1901
5-39, 6-145	W. Rhodes	Somerset	Leeds	1901
7-20, 5-66	W. Rhodes	Gloucestershire	Hull	1901
7-12, 5-17	G. H. Hirst	Essex	Leyton	1901
6-48, 5-18	S. Haigh	Warwickshire	Birmingham	1902
7-123, 5-72	W. Rhodes	Essex	Bradford	1902
5-22, 7-36	W. Rhodes	Gloucestershire	Leeds	1902
5-39, 7-40	S. Haigh	Middlesex	Lord's	1902
6-36, 6-59	S. Haigh	Worcestershire	Leeds	1905
6-34, 6-21	S. Haigh	Nottinghamshire	Sheffield	1905
5-48, 5-26	W. Rhodes	Warwickshire	Dewsbury	1905
6-12, 6-7	G. H. Hirst	Northamptonshire	Northampton	1908
5-44, 5-48	J. T. Newstead	Surrey	Oval	1908
9-25, 5-40	S. Haigh	Gloucestershire	Leeds	1912
5-37, 5-57	S. Haigh	Worcestershire	Dewsbury	1912
6-30, 6-37	G. H. Hirst	Somerset	Taunton	1912
7-50, 5-69	M. W. Booth	Essex	Leyton	1912
6-58, 6-68	A. Waddington	Gloucestershire	Leeds	1919
5-80, 5-42	W. Rhodes	Middlesex	Leeds	1919
6-8, 5-23	G. G. Macaulay	Northamptonshire	Northampton	1922
5-29, 6-22	R. Kilner	Essex	Harrogate	1922
5-106, 5-52	A. Waddington	Kent	Maidstone	1922
7-47, 5-29	G. G. Macaulay	Gloucestershire	Dewsbury	1922
5-11, 5-58	G. G. Macaulay	Worcestershire	Harrogate	1923
5-25, 6-27	G. G. Macaulay	Hampshire	Portsmouth	1923
5-19, 7-21	G. G. Macaulay	Gloucestershire	Gloucester	1924
5-33, 6-15	R. Kilner	Hampshire	Portsmouth	1924
5-18, 7-37	R. Kilner	Sussex	Brighton	1924
5-36, 6-68	G. G. Macaulay	Surrey	Bradford	1925

FIVE WICKETS IN EACH INNINGS—*continued*

Analyses	Player	Against	Ground	Season
5-71, 5-96	G. G. Macaulay	Worcestershire	Harrogate	1925
5-39, 6-63	W. E. Bowes	Middlesex	Lord's	1931
5-64, 5-68	W. E. Bowes	Hampshire	Portsmouth	1931
6-21, 8-33	H. Verity	Glamorgan	Swansea	1931
6-52, 7-93	H. Verity	Sussex	Brighton	1931
5-49, 5-56	W. E. Bowes	Gloucestershire	Bristol	1932
5-8, 5-45	H. Verity	Essex	Leyton	1932
6-32, 5-37	H. Verity	Derbyshire	Leeds	1932
6-12, 6-41	H. Verity	Derbyshire	Hull	1933
5-34, 6-40	H. Verity	Essex	Dewsbury	1933
6-25, 6-22	G. G. Macaulay	Leicestershire	Bradford	1933
6-44, 6-93	W. E. Bowes	Kent	Leeds	1933
7-28, 5-21	G. G. Macaulay	Lancashire	Manchester	1933
7-89, 6-87	W. E. Bowes	Nottinghamshire	Nottingham	1933
7-68, 5-72	W. E. Bowes	Surrey	Sheffield	1933
7-35, 6-67	H. Verity	Northamptonshire	Leeds	1933
8-47, 9-44	H. Verity	Essex	Leyton	1933
5-43, 6-49	H. Verity	Middlesex	Lord's	1933
5-118, 5-74	H. Verity	Derbyshire	Chesterfield	1935
8-40, 5-48	W. E. Bowes	Worcestershire	Sheffield	1935
7-31, 7-47	H. Verity	Hampshire	Hull	1935
5-69, 8-28	H. Verity	Leicestershire	Leeds	1935
8-18, 8-17	W. E. Bowes	Northamptonshire	Kettering	1935
6-16, 6-83	W. E. Bowes	Lancashire	Bradford	1935
6-32, 6-49	W. E. Bowes	Warwickshire	Bradford	1935
6-53, 5-20	H. Verity	Middlesex	Leeds	1935
6-52, 7-55	H. Verity	Hampshire	Portsmouth	1935
5-53, 5-60	H. Verity	Worcestershire	Stourbridge	1937
6-46, 5-82	H. Verity	Kent	Tonbridge	1937
9-43, 5-49	H. Verity	Warwickshire	Leeds	1937
5-76, 5-71	H. Verity	Glamorgan	Scarborough	1937
8-80, 6-52	H. Verity	Sussex	Eastbourne	1937
6-35, 8-68	T. F. Smailes	Glamorgan	Hull	1938
5-114, 5-52	H. Verity	Northamptonshire	Scarborough	1938
7-50, 5-49	W. E. Bowes	Warwickshire	Birmingham	1939
7-48, 7-20	H. Verity	Glamorgan	Bradford	1939
5-60, 5-59	E. P. Robinson	Glamorgan	Cardiff	1939
5-80, 8-35	E. P. Robinson	Lancashire	Leeds	1939
8-76, 5-88	E. P. Robinson	Surrey	Oval	1946
5-29, 7-24	E. P. Robinson	Hampshire	Scarborough	1946

Summary

No. of Times		No. of Times	
21	H. Verity	4	E. P. Robinson
15	W. Rhodes	2	E. Wainwright
10	W. E. Bowes	2	A. Waddington
9	G. G. Macaulay	1	M. W. Booth
8	S. Haigh	1	J. T. Newstead
5	G. H. Hirst	1	T. F. Smailes
4	R. Kilner		

Yorkshire's opponents performed the feat on 23 occasions.

AVERAGES

of cricketers who played for Yorkshire in the 22 Championship seasons, the figures being exclusive of those recorded in non-Championship years

Player	Mtchs.	Inns.	Not Out	Runs	Hghst Inns.	100's	50's	Aver.	Wkts.	Runs	5 Wkts. in Inns.	Aver.	Ctchs.
Allen, S.	1	2	—	8	6	—	—	4·00	2	116	—	58·00	—
Anson, C. S.	1	2	—	27	14	—	—	13·50	—	—	—	—	1
Badger, H. D.	1	2	1	6	6*	—	—	6·00	—	34	—	—	—
Bates, W. E.	32	44	4	618	64	—	3	15·45	9	222	—	24·66	15
Bayes, G.	4	4	2	25	14	—	—	12·50	6	123	—	20·50	1
Beaumont, H.	16	25	3	432	59	—	2	19·63	—	—	—	—	7
Bell, J. T.	5	5	1	125	54	—	—	31·25	—	—	—	—	—
Barber, W.	197	279	27	9282	255	21	38	36·83	5	224	—	44·80	91
Birtles, T. J.	5	7	—	127	42	—	—	18·14	—	—	—	—	1
Blackburne, W. E.	6	7	1	15	5*	—	—	2·50	30	596	2	19·86	8
Booth, A.	24	24	10	96	29	—	—	6·75	85	1041	2	12·24	9
Booth, M. W.	27	35	5	608	75	—	4	20·26	85	1535	6	18·05	13
Bottomley, T.	1	1	—			—	—	—	—	—	—	—	1
Bowes, W. E.	175	138	66	825	43*	—	—	11·45	857	12910	68	15·06	63
Brearley, H.	1	2	—	17	9	—	—	8·50	—	—	—	—	—
Brooke, J. W.	1	1	—	0	—	—	—	—	—	—	—	—	—
Brown, J. T., sen.	140	222	19	6600	300	11	29	32·51	96	2555	2	26·61	73
Brown, J. T., jun.	11	12	1	81	17*	—	—	7·36	34	641	1	18·85	8
Brown, W.	1	1	—	2	2	—	—	2·00	3	61	—	20·33	—
Brumfitt, J.	1	1	—	9	9	—	—	9·00	—	—	—	—	—
Burton, D. C. F.	22	23	2	530	142*	1	1	25·23	—	6	—	—	9
Cawthray, G.	2	3	—	57	29	—	—	19·00	1	139	—	139·00	1
Chichester-Constable, R. C.	1	1	—			—	—	—	—	—	—	—	—
Claughton, H. M.	3	4	—	32	15	—	—	8·00	2	144	—	72·00	1

* Not out.

AVERAGES—*continued*

Player	Mtchs.	Inns.	Not Out	Runs	Hghst Inns.	100's	50's	Aver.	Wkts.	Runs	5 Wkts. in Inns.	Aver.	Ctchs.
Coxon, A.	23	26	8	322	51*	—	1	17·88	63	1154	3	18·31	19
Crawford, G. H.	1	1	—	17	17	—	—	17·00	5	95	—	19·00	1
Crowther, F.	1	2	—	0	0	—	—	—	—	—	—	—	1
†Davidson, K. R.	5	6	1	90	47	—	—	18·00	—	—	—	—	4
Dennis, F.	16	19	1	298	44	—	—	16·55	6	378	—	63·00	8
Denton, D.	232	343	21	11035	221	21	54	35·36	7	289	1	41·28	124
Deyes, G.	1	1	0	0	0	—	—	—	5	110	—	22·00	1
Douglas, S.	5	4	—	44	19	—	—	11·00	9	308	—	34·22	6
Drake, A.	26	36	2	629	65	—	4	18·50	67	1110	6	16·56	18
Drake, J.	3	4	1	21	10	—	—	7·00	1	117	—	117·00	2
Elam, F. W.	2	3	1	48	28	—	—	24·00	—	—	—	—	2
Elms, J. E.	1	2	—	20	20	—	—	10·00	1	28	—	28·00	1
Fisher, H.	30	31	6	389	76*	—	1	15·56	58	1480	2	25·51	13
Frank, R. W.	1	1	—	7	7	—	—	7·00	—	—	—	—	—
‡Gibb, P. A.	27	39	4	1171	157*	2	5	33·45	1	42	—	42·00	6
Greenwood, F. E.	33	35	5	698	97	—	2	23·66	—	—	—	—	22
Grimshaw, C. H.	20	26	—	415	71	—	1	17·29	3	73	—	24·33	26
Haigh, S.	177	230	30	3726	159	1	16	18·63	740	10704	58	14·46	97
Hall, C. H.	11	7	1	23	10*	—	—	3·83	22	576	2	26·18	6
Halliday, H.	11	14	—	167	36	—	—	11·92	1	4	—	4·00	4
Hamer, A.	2	2	—	3	3	—	—	1·50	1	64	—	64·00	2
Hampshire, J.	3	2	—	5	5	—	—	2·50	5	109	—	21·80	1
Harbord, W. E.	8	10	—	161	46	—	—	16·10	—	—	—	—	6
Hardisty, C. H.	17	27	4	595	84	—	2	25·86	—	—	—	—	9
Hargreaves, H. S.	5	6	—	14	9	—	—	2·80	7	165	—	23·57	—
Hawke, Lord	151	197	33	3710	166	5	13	22·62	—	—	—	—	48
Hayley, H.	2	3	1	29	18	—	—	14·50	—	18	—	—	—

* Not out.   † Played both as amateur and professional.   ‡ See also under "Wicketkeepers."

AVERAGES—*continued*

Player	Mtchs.	Inns.	Not Out	Runs	Hghst Inns.	100's	50's	Aver.	Wkts.	Runs	5 Wkts. in Inns.	Aver.	Ctchs.
Hirst, G. H.	238	329	42	10241	341	18	60	43·21	734	13524	42	18·42	163
Holmes, P.	217	302	27	10857	315*	26	43	39·48	1	13	—	13·00	131
Hutton, L.	92	138	19	6049	280*	19	21	50·83	79	1885	3	23·86	72
Jackson, Rt. Hon. Sir F. S.	70	103	7	3582	160	10	14	37·31	180	3015	8	16·75	47
Jacques, T. A.	3	2	1	10	7*	—	—	10·00	11	248	1	22·54	2
Jakeman, F.	1	1	—	3	3	—	—	3·00	—	—	—	—	1
Johnson, J.	2	2	1	5	4*	—	—	5·00	5	16	1	3·20	—
Kaye, H. S.	4	5	—	25	15	—	—	5·00	—	—	—	—	4
Kilburn, S.	1	1	—	8	8	—	—	8·00	—	—	—	—	—
Kilner, N.	33	32	3	601	102*	1	3	20·72	—	—	—	—	16
Kilner, R.	158	192	22	4824	124	5	25	28·37	520	7126	27	13·70	105
Lester, E.	1	1	—	47	47	—	—	47·00	—	—	—	—	—
Leyland, M.	293	385	47	13036	210*	26	65	38·56	174	4118	2	23·66	102
Lupton, A. W.	33	24	4	190	31*	—	—	9·50	—	40	—	—	9
Macaulay, G. G.	201	183	42	2348	101*	1	3	16·65	879	12791	62	14·55	161
Milligan, F. W.	38	52	7	902	74	—	7	20·04	47	1156	—	24·59	16
Mitchell, A.	184	259	31	7982	177*	15	39	35·00	1	105	—	105·00	230
Mitchell, F.	27	38	4	1674	162*	7	6	49·23	—	—	—	—	12
Moorhouse, R.	44	59	7	1082	113	—	3	20·80	5	266	—	53·20	17
Mounsey, J.	22	29	6	454	58	—	2	19·73	—	47	—	—	8
Myers, H.	45	65	8	1104	75	—	4	19·36	72	1547	3	21·48	28
Newstead, J. T.	28	37	6	745	100*	1	3	24·03	123	1758	9	14·29	21
Oldroyd, E.	157	204	25	6428	194	10	35	35·91	7	160	—	22·85	90
Oyston, C.	9	12	4	60	22	—	—	7·50	25	583	—	23·32	2
Pearson, J. H.	1	1	—	44	44	—	—	44·00	—	—	—	—	—
Peel, R.	39	58	4	1478	210*	3	4	27·37	162	2772	12	17·11	15
Rawlin, E. R.	5	5	1	21	11	—	—	5·25	19	389	—	20·47	2

* Not out.

AVERAGES—*continued*

Player	Mtchs.	Inns.	Not Out	Runs	Hghst Inns.	100's	50's	Aver.	Wkts.	Runs	5 Wkts. in Inns.	Aver.	Ctchs.
Render, G.	1	1		5	5			5·00					
Rhodes, A. C.	49	55	16	757	64*			19·41	74	2372	3	32·05	37
Rhodes, W.	313	404	67	10342	201	17	50	30·68	1388	18976	106	13·66	211
Richardson, J. A.	4	7	1	170	54*		1	28·33	1	54		54·00	1
Riley, W.	3	4	1	36	25*			12·00	61	1237	5	20·27	1
Ringrose, W.	16	22	4	92	19			5·11	350	6741	13	19·26	5
Robinson, E.	167	173	33	3270	112*	2	15	23·35	407	7582	27	18·62	143
Robinson, E. P.	104	124	21	1954	75*		5	18·97					118
Rothery, J. W.	43	65	3	1387	161	2	9	22·37					5
Rudston, H.	4	5		42	21			8·40					2
Ryder, L.	2	2	1	1	1			1·00	4	151		37·75	
Sellers, A.	15	25		678	105	2	3	27·12	5	256		51·20	11
Sellers, A. B.	188	239	32	5222	109	2	26	25·22	3	62		20·66	148
Shaw, J.	1	1		1	1			1·00					
Smailes, T. F.	116	148	13	2785	117	3	9	20·62	356	7526	16	21·70	77
Smith, Ernest	54	78	11	1302	116*	1	5	19·43	89	2069	4	23·24	36
Smith, E.	8	10	3	94	49			13·42	15	514	1	34·26	3
Smithson, G. A.	1	1		16	16			16·00					3
Smurthwaite, J.	5	7	5	24	20*			12·00	7	152		21·71	
Stephenson, J. S.	7	7		45	28			6·42	5	151		30·20	3
Sutcliffe, H.	309	438	43	20635	313	60	75	52·24					203
Tait, T.	1	1	1	3	3			3·00					
Tasker, J.	18	24		318	52		2	13·82					7
Tattersall, G.	1	11		26	26			13·00					1
Taylor, H.	8	11		141	36			12·81					
‡Taylor, T. L.	54	76	7	2799	156	7	17	40·56	99	2629	4	26·55	24
Turner, C.	100	135	17	3248	97		25	27·52					94

* Not out.   ‡ See also under " Wicketkeepers."

AVERAGES—continued

Player	Mtchs.	Inns.	Not Out	Runs	Hghst Inns.	100's	50's	Aver.	Wkts.	Runs	5 Wkts. in Inns.	Aver.	Ctchs.
Turner, I.	5	7	—	33	12	—	—	4.71	—	—	—	—	2
Tunnicliffe, J.	170	269	25	7909	243	13	44	32.41	1	73	—	73.00	256
Ulyett, G.	15	22	2	342	73	—	3	17.10	—	12	—	—	12
Verity, H.	175	173	40	2004	78*	—	5	15.06	1020	13471	93	13.21	118
Waddington, A.	106	115	37	893	64*	—	1	11.44	422	7595	24	19.99	122
Wainwright, E.	114	163	11	3369	145	5	12	22.16	269	4541	17	16.88	107
Wainwright, W.	2	3	—	42	35	—	—	14.00	—	—	—	—	—
Waller, G.	1	1	—	1	1	—	—	1.00	2	10	—	5.00	—
Wardall, T.	8	13	—	174	106	1	—	13.38	14	209	—	14.92	6
Wardle, J. H.	2	2	2	12	10*	—	—	—	—	10	—	—	—
Washington, I.	36	51	5	1157	100*	1	6	25.15	—	—	—	—	14
Watson, W.	12	18	—	263	43	—	—	14.61	—	—	—	—	5
White, Sir A. W.	26	31	9	437	54*	—	1	19.86	—	19	—	—	10
Whitehead, J. P.	1	1	1	5	5*	—	—	—	—	—	—	—	—
Whitehead, L.	1	2	—	13	13	—	—	6.50	—	—	—	—	—
Whitehead, Lees	31	38	8	707	67*	—	6	23.56	8	284	—	35.50	19
†Wilkinson, F.	12	12	1	58	18*	—	—	5.27	26	524	1	20.15	11
Wilkinson, H.	12	20	—	414	81	—	4	20.70	—	28	—	—	4
Wilkinson, W. H.	34	52	3	1338	99	—	9	27.30	1	133	—	133.0	26
Williams, A. C.	9	9	7	73	48	—	—	36.50	25	472	2	18.88	4
Wilson, B. B.	27	42	3	1195	150	2	3	30.64	—	33	—	—	2
Wilson, C. E. M.	2	4	1	47	27	—	—	15.66	4	53	—	13.25	1
Wilson, E. R.	28	29	6	317	63	—	2	13.78	56	1006	2	17.96	5
Wilson, G.	80	80	12	867	70	—	3	12.75	—	11	—	—	26
Wilson, G. A.	10	18	4	276	55*	—	2	19.71	—	66	—	—	7
Wilson, J. P.	1	—	—	—	—	—	—	—	—	—	—	—	1
Wilson, J. V.	5	8	—	71	24	—	—	8.87	—	—	—	—	4
Yardley, N. W. D.	63	92	10	2320	137	4	10	28.29	28	1125	—	40.17	45

* Not out. † Played both as amateur and professional.

AVERAGES—continued

WICKETKEEPERS

Player	Matches	Innings	Not out	Runs	Highest Innings	100's	50's	Average	Stumped	Caught	Total
Allen, W. R.	10	10	3	196	95*	—	1	28·00	2	13	15
Bairstow, A. L.	8	8	5	26	10*	—	—	8·66	12	18	30
Binns, J.	1	1	—	4	4	—	—	4·00	3	—	3
Crick, H.	2	1	—	18	16	—	—	9·00	—	4	4
Dolphin, A.	162	146	51	1101	62*	—	1	11·58	112	204	316
Earnshaw, W.		1	—	1	1	—	—	1·00	1	1	2
Gibb, P. A.	27	39	4	1171	157*	2	5	33·45	8	15	23
Higgins, H. J.	5	7	1	42	15	—	—	7·00	3	3	6
Hoyle, T. H.	1	2	—	7	7	—	—	3·50	—	1	1
Hunter, D.	162	210	99	1469	58*	—	1	13·23	127	293	420
Taylor, T. L.	54	76	7	2799	156	7	17	40·56	2	4	6
Watson, H.	8	11	4	30	16*	—	—	4·28	1	24	25
Wood, A.	195	232	45	4294	123*	1	19	22·96	124	291	415

* Not out.

100 YORKSHIRE RECORDS

(All records and figures are complete to October 1, 1947)

At Edgbaston in 1896 Yorkshire scored 887 runs in an innings against Warwickshire. This is the fourth biggest total in first-class cricket and a record in a county match.

In two successive series of Test matches v. Australia, W. Rhodes took 22 wickets for 15·27 runs each (1902), and 31 wickets for 15·74 runs each (1903–04). The latter is the best performance, statistically, for a single series of England-Australia Tests in Australia.

G. H. Hirst was the first professional cricketer to score 2,000 runs and take 100 wickets in a season—in 1904 he scored 2,501 runs and took 132 wickets.

Five Yorkshire bowlers have taken 200 wickets in a season—W. Rhodes (three times), H. Verity (three times), G. H. Hirst, G. G. Macaulay and E. Peate.

In 1904 three Yorkshire cricketers (Hirst, Rhodes and Haigh) scored 1,000 runs and took 100 wickets in the season.

During the period 1919–39, H. Sutcliffe made every score from 0 to 127 inclusive. No other cricketer has equalled this feat.

In 1902, Rhodes went in No. 11 in five Tests v. Australia and headed the England batting averages in the series. He scored 67 runs in seven innings and was not out in six.

In 1935 at Kettering, W. E. Bowes took sixteen Northants wickets for 35 runs—eight for 16 and eight for 17.

H. Sutcliffe is the only English batsman who has scored 50 or more runs in an innings six times in a series of England-Australia matches. In 1924–25 he scored 59, 115, 176, 127, 59, 143 in Australia.

In only 12 of the 148 Test matches against Australia has the England team contained no Yorkshireman, and 5 of these matches were in Australia in 1901–02, when the touring side included no Yorkshire cricketer.

In five seasons in succession (1919–23), W. Rhodes was top of the English bowling averages four times and second once. In each season he scored over 1,000 runs. Rhodes was 42 in 1919.

On eleven occasions, Hobbs and Sutcliffe scored more than 100 runs for England's first wicket v. Australia. Hobbs and Rhodes did so four times.

In 1903, G. H. Hirst was third in the batting averages and sixth bowler—probably the finest single season all-round performance.

In the fifth Test match at Durban in 1938–39, H. Verity bowled 766 balls—a record number in one Test match.

Ten Yorkshiremen have completed " doubles " 41 times—W. Rhodes (16), G. H. Hirst (14), R. Kilner (4), and R. Peel, E. Wainwright, Sir F. S. Jackson, S. Haigh, M. W. Booth, A. Drake and T. F. Smailes.

G. H. Hirst is the only cricketer who has scored two separate centuries and taken five or more wickets in each innings of the same match. In 1906 v. Somerset at Bath he scored 111 and 117 not out, and took eleven wickets for 115 runs (six for 70 and five for 45).

Sir F. S. Jackson is the only batsman who has scored five hundreds *v.* Australia in Test matches in England.

H. Verity took 100 wickets in Test cricket in less time than any other English bowler. He played in his first Test match (*v.* New Zealand) in 1931, and took his 100th Test wicket in Australia in 1937.

H. Sutcliffe is the only English cricketer who has scored four hundreds in a series of Test matches twice—*v.* Australia in 1924-25, and *v.* South Africa in 1929.

W. Rhodes shared 158 partnerships of 100 or more runs : first wicket, 29 ; second, 27 ; third, 13 ; fourth, 26 ; fifth, 24 ; sixth, 15 ; seventh, 9 ; eighth, 7 ; ninth, 7 ; tenth, 1.

At Southampton in 1921, C. Tyson scored 100 not out and 80 not out against Hampshire in his first two innings in first-class cricket. This is the nearest any English debutant has got to scoring two separate hundreds in his first match.

W. Rhodes and H. Verity are the only English bowlers who have taken as many as fifteen wickets in an England-Australia match—Rhodes, fifteen for 124 runs at Melbourne, 1904 ; Verity, fifteen for 104 runs at Lord's, 1934.

On September 1, 1935, A. Wood kept wicket in his 220th consecutive county match. During the period covered by these matches Yorkshire played 267 matches, and Wood kept wicket in 266 of them.

In his first season, H. Verity was top of the English bowling averages with 64 wickets for 12·42 runs each.

In England-Australia matches, 30 Yorkshiremen have made 284 appearances. In addition, P. A. Gibb and T. F. Smailes were among England's "thirteen" at Manchester in 1938 when the match was abandoned without a ball being bowled.

H. Sutcliffe is the only English cricketer who has scored two separate hundreds in a Test match twice—176 and 127 *v.* Australia at Melbourne (1925), 104 and 109 not out *v.* South Africa at the Oval (1929).

In 1908 at Northampton, Yorkshire dismissed Northamptonshire for 27 and 15—the smallest aggregate for two innings on record in a County Championship match.

In 1883, E. Peate took eight wickets for 5 runs *v.* Surrey at Holbeck.

G. H. Hirst is the only cricketer who has scored 2,000 runs and taken 200 wickets in the same season. In 1906 he scored 2,385 runs and took 208 wickets.

In 44 seasons (1893-1946), Yorkshire won the County Cricket Championship 22 times. The county has been champions in four consecutive seasons (1922-23-24-25 and 1937-38-39-46), and in three consecutive seasons twice (1900-01-02 and 1931-32-33).

W. Rhodes took a wicket with his first ball in Australia and with his last ball in first-class cricket.

In 1933 at Leyton, H. Verity took seventeen wickets *v.* Essex—eight wickets for 47 and nine for 44—in one day.

H. Sutcliffe is the only batsman who has averaged 16 runs an innings more against Australia than in county cricket. On October 1, 1939, his average *v.* Australia was 66·85 and in county matches 50·71—a difference of 16·14 runs per innings.

W. Rhodes is the only cricketer who has scored over 30,000 runs and taken 4,000 wickets in first-class cricket.

In county matches, David Hunter dismissed 1,272 opponents—352 stumped, 920 caught.

J. B. Hobbs and H. Sutcliffe are the only English batsmen who have scored 400 runs in six series of Test matches. Sutcliffe's six were *v.* Australia in 1924-25, 1926, 1930, 1932-33, and *v.* South Africa in 1927-28, 1929.

In his first Test match (*v.* South Africa at Johannesburg in 1938), P. A. Gibb scored 93 and 106—a record début in Test cricket.

In eleven successive seasons, G. H. Hirst completed " doubles "— 1903 to 1913.

H. Sutcliffe is the only Yorkshire cricketer who has scored 100 centuries in Yorkshire matches, 4,000 runs in Test cricket, and 50,000 runs in first-class cricket.

In 1902, Yorkshire bowlers dismissed Australia in successive matches for 36 and 23. For England *v.* Australia at Birmingham, Hirst and Rhodes dismissed Australia in the first innings of the match for 36. In the next game at Leeds the same eleven Australians scored 23 against Hirst and F. S. Jackson in their second innings.

During his 9½ years of first-class cricket, H. Verity took 1,956 wickets —an average of 205 wickets per year. No other bowler has equalled this figure throughout his career.

The only instance of two cricketers from the same county scoring hundreds in the same innings *v.* Australia was provided by L. Hutton (364) and M. Leyland (187) at the Oval in 1938.

H. Sutcliffe was the first English batsman to (1) make four hundreds in a series of Test matches *v.* Australia ; (2) score two separate hundreds in an England-Australia match ; (3) score three hundreds in consecutive innings in Test cricket ; (4) score over 700 runs in a series of England-Australia matches.

In 1905, Sir F. S. Jackson captained England against Australia, won the toss five times, and headed the England batting and bowling averages for the series.

On May 1st, 1939, H. Verity had dismissed D. G. Bradman eight times in Test matches—more frequently than any other bowler.

W. E. Bowes is the only bowler who has clean-bowled D. G. Bradman four times in Test matches.

On June 25, 1934, H. Verity took fourteen Australian wickets for 80 runs in one day at Lord's.

In the Yorkshire-Somerset match at Sheffield in 1932, H. Fisher did the hat-trick, all three batsmen being lbw.

In the Yorkshire-Glamorgan match at Sheffield in 1930, Holmes and Sutcliffe scored 235 for Yorkshire's first wicket, and W. E. Bates and A. H. Dyson 233 for Glamorgan's first wicket. Each of the four players was born in Yorkshire.

W. Rhodes scored 1,000 runs in a season twenty times and took 100 wickets in a season twenty-three times. In sixteen seasons he completed both performances.

In three seasons, two being consecutive, H. Sutcliffe scored over 3,000 runs—3,002 (1928), 3,006 (1931), 3,336 (1932).

At Nottingham in 1932, H. Verity took ten wickets in an innings for 10 runs against Nottinghamshire.

On 95 occasions Yorkshire has dismissed opponents for 50 runs or fewer in an innings, Lancashire having suffered eight of these disasters.

W. E. Bowes took 1,000 wickets before he scored his 1,000th run. He made his first appearance for Yorkshire in 1928, took his 1,000th wicket in 1935, and completed 1,000 runs in 1937.

Three Yorkshire bowlers have taken four wickets with consecutive balls—G. Ulyett, for England v. New South Wales at Sydney (1878-79); S. Haigh, for M.C.C. v. Army at Pretoria (1905-06); and A. Drake, Yorkshire v. Derbyshire at Chesterfield (1914).

W. Rhodes and H. Verity each took 200 wickets in a season in three consecutive seasons—Rhodes in 1900-01-02, Verity in 1935-36-37.

In his first Test match (England v. South Africa at Cape Town in 1923), G. Macaulay took a wicket with his first ball, and made the winning hit when England won by one wicket.

In ten consecutive seasons, H. Verity was never lower than third in the season's bowling averages, 40 wickets being taken as a minimum. He was first in 1930 and 1939, second in 1931, 1932, 1935, 1936, 1937, 1938, and third in 1934.

G. H. Hirst appeared in the first twenty in the English batting and bowling averages in four consecutive seasons—1903, 1904, 1905, 1906.

In 1932 at Leyton, P. Holmes and H. Sutcliffe scored 555 for Yorkshire's first wicket against Essex. At Chesterfield in 1898, J. T. Brown and J. Tunnicliffe scored 554 for the first wicket against Derbyshire. No other first wicket partnerships exceeding 500 runs have been scored in first-class cricket.

Yorkshire is the only county that has twice beaten the Rest in the Champion County v. Rest of England match at the Oval. In 1905, Yorkshire won by 65 runs, and in 1935 by 149 runs.

During his career, W. Rhodes took 4,188 wickets in first-class cricket—3,960 in England, 114 in Australia, 52 in South Africa, 39 in West Indies, and 23 in India.

In two Test matches (v. Australia) L. Hutton has shared century first wicket partnerships in each innings (with C. Washbrook).

The first time he bowled in first-class cricket, H. Sedgwick took five wickets for 8 runs for Yorkshire v. Worcestershire at Hull in 1906.

M. Leyland is the only English batsman who has scored three hundreds against Australia in a series of Test matches in England. In 1934 he scored 109 at Lord's, 153 at Manchester, and 110 at the Oval.

H. Sutcliffe is the only cricketer who has scored 50 or more runs in each innings of a Test match seven times.

W. Rhodes is the only English cricketer who has scored 1,000 runs and taken 100 wickets in Test matches against Australia.

In 1908, four Yorkshire bowlers finished in the first seven in the English averages, and each took 100 wickets : S. Haigh, 103 wickets (average 13·39); G. H. Hirst, 174 (14·05); W. Rhodes, 115 (16·13); J. T. Newstead, 140 (16·50). In 1922, Rhodes, Macaulay, R. Kilner and Waddington each took 100 wickets in the season.

On 17 occasions in fourteen seasons (1878-91), Louis Hall carried his bat through the innings for Yorkshire.

In 1930, for the first time in cricket history, cricketers from the same county (H. Sutcliffe and H. Verity) headed the English batting and bowling averages.

L. Hutton is the youngest English cricketer to score over 300 runs in an innings in a first-class match, and also the only batsman who has shared partnerships of 300 and 200 runs in the same Test innings.

W. Rhodes and H. Verity are the only professional cricketers who have gone in last and first for England, against Australia.

On 74 occasions (69 being in Yorkshire matches), P. Holmes and H. Sutcliffe scored 100 runs or more for the first wicket.

In all Test cricket, thirty-nine Yorkshiremen have scored 21,134 runs, including 44 hundreds, taken 776 wickets, and caught or stumped 311 opponents.

L. Hutton's 364 v. Australia at the Oval (1938) is (a) the biggest innings in Test cricket, (b) the biggest innings by a professional in first-class cricket, (c) the biggest innings by a Yorkshire cricketer, (d) the longest innings in first-class cricket.

Since 1874, Yorkshire has distributed over £77,000 in the form of benefits, testimonials and grants to players.

W. Rhodes took more wickets in England-Australia matches (109) than any other English bowler.

In 1935, Yorkshire scored the highest and lowest innings of the season—582 for seven wickets v. Surrey at Sheffield, and 31 v. Essex at Huddersfield.

On three occasions five Yorkshiremen have appeared in the same England Test XI : G. Ulyett, T. Armitage, T. Emmett, A. Greenwood, A. Hill twice v. Australia at Melbourne in 1877 ; and L. Hutton, M. Leyland, H. Verity, A. Wood and W. E. Bowes v. Australia at the Oval in 1938.

In consecutive seasons (1937 and 1938), L. Hutton and H. Verity were third in the English batting and bowling averages.

In 1933, Yorkshire dismissed three counties for less than 80 runs an innings in three consecutive matches : Derbyshire, 51, 78 ; Essex, 64, 68 ; Leicestershire, 65, 39—average innings, 61.

For fifty-five years Lord Hawke was a leader of Yorkshire cricket. From 1883 to 1910 he was Captain, from 1898 to 1938 President, and for thirteen years (1898 to 1910) both President and Captain.

Six Yorkshire bowlers have taken over 50 wickets in Test cricket—H. Verity 144, W. Rhodes 127, R. Peel 102, W. E. Bowes 67, G. H. Hirst 59, G. Ulyett 51.

In 1931, H. Sutcliffe scored four hundreds in consecutive innings, and later in the season three other hundreds in succession.

In 1923, Yorkshire bowlers occupied the first three places in the season's bowling averages—W. Rhodes, 134 wickets (average 11·54); R. Kilner, 158 (12·91); G. Macaulay, 166 (13·83). E. Robinson was ninth with 96 wickets for 15·61 runs each.

Yorkshire is the only county that has provided a captain for one of the other Test-playing countries. After playing for Yorkshire and England, F. Mitchell captained South Africa in the Triangular Tournament in 1912.

On two occasions P. Holmes and H. Sutcliffe scored 100 runs for the first wicket in each innings of a match—105 and 265 (unfinished) v. Surrey at the Oval in 1926, and 184 and 210 (unfinished) v. Nottinghamshire at Nottingham in 1928.

In five consecutive seasons (1922-26) five Yorkshire bowlers (Rhodes, Macaulay, R. Kilner, Waddington and E. Robinson) took 2,675 wickets in county matches for 16·10 runs each. For consistent success over a long period, these figures have never been surpassed.

W. Rhodes is the only cricketer who has scored 2,000 runs and taken 100 wickets in Test matches—2,325 runs (average 30·19), 127 wickets (average 26·96).

In each of six consecutive series of England-Australia Test matches (1924-34), H. Sutcliffe averaged over 50 runs per innings.

At Melbourne in 1883, W. Bates scored 55 in the English innings and took thirteen Australian wickets for 102 runs in the match.

On four occasions, P. Holmes and H. Sutcliffe scored over 300 runs for Yorkshire's first wicket—555 v. Essex (1932), 347 v. Hampshire (1920), 323 v. Lancashire (1931), 309 v. Warwickshire (1931).

L. Hutton and M. Leyland are the only English cricketers from the same county who have shared a partnership of 300 runs in a Test match—382 v. Australia at the Oval in 1938. This partnership is also an English record for any wicket in Test cricket.

R. Peel is the only cricketer who has been dismissed without scoring in each innings of a Test match three times. In three out of four consecutive Tests v. Australia in 1895 and 1896 he " bagged a brace."

In his first season (1919), H. Sutcliffe finished twelfth in the English batting averages.

D. Denton scored over 1,000 runs during the month of July in 1912. In August 1932, M. Leyland and H. Sutcliffe both scored over 1,000 runs.

Only two English batsmen have scored over 50 runs in each of their first three innings in Test cricket—H. Sutcliffe (64, 122, 83) v. South Africa in 1924, and P. A. Gibb (93, 106, 58) v. South Africa in 1938-39.

W. Rhodes shared record partnerships for the first and last wickets in Test cricket—323 (with J. B. Hobbs) at Melbourne in 1912, and 130 (with R. E. Foster) at Sydney in 1903.

At Dewsbury in 1894, E. Wainwright took the last five Sussex wickets in seven balls in the second innings.

In fourteen consecutive seasons, H. Sutcliffe scored 2,000 runs or more (1922-35).

Yorkshire is the only county that has won more than half the county matches it has played.

In 1934, W. Barber scored his 1,000th run on June 13.

At Scarborough in 1932, H. Sutcliffe and M. Leyland hit the Essex bowling for 102 runs in six successive overs. During this innings Sutcliffe raised his score from 100 to 182 in 20 minutes.

Three Yorkshire bowlers have taken all ten wickets in an innings in a County Championship match : H. Verity (*v.* Warwickshire in 1931 and *v.* Nottinghamshire in 1932—his second and third seasons) ; A. Drake *v.* Somerset in 1914 ; and T. F. Smailes *v.* Derbyshire in 1939.

H. Sutcliffe scored his 1,000th run in Test cricket in his ninth Test match (in one of the games he did not bat)—the quickest 1,000 runs in Test cricket by an English batsman.

In England's second innings in the fifth Test *v.* South Africa in 1939, P. A. Gibb scored 120 in 7 hours 31 minutes (just under 16 runs per hour). This is the slowest century scored by an English batsman in Test cricket.

W. Rhodes holds the record for the longest career in Test cricket. He played his first Test match (*v.* Australia) in June 1899 and his last (*v.* West Indies) in April 1930.

In 1931 (a wet season), H. Sutcliffe scored 3,006 runs and averaged 96·96—the highest average ever obtained by an English batsman. The next most successful batsman in 1931 averaged 69·23.

In 1923, Yorkshire won 25 of their 32 county matches. Thirteen of the games were won with an innings to spare.

The Yorkshire-Middlesex match at Leeds in 1947 was W. E. Bowes' Benefit. With subscriptions, Bowes received £8,083.

In South Africa's two innings at Leeds in 1935, H. Verity bowled twenty-four overs, of which 20 were maidens.

Against Gloucestershire at Gloucester in 1887, J. Hunter made nine catches at the wicket—three in the first innings and six in the second.

During his career (17 seasons), J. Tunnicliffe caught 691 opponents —an average of 41 dismissals a season. All his catches were made in England.

In his first four innings (two matches) *v.* Australia, H. Sutcliffe scored 59, 115, 176, 127, and shared three consecutive first wicket partnerships of over 100 runs with J. B. Hobbs.

R. T. Stanyforth is the only wicketkeeper who has captained England in Test cricket (*v.* South Africa, 1927-28).

H. Sutcliffe is the oldest cricketer to (*a*) carry his bat through the innings while scoring the first hundred of the season (1939), and (*b*) score four hundreds in consecutive innings (1939).

In twenty-one seasons (1919-39), Yorkshire fielders dismissed 6,359 opponents—an average of 301 per season. The modes of dismissal were : caught, 5,646 ; stumped, 451 ; run out, 262.

INDEX

of cricketers who played for Yorkshire in the 22 Championship seasons.
Names of amateurs are inset. An asterisk indicates that the player
appeared in Test cricket.

Allen, W. R.	1922, 1923, 1925
Allen, S.	1924
Anson, C. S.	1924
Badger, H. D.	1922
Bairstow, A. L.	1896, 1898, 1900
*Barber, W.	1931, 1932, 1933, 1935, 1937, 1938, 1939, 1946
Bates, W. E.	1908, 1912
Bayes, G.	1912
Beaumont, H.	1946
Bell, J. T.	1923
Binns, J.	1898
Birtles, T. J.	1919, 1924
Blackburne, W. E.	1919
Booth, A.	1931, 1946
*Booth, M. W.	1908, 1912
Bottomley, T.	1935
*Bowes, W. E.	1931, 1932, 1933, 1935, 1937, 1938, 1939, 1946
Brearley, H.	1937
Brooke, J. W.	1923
*Brown sen., J. T.	1893, 1896, 1898, 1900, 1901, 1902
Brown jun., J. T.	1898, 1900, 1901, 1902
Brown, W.	1902
Brumfitt, J.	1938
Burton, D. C. F.	1919
Cawthray, G.	1939
Chichester-Constable, R. C.	1919
Claughton, H. M.	1919
Coxon, A.	1946
Crawford, G. H.	1925
Crick, H.	1937
Crowther, F.	1905
†Davidson, K. R.	1933, 1935
Dennis, F.	1931, 1932, 1933
*Denton, D.	1896, 1898, 1900, 1901, 1902, 1905, 1908, 1912, 1919
Deyes, G.	1905
*Dolphin, A.	1905, 1912, 1919, 1922, 1923, 1924
Douglas, S.	1925, 1933
Drake, A.	1912
Drake, J.	1923, 1924
Earnshaw, W.	1896
Elam, F. W.	1900, 1902
Elms, J. E.	1905
Fiddling, K.	1939, 1946
Fisher, H.	1931, 1932, 1935
Frank R. W.	1893
*Gibb, P. A.	1935, 1937, 1938, 1946
Greenwood, F. E.	1931, 1932
Grimshaw, C. H.	1905, 1908

† Also played as a professional.

* *Haigh, S.   1896, 1898, 1900, 1901, 1902, 1905, 1908, 1912
  Hall, C. H.   1932, 1933
  Halliday, H.   1938, 1946
  Hamer, A.   1938
  Hampshire, J.   1937
    Harbord, W. E.   1932, 1933, 1935
  Hardisty, C. H.   1908
  Hargreaves, H. S.   1937, 1938
    *Hawke, Lord   1893, 1896, 1898, 1900, 1901, 1902, 1905, 1908
  Hayley, H.   1893, 1898
  Higgins, J.   1901, 1902, 1905
*Hirst, G. H.   1893, 1896, 1898, 1900, 1901, 1902, 1905, 1908, 1912, 1919
*Holmes, P.   1919, 1922, 1923, 1924, 1925, 1931, 1932, 1933
  Hoyle, T. H.   1919
  Hunter, D.   1893, 1896, 1898, 1900, 1901, 1902, 1905, 1908
*Hutton, L.   1935, 1937, 1938, 1939, 1946
    *Jackson, Rt. Hon. Sir F. S.   1893, 1896, 1898, 1902, 1905
  Jacques, T. A.   1931, 1933, 1935
  Jakeman, F.   1946
  Johnson, J.   1938, 1939
    Kaye, H. S.   1908
  Kilburn, S.   1896
  Kilner, N.   1919, 1922, 1923
*Kilner, R.   1912, 1919, 1922, 1923, 1924, 1925
  Lester, E.   1946
*Leyland, M.   1922, 1923, 1924, 1925, 1931, 1932, 1933, 1935, 1937, 1938, 1939, 1946
  Lupton, A. W.   1908, 1915
*Macaulay, G. G.   1922, 1923, 1924, 1925, 1931, 1932, 1933, 1935
    *Milligan, F. W.   1896, 1898
*Mitchell, A.   1924, 1925, 1931, 1932, 1933, 1935, 1937, 1938, 1939
    *Mitchell, F.   1901
  Moorhouse, R.   1893, 1896, 1898
  Mounsey, J.   1893, 1896
  Myers, H.   1901, 1905, 1908
  Newstead, J. T.   1908, 1912
  Oldroyd, E.   1912, 1922, 1923, 1924, 1925, 1931
  Oyston, C.   1900, 1902, 1905
  Pearson, J. H.   1935
*Peel, R.   1893, 1896
  Rawlin, E. R.   1935
  Render, G.   1919
  Rhodes, A. C.   1932, 1933
*Rhodes, W.   1898, 1900, 1901, 1902, 1905, 1908, 1912, 1919, 1922, 1923, 1924, 1925
  Richardson, J. A.   1937
  Riley, W.   1900
  Ringrose, W.   1902, 1905
  Robinson, E.   1919, 1922, 1923, 1924, 1925, 1931
  Robinson, E. P.   1935, 1937, 1938, 1939, 1946
  Rothery, J. W.   1905, 1908
  Rudston, H.   1905
  Ryder, L.   1924
    Sellers, A.   1893
    Sellers, A. B.   1932, 1933, 1935, 1937, 1938, 1939, 1946
  Shaw, J.   1896
*Smailes, T. F.   1932, 1933, 1935, 1937, 1938, 1939, 1946
    Smith, E.   1896, 1898, 1900, 1901, 1902, 1905

Smith, E.	1919
*Smithson, G. A.	1946
Smurthwaite, J.	1938, 1939
Stephenson, J. S.	1923, 1924
*Sutcliffe, H.	1919, 1922, 1923, 1924, 1925, 1931, 1932, 1933, 1935, 1937, 1938, 1939
Tait, T.	1898
Tasker, J.	1912
Tattersall, G.	1905
Taylor, H.	1924, 1925
Taylor, T. L.	1900, 1901, 1902
Turner, C.	1925, 1931, 1932, 1933, 1935, 1937, 1938, 1939, 1946
Turner, I.	1924
Tunnicliffe, J.	1893, 1896, 1898, 1900, 1901, 1902, 1905
*Ulyett, G.	1893
*Verity, H.	1931, 1932, 1933, 1935, 1937, 1938, 1939
*Waddington, A.	1919, 1922, 1923, 1924, 1925
*Wainwright, E.	1893, 1896, 1898, 1900, 1901
Wainwright, W.	1905
Waller, G.	1893
Wardall, T.	1893
*Wardle, J. H.	1946
Washington, I.	1900, 1902
Watson, H.	1908, 1912
Watson, W.	1939, 1946
White, Sir A. W.	1912
Whitehead, J. P.	1946
Whitehead, Lees	1900, 1901, 1902
Whitehead, L.	1893
†Wilkinson F.	1937, 1938
Wilkinson, H.	1905
Wilkinson, W. H.	1905, 1908
Williams, A. C.	1919
Wilson, B. B.	1908, 1912
*Wilson, C. E. M.	1896, 1898
*Wilson, E. R.	1900, 1902, 1919, 1922, 1923
Wilson, G.	1919, 1922, 1923, 1924
Wilson, G. A.	1937, 1938, 1939
Wilson, J. P.	1912
Wilson, J. V.	1946
*Wood, A.	1931, 1932, 1933, 1935, 1937, 1938, 1939, 1946
*Yardley, N. W. D.	1937, 1938, 1939, 1946

† Also played as a professional.